CENTRAL ISSUES IN CONTEMPORARY ECONOMIC THEORY AND POLICY

General Editor: **Gustavo Piga**, *Managing Editor, Rivista di Politica Economica, Rome, Italy*

Published titles include:

Mario Baldassarri (*editor*)
HOW TO REDUCE UNEMPLOYMENT IN EUROPE

Mario Baldassarri (*editor*)
THE NEW WELFARE
Unemployment and Social Security in Europe

Mario Baldassarri, Michele Bagella and Luigi Paganetto (*editors*)
FINANCIAL MARKETS
Imperfect Information and Risk Management

Mario Baldassarri and Bruno Chiarini (*editors*)
STUDIES IN LABOUR MARKETS AND INDUSTRIAL RELATIONS

Mario Baldassarri and Pierluigi Ciocca (*editors*)
ROOTS OF THE ITALIAN SCHOOL OF ECONOMICS AND FINANCE
From Ferrara (1857) to Einaudi (1944) (three volumes)

Mario Baldassarri and Massimo Di Matteo (*editors*)
INTERNATIONAL PROBLEMS OF ECONOMIC INTERDEPENDENCE

Mario Baldassarri, Cesare Imbriani and Dominick Salvatore (*editors*)
THE INTERNATIONAL SYSTEM BETWEEN NEW INTEGRATION AND
NEO-PROTECTIONISM

Mario Baldassarri and Luca Lambertini (*editors*)
ANTITRUST, REGULATION AND COMPETITION

Mario Baldassarri, Alfredo Macchiati and Diego Piacentino (*editors*)
THE PRIVATIZATION OF PUBLIC UTILITIES
The Case of Italy

Mario Baldassarri, Luigi Paganetto and Edmund S. Phelps (*editors*)
EQUITY, EFFICIENCY AND GROWTH
The Future of the Welfare State

Mario Baldassarri, Luigi Paganetto and Edmund S. Phelps (*editors*)
THE 1990s SLUMP
Causes and Cures

Mario Baldassarri, Luigi Paganetto and Edmund S. Phelps (*editors*)
WORLD SAVING, PROSPERITY AND GROWTH

Mario Baldassarri, Luigi Paganetto and Edmund S. Phelps (*editors*)
INTERNATIONAL DIFFERENCES IN GROWTH RATES
Market Globalization and Economic Areas

Mario Baldassarri and Paolo Roberti (*editors*)
FISCAL PROBLEMS IN THE SINGLE-MARKET EUROPE

Mario Baldassarri and Franco Modigliani (*editors*)
THE ITALIAN ECONOMY
What Next?

Mario Baldassarri (*editor*)
MAFFEO PANTALEONI
At the Origin of the Italian School of Economics and Finance

Mario Baldassarri, Luigi Paganetto and Edmund S. Phelps (*editors*)
INSTITUTIONS AND ECONOMIC ORGANIZATION IN THE ADVANCED ECONOMIES
The Governance Perspective

Stefano Manzocci (*editor*)
THE ECONOMICS OF ENLARGEMENT

Central Issues in Contemporary Economic Theory and Policy
Series Standing Order ISBN 0–333–71464–4
(*outside North America only*)

You can receive future titles in this series as they are published by placing a standing order. Please contact your bookseller or, in case of difficulty, write to us at the address below with your name and address, the title of the series and the ISBN quoted above.

Customer Services Department, Macmillan Distribution Ltd, Houndmills, Basingstoke, Hampshire RG21 6XS, England

The Economics of Enlargement

Edited by

Stefano Manzocchi
Professor of International Economics
University of Perugia
Italy

in association with
Rivista di Politica Economica, SIPI, Rome

First published 2003 by
PALGRAVE MACMILLAN
Houndmills, Basingstoke, Hampshire RG21 6XS and
175 Fifth Avenue, New York, N. Y. 10010
Companies and representatives throughout the world

PALGRAVE MACMILLAN is the global academic imprint of the Palgrave Macmillan division of St. Martin's Press, LLC and of Palgrave Macmillan Ltd. Macmillan® is a registered trademark in the United States, United Kingdom and other countries. Palgrave is a registered trademark in the European Union and other countries.

ISBN 1–4039–1516–4

This book is printed on paper suitable for recycling and made from fully managed and sustained forest sources.

A catalogue record for this book is available from the British Library.

Library of Congress Cataloging-in-Publication Data
The economics of enlargement / edited by Stefano Manzocchi.
    p. cm. -- (Central issues in contemporary economic theory & policy)
  Includes bibliographical references and index.
  ISBN 1–4039–1516–4
    1. Europe, Eastern--Economic integration. 2. Europe, Central--Economic integration. 3. Europe--Economic integration. 4. International economic integration. I. Manzocchi, Stefano. II. Central issues in contemporary economic theory and policy

  HC244.E24478 2003
  337.1'42--dc21

                                        2003049800

10   9   8   7   6   5   4   3   2   1
12   11   10   09   08   07   06   05   04   03

Printed and bound in Great Britain by
Antony Rowe Ltd, Chippenham and Eastbourne

Contents

Introduction

Stefano Manzocchi*

Università di Perugia

A sound and popular economic argument nowadays is that, in the last two decades, the United States have taken the global lead in product and process innovation with the gestation and birth of the so-called *Information Technology Revolution*, and that this has contributed to the outstanding performance of the American economy in the 1990s *vis-à-vis* other industrial partners, notably the European Union (EU) and Japan (see for instance Schreyer [9]). On different grounds, one can argue that in the past decade the EU has taken the leadership in another sort of innovative activity, namely institution-building and institutional change. First, the creation of a true single market for goods, services and factors, still under way but remarkably advanced today relative to the early 1990s; and second, the launch of the monetary union and the euro, have correctly endorsed the vision of Europe as being «under construction». We can now say that, ten years later, institutional innovation has progressively shaped an Economic and Monetary Union that, although still imperfect, is much closer to the ideal of «one money, one market». The debate is open on whether this is contributing, or will soon contribute, to European growth.

While the completion of the single market is not fully behind us — think for instance of financial integration — the European

---

* Stefano Manzocchi is Professor of Economics at the Department of Economics.

Union is on the eve of a new step in institutional transformation. After the launch of the euro, it is now time for shifting the Union's border to the East[1]. The challenge facing the Union at the start of the Eastern enlargement, whose first wave should be decided at the end of 2002 and implemented in 2004-2006, cannot be underestimated. A region of about 100 million inhabitants will be integrated into the EU; but, given the existing income gap between the two halves of Europe, the Union's GDP will increase by only 5% after enlargement. Populations deeply involved in European history will become again part of the continental *polis*, but ten years ago these same populations emerged from about half a century of Soviet domination and planned economy. A complex net of similarities and differences makes the Eastern enlargement something different from previous episodes of EU expansion.

The last two enlargements of the EU were, first, to the South, and then, to the North. The accession of Greece, Portugal and Spain in the 1980s brought relatively low-income partners in the Union, and this changed the economic geography and the budgetary structure of the EU. However, both the population size and the average income gap of the countries then involved in the Southern enlargement were about half of those of the current candidate countries. The Northern enlargement of the 1990s actually raised the average per capita income of the EU, and the accession of Austria, Finland and Sweden brought a net positive contribution to the Union's budget. This time the picture is completely different. The future members of the EU are, and will be for quite a long time, significantly poorer than the existing members. Their average wages will be lower than those of the incumbents, hence there could be an incentive for workers to move westward, and for capital to go eastward. Their core inflation rates will probably be higher, due to the rise in the relative price of services: productivity in the tertiary sector cannot grow as quickly as in manufacturing, while the demand for services is evolving at a faster-than-average

---

[1] The current enlargement process concerns ten formerly planned economies of Central Eastern Europe (CEE), plus Malta and Cyprus which will be usually neglected in this volume.

pace. Finally, their net contribution to the EU budget should be persistently negative. All this will impact on a number of EU policies and institutions, in the fields of migration and border flows, financial and budgetary provisions, monetary policy and the working of the European Central Bank (ECB), product and labour market regulations, just listing the economic aspects.

Forced by the prospect of future admission, the Eastern candidates have reformed their societies, and their economies have become more similar to their Western counterparts in the last decade. Future accession has played a role in shaping the expectations of economic agents, both in the candidate countries and on international markets, and has then contributed to shelter the candidates from the financial turmoil following the crises in Russia (1998), Brazil (1999) and Turkey (2001).[2] It is not surprising that economists have reached different conclusions on the impact of the next enlargement, depending on whether they have put more emphasis on the achievements of CEE's transition, or on the road ahead before reaching Western standards (for a review centred on trade aspects, see Brenton and Manzocchi [4]).

Of course, a number of studies have been released on the feasible effects, costs and benefits of the Eastern Enlargement, and more will be published as its start approaches.[3] In this volume, we will not focus on the costs and benefits of the next enlargement, nor on their distribution among incumbents and newcomers. Rather, this volume has a different, twofold aim. First, to introduce and discuss a number of «sensitive» economic chapters along the way to enlargement, for instance real and nominal convergence before accession to the EU and Euroland, or agricultural and structural policies in an enlarged Union. The Eastern Enlargement will necessarily lead to another round of deep political and institutional reform and adjustment within the EU. This was clear at the time the political decision was taken to encourage the countries of Central Eastern Europe to apply for accession to the

---

[2] The negative spill-overs of the Argentinian crisis of 2001 have in general been more limited.

[3] Among the most quoted works, see BALDWIN R. *et* AL. [1], BOERI T. - BRUECKER H. [3], EUROPEAN COMMISSION [6], GROS D. *et* AL. [7].

EU, namely in early 1990s. Since then, however, other priorities
have ranked high in the list of European policymakers, first of all
the process leading to monetary unification. At the same time, the
enlargement countdown has not been stopped, and the need for
EU institutional and political reforms has become even clearer.
The *Nice Treaty* makes some steps in the direction of adapting the
institutional framework to a 27 members EU, but the Treaty falls
short of fulfilling the reform requirements of the enlargement.[4]
The *Laeken Council* of 2000 made another step forward with the
launch of a *Convention*, whose purpose is to make constitutional
reform proposals to be debated in the next Intergovernmental Conference. At the same time, the Commission released a *White Book*
on European governance with a number of suggestions to make
European institutions more effective. A key issue for the future of
the EU is how the Union will accommodate the increasing heterogeneity of its member states.

The second aim of the volume is to offer a representative sample of what can be defined by the *Economics of Transition and
Enlargement*. More than ten years ago, the exit from planning towards a market economy in most of Central Eastern Europe and
Asia (China only partially excluded) has prompted a wave of economic research on the features of this transformation, and on the
problems facing the countries involved in it. This has become
known as the *Economics of Transition*, and has been recognised
as a specific field of analysis, with scholars and journals devoted
to it.[5] This field has yielded remarkable spill-overs and cross-fer-
tilisation with other branches of the economic profession, and is
currently been revitalised by the next enlargement, which adds to
the number of open questions and developments therefore requiring more research, and of even more sophisticated nature.

Hence, in this special issue of the Rivista di Politica Economica we look at the «economics of enlargement» both as a
range of critical themes, open for political assessment and decision, and as new lines of economic thinking stimulated by the

---

[4] See BALDWIN R. et AL. [2] for a discussion.
[5] See CAMPOS N. F., CORICELLI F. [4] for a recent survey, and JOURNAL OF ECO-
NOMIC PERSPECTIVES [8] for a number of recent contributions.

complex process of former planned economies entering the European Union, by itself a unique experiment in contemporary history and possibly the most original innovation in institutional design in the last century. In asking such a distinguished panel of authors to contribute to the volume, my purpose was to accomplish a good balance between the relevance of the topics covered and the novelty of the instruments and methodologies adopted. The reader can judge whether such balance has been reached.

The first two essays provide a broad and insightful analysis of respectively, production and trade aspects, and nominal and financial developments, in Central Eastern Europe (CEE) on the eve of enlargement. Michael Landesmann and Robert Stehrer explore the process of industrial transformation and the evolution of trade competitiveness in CEE. They put forward an original interpretation of the dynamics of comparative advantage, based on the potential for catching-up and the relative evolution of productivity and wage costs at the sectoral level. Applying Gerschenkron's concept of «backwardness' advantage» to the dynamics of sectoral, instead of aggregate, productivity, Landesmann and Stehrer argue that not only price competitiveness, but also foreign investment attractiveness and quality upgrading, are driven by the sectoral potential for catching-up in CEE. The key message of their paper is that trade specialisation changes in CEE according to the potential for catching-up in different industries, and the «social capabilities» available for exploiting such potential. Their paper also discards simple views of CEE as a single backward region. Instead, it shows that a more advanced area whose trade specialisation has evolved towards high and medium tech industries (Central Europe and Slovenia), coexists with a region more oriented towards traditional sectors (the Balkans). Enlargement could trigger, they argue, another step in structural change and real convergence in both the more and the less advanced countries of Central Eastern Europe.

The paper by Daniel Gros tackles the issue of nominal convergence between CEE and the EU. The most advanced among candidate countries, he reminds us, could be only four years away from entering the European Monetary Union (EMU), and in fact

their performance in terms of nominal admittance criteria is good
compared to that of Mediterranean countries (Spain, Italy and
Portugal) before their accession in the 1990s. However, the recent
history of financial and currency distress in Western Europe and
emerging countries warns us not to downplay the risk of speculative attacks before CEE enters Euroland. In this respect, Gros
suggests that fiscal policies and current accounts must be kept under scrutiny in Eastern Europe, and that careful attention must
be paid to the real exchange rate in order to avoid unsustainable
appreciation. As noted before, CEE's currencies have shown remarkable resilience during the recent financial turmoil following
emerging market crises in Russia, Brazil and Turkey. Nonetheless,
the expectation of a devaluation at the time of fixing the conversion rate with the euro could trigger speculative attacks as EMU
membership becomes feasible.

The dynamics of the real exchange rate is at the core of the
paper by Fabrizio Coricelli and Bostjan Jazbec. They model the
so-called *Balassa-Samuelson effect* of real appreciation under productivity growth in the tradable sector: when productivity gains
are lower in the non-tradable service sector, but wages are
equalised, the price of services tends to increase leading to inflation and real appreciation. The value added of their contribution
stands in the special way the dynamics of the real exchange rate
is modelled. Coricelli and Jazbec take into account the distortions
inherent in Soviet economies, especially the excessive output of
industrial goods and the insufficient amount of services, relative
to demand, under central planning. A key point of Coricelli and
Jazbec is that, even once such distortions are removed, equilibrium real exchange rate appreciation can yield large inflation differentials between CEE and Euroland. The reason is that growth
and catching up in the most advanced among CEE countries are
mainly driven by productivity gains in the tradable industrial sectors (see Landesmann and Stehrer), and this could foster inflation
according to the Balassa-Samuelson effect. In a word, *real convergence* may come along with *nominal divergence* in an enlarged
Europe. Coricelli and Jazbec argue that an early adoption of the
euro in CEE could reduce inflation differentials, but not eliminate

them. In order to adjust for an increasing heterogeneity of core inflation rates in the enlarged Union, new arrangements within the ECB and new frameworks for monetary policy will have to be conceived.

Tito Boeri and Joaquim Oliveira Martins provide another essay in what we have defined as the *Economics of Transition and Enlargement*. They set up a theoretical model that relates the output collapse at the beginning of the post-communist age, with the mismatch between an increasing «love for variety» in consumer's preferences and a rigid supply structure in CEE. Here, similarly to the Coricelli-Jazbec model, central planning distortions, namely the bias towards heavy industry producing standardised goods, leave a heavy heritage for the transition process. Boeri and Oliveira Martins convincingly argue that successful transition is conditional on the creation of new enterprises, which can gradually match the excess demand for differentiated goods without incurring balance-of-payments problems. Unemployment benefits can support this process by providing seed capital for self-employment choices; if they are too high, however, job search can be discouraged. Boeri and Oliveira Martins also observe that, compared with the EU, the economic environment in CEE is still unfavourable to enterprise creation due to the weakness of the financial and infrastructure systems. As enlargement is approaching, they suggest that EU structural programs towards CEE should be focused on the removal of these bottlenecks.

The paper by Cinzia Alcidi, Gianmarco Ottaviano and Stefano Manzocchi emphasises another element of economic disadvantage of Eastern vis-i-vis Western Europe, namely the different size of their respective «internal» markets. Despite the Association Agreements of the early 1990s that lowered tariff barriers between the two halves of Europe, the exclusion of CEE from the Internal Market and the Monetary Union has raised the relative cost of making business in Eastern Europe. Enterprise location on the Western side has become more profitable because a larger market has become available at ever lower trade and foreign exchange costs. Alcidi and others run numerical simulations showing that the welfare cost of EU exclusion might have been quite high for CEE, and that it might not have been fully counterbalanced by the progress in economic transition. From this perspective, the Eastern Enlargement (and the adoption of the euro) will level the competition field, as a single internal market will be available for firms located on both sides of Europe. In the medium run, this could provide an incentive for enterprise delocalisation from the EU towards CEE, and therefore trigger some political opposition in Western Europe.

However, one has to recall that the process of industrial integration between CEE and the EU will not start after enlargement, but has been under way for a more than a decade and is now reality. Salvatore Baldone, Fabio Sdogati and Lucia Tajoli analyse the pattern of productive integration from an original perspective, namely that of the competitiveness gains attainable by EU companies through a so-called «fragmentation» process. Fragmentation stands for the vertical re-organisation of the industrial chain on a multinational scale: in the case of pan-European relations, it is usually aimed at a reduction in global costs obtained by moving the more labour-intensive phases to Eastern Europe. The empirical results of Baldone and others are surprising: they find that — in a so-called «traditional» sector like textiles and apparel — EU-CEE industrial fragmentation has led to cost savings of the order of 40-50 % for Italian firms, and even more for German firms. This has allowed these companies to face the competition coming from low-cost regions like Southern and Eastern Asia. An important message one gets from the paper by Baldone and others is that East-West industrial competitiveness cannot be simply assessed on the basis of bilateral trade balances, or the dynamics of export shares: more complex industrial strategies, including «fragmentation», require new types of conceptual and empirical analysis.

The two following papers are devoted to «hot» issues in the negotiations between candidate countries and the EU, as well as among the current EU members. In his essay on structural policies and enlargement, Giuseppe Mele argues that the time is ripe for a comprehensive debate on the meaning, working and financing of EU structural and regional policies. First of all, a number of ambiguities concerning the role and effectiveness of structural funds need to be solved. The way Mele summarises the current argument on structural policies is the following: *a)* per capita income dispersion at the EU regional level has not decreased in the past fifteen years; *b)* the Eastern Enlargement will lead to more regional inequality; *c)* hence, structural and regional policies have to be maintained although their impact on the EU budget must be carefully assessed. The alternative, and more convincing, logical sequence suggested by Mele runs as follows: *a')* have EU structural policies been successful in reducing regional inequality in the past? *b')* how should they be modified, provided enlargement will magnify income inequality? *c')* what kind of compromise can be found between the financial expectations of new members, and the need of avoiding a much heavier burden for current members? Behind these alternative ways of thinking at regional policy reform, there is perhaps a more fundamental ambiguity in the nature of EU structural policies, to be intended either as a «common» pool of resources to be managed by the Union, or as a «common» set of rules to be agreed on and respected by member states when implementing their own regional policies.

The impression one gets from the paper by Fabrizio De Filippis and Luca Salvatici is that a similar, possibly even more arduous, set of pending issues is involved in the current debate on the reform of the EU agricultural policy. Here again, the next enlargement is having a disruptive effect on long-standing politico-economic equilibria that for many years prevented the radical reform of an inefficient set of policies. Such politico-economic equilibria were a key element of the founding contract of the European Community, and have afterwards been preserved to avoid political turmoil, at the EU and/or at the individual member state level. For instance, the current system of direct payments to EU farmers was initially justified with the need of compensating them for the lower revenues they would have obtained in the transition to world market prices. Afterwards, it has been maintained despite its huge costs, in order to preserve the politico-economic equilibrium among large EU member countries, on the one hand, and to appease the strong agricultural lobbies inside some of these countries, on the other hand. Now, as stressed by De Filippis and Salvatici, the Eastern Enlargement calls for a deep reform in the direction of a re-nationalisation of the Common Agricultural Policy (CAP) for at least three reasons. First, the application the current agricultural policies to the new Eastern members would undermine their incentive for restructuring inefficient farms, as it would immediately raise net farmers' revenues and loosen their budget constraint. Second, in the case of some candidate countries whose agricultural sector is mildly protected, applying current CAP provisions will lead to a de-liberalisation of the CEE markets, clearly at odds with WTO obligations recently subscribed by the EU. Third, if current CAP provisions are extended to newcomers, the enlargement will lead to a jump in the EU agricultural budget and to big distributive conflicts among member states.

The final essay by Friedrich Heinemann takes us more deeply into the realm of bureaucratic interest and lobbying. This enlargement, he argues, threatens the vested interests of politicians and lobbyists in many ways, and a politico-economic perspective is required in order to supplement the conventional view economists offer of this event. Many aspects of the enlargement process can be interpreted in a different light, and what is often presented by economists as a win-win outcome may bring about costs, as well as benefits, for incumbents and entrants. For instance, according to Heinemann the reforms of the EU institutions decided in Nice, or the rules for the participation of candidate countries in the Convention, were clearly designed to protect the interests of EU-15 representatives relative to future members. Similarly, the transition periods envisaged by the EU in the negotiations concerning «sensitive» enlargement chapters such as labour mobility or the extension of direct farm payments to candidate countries, tend to shift the burden of potential conflict beyond the relevant time horizon of EU politicians and bureaucrats — that of the next elections or the next round of appointments — but at the same time tend to postpone essential reforms.

At the beginning of the XIX century, the Prince of Metternich used to say that Asia started just beyond the *Rennweg*, the avenue that crosses Vienna. The essays collected in this volume prove that, provided it was true at that time, this is no longer the case even after fifty years of separation. Enlargement will make Central Eastern Europe even closer to the European Union, and may have beneficial effects on competitiveness and welfare in the EU as well, but a supplement of institutional change is needed. When the political decision of rejoining the two halves of Europe was taken more than a decade ago, it was implicitly decided that the European Union would have undertaken a deep process of reshaping. This reform process was needed in order to allow the Union to work with 27 or more members, and to employ its resources more effectively to promote growth, convergence and welfare. Institutional and political innovation must now advance, in such diverse fields like the conduct of monetary policy, the working of structural funds or the composition of EU institutions, to adjust for the accession of new members and to make the Union more effective. The Eastern Enlargement is now reality, and new governance solutions must be thought and implemented to the advantage of Easterners and Westerners alike: it is not yet time for Europe to give up its lead in institutional innovation.

BIBLIOGRAPHY

[1] BALDWIN R. - FRANCOIS J. F. - PORTES R. «The Costs and Benefits of Eastern Enlargement: The Impact on the EU and Central Europe», *Economic Policy*, n. 24, 1997, pp. 127-70.

[2] BALDWIN R. - BERGLOF E. - GIAVAZZI F. - WINDGREN M. «Nice Try: Should the Treaty of Nice be Ratified?» London, Centre for Economic Policy Research, *CEPR Monitoring European Integration*, n. 11, 2001.

[3] BOERI T. - BRUECKER H., *The Impact of Eastern on Employment and Labour Markets in the EU Member State*, Report to the Employment and Social Affairs Directorate General of the European Commission, Brussels, 2001.

[4] BRENTON P. - MANZOCCHI S. (eds), *Enlargement, Trade and Investment*, Cheltenham, Edward Elgar, (UK), forthcoming 2002.

[5] CAMPOS N. F. - CORICELLI F., «Growth in Transition: What We Know, What We Don't and What We Should», London, Centre for Economic Policy Research, *CEPR Discussion Paper*, n. 3246.

[6] EUROPEAN COMMISSION, «The Economic Impact of Enlargement», *Enlargement Papers*, n. 4, June 2001.

[7] GROS D. - NÙÑEZ FERRER R.J. - PELKMANS J., «Long Run Economic Aspects of the European Union's Eastern Enlargement», *WRR Working Document*, n. 109, The Hague, Netherlands Scientific Council for Government Policy, 2000.

[8] JOURNAL OF ECONOMIC PERSPECTIVES, *Symposium on Transition Economies*, vol. 16, n. 1, Winter 2002, pp. 3 - 124.

[9] SCHREYER P. «Contribution of Information and Communication Technology to Output Growth: a Study of the G7 Countries», OECD Directorate for Science, Technology and Industry, Paris, *OECD, DSTI/DOC 2000/2*, 2000.

Evolving Competitiveness of CEEC's in an Enlarged Europe

Michael A. Landesmann - Robert Stehrer*

The Vienna Institute for International Economics Studies WIIW

Questo lavoro ripercorre l'evoluzione della competitività e della specializzazione produttiva e commerciale dei paesi dell'Europa Centro-Orientale. I sentieri di specializzazione intrapresi da tali paesi si possono interpretare utilizzando una combinazione tra un modello di catching-up ed uno di vantaggi comparati. In particolare, mostriamo come la dinamica della produttività e dei costi salariali nei diversi settori industriali dia luogo ad un complesso quadro evolutivo della competitività. Nel complesso, si delinea un panorama interessante ed anche inatteso della specializzazione in un'Europa allargata.

This paper discusses the evolution of competitiveness, industrial and trade specialisation of the countries of Central and Eastern Europe (CEECs). It is shown that the paths taken by the different CEECs have been quite diverse and we attempt to show that a combination of a catching-up plus trade specialisation model is required to understand the patterns of specialisation emerging in Central and Eastern Europe. We add information about the industrial allocation of FDI and comparative educational attainment. All the above yields an interesting (and at times unexpected) picture of the evolving division of labour in an enlarged Europe. [JEL Code: F02, F14, L6, O57, P52]

1. - Introduction

In this paper we analyse structural developments and the evolution of competitiveness in the countries of Central and Eastern Europe (CEECs). Since the beginning of the transition in 1989 the

---

* Michael A. Landesmann is Director and Robert Stehrer is Research Fellow.
N.B., the numbers in square brackets refer to the Bibliography at the end of the paper.

CEECs have gone through a dramatic process of systemic change and structural adjustment in which their integration into trade and production links with Western Europe has played a major role. This paper describes the processes of structural adjustment which have taken place and we shall take a particular stance with regard to the patterns of production and trade specialisation which have emerged in this process of East-West European integration. EU Enlargement will of course be a major step in this process towards full integration, but the basic outlines of the division of labour which is emerging in this 'enlarged Europe' have already become visible prior to that.

Underlying our analysis is a theoretical model (see Landesmann and Stehrer [21] [22]) which attempts to combine a model of catching-up with international trade specialisation and thus falls into the category of the dynamic modelling of trade and growth (for other approaches, see Krugman [19], Grossman and Helpman [14]). The basic outlines of the model are simple and have been guided by the 'stylized facts' observed in growth patterns of successful and less successful catching-up economies. Such economies start off with substantial productivity (and product quality) gaps which are not the same across all industrial branches. Typically, the gaps are greater in the technologically more advanced branches and less in the technologically less demanding ones. This has the following implications: full catching-up has a longer way to go in the technologically more advanced branches and this can be interpreted in two ways. On the one hand, it is 'more difficult' to catch up fully in such branches as it requires a much greater effort in learning, skill acquisition and often a big jump in organisational and managerial capacities; on the other hand, it means that the scope for differential productivity growth (and for product quality upgrading) between the 'technology leader' and the catching-up economy ('the laggard') is higher where the initial gap is larger.

This is a simple application of the Gerschenkron hypothesis ('advantage of backwardness') which states that the 'potential' for growth is highest where the 'initial gap' is the highest (Gerschenkron [12]). This principle has, of course, been widely applied at the aggregate level and is the background for the much tested 'convergence' hypothesis in the many recent aggregate growth studies (for a survey of such studies see Temple [28]). What is special in our model is that we apply this principle at the industrial level with the implication that those industries have the greatest potential for productivity growth and product quality up-grading that start off with the biggest 'initial gaps'. Of course, as pointed out early on by Abramovitz [2], actual growth is not necessarily equal to potential growth as countries (and in our case industries) might not be able to exploit this potential. Abramovitz emphasised here the importance of 'social capabilities', i.e. a wide range of institutional and behavioural requirements which are necessary such that actual catching-up comes as close as possible to potential catching-up. This analysis opens a wide range of possible catching-up patterns. In the case of our more disaggregated analysis it also means that the dynamics of comparative advantages which determines a country's position in the international division of labour can follow quite different patterns for catching-up economies. At a more concise level, the dynamics of specialisation advantages and disadvantages is determined by the timing of 'switchovers' in the comparative cost structures across industrial branches. Here the dynamics of relative productivity growth rates and of wage rates across industrial branches plays a decisive role. We have examined these patterns of comparative advantages across the historical experiences of a wide range of catching-up economies in a number of analytical and empirical studies (see Landesmann and Stehrer [22], and Stehrer and Woerz [27]) and will show in this paper that the approach gets also validated in the analysis of patterns of catching-up and trade specialisation of CEECs after the transition.

In an extension of this approach, it is possible to show that the allocation of Foreign Direct Investment (FDI) across industrial branches is similarly affected by the dynamics of comparative advantages although in this context we also emphasise the role which price-cost margins (Schumpeterian profits) play in determining (particularly foreign) investment activity. In the present paper we shall also show that — similarly to the uneven productivity dynamics mentioned above — product quality up-grading also proceeds at different speeds across industrial branches and this also represents another important aspect of catching-up. Just as the model implies that the range of experiences with respect to catching-up patterns and hence of the positions that economies occupy in the international division of labour can be quite wide, this is borne out by the diversity of experiences we observe in Central and Eastern Europe.

We shall now give an overview of the structure of the paper: Section 2 summarises the broad patterns of structural shifts (across the primary, secondary and tertiary sectors) which we observed since the beginning of the transition and it also reviews some aggregate developments with regard to output, employment and productivity growth. Section 3 takes a closer look at structural change within the manufacturing sector and reveals at this level some of the interesting emerging patterns of industrial specialisation of CEECs. Section 4 reports on the main determinants of industrial cost competitiveness, i.e. productivity, wage rates and labour unit costs and shows in which industry groupings (lower tech, resource based, higher tech) the strongest inroads were made in relative productivity and unit cost developments. Section 5 discusses trade performance and uses various classifications guided by industrial organisation and skill content criteria to show the qualitative pattern of trade specialisation emerging in CEECs in relation to the European Union (EU). We also discuss in some detail the patterns of product quality up-grading mentioned above. Section 6 finally gives some evidence on FDI allocation across industrial branches as well as on educational attainment in the CEECs as two of the important factors which affect the patterns of catching-up and industrial specialisation. It also provides an outlook on the impact which EU Enlargement will have on the further integration processes between Central and Eastern and Western Europe.

2. - Broad Patterns of Structural Change: Deindustrialisation - Tertiarisation - De- (and Re-) Agrarisation

In this Section we review shortly the patterns of structural change which took place in the CEECs at the broad sectoral level. Overall employment drops since the beginning of the transition were very substantial in the CEECs. The employment reductions were concentrated in some countries (Hungary, Poland) in the early phases of the transition, 1990-1993, while in other economies, such as Romania and the Slovak Republic, substantial overall employment declines took place also in periods after 1993. GDP experienced in all transition economies dramatic early declines (Janos Kornai coined these the 'transformational recessions') and most of the economies also experienced further — at times — sharp interruptions in their growth processes due to delayed corporate restructuring and banking crises (often called 'secondary transformational recessions') and/or macroeconomic imbalances, most often caused by unsustainable current account deficits.

At the broad sectoral level also quite strong shifts took place which can be interpreted as structural convergence with more advanced Western economies and can be summarised under the headings 'deindustrialisation' and 'tertiarisation'. It is well-known that the Communist economies emphasised industry at the cost of services and, furthermore, service activities were often supplied within big industrial combines which meant that these service activities were classified under industry. With the transition a strong move towards the expansion of the service sector took place and a scaling down of the industrial sector. With respect to agriculture a somewhat more complex picture emerged which will be discussed below.

Graphs 1 and 2 demonstrate the evolution over the period 1989 to 2000 of the shares of the three classic sectors (agriculture, industry, services) in value added and employment respectively. Graph 3 allows a comparison of the sectoral employment structures after a decade of adjustment between the CEECs and two groups of EU countries, the 'EU North' (composed of Belgium, France, Germany, UK) and the 'EU South' (composed of Greece, Portugal, Spain). We can observe the following tendencies:

GRAPH 1

COMPARISON OF CEEC'S VALUE ADDED STRUCTURES
IN 1989, 1993 AND 2000

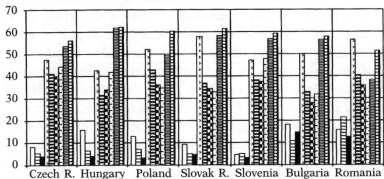

Agriculture & Fishing
☐ 1989 ⊟ 1993 ■ 2000

Industry & Construction
▣ 1989 ⊟ 1993 ◪ 2000

Services
▯ 1989 ⊟ 1993 ⊟ 2000

Source: WIIW.

GRAPH 2

COMPARISON OF CEEC'S EMPLOYMENT STRUCTURES
IN 1989, 1993 AND 2000
(based on registration data)

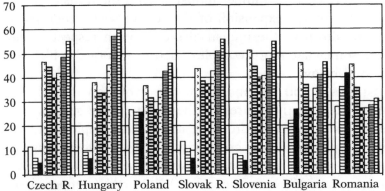

Agriculture & Fishing
☐ 1989 ⊟ 1993 ■ 2000

Industry & Construction
▣ 1989 ⊟ 1993 ◪ 2000

Services
▯ 1989 ⊟ 1993 ⊟ 2000

Source: WIIW.

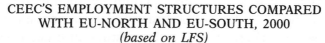

GRAPH 3

CEEC'S EMPLOYMENT STRUCTURES COMPARED
WITH EU-NORTH AND EU-SOUTH, 2000
(based on LFS)

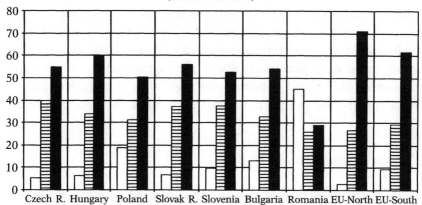

☐ Agriculture & Fishing
▤ Industry & Construction
■ Services
Source: WIIW.

2.1 De - and Re-Agrarisation

While there was a tendency in most of the CEECs to reduce the size of the agricultural sector, there are/were exceptions to this: in some economies the share of the labour force in agriculture (and in Romania even the absolute number) has actually increased! This is true for Bulgaria and Romania, while for all the other CEECs there were losses in the shares (and dramatic losses in absolute numbers) of agricultural employment. Interestingly, the economies with the larger agricultural sectors (Poland, Bulgaria, Romania) had smaller percentage declines (or even increases) in the employment shares of this sector than the countries which started off with a smaller agricultural sector (Czech and Slovak Republics, Hungary, Slovenia). Hence, regarding the 'primary sector', the transition brought about processes both of 'deagrarisation' as well as — in some countries — of 'reagrarisation'. The second type of pattern should be considered a transitory phenomenon, resulting from the severe employment crisis in the industrial sector (especially in countries such as Bulgaria and Romania) and — so far — the limited absorption capacity in the services sector. There are also interesting discrepancies in the movements of value added shares and employment shares in agriculture: in value added, the shares of the agricultural sectors are declining in the most recent period also in those economies in which there were previously signs of 'reagrarisation' (Bulgaria and Romania); this trend supports the view that the phenomenon reflects mostly the dramatic overall jobs crisis in these countries.

2.2 Deindustrialisation

Broadly, one can also speak of a general process of 'deindustrialisation' with falling absolute employment levels in the industrial sectors (comprising manufacturing, mining, water and electricity supply, construction). In share terms, however, there are some interesting exceptions to the general decline of employment in the industrial sector. In Hungary the employment shares of the industrial sector have recovered after the initial drop at the beginning of the transition and value added shares have risen again in Hungary and the Czech Republic and stabilised in Slovenia. In relation to both the EU North and the EU South, some of the CEECs maintain, also at the end of the first decade of transition, a high share of industry in both value added and employment (for employment shares compared to EU-North and EU-South see Graph 3). There are again differences in value added and employment shares: the Czech Republic and Slovenia, followed by the Slovak Republic and Hungary are the countries with the highest employment shares in industry, while the Czech Republic, Slovenia and Romania, followed by Poland are the countries with the highest shares in value added. These differences reflect, of course, differences in relative sectoral productivity levels, e.g. the extremely low productivity level in Romanian agriculture would push up industry's share in value added in spite of its own low level of productivity. The levelling off of relative employment losses in manufacturing in some of the CEECs (such as Hungary and Poland) and persistence of manufacturing's relatively high value added shares could be an indication of the attractiveness of some of the CEECs as locations for some of Europe's industries within the context of an overall European division of labour.

2.3 *Tertiarisation*

As regards the 'tertiary sector', there are clear signs of a catching-up process of the CEECs in the relative size of this sector (although, just as in the West, the changes are partially due to statistical reclassifications and outsourcing of service activities previously undertaken within the other sectors). Again, the relative increase of the importance of the services sector in the CEECs over the last decade has not necessarily been in line with the size of the initial gap (relative to the Western European employment structure). Thus, countries such as Hungary, Slovenia, Slovakia and the Czech Republic experienced very substantial increases in the shares of the services sector, while countries such as Romania and Poland where the initial shares of the services sector in overall employment were relatively low, experienced rather modest share increases. In absolute terms, the employment gains in the services sector were however far from sufficient to compensate for the employment losses in the other two sectors.

3. - Convergence and Divergence in Manufacturing Structure

Let us now look more closely at the ongoing structural change within the manufacturing sector in the CEECs. We use data from the the Vienna Institute for International Economic Studies (WI-IW) industrial database which reports several variables at the NACE rev. 1, 2-digit level (DA-DN) for seven Central and Eastern European countries. In this paper we restrict the analysis to the period 1993-2000, i.e. after the transformational crises. The data, which are partly collected from international and from national sources are likely to be at times inconsistent over the years (e.g. as data sources changed or for methodological reasons, such as coverage of the small enterprise sector). To avoid these problems we tested the series for a significant change in the growth rate when a structural break was indicated by using dummies in the estimates on growth rates. If this procedure indicated a significant break the data series were adjusted accordingly.

Let us first get an overview of growth processes in aggregate manufacturing over the period 1993-2000, i.e. after the immediate impact of the 'transformational recession'. Graph 4 shows the trend (*per annum*) growth rates of output, employment and labour productivity. We can see that trend employment growth over this period in manufacturing was negative in all of the transition countries. It ranged from –8.1 and –7.1% in Bulgaria and Romania to –1.4% in Poland. Output growth was even more diverse, with still negative growth over that period in Bulgaria and Romania and a wide spectrum of growth rates amongst the 'more advanced' of the candidate countries. The relatively high growth rates in manufacturing output in Hungary (11.9) and Poland (9.4) are particularly striking with rather modest trend growth in the other three economies. (Labour) productivity growth results directly from the difference in output and employment growth and shows again a quite wide range of diversity, with Hungary and Poland again the forerunners driven by high output growth, followed by a range of economies with *per annum* average growth rates in labour productivity of 5-7%. It is clear from these figures that the relationship between output and employment growth is quite differentiated across the transition countries and, most likely (as would be seen if the time series were analysed more closely) unstable across time, reflecting major periods of restructuring and other periods when labour hoarding takes place in the wake of output declines.

We now move on to present a qualitative picture of the ongoing structural changes within manufacturing. For this purpose we do not report developments in all the 14 industries contained in the database but aggregated the industries into three broader categories (note that these do not cover all manufacturing industries):

GRAPH 4

GROWTH RATES OF EMPLOYMENT, OUTPUT, AND PRODUCTIVITY
(1993-2000)

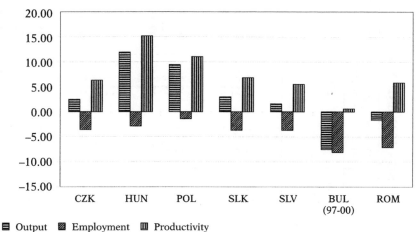

■ Output   ▨ Employment   ▥ Productivity

Source: WɪɪW industrial database; own calculations.

1) *low-tech, labour-intensive industries:* food products, beverages and tobacco (*DA*), textiles and textile products (*DB*), and
leather and leather products (*DC*)

2) *resource-intensive industries:* wood and wood products
(*DD*), coke, refined petroleum products and nuclear fuel (*DF*),
chemicals, chemical products and man-made fibres (*DG*), and other non-metallic mineral products (*DI*)

3) *medium-, to high-tech industries:* machinery and equipment
(*DK*), electrical and optical equipment (*DL*), and transport equipment (*DM*)

Table 1 reports data on employment and output shares (both
at prices 1996 and at current prices) and the wage structure for
the seven Central and Eastern European countries and Austria as
the benchmark[1]. Further Table 2 shows deviations of the variables
from Austria in percentage points.

---

[1] An average of EU economies would have been preferable for this comparison, but Austria was singled out as a benchmark country for reasons of data availability.

TABLE 1

CHANGES IN THE STRUCTURE OF MANUFACTURING - 1993 AND 2000

	Employment shares			Output (at prices 1996)			Output structure (at current prices)		Wage structure	
	1993	2000	Employment growth (p.a.)	1993	2000	Output growth (p.a)	1993	2000	1993	2000
Austria[1]										
Low tech	19.64	18.21	-2.39	20.51	17.08	2.36	21.59	16.91	84.57	79.35
Resource intensive	17.00	16.17	-1.79	23.66	20.72	3.00	23.30	21.74	103.01	104.86
Medium-high tech	29.22	30.66	-0.17	27.08	34.05	9.23	26.74	33.08	108.48	112.32
Czech Republic[1]										
Low tech	24.65	22.69	-4.80	27.07	19.94	-0.81	28.31	22.39	88.54	83.20
Resource intensive	14.22	17.16	-1.72	20.60	18.00	1.97	18.59	18.60	105.63	113.70
Medium-high tech	31.53	33.05	-3.28	25.60	36.35	7.76	26.37	30.16	99.46	106.84
Hungary										
Low tech	39.20	36.95	-3.91	34.73	16.64	1.83	34.66	19.17	85.44	77.15
Resource intensive	16.55	15.27	-4.11	27.58	11.28	-0.73	25.95	17.18	124.54	133.67
Medium-high tech	22.67	32.01	1.32	16.70	56.80	24.40	18.61	46.76	101.93	111.51
Poland[1]										
Low tech	35.56	33.08	-2.59	34.86	27.49	5.61	35.91	30.53	88.55	81.92
Resource intensive	15.63	16.82	-0.54	21.76	19.56	7.31	22.80	20.07	106.47	110.55
Medium-high tech	26.22	22.70	-3.51	19.22	24.40	12.10	18.64	23.09	105.16	113.94

[1] 1999 instead of 2000 for current output

TABLE 1 (cont.)

	Employment shares			Output (at prices 1996)			Output structure (at current prices)		Wage structure	
	1993	2000	Employment growth (p.a.)	1993	2000	Output growth (p.a)	1993	2000	1993	2000
Slovakia										
Low tech	27.52	26.85	-0.03	26.38	17.83	-0.78	25.22	18.52	85.59	85.60
Resource intensive	17.08	16.18	-1.27	24.27	20.87	2.94	25.26	19.61	111.33	103.71
Medium-high tech	31.70	28.62	-1.68	18.10	32.90	9.99	18.46	27.29	95.74	105.39
Slovenia[1]										
Low tech	29.21	26.08	-3.83	27.10	23.67	0.11	26.78	23.65	95.44	86.41
Resource intensive	14.29	15.40	-0.89	18.90	19.63	1.76	20.09	18.35	110.85	113.48
Medium-high tech	26.84	25.88	-2.69	25.29	29.61	4.30	25.51	28.94	97.20	101.06
Bulgaria										
Low tech	29.22	43.28	-3.73	29.82	31.37	-4.15	32.67	29.60	97.38	81.21
Resource intensive	13.46	14.22	-8.61	25.58	31.72	-2.26	25.25	36.66	128.30	135.91
Medium-high tech	29.21	22.31	-13.33	14.59	13.58	-6.82	17.82	12.39	105.94	102.52
Romania										
Low tech	32.05	37.90	-4.80	29.54	33.71	0.09	33.77	29.95	86.96	76.62
Resource intensive	15.60	15.49	-7.54	28.76	23.11	-5.06	24.49	26.72	110.97	114.15
Medium-high tech	28.92	24.66	-9.63	14.42	18.77	1.65	19.79	14.75	103.96	127.10

[1] 1999 instead of 2000 for current output

TABLE 2

CHANGES IN THE STRUCTURE OF MANUFACTURING (AUSTRIA = 100) - 1993 AND 2000

	Employment			Output (at prices 1996)			Output structure (at current prices)		Wage structure	
	1993	2000	Employment growth (p.a.)	1993	2000	Output growth (p.a)	1993	2000	1993	2000
Czech Republic[1]										
Low tech	5.01	4.48	-2.42	6.56	2.86	-3.17	6.72	5.48	3.97	3.86
Resource intensive	-2.78	0.99	0.07	-3.06	-2.72	-1.04	-4.71	-3.13	2.62	8.83
Medium-high tech	2.31	2.39	-3.12	-1.47	2.30	-1.47	-0.37	-2.92	-9.03	-5.48
Hungary										
Low tech	19.56	18.74	-1.52	14.22	-0.43	-0.53	13.07	2.26	0.87	-2.19
Resource intensive	-0.46	-0.90	-2.32	3.93	-9.44	-3.73	2.65	-4.56	21.53	28.81
Medium-high tech	-6.54	1.35	1.49	-10.38	22.75	15.17	-8.13	13.68	-6.55	-0.81
Poland[1]										
Low tech	15.92	14.87	-0.21	14.35	10.41	3.25	14.32	13.62	3.98	2.57
Resource intensive	-1.37	0.65	1.25	-1.89	-1.16	4.30	-0.50	-1.66	3.46	5.68
Medium-high tech	-3.00	-7.96	-3.34	-7.86	-9.65	2.87	-8.10	-9.99	-3.33	1.62
Slovakia										
Low tech	7.87	8.63	2.35	5.87	0.75	-3.14	3.63	1.61	1.02	6.25
Resource intensive	0.08	0.01	0.53	0.62	0.15	-0.06	1.96	-2.13	8.32	-1.15
Medium-high tech	2.48	-2.04	-1.52	-8.98	-1.16	0.76	-8.28	-5.79	-12.74	-6.93

[1] 1999 instead of 2000 for current output.

TABLE 2 (cont.)

	Employment			Output (at prices 1996)			Output structure (at current prices)		Wage structure	
	1993	2000	Employment growth (p.a.)	1993	2000	Output growth (p.a)	1993	2000	1993	2000
Slovenia[1]										
Low tech	9.57	7.86	-1.45	6.58	6.59	-2.25	5.19	6.75	10.86	7.06
Resource intensive	-2.71	-0.77	0.90	-4.76	-1.09	-1.25	-3.21	-3.38	7.84	8.62
Medium-high tech	-2.38	-4.78	-2.52	-1.78	-4.45	-4.93	-1.23	-4.14	-11.29	-11.26
Bulgaria										
Low tech	9.58	25.07	-1.34	9.31	14.29	-6.52	11.08	12.70	12.81	1.86
Resource intensive	-3.54	-1.95	-6.82	1.92	11.00	-5.26	1.95	14.92	25.29	31.05
Medium-high tech	-0.01	-8.36	-13.16	-12.49	-20.47	-16.05	-8.92	-20.69	-2.54	-9.80
Romania										
Low tech	12.40	19.69	-2.41	9.03	16.64	-2.27	12.18	13.04	2.39	-2.73
Resource intensive	-1.40	-0.68	-5.75	5.10	2.39	-8.06	1.19	4.98	7.96	9.29
Medium-high tech	-0.30	-6.00	-9.46	-12.65	-15.28	-7.58	-6.96	-18.33	-4.53	14.78

One can see that all countries started in 1993 with high shares in low-tech industries relative to Austria. In employment Hungary and Poland with more than about 20 and 16 percentage points above Austrian shares were the countries with the highest shares in low-tech industries. The lowest deviation from Austria can be observed for the Czech Republic. This corresponds to the data on output shares (either at current or constant 1996 prices). With regard to employment shares in medium-/high-tech industries only the Czech Republic and Slovakia showed initially higher employment shares than Austria reflecting a strong position of the engineering sector in these two economies. In terms of output shares, the medium-/high-tech sectors had in all countries lower output shares than the benchmark Austria (although for some countries these deviations were quite small). In the resource intensive sectors the shares relative to Austria are smallest on average both in terms of employment and output shares[2].

More interesting than these starting values are, however, the trends over time. Employment shares in low-tech sectors have been declining slightly in the Czech Republic, Hungary, Poland, Slovakia and Slovenia but have increased dramatically in Bulgaria (from about 30% to about 43%(!)) and in Romania. On the other hand one can see slight increases of employment shares in the medium-/high-tech sectors in the Czech Republic but very large increases in Hungary (from 23% to 32%). Relative to Austria all countries except Czech Republic and Hungary now show lower employment shares in medium-/high-tech sectors than in 1993. For the resource-intensive sectors there are no clear trends across countries and changes are small.

These trends in employment shares can either result from changes in output or changes in (labour) productivity (ignoring possible interactions between these two variables). Compared to Austria the output shares of low tech industries at constant 1996 prices have fallen dramatically in the Czech Republic, Hungary, Poland and Slovakia and remained almost stable for Slovenia. On

---

[2] One reason for this pattern is the relatively large share of resource intensive industries in Austria.

the other hand the shares of these industries compared to Austria have risen in Bulgaria and Romania from nine to about 16%[3]. This shows a clear pattern of specialisation amongst the CEECs. Regarding the medium-/high-tech sectors one can see the opposite tendencies for output measured at constant prices. Hungary increased its share dramatically from about 17% to more than 55%! The Czech Republic from 25 to 36%, and Slovakia from 18 to about 33%. In the other countries output shares of high-tech industries also increased, but at lower rates and remained more or less stable in Bulgaria. The rising share of high-tech output in Romania is due to the decreasing share of resource intensive industries (especially chemicals and chemical products (*DG*)). Output shares of high-tech industries at current prices were rising in all countries except for Bulgaria and Romania. Again a clear and diverse pattern of industrial specialisation gets revealed.

With respect to the wage structure one would expect that on average wage rates are relatively higher in the higher tech sectors (e.g. by the assumption that the skill-intensity is higher for these sectors or the higher productivity of these sectors). However, the general picture in 1993 was that average wages have been highest in all countries in the resource intensive sectors and lowest in the low-tech sectors. Comparing this with the year 2000 we can indeed see a catching-up of relative wage rates in the medium-high tech branches and a falling behind in the low tech branches. The question for comparative costs is whether such changes proceed above or below relative productivity level adjustments which will be explored in the next section of the paper. One can also find a trend towards a convergence of wage structures (e.g. compared to the Austrian as a representative of a Western European wage structure) although this process seems to be slow.

Note that the analysis of output and employment patterns already points towards our initial (Gerschenkron) hypothesis that specialisation patterns of catching-up economies may get direct-

---

[3] It is however interesting to see that the output shares of the low-tech industries at current prices have fallen in all countries (the highest again in Hungary and the Czech Republic) the difference to the constant price output shares being driven by changes in relative prices.

ed towards the medium-/higher-tech branches as was the case especially in Hungary where initially the gap might be the largest; but this requires the utilisation of a potential and this in turn depends on the existence or mobilisation and utilisation of 'capabilities' (to use Abramovitz' terms) in these areas. This was apparently not the case in Bulgaria and Romania and the experience in this respect was also quite differentiated amongst the other (more advanced) candidate countries. We now turn to the productivity and cost side of production in order to look at the development of productivity gaps and the evolution of comparative cost structures more directly. After that we study the emerging patterns of trade specialisation.

4. - Productivity, Wage Rates and Unit Labour Costs

Not only productivity matters for competitiveness but also wage rates play their role in shaping relative cost structures and hence the competitive position of different industries from the cost side. In Table 3 and 4 we have summarised the data again for the three types of industries (low-tech, resource-intensive, and high-tech).

Using the same database as before, we focus now on productivity, wage rates and unit labour costs. For productivity levels we use employment and data on output which are first expressed in national currency units (NCU) at prices 1996. For comparative analysis these can be converted either by using nominal exchange rates (EXR) or PPP rates (PPP) for the year 1996[4]. Output for industry i in country c in year t is denoted as $PR^c_{i,t}$. Data on wages and salaries $W^c_{i,t}$ are first obtained in NCU at nominal values. These data are converted into a common currency (Euro) using either current EXR or current PPP[5]. Data on employees $E^c_{i,t}$

---

[4] For this analysis we are constrained to using PPP rates for GDP as a whole. For selective countries we have been able to obtain industry-level unit value ratios to adjust for industry level differences in price levels, but this database is not large enough to allow the more extensive comparative analysis presented here.

[5] One might ask why one should look at wage rates also in PPP terms as one is interested in comparative actual wage costs. The reason could be that one might

refer to average employment levels over the years. Labour productivity $LPR^c_{i,t}$ is calculated as:

$$LPR^c_{i,t} = \frac{PR^c_{i,t}}{E^c_{i,t}}$$

Further, unit labour costs are defined as:

$$ULC^c_{i,t} = \frac{LPR^c_{i,t}}{W^c_{i,t} \Big/ E^c_{i,t}}$$

In Tables 3 and 4 wage rates, productivity levels and unit labour costs are compared to Austria (=100). The variables for Austria have been calculated analogously. Table 3 presents the data using the nominal exchange rates (EXR) conversion and in Table 4 the gaps are derived from PPP comparisons (both wage rates and productivity levels). The difference between the two tables thus reflects the development of the ratio between the exchange rate and the PPP rate. In the following we shall discuss first the three variables expressed at exchange rates.

4.1 Productivity

Expressed in nominal exchange rates all countries showed a large gap in 1993. The best performing country was Slovenia reaching a productivity level of about 27% (relative to Austria). Bulgaria and Romania only reached a productivity level of about 5 to 6 % the Austrian level.

---

want to conjecture what wage costs would be when price levels between the CEECs and the EU have converged. One could see such a comparison as an exercise multinationals might be interested in if they want to judge relative wage cost differentials also for the longer-run when the severe undervaluation of the CEECs national currencies would get eroded. In this case, workers would still ask at least for the same real wage rate as they now obtain, an estimate for which would be the wage rate at PPP rates.

TABLE 3

PRODUCTIVITY, WAGE AND UNIT LABOUR COST GAPS AT EXR - 1993 AND 1999

	Wage			Productivity			Unit labour costs		
	gap 1993	growth rate	gap 1999	gap 1993	growth rate	gap 1999	gap 1993	growth rate	gap 1999
Czech Republic									
Manufacturing total	7.79	-8.72	13.14	13.70	-1.05	14.58	48.10	-3.63	59.80
Low tech	8.49	-8.79	14.60	16.52	1.32	16.39	47.39	-4.77	58.90
Resource intensive	7.00	-9.31	12.39	15.49	-4.03	16.56	58.54	0.20	55.35
Medium-high tech	7.36	-9.58	12.85	11.90	-2.37	13.88	50.45	-5.45	68.65
Hungary									
Manufacturing total	11.22	0.64	10.80	17.91	-8.01	28.96	62.19	10.68	32.77
Low tech	12.01	-0.07	12.00	17.34	-1.93	19.35	77.75	7.10	53.80
Resource intensive	11.54	0.05	11.58	16.48	2.60	13.66	113.90	3.27	82.35
Medium-high tech	10.73	0.11	10.51	14.07	-15.04	48.40	66.66	14.77	22.36
Poland									
Manufacturing total	7.94	-8.67	13.36	15.31	-3.45	18.84	51.67	-4.12	66.15
Low tech	8.42	-9.12	14.72	15.97	-2.74	19.02	57.26	-4.11	71.18
Resource intensive	7.89	-9.03	13.64	14.05	-1.64	16.02	58.36	-6.14	82.88
Medium-high tech	7.88	-9.19	13.76	11.71	-6.34	17.23	69.00	-2.02	75.34
Slovak Republic									
Manufacturing total	6.71	-6.02	9.63	15.15	3.19	12.52	50.77	-2.51	59.04
Low tech	7.12	-8.34	12.02	17.86	6.74	12.21	57.02	-6.67	82.42
Resource intensive	6.18	-5.52	8.50	12.05	-0.40	11.57	63.28	-2.52	73.31
Medium-high tech	5.98	-7.14	9.79	9.28	-2.05	19.39	72.14	-0.04	58.30

TABLE 3 (cont.)

	Wage			Productivity			Unit labour costs		
	gap 1993	growth rate	gap 1999	gap 1993	growth rate	gap 1999	gap 1993	growth rate	gap 1999
Slovenia									
Manufacturing total	21.65	-5.74	30.54	27.13	2.64	23.16	87.53	-1.71	97.00
Low tech	27.46	-5.26	38.64	34.76	3.01	30.03	105.55	-1.09	104.70
Resource intensive	23.92	-5.27	34.59	33.32	4.86	29.82	80.35	-6.01	104.12
Medium-high tech	19.63	-5.96	27.93	29.25	0.80	27.16	75.57	-0.22	83.73
Bulgaria									
Manufacturing total	4.24	0.66	4.08	6.61	5.18	4.84	80.17	3.60	64.58
Low tech	5.57	2.82	4.63	7.65	6.17	5.28	90.53	4.89	71.85
Resource intensive	5.06	1.90	4.43	7.28	4.84	4.61	111.54	3.62	89.04
Medium-high tech	4.31	1.80	3.74	3.55	2.85	3.23	125.74	3.69	93.27
Romania									
Manufacturing total	2.93	-2.32	3.36	5.25	0.95	4.96	52.06	0.26	51.27
Low tech	3.26	-2.20	3.74	7.08	-2.34	8.66	49.55	-0.14	49.42
Resource intensive	2.77	-2.85	3.23	5.97	5.16	3.95	60.20	0.75	57.13
Medium-high tech	2.88	-3.46	3.55	2.70	-3.81	3.71	87.14	-1.55	86.13

TABLE 4

PRODUCTIVITY, WAGE AND UNIT LABOUR COST GAPS AT PPP - 1993 AND 1999

	Wage			Productivity			Unit labour costs		
	gap 1993	growth rate	gap 1999	gap 1993	growth rate	gap 1999	gap 1993	growth rate	gap 1999
Czech Republic									
Manufacturing total	28.91	-3.16	34.94	40.80	-1.05	43.44	48.10	-3.63	59.80
Low tech	31.53	-3.23	38.82	49.21	1.32	48.82	47.39	-4.77	58.90
Resource intensive	25.99	-3.76	32.96	46.14	-4.03	49.33	58.54	0.20	55.35
Medium-high tech	27.32	-4.02	34.18	35.45	-2.37	41.35	50.45	-5.45	68.65
Hungary									
Manufacturing total	28.28	0.58	27.32	48.32	-8.01	78.12	62.19	10.68	32.77
Low tech	30.28	-0.14	30.36	46.78	-1.93	52.21	77.75	7.10	53.80
Resource intensive	29.10	-0.01	29.31	44.46	2.60	36.85	113.90	3.27	82.35
Medium-high tech	27.05	0.04	26.60	37.94	-15.04	130.56	66.66	14.77	22.36
Poland									
Manufacturing total	22.61	-5.44	31.34	38.81	-3.45	47.74	51.67	-4.12	66.15
Low tech	23.99	-5.89	34.55	40.47	-2.74	48.20	57.26	-4.11	71.18
Resource intensive	22.47	-5.79	32.02	35.61	-1.64	40.59	58.36	-6.14	82.88
Medium-high tech	22.44	-5.95	32.30	29.67	-6.34	43.65	69.00	-2.02	75.34
Slovak Republic									
Manufacturing total	24.22	-3.61	30.08	48.85	3.19	40.35	50.77	-2.51	59.04
Low tech	25.69	-5.93	37.55	57.57	6.74	39.37	57.02	-6.67	82.42
Resource intensive	22.29	-3.11	26.56	38.83	-0.40	37.30	63.28	-2.52	73.31
Medium-high tech	21.59	-4.73	30.57	29.91	-2.05	62.49	72.14	-0.04	58.30

TABLE 4 (cont.)

	Wage			Productivity			Unit labour costs		
	gap 1993	growth rate	gap 1999	gap 1993	growth rate	gap 1999	gap 1993	growth rate	gap 1999
Slovenia									
Manufacturing total	43.39	-2.49	50.40	48.51	2.64	41.41	87.53	-1.71	97.00
Low tech	55.03	-2.02	63.76	62.14	3.01	53.69	105.55	-1.09	104.70
Resource intensive	47.94	-2.03	57.07	59.57	4.86	53.31	80.35	-6.01	104.12
Medium-high tech	39.34	-2.72	46.08	52.30	0.80	48.55	75.57	-0.22	83.73
Bulgaria									
Manufacturing total	7.19	-12.19	14.94	30.92	5.18	22.66	80.17	3.60	64.58
Low tech	9.44	-10.02	16.96	35.78	6.17	24.73	90.53	4.89	71.85
Resource intensive	8.57	-10.94	16.22	34.09	4.84	21.59	111.54	3.62	89.04
Medium-high tech	7.30	-11.04	13.70	16.59	2.85	15.13	125.74	3.69	93.27
Romania									
Manufacturing total	15.67	1.94	13.95	28.54	0.95	26.96	52.06	0.26	51.27
Low tech	17.48	2.06	15.50	38.52	-2.34	47.10	49.55	-0.14	49.42
Resource intensive	14.85	1.41	13.40	32.47	5.16	21.47	60.20	0.75	57.13
Medium-high tech	15.44	0.80	14.70	14.67	-3.81	20.21	87.14	-1.55	86.13

There are however differences when looking at industry groups. In all countries the gaps to Austria were the largest in the high-tech industries and smallest in the low-tech industries, the measured difference in the productivity gaps between these two sets of industries was generally between 5 to 10 percentage points.

Over time rapid changes in these patterns occurred. All countries experienced positive productivity growth from 1993 to 2000 (see Graph 4 earlier in the paper). But not all countries succeeded in closing the gap relative to the benchmark Austria. In aggregate manufacturing only the Czech Republic, Hungary, and Poland had higher productivity growth than Austria. All other countries had lower productivity growth and thus the gap widened.

But here again there are marked differences across types of industries. Hungary closed the gap in the high-tech industries with a (per annum) rate of closure of the gap of 15% and reached a level of about 50% that of Austria. Similarly Poland closed the gap most rapidly in the high-tech sector with a rate of 6% and the Slovak Republic of 2%. Slovenia and Bulgaria were falling back relative to Austria in all three sectors, but the gap widened more (at a higher rate) in the low tech and resource intensive industries than in the medium-high-tech industries. Finally, also Romania succeeded in closing the gap in the low and the medium-high-tech industries but started from an extremely low level.

4.2 Wage Rates

With respect to wage rates one can see the following. First, the gaps in wage rates are much more even across sectors than was the case with productivity. The gaps in wage rates (at current nominal exchange rates) extended from Slovenia with a level of about 20% the Austrian wage rate level in 1993 to Romania with only 3%. Secondly, and this is a very important point for the comparative cost dynamic, the growth (or closure) rates for wage rates were much more similar across sectors than was the case for the (differential) productivity growth rates.

4.3 *Unit Labour Costs*

The relative movements of wage rates and productivity determine the evolution of unit labour costs which is, of course, an important measure of the general (cost) competitiveness of countries but more importantly, for our purposes, of the relative competitiveness of different industries.

Looking at the dynamics, we can see that in aggregate manufacturing the wage versus productivity growth was such that over the period 1993-1999 unit labour costs were rising (relative to Austria) in the Czech Republic, Poland, Slovak Republic, and Slovenia. They were falling quite strongly in Hungary and Bulgaria, but for quite different reasons as a comparison of productivity and wage rate movements at both current and PPP exchange rates shows. In Hungary this was due to a very strong performance in relative productivity growth and very moderate relative wage growth (at current exchange rates), while in Bulgaria there was actually a fall in the productivity position (relative to Austria) but combined with a much sharper fall in relative wage levels (again measured at the current exchange rate and this was due to a sharp devaluation of the Bulgarian currency).

Differences in the dynamics across industry groupings are remarkable especially for those sectors in which countries experienced large productivity growth rates (as wage growth is rather similar across sectors). Especially Hungary reduced relative unit labour costs in the high-tech sectors from 66% (the Austrian level) in 1993 to about 22% in 1999!

The important point which emerges from cross-industry comparisons is that for some countries the productivity catching-up (closure of the gap) is rather rapid in the medium-high-tech industries in which the initial gaps were the highest. This pattern very much confirms the 'Gerschenkron hypothesis' as applied to the industry level (and as stated in the introduction of the paper). For other countries no such differential productivity catch-up can be observed; in the language of Abramovitz, such countries either did not have the 'capabilities' or did not mobilise these to make use of the high learning (and technology transfer) potential in those industries in which the initial technological gaps were the highest. On the other hand, we observe that the pattern of wage catching-up (or wage growth) is much more even — than productivity growth — across sectors, and hence comparative cost structures move in favour of those sectors which experience faster productivity catching-up; in Hungary and to a lesser degree also in a number of other CEECs these are the medium- to high-tech sectors. This is exactly the pattern which was also found in research on the dynamics of comparative costs across a much wider range of catching-up economies (Landesmann and Stehrer [22]). Let us now move on to examine whether these underlying patterns of comparative cost dynamics get also revealed in the evolving trade structures of CEE economies.

5. - Trade Performance and Trade Specialisation

In this Section we start with an overview of broad sectoral patterns of trade performance and then move towards a more detailed qualitative examination of trade specialisation. As will be seen below, the analysis of evolving patterns of trade specialisation will turn out to be consistent with the previous observations regarding the dynamics of differentiated productivity catching-up (across countries and industries) and the implications drawn from this regarding comparative cost dynamics. To complete the analysis of trade performance we shall show that indicators of product quality up-grading (measured by the closure of export price gaps) also support the picture drawn here regarding the evolution of comparative advantage dynamics across the different CEE economies.

5.1 *Current Accounts: Structures and Developments*

We shortly review the broad outlines of the current accounts in the CEECs. Table 5 shows the four broad components of the current accounts (all expressed in per cent of GDP) over the period 1989-1998. We can see that all countries (with the exception of Slovenia) experienced at times dramatic — and unsustainable — deficits in the current accounts. In general, the CEECs are performing better in the trade accounts on services than on goods. However, at closer examination (Roemisch [25]), it emerges that this good performance in services trade is predominantly due to the *travel account*, i.e. tourism income which is a very strong net contributor to the current accounts in countries such as the Czech Republic, Slovenia, and — potentially — Bulgaria. Also the transport services sector contributes positively in many CEECs to the current account due particularly to the wage cost advantages in road haulage. In other services, in which financial, insurance and all types of business services (accountancy, marketing, consultancy, etc.) are the main components, the CEECs are predominantly net importers. In previous studies it has been shown that in the business services area, advanced economies retain a strong comparative advantage *vis-á-vis* catching-up economies after they have lost comparative advantages even in relatively advanced areas of manufacturing (such as in electronics). We thus expect the net import position in the business services area to persist between the CEECs and the advanced countries of Western Europe in the longer-run. To some extent high deficit positions in these areas (especially in financial services) get reduced in those countries which were most successful to attract foreign firms to set up local subsidiaries.

The income accounts also show mostly a negative balance (again with the exception of Slovenia) which is mostly due to high interest payments on debt as well as — in countries which managed to attract a lot of FDI such as Hungary — the repatriation of profits. In most countries there is a positive balance on transfers.

Although a differentiated analysis of the non-manufacturing parts of the current accounts across the CEECs would be very interesting in itself we shall now — for reasons of space — move towards a more detailed examination of trade specialisation within manufacturing.

TABLE 5

CURRENT ACCOUNT IN % OF GDP

		1989	1990	1991	1992	1993	1994	1995	1996	1997	1998
Czech Republic	Current account balance	.	.	.	.	1.35	-2.05	-2.64	-7.42	-6.17	-1.89
	Balance on goods	.	.	.	.	-1.50	-3.53	-7.08	-10.15	-8.66	-4.65
	Balance on services	.	.	.	.	2.94	1.21	3.54	3.31	3.29	3.37
	Balance on incomes	.	.	.	.	-0.34	-0.05	-0.20	-1.25	-1.49	-1.32
	Balance on transfers	.	.	.	.	0.25	0.32	1.10	0.66	0.69	0.72
Hungary	Current account balance	-2.02	1.15	1.21	0.94	-11.06	-9.76	-5.68	-3.74	-2.15	-4.85
	Balance on goods	3.58	1.62	1.07	-0.03	-10.43	-8.95	-5.45	-5.87	-3.79	-4.47
	Balance on services	-1.26	1.47	1.60	2.05	0.56	0.38	1.44	3.31	2.58	1.43
	Balance on incomes	-4.78	-4.32	-4.06	-3.38	-3.09	-3.39	-4.04	-3.22	-3.12	-3.96
	Balance on transfers	0.45	2.38	2.60	2.30	1.90	2.19	2.37	2.04	2.18	2.14
Poland[1]	Current account balance	-1.72	5.20	-2.81	-3.68	-6.74	1.03	0.68	-2.28	-4.01	.
	Balance on goods	0.06	6.09	-0.93	-0.16	-4.08	-0.62	-1.30	-5.10	-6.87	.
	Balance on services	0.18	0.60	0.91	0.86	0.66	3.07	2.80	2.38	2.22	.
	Balance on incomes	-3.93	-5.74	-3.79	-4.94	-4.21	-2.77	-1.58	-0.75	-0.79	.
	Balance on transfers	1.97	4.26	1.00	0.55	0.89	1.35	0.76	1.19	1.42	.
Slovakia	Current account balance	.	.	.	.	-4.84	4.88	2.24	-11.13	-10.08	-10.44
	Balance on goods	.	.	.	.	-7.61	0.44	-1.32	-12.15	-10.72	-11.54
	Balance on services	.	.	.	.	2.27	4.81	3.11	0.20	0.38	0.08
	Balance on incomes	.	.	.	.	-0.32	-0.87	-0.08	-0.25	-0.63	-0.78
	Balance on transfers	.	.	.	.	0.82	0.50	0.53	1.07	0.89	1.80

Source: IMF, BoP; cited from RÖMISCH R. [25].
[1] Data for 1998 were not available.

TABLE 5 (cont.)

	1989	1990	1991	1992	1993	1994	1995	1996	1997	1998
Slovenia										
Current account balance	·	·	·	7.81	1.51	4.17	-0.12	0.21	0.20	-0.02
Balance on goods	·	·	·	6.30	-1.22	-2.35	-5.09	-4.67	-4.24	-3.97
Balance on services	·	·	·	1.45	2.96	4.70	3.37	3.73	3.24	2.63
Balance on incomes	·	·	·	-0.31	-0.41	1.18	1.12	0.82	0.72	0.75
Balance on transfers	·	·	·	0.37	0.17	0.64	0.48	0.33	0.48	0.57
Romania										
Current account balance	4.69	-8.51	-3.51	-7.69	-4.45	-1.42	-5.00	-7.28	-6.12	-7.65
Balance on goods	3.82	-8.74	-3.83	-6.10	-4.28	-1.37	-4.45	-6.99	-5.67	-6.88
Balance on services	0.72	-0.46	-0.48	-1.47	-0.44	-0.57	-0.92	-1.09	-1.18	-1.71
Balance on incomes	0.15	0.42	0.05	-0.46	-0.55	-0.43	-0.68	-0.87	-0.92	-1.03
Balance on transfers	·	0.28	0.76	0.33	0.81	0.94	1.04	1.68	1.66	1.97
Bulgaria										
Current account balance	-1.64	-2.96	-0.95	-4.18	-10.16	-0.33	-0.20	0.16	4.20	-2.06
Balance on goods	-1.47	-2.27	-0.39	-2.47	-8.19	-0.17	0.92	1.89	3.74	-2.57
Balance on services	0.93	0.41	-1.06	-1.10	-0.54	0.11	1.17	1.21	1.64	1.21
Balance on incomes	-1.26	-1.31	-0.35	-1.11	-1.78	-1.99	-3.30	-3.98	-3.51	-2.56
Balance on transfers	0.16	0.22	0.85	0.50	0.34	1.72	1.01	1.05	2.33	1.87

5.2 *Trade Specialisation in Manufacturing*

In order to analyse structures and tendencies of trade specialisation of CEECs within manufacturing we use the COMEXT
database which collects all trade with the EU countries as reporting countries. The database includes data at a very detailed
(8-digit) level. The very detailed level will be used in Section 5.3
when examining relative export prices as indicators for relative
product quality. In this Section we shall examine trade structures
at the level of industry groupings which themselves are constructed as aggregates of industries defined at the 3-digit NACE
level. The industry groupings used are the same ones which were
defined for the series of *European Competitiveness Reports* (see
European Commission [7] and [8]) and the WIIW [30].

Earlier studies (see e.g. Landesmann [20]) have shown that
the Central and East European countries' trading structure with
the EU(12) started in 1989 with a profile typical of less developed
economies: the representation of exports of the labour-intensive
industrial branches was above-average (in relation to EU imports
as a whole), in the capital-, R&D- and skill-intensive branches below-average (particularly in the latter two), while the representation of exports of energy-intensive branches was above-average —
which reflected the heritage of cheap energy supplies within the
CMEA. Over time, important changes took place in the CEECs'
export structure to the EU and in the revealed comparative advantage indicators (RCAs) in the different categories of industries.
The most remarkable change took place in Hungary: from sizeable deficits in its export structure in the areas of capital-, R&D-
and skill-intensive industries, these deficits were either completely eroded to zero or turned into surpluses. This pattern was followed in a much less spectacular manner by the Czech Republic
and Poland, where deficits in the representation of skill-, R&D-
and capital-intensive branches had been reduced. For these
economies and also for the Slovak Republic the relatively strong
presence of energy-intensive branches got substantially reduced
while this was not the case with Romanian and Bulgarian exports
to the EU (particularly in the latter case, dependence upon ener-

gy-intensive exports to the EU had increased markedly until 1998). Also the picture with respect to labour-intensive industries was remarkably different in the cases of Romania and Bulgaria, on the one hand, and the CEEC-5 on the other: in the first two labour-intensive branches became the predominant segment of their exports to the EU while the dependence upon labour-intensive branches got somewhat reduced in the other branches.

Discontinuity in statistics do not allow us to present a full analysis of patterns of trade specialisation going back to 1989 over here and we focus instead on the period 1995 to 2000 (from 1995 onwards 15 EU reporting countries are represented in the COMEXT database and consistent CN-NACE classification converters can be used). As mentioned above we shall employ for this analysis a qualitative grouping of industries (derived from an aggregation of 3-digit NACE industries) which was being used in the EU Competitiveness Reports and has hence the advantage of immediate comparability with the analysis conducted there for the EU member countries. Two 'taxonomies' are applied: one based on the use of cluster-analytic techniques where industries are clustered (and industry groupings identified) by the use of a number industrial organisation and input use criteria (taxonomy 1). This led to the distinction of 5 industry groupings: mainstream, labour-intensive, capital-intensive, marketing-driven and technology-driven. In the other taxonomy (taxonomy 2) industries are grouped by skill intensity (low skill, medium skill/blue collar, medium skill/white collar, high skill). The correspondence between NACE 3-digit industries and the two taxonomies can be seen in Appendix Table A.1 and more detail on the underlying methodology can be obtained from Peneder [24].

In Table 6 and 7 we have calculated (in Table 6 for taxonomy 1 and in Table 7 for taxonomy 2) by which percentage points certain industry groupings are more or less represented in the export structures of the CEECs compared to the export structure of the EU Northern countries (all EU countries except for Spain, Portugal and Greece). The Graphs for the EU Southern cohesion countries have been similarly calculated as differences in the percentage representation of their exports to the EU in the different

TABLE 6

EXPORT STRUCTURE OF CEEC'S COMPARED TO EU-NORTH AND EU-SOUTH*
EXPORT SHARES (TAXONOMY I - FACTOR INTENSITIES) - DIFFERENCES TO EU-NORTH

	Czech Republic		Hungary		Poland		Slovak Republic		Slovenia		Bulgaria		Romania	
	1995	2000	1995	2000	1995	2000	1995	2000	1995	2000	1995	2000	1995	2000
1 Mainstream	7.65	8.95	-0.83	-3.42	-4.37	-0.56	-1.34	2.02	6.96	7.84	-10.32	-8.95	-7.28	-5.13
2 Labour-intensive	14.37	8.13	11.11	2.07	25.88	19.44	13.59	8.90	16.64	12.58	10.46	21.50	32.33	35.84
3 Capital intensive	0.36	-4.10	-3.09	-10.15	1.70	-3.35	13.79	1.96	-5.52	-3.09	25.41	16.53	3.68	-7.99
4 Marketing-driven	-6.22	-4.47	-1.07	-4.85	-5.44	-2.73	-7.80	-4.94	-7.99	-5.01	-0.58	-0.03	-2.59	3.08
5 Technology driven	-16.16	-8.51	-6.12	16.35	-17.77	-12.80	-18.24	-7.95	-10.10	-12.32	-24.97	-29.05	-26.14	-25.79

	Estland		Latvia		Lithuania		EU-South		EU-North (Shares)	
	1995	2000	1995	2000	1995	2000	1995	2000	1995	2000
1 Mainstream	-10.66	-12.24	-14.21	-15.27	-14.88	-12.46	-6.60	-7.37	21.67	20.82
2 Labour-intensive	27.39	18.06	20.75	46.93	22.49	34.18	12.37	1.84	11.39	11.60
3 Capital intensive	8.01	-5.51	31.36	7.99	22.38	9.33	-3.23	2.56	23.81	23.37
4 Marketing-driven	-8.00	-6.33	-10.90	-8.12	-6.26	-3.63	4.56	7.00	15.53	11.62
5 Technology driven	-16.73	6.01	-27.00	-31.53	-23.74	-27.42	-7.11	-4.02	27.60	32.59

Source: COMEXT data base and own calculations.
* Differences of export shares between CEEC's and EU-South to EU-North; Export shares for EU-North.

TABLE 7

EXPORT STRUCTURE OF CEEC'S COMPARED TO EU-NORTH AND EU-SOUTH*
EXPORT SHARES (TAXONOMY II - SKILL INTENSITIES) - DIFFERENCES TO EU-NORTH

	Czech Republic		Hungary		Poland		Slovak Republic		Slovenia		Bulgaria		Romania	
	1995	2000	1995	2000	1995	2000	1995	2000	1995	2000	1995	2000	1995	2000
1 Low skill	6.54	-3.32	9.41	-7.79	17.08	4.77	12.68	1.42	3.94	-0.08	38.28	45.81	38.06	36.64
2 Medium skill/blue collar	7.33	16.52	3.92	9.36	11.27	20.15	5.80	13.82	12.85	16.61	-13.42	-14.23	-3.90	-5.40
3 Medium skill/white collar	-7.11	-8.09	-2.34	0.92	-14.05	-11.91	-5.43	-7.53	-6.39	-7.20	-11.90	-20.14	-19.28	-17.64
4 High skill	-6.77	-5.11	-10.99	-2.49	-14.30	-13.01	-13.05	-7.71	-10.40	-9.34	-12.96	-11.44	-14.87	-13.60

	Estland		Latvia		Lithuania		EU-South		EU-North (Shares)	
	1995	2000	1995	2000	1995	2000	1995	2000	1995	2000
1 Low skill	13.29	4.01	3.68	2.10	19.75	22.05	23.36	14.88	29.41	26.97
2 Medium skill/blue collar	2.76	7.95	3.08	24.77	-5.28	-1.34	1.67	-2.75	19.59	20.56
3 Medium skill/white collar	-7.50	3.26	11.25	-9.75	4.07	-3.56	-11.49	-7.28	32.00	33.62
4 High skill	-8.55	-15.21	-18.00	-17.12	-18.53	-17.15	-13.54	-4.85	19.00	18.86

Source: COMEXT data base and own calculations.
* Differences of export shares between CEEC's and EU-South to EU-North; Export shares for EU-North.

GRAPH 5

SHARES OF DIFFERENT INDUSTRY GROUPING IN EXPORTS TO EU

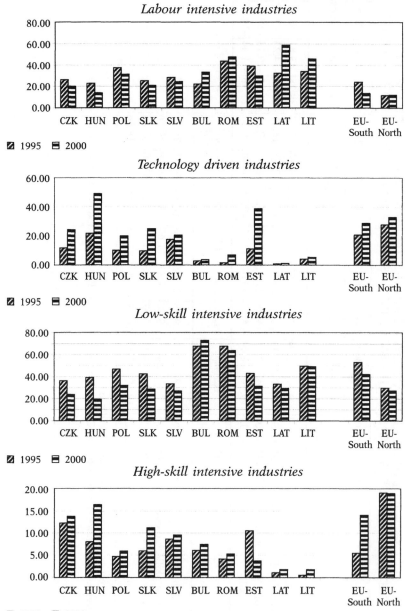

Source: Comext database; own calculations

industry groupings relative to that of the EU-North. Finally for the EU Northern countries the actual percentage representation of the industry groupings in their total (intra-EU) exports are presented. In Graph 5 we have picked out the shares in countries' exports to the EU of those industry groupings where the qualitatively most striking differences can be observed: the labour-intensive and technology-driven groupings of taxonomy 1 and the low-skill and the high-skill groupings of taxonomy 2.

We can see the following:

1) In general there is still a relatively stronger representation of the labour-intensive branches in the CEECs export structures to the EU (compared to the EU Northern countries' export structures). For Poland, Bulgaria, Romania and the Baltic states this dependence is very strong — in fact much stronger than for the EU-South — and for Bulgaria, Romania, Latvia and Lituania this dependence has, furthermore, sharply increased over the period 1995 to 2000. For the other countries, this 'overrepresentation' of labour-intensive branches — relatively to the advanced EU member countries — has declined, for some quite sharply. For Hungary a (branch) specialisation in this direction no longer exists.

2) With respect to technology-intensive branches which accounted for about 33% of EU Northern EU exports, the CEECs started off in 1995 (earlier figures would indicate that this was even more the case before that) with sizable 'deficits' in these areas. Over the period 1995 to 2000 these deficits have declined substantially in Hungary, the Czech and Slovak Republics, Estonia (in fact, in Hungary and Estonia they have turned into surpluses) and in Poland more mildly. In Bulgaria, Romania, Latvia and Lithuania these deficits have remained at very high levels and in most cases have further increased.

3) The picture is similar if we look at the two extreme categories of taxonomy 2, i.e. the relative representation of low-skill and high-skill intensive industries respectively in the countries export structures to the EU. Again we can see that the CEECs all started off with an over-representation of the low-skill intensive branches in their exports to the EU (just as the Southern EU coun-

tries do). This overrepresentation falls quite dramatically in the case of a number of CEECs (the Czech and Slovak Republics, Hungary, Poland, Slovenia and Estonia) and stays at a low level in Latvia, but again remains at a very high level in Bulgaria, Romania and Lithuania.

4) In the high-skill industries, deficits remain in all CEECs (as they do in the Southern EU countries) but the picture shows again quite a bit of differentiation across the CEECs, so that the percentage differences (to EU North) are below 10% in the case of the Czech and Slovak Republics, Hungary and Slovenia.

Thus the picture which emerges is of strong differentiation across the CEECs by a number of indicators of revealed comparative advantage (see the WIIW Competitiveness Report, WIIW, [30], for further indicators and analysis) in their structures and, furthermore, tendencies of trade specialisation. While some of the CEECs have reduced dramatically (or even lost completely) their inter-industry specialisation towards labour-intensive, low-skill branches and made some inroads into technology-driven and skill-intensive branches, others show clearly that their specialisation structures got locked in (at least so far) in the labour-intensive, low-skill sectors. We take this as support of our basic hypothesis that catching-up patterns can give rise to 'comparative advantage switchovers' if countries can utilise the high potential for productivity growth (and, as we shall see below, of product quality up-grading) in industries in which the initial technological (and product quality) gaps are rather high. Alternatively, countries which cannot utilise this potential remain locked in a specialisation pattern which remains the typical one between (technologically) advanced and less advanced economies.

However, we have still to be cautious at this stage: What we have analysed in this section was a distinct pattern of inter-industry specialisation which emerges in trade between the CEECs and the EU. However, the analysis of inter-industry specialisation is only one aspect of trade specialisation, the other would be intra-industry specialisation, i.e. the specialisation on particular production stages or on product quality segments within an industry. This will be the subject of the next Section 5.3.

Before we come to this, we just want to point out that there is established strong evidence (Landesmann [20] and WIIW [30]) for growing intra-industry trade between the more advanced CEECs and the EU. This is in line with the 'new' trade theory which suggests that trade among industrialised countries is motivated by product differentiation and economies of scale. Measured by Grubel-Lloyd indices, intra-industry trade has been most pronounced in EU trade of the Czech Republic, Slovenia and Hungary whereas it has been lowest in Latvia, Lithuania and Romania. Moreover, intra-industry trade has been growing most rapidly in the Czech Republic and (less pronounced) in Poland; it stagnated either at a relatively high level in Hungary, Slovenia and the Slovak Republic, or at a low level in the remaining candidate countries. Compared to the early period of transition (and even more so with the pre-transition period), intra-industry trade between the more advanced CEECs (the Czech and Slovak Republics, Hungary and Poland) and the EU has increased further whereas it has more or less stagnated in Bulgaria and Romania. Judging also by the high shares in exports and imports, intra-industry trade (including outward processing trade) has been of particular importance in textiles as well as in electrical, optical and transport equipment. Hence, again, the evidence on the levels and rates of change of intra-industry trade points towards a strong differentiation amongst the CEECs.

5.3 *Product Quality and Quality Up-Grading of CEE Exports to the EU*

In this Section we use export unit values to proxy differences in product quality of different producers of tradable goods (in our case CEE exporters and EU producers). If products are defined at a very detailed level and comparisons are made in the same market (in our case, the EU market) then — under certain conditions concerning market structure — differences in price do reveal differences in 'product quality' (including consumer loyalty to particular producers, marketing and product design differences, after sales services, etc.). The importance of price differences in trade even at the most detailed level of product classifications (in our case at the 8-digit CN level) has given rise to a number of studies of the phenomenon of 'vertical intra-industry trade', i.e. trade in products with quality differences (Greenaway, Hine and Milner [13], Fontagné and Freudenberg [11], Jansen and Landesmann [18]). It has been pointed out in previous studies that 'vertical intra-industry trade' is particularly relevant in trade relations between East and West European countries (Burgstaller and Landesmann [6], Aturupane, Djankov and Hoekman [3]).

We shall present some of the most recent evidence on the present position of the CEE producers in vertical intra-industry trade relations with the EU. The analysis of whether CEE producers trade at the low-, medium- or high-quality end of the product range and in which industries can serve as an important indicator for industrial strengths and weaknesses of CEE producers and, furthermore, can give rise to interesting analyses of emerging production networks (Baldone *et al.*, [4]). We shall also analyse whether there is evidence for closures in the 'price/quality gaps' between CEE and EU producers and how this 'product quality catching-up' is proceeding across the different candidate countries. In the following we shall briefly introduce the methodology adopted to analyse product quality gaps at the product and industry level.

5.3.1 Methodology of the Calculation of Relative Unit Values

In the calculation of relative unit values of traded products we use the COMEXT trade database at the most detailed 8-digit level. Denoting the value of exports to the EU of commodity i by country c in year t by v_{it}^c and the quantity (measured in tons) by x_{it}^c, the export unit value is defined as

$$(1) \qquad\qquad u_{it}^c = v_{it}^c / x_{it}^c$$

The unit values of country c's exports to the EU is then compared to the unit values of total EU imports (from the world, including intra-EU trade) by calculating the logs of the unit value ratios

$$(2) \qquad r^c_{it} = ln \ (u^c_{it}/u^{EU}_{it})$$

where: u^{EU}_{it} denotes the unit value of total EU imports for a particular commodity i in year t.

Taking the logarithm of (u^c_{it}/u^{EU}_{it}) ensures a symmetric aggregation across products for ratios larger and smaller than 1 (see below). In logs, the ratio is thus larger (smaller) than zero if the export unit value of country c is larger (smaller) than the unit value of total EU imports.

We shall not present information at the very detailed (8-digit) product level but aggregate the unit value ratios to the level of (3-digit NACE) industries and further to industry groupings. This is done by constructing a weighted sum of the unit value ratios r^c_{it} across the products belonging to a particular industry j (or an industry group). The weight used for a particular commodity i in such an aggregation is the share of its export value in the industry's exports of country c. Denoting the set of commodities i belonging to an aggregate j (industry or industry grouping) by $i \in I \ (j)$ the weights are calculated as

$$(3) \qquad w^c_{it} = v^c_{it}/\Sigma_{i \in I \ (j)} \ v^c_{it}$$

The unit value ratio for a particular aggregate j is then

$$(4) \qquad r^c_{jt} = \Sigma_{i \in I \ (j)} r^c_{it} w^c_{it}$$

This measure can be interpreted analogously to the unit value ratios for a particular commodity as mentioned above. For ease of interpretation we report however

$$(5) \qquad uvr^c_{jt} = exp \ (r^c_{jt}) - 1$$

to which we also refer as *unit value ratios* of industry (or industry grouping) j. This measure can then be interpreted more easily than the log values, namely as the percentage deviation from the average EU import unit value. We shall also refer to these ratios as 'export price/quality gaps'; they can be positive or negative[6].

5.3.2 Aggregate Export Price Gaps and Numbers of Products Exported to the EU

To present a first overview of relative unit value ratios uvr_t^c (or 'export price/quality gaps') at the aggregate level (i.e. calculated across all manufacturing products traded with the EU) we can see a comparison in Graphs 6 and 7 of these unit value ratios between the 10 CEE candidate countries and the EU members for the years 1995 to 2000[7]. Remember that the zero level refers to the average price line for total EU imports and the values off the zero price line can be interpreted as (positive or negative) export price gaps (in %) relative to that average.

In the first instance, we can see that — in the aggregate — EU members sell their products at prices above those of total EU imports, while candidate countries sell their products on EU markets below those of total EU trade. Exceptions amongst the EU

---

[6] As the COMEXT trade data can contain errors at the detailed product level, we have — in our procedure of calculating unit value ratios — deleted very extreme levels of relative unit values. The criterion we used to classify an observation as an outlier was derived from the levels of the so-called 'adjucant values' in the distribution of the unit value ratios in the following way: The lower (upper) adjucant values are defined as the 25th (75th) percentile of the data minus (plus) 1.5 times the interquartile range (i.e. the range from the 25th to the 75th percentile). The lowest adjucant value in the data was found for Bulgaria in 1995 with about 2.5 ($\approx$ – ln 12) and the highest adjucant value for Slovenia in 1999 with about 1.75 ($\approx$ ln 5.75). In the calculations we dropped observations where $r_{jt}^c > \ln \mid 20 \mid$, i.e. at a value larger than the highest and lowest adjucant values in the sample. This means that observations where the ratio ($u_{it}^c \mid u_{it}^{EU}$) was higher than 20 or lower than 1/20 have been classified as outliers and removed from the sample. Using this criterion we think that extreme outlier values have been removed without biasing the data.

[7] Because of a break in the NACE industry classification and hence in the product-to-industry converters, we shall limit our analysis in this section to the years 1995 to 2000. For an analysis of developments over the earlier period, see the studies by BURGSTALLER J. - LANDESMANN M. [6], and STEHRER R. - LANDESMANN M.A. and BURGSTALLER J. [26].

GRAPH 6

EXPORT PRICE GAPS - ALL MANUFACTURING PRODUCTS TRADED WITH THE EU CEE CANDIDATE COUNTRIES

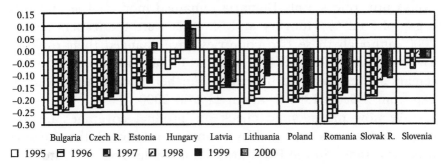

□ 1995 ⊟ 1996 ◪ 1997 ◪ 1998 ■ 1999 ▨ 2000

GRAPH 7

EU*

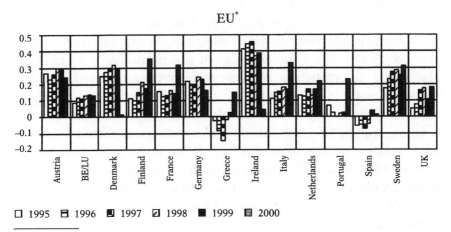

□ 1995 ⊟ 1996 ◪ 1997 ◪ 1998 ■ 1999 ▨ 2000

Source: own calculations based on EUROSTAT COMEXT DATABASE;
* Export price gaps have been calculated from detailed product-by-product comparisons and are expressed in percentage deviations from the average price of the products traded in EU markets (i.e. all imports to the EU including intra-EU).

member states are the Southern EU countries (Greece, Spain and Portugal) which sell at or just below the measured average (and weighted) price levels of total EU imports.

One can see some remarkable differences across the candidate countries. In 1995 the best performing country has been Slovenia with a gap of about 6.4% and Hungary with 7.5%. Latvia performed third with about 16% followed by Slovakia with a 20% gap. The other countries experienced gaps of 22% (Latvia) to 29% (Romania). Over time all countries succeeded in catching-up in export unit prices, only Bulgaria remained more or less stable at a gap of 23-25%. Hungary and Slovenia were the leaders also in 2000, although these two countries have changed their ranking. The two Baltic countries (Estonia and Lithuania) also experienced remarkable catching-up processes. Further, Romania reduced its gap from 29% in 1995 to about 17% in 2000.

We now move on to check on 'product coverage', i.e. the range of products exported by country *c* relative to the range of products traded in the EU market as a whole. This indicator can be seen as a measure to which degree a country participates in the range of (horizontally or vertically) product differentiated trade (within an industry or industry grouping or in the aggregate). The number of products exported by a country depends, of course, on the size of the economy (one expects that smaller economies export a smaller range of goods than larger ones) but also other determinants such as technologies adopted, abilities to participate in horizontal product differentiation, transport costs, market barriers, etc. Graphs 8 and 9 present the product coverage ratios (i.e. the number of products exported by country c relative to the total number of products imported by the EU) in 1995 and 2000. Such product coverage ratios have also been calculated for individual industries and industry groupings but will not be presented here, although we shall refer to these in the text.

We can see that the CEE candidate countries with the highest coverage ratios (Czech Republic, Hungary and Poland) have product coverage ratios in line with those for Austria, Denmark and Sweden, but substantially below the smaller EU countries, Belgium and Netherlands, as well as the larger EU member states (France, Germany, Italy, Spain, UK). Romania, the Slovak Republic and Slovenia have product coverage ratios in line with Finland, Ireland and Portugal, while the small Baltic states and Bulgaria show coverage ratios below that of Greece (the EU country with the smallest coverage). At this aggregate level, we can con-

GRAPH 8

PRODUCT COVERAGE OF CEE EXPORTS, EU (15) IMPORTS = 1

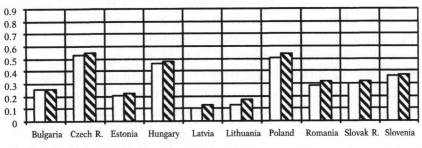

□ 1995   ▨ 2000

GRAPH 9

PRODUCT COVERAGE OF EU EXPORTS, EU (15) IMPORTS = 1*

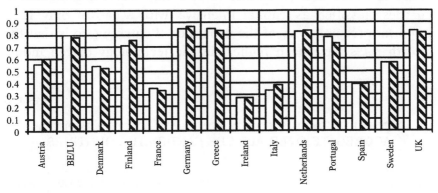

□ 1995   ▨ 2000

Source: own calculations based on Eurostat Comext Database;
* Product coverage refers here to the share of product items exported by a country to the EU relative to the total number of product items traded in EU markets (i.e. in total EU imports including intra-EU trade).

clude that CEE candidate countries have reached coverage ratios below the 'old' EU member states, but quite close to the more recent entrants. Except for Bulgaria, the coverage ratios have increased for all candidate countries over the period 1995 to 2000, although at slow rates.

5.3.3 *Unit Value Ratios at the Level of Industry Groupings*

We now return to the taxonomies used in section 5.2. which led to the identification of different industry groupings either by factor input criteria or industrial organisation features and look at variations in the positions of CEE producers in unit value ratios across the different industry groupings thus identified.

Table 8 presents the calculated unit value ratios uvr_{jt} ('export price gaps') across the five identified industry clusters and for the whole group of CEE candidate countries. The last column also shows the (per annum) growth rates of unit value ratios over the period 1995 to 2000.

We can see the following: The highest gap in 1995 was in the industries classified as 'mainstream' with a gap of about 35%. In labour intensive and technology driven industries the gap was about 23%. The best performer in 1995 has been the group of industries classified as 'capital intensive' with a gap of only 12%. Important for our story of the dynamics of catching-up is that the growth rates have been highest in the technology driven indus-

TABLE 8

UNIT VALUE RATIOS FOR TAXONOMY I (FACTOR INPUTS) –
AGGREGATE OVER ALL CEE CANDIDATE COUNTRIES
(in %)*

Industry clusters	1995	1996	1997	1998	1999	2000	p.a. growth 1995 -2000
1 Mainstream	−35.5	−37.2	−34.2	−29.3	−26.8	−28.2	1.46
2 Labour-intensive	−23.7	−18.5	−21.9	−16.0	−14.4	−14.0	1.94
3 Capital-intensive	−12.3	−12.9	−12.3	−13.1	−11.7	−7.7	0.91
4 Marketing-driven	−16.6	−15.6	−16.8	−13.2	−16.1	−15.2	0.29
5 Technology-driven	−23.4	−21.3	−16.2	−10.2	−2.5	0.1	4.71

Source: own calculations based on Eurostat Comext Database.
* Unit value ratios refer here to the ratios of export prices sold by a particular country to the EU (in the different industry categories) relative to the average import prices in total EU trades (in the respective industry categories).

tries with an exponential (per annum) growth rate of about 4.7%, second highest in the mainstream industries with 1.5% and the labour intensive industries with 1.9%. This pattern of growth has changed the ranking of industries in 2000, where the technology driven industries reached the average level. The mainstream industries show now the biggest gap with about 28%.

The pattern of the gaps and the catching-up in the particular classes for the individual candidate countries can be seen in Graph 10. In this figure the y-axes are scaled identically for all groupings of industries. The figures thus allow to compare levels and developments for countries and industry groups simultaneously. We can see that:

1) In the technology driven industries the most successful countries are Hungary, the Slovak Republic and Slovenia where the unit value ratios uvr^c_{jt} are at a level of about zero and have been strongly increasing for Hungary. The other countries had a gap in 1995 between 20% (Poland) and more than 70% in Estonia. There have been catching-up processes taking place in almost all countries (especially remarkable for Estonia). All the countries succeeded in diminishing the gaps which have been between 10 and 30% in 2000. Hungary achieved above average unit value ratios in this industry grouping (+20% in 2000).

2) Such a catching-up process cannot be observed in the marketing driven industries where the gap for most countries is more or less stable at about 10% to 20% for most countries. The best performers are again Hungary and Lithuania that succeeded in fully catching-up with the average price levels. Other quite well performing countries are Estonia, Latvia, the Slovak Republic and Slovenia. On the other hand, Bulgaria, the Czech Republic and Romania show a gap of about 20% or even more.

3) The capital intensive industries were the industries for which the gap in 1995 was smallest with a gap of about only 12% as stated above. Here only very little convergence can be observed with the remarkable exception of Lithuania.

4) In the labour intensive industries the gap in 1995 ranges from 10% (Czech Republic, Estonia, Romania, Slovak Republic) to about 30 % in Bulgaria. Here Slovenia sticks out with 'positive

GRAPH 10

UNIT VALUE RATIOS BY TAXONOMY I (FACTOR INPUTS)*

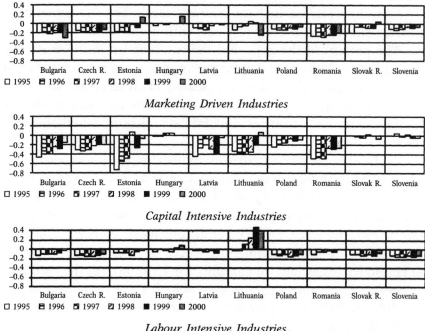

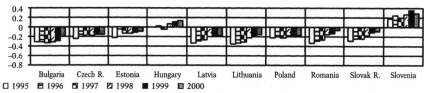

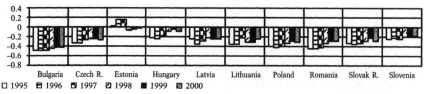

Source: own calculations based on EUROSTAT COMEXT DATABASE.

* Unit value ratios refer here to the ratios of export prices sold by a particular country to the EU (in the different industry categories) relative to the average import prices in total EU trades (in the respective industry categories).

gaps' of +25% and Hungary also reached a level above the average[8].

5) Finally, the industries classified as mainstream show high gaps in 1995 (on average 35%) with at times remarkable catching-up processes taking place in all countries so that the gaps reach about 25 % on average in 2000. Here the best performing country is Estonia with export unit values comparable to the EU average.

Further one may look at the number of products exported to the EU over time. The catching-up process in quality levels may stem from either an increase in quality of particular commodities or from the widening of the range of products exported in the more sophisticated types of industries.

Thus we take a look at the product coverage ratios in the five industry groupings. In order to control for a country's overall product coverage ratio, we look at the product coverage ratios in each of the industry groupings relative to the national average. Taking an (arithmetic) average of these relative coverage ratios in the different industry groupings across all candidate countries, we find that they have high relative coverage ratios in mainstream and labour-intensive branches (on average +37% and +75% respectively above the national average in 2000) and have — again relative to the respective national product coverage ratios — a relatively low product coverage in the marketing- and the technology-driven industries (–36% and –34% respectively). Over time (i.e. over the period 1995-2000), however, the product coverage ratios increased (relative to the national average) the most in two areas: labour-intensive products (+7%) and in technology-driven products (+8%) and fall in the capital-intensive industries (–12%). We shall return with a summary assessment of these developments in coverage ratios after presenting the equivalent results obtained from applying taxonomy II based on skill-groupings.

Utilizing the alternative classification (taxonomy II introduced

---

[8] We should remark here that high relative export prices can also reveal that producers have become uncompetitive in certain branches. A closer analysis requires a joint examination of price and market share movements, a point developed by Aiginger in his analysis (AIGINGER K. [1]).

TABLE 9

UNIT VALUE RATIOS FOR TAXONOMY II (LABOUR SKILLS) –
AGGREGATE OVER ALL CEE CANDIDATE COUNTRIES
(in %)*

Industry clusters	1995	1996	1997	1998	1999	2000	p.a. growth 1995 -2000
1 low skill	–13.7	–13.6	–12.9	–8.9	–8.0	–7.6	1.2
2 medium skill/ blue collar	–29.0	–22.5	–24.8	–19.2	–15.6	–14.0	3.0
3 medium skill/ white collar	–18.4	–21.8	–20.0	–13.5	–15.0	–7.2	2.2
4 high skill	–53.7	–51.9	–44.1	–42.1	–26.4	–34.6	3.8

Source: own calculations based on EUROSTAT COMEXT DATABASE.
* Unit value ratios refer here to the ratios of export prices sold by a particular country to the EU (in the different industry categories) relative to the average import prices in total EU trades (in the respective industry categories).

above) industry groups are classified according to relative labour skill requirements. Again we first present in Table 10 the 'export price gaps' for the aggregate of the candidate countries by these four industry groupings over the period 1995-1999 and again the p.a. growth rates in the last column. The export price gaps for the different accession countries are then given in Graph 11 (the y-axes are again scaled identically to allow cross-industry comparisons).

Table 9 shows that for candidate countries as a whole the largest gap in 1995 could be measured in the industries classified as 'high-skill intensive' industries with a gap of about 50%. The smallest gap in 1995 could be observed in the 'low-skill intensive' industries. Between the two medium-skill intensive industry groupings the gap is smaller in the medium/white collar industries (with about 18%) compared to the medium/blue collar industries with about 30%. The highest growth rates of the unit value ratios over the period 1995 to 2000 occurred in the high skill industries (the class of industries with the highest gaps in 1995)

GRAPH 11

UNIT VALUE RATIOS BY TAXONOMY II (LABOUR SKILLS)*

High Skill Industries

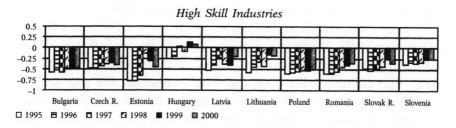

□ 1995 ☰ 1996 ◪ 1997 ▨ 1998 ■ 1999 ▩ 2000

Medium Skill/white Collar Workers Industries

□ 1995 ☰ 1996 ◪ 1997 ▨ 1998 ■ 1999 ▩ 2000

Medium Skill/blue Collar Workers Industries

□ 1995 ☰ 1996 ◪ 1997 ▨ 1998 ■ 1999 ▩ 2000

Low Skill Industries

□ 1995 ☰ 1996 ◪ 1997 ▨ 1998 ■ 1999 ▩ 2000

Source: own calculations based on EUROSTAT COMEXT DATABASE.
* Unit value ratios refer here to the ratios of export prices sold by a particular country to the EU (in the different industry categories) relative to the average import prices in total EU trades (in the respective industry categories).

with an exponential growth rate of about 3.8% and for the medium/blue collar industries with a growth rate of about 3%.

Looking at Graph 11 we can again observe that the highest gaps in 1995 can be observed in the high skill and medium skill/blue collar workers industries with gaps of about or even more than 50% in some countries (especially in Bulgaria, Estonia, Poland and Romania). In the other two categories, medium skill/white collar workers and low skill industries, the gap in 1995 was about 20 to 25%. But here are some remarkable country differences. Especially Hungary performed better than the other countries in all four categories and has by 2000 no negative export price gaps in any of the industry groupings and a particularly good performance in the high-skill grouping.

As to product coverage ratios, we only want to mention again the fact that with regard to movements over time, it is in the high skill industries that the CEE product coverage ratios are rising the fastest compared to the other types of industry groupings; this is the case in all countries with the exception of Bulgaria. This means that in the high skill industries it is the other component of a catching-up process which is particularly important (beside the quality improvement of individual commodities) and that is the widening of the range of exported products. This is in line with what we mentioned earlier for the technology-driven industries.

6. - The Allocation of Foreign Direct Investment and Educational Attainment

We finally look at two important factors which are generally regarded as important in determining the course of catching-up and the pattern of specialisation of the Central and Eastern European countries. We refer here, firstly, to the role of foreign direct investments (FDI) as important carriers of technological and managerial know-how transfer and, secondly, to the role of human capital whose existence is seen as crucial in facilitating the adoption of new technologies and as influencing a country's pattern of trade and industrial specialisation.

6.1 *The Role of Foreign Direct Investment (FDI)*

There is broad agreement in the literature that FDI is playing an important role in restructuring and improving the competitiveness of manufacturing (see the general evidence worldwide e.g. in UNCTAD [29], Barrel and Holland [5], and Hunya
[15], [16], for CEECs). Table 10 reports data on FDI stocks in 2000
for seven Central and Eastern European countries. These data
were collected from national sources and/or foreign investment
agencies. As there are methodological problems in comparing the
data across countries (especially for Hungary and Poland) we shall
only discuss the structure of FDI within the countries.

Manufacturing industry has been an important target of FDI
in most candidate countries attracting nearly half of all inward
FDI stock as of end-2000 (except for Estonia, Latvia and Lithuania; no data are available for Bulgaria and Romania; see Table
10). The sectoral distribution of FDI is highly uneven, reflecting
the varying attractiveness of individual branches for foreign in-
vestors and their investment motives as well as differences in the
privatisation policies pursued by the individual candidate countries (Hunya [17]). Generally FDI inflows have been high in both
the domestically oriented food, beverages and tobacco industry
(*DA*) especially in the Czech Republic, Hungary, Poland, Slovakia,
Latvia and Lithuania and in other non-metallic minerals (*DI*), as
well as in export-oriented branches such as electrical, optical (*DL*)
and transport equipment (*DM*) industries. FDI penetration of the
manufacturing industry (FDI stock per employee) is high in the
Czech Republic, Hungary, Poland and also in Slovenia. Table 11
reports the FDI stock per employee which gives a crude measure
(as it is not by itself adjusting for differences in general capital
intensity) of the importance of FDI in different branches. Table
12 gives the ratio of FDI relative to total manufacturing. FDI is
mainly concentrated in most countries in food products (*DA*),
chemicals and man-made fibres (*DG*), other non-metallic products
(*DI*) and finally in transport equipment (DM).

There are two points we want to make with regard to FDI:
a) the presence of FDI across CEECs remains very uneven

TABLE 10

FOREIGN DIRECT INVESTMENT (FDI) STOCK IN MANUFACTURING INDUSTRY, 2000*
USD million

NACE activities	Czech Republic[1]	Hungary	Poland	Slovak Republic	Slovenia	Estonia	Latvia	Lithuania
DA Food products; beverages and tobacco	1125.6	918.4	4961.9	229.0	38.5	128.2	100.2	269.3
DB Textiles and textile products	203.6	142.6	254.4	20.6	12.7	78.6	32.5	108.6
DC Leather and leather products	4.1	22.8	17.2	15.3	12.4	.	1.8	0.3
DD Wood and wood products	89.7	40.4	240	17.1	5.6	93.6[3]	57.9	33.0
DE Pulp, paper & paper products, publishing & printing	587.7	159.4	1470.3	105.9	191.6	.	17.9	25.2
DF Coke, refined petroleum products & nuclear fuel	210.9	515.9[2]	.	151.6	.	6.0	0.0	42.8
DG Chemicals, chemical products and man-made fibres	398.0	.	1285.1	117.1	173.2	49.6	38.1	.
DH Rubber and plastic products	104.2	176.7	591.4	21.3	141.4	6.3	10.5	26.7
DI Other non-metallic mineral products	1467.8	233.6	2785.7	97.9	73.3	.	23.7	37.6
DJ Basic metals and fabricated metal products	624.2	194.6	403.4	819.2	88.5	22.3	25.7	11.6
DK Machinery and equipment n.e.c.	218.7	199.1	317.1	80.4	144.7	18.5	21.5	7.4
DL Electrical and optical equipment	662.2	680.6	1575.1	80.0	122.4	16.6	5.9	53.0
DM Transport equipment	989.5	366.0	5167.7	122.3	133.9	39.1	1.3	48.1
DN Manufacturing n.e.c.	100.5	38.3	393.5	7.8	4.5	.	8.1	7.9
D Manufacturing	6786.7	3688.4	19462.8	1885.4	1142.7	567.7	345.0	671.5
FDI total	17552.1	10104.0	45772.0	3692.2	2808.5	2645.4	2081.3	2334.3

[1] 1999
[2] includes DF+DG
[3] includes DD+DE

Source: NATIONAL BANKS, STATISTICAL OFFICES and FOREIGN INVESTMENT AGENCIES.

* Czech Republic: nominal capital based on corporation-tax declarations. Hungary: equity capital, reinvested earnings, loans. Poland: equity capital, reinvested earnings gross; projects over USD 1 million capital based on PAIZ data. Slovak Republic: equity capital, reinvested earnings - in the corporate sector. Slovenia: equity capital, reinvested earnings, loans. Estonia: equity capital, reinvested earnings, loans. Latvia: equity capital, reinvested earnings, loans. Lithuania: equity capital, reinvested earnings, loans. Croatia: equity capital.

TABLE 11

FDI STOCK PER EMPLOYEE IN USD, 2000

NACE activities	Czech Rep.	Hungary	Poland	Slovak Rep.	Slovenia	Latvia	Lithuania
DA Food products; beverages and tobacco	7484	8815	8552	4205	5148	1787	3176
DB Textiles and textile products	2054	1716	585	226	961	779	1322
DC Leather and leather products	159	1075	.	500	241	259	
DD Wood and wood products	2104	3318	3228	384	1316	962	973
DE Pulp, paper & paper products, publishing & printing	12623	7505	11079	675	19279	698	1448
DF Coke, refined petroleum products & nuclear fuel	58230	16560	.	9164	0		14519
DG Chemicals, chemical products and man-made fibres	7788	10362	9735	5037	18442	4088	
DH Rubber and plastic products	6915	5818	3864	1078	14851	1707	5348
DI Other non-metallic mineral products	19306	8740	11777	2654	8192	2578	3042
DJ Basic metals and fabricated metal products	2475	5856	1075	3073	1944	4030	780
DK Machinery and equipment n.e.c.	1311	3391	2198	774	6037	1195	452
DL Electrical and optical equipment	5703	6018	5659	1506	4686	709	1779
DM Transport equipment	11095	11620	18203	3526	18465	162	7358
DN Manufacturing n.e.c.	1232	2056	1331	315	471	320	291
D *Manufacturing*	*5756*	*6290*	*5681*	*2026*	*6276*	*1346*	*2097*

Michael A. Landesmann - Robert Stehrer

TABLE 12

FDI STOCK PER EMPLOYEE IN USD, 2000
(Manufacturing = 1)

NACE activities	Czech Rep.	Hungary	Poland	Slovak Rep.	Slovenia	Latvia	Lithuania
DA Food products; beverages and tobacco	1.30	1.40	1.51	2.08	0.82	1.33	1.51
DB Textiles and textile products	0.36	0.27	0.10	0.11	0.15	0.58	0.63
DC Leather and leather products	0.03	0.17		0.25	0.04	0.19	0.00
DD Wood and wood products	0.37	0.53	0.57	0.19	0.21	0.71	0.46
DE Pulp, paper & paper products, publishing & printing	2.19	1.19	1.95	0.33	3.07	0.52	0.69
DF Coke, refined petroleum products & nuclear fuel	10.12	2.63		4.52	0.00	0.00	6.92
DG Chemicals, chemical products and man-made fibres	1.35	1.65	1.71	2.49	2.94	3.04	0.00
DH Rubber and plastic products	1.20	0.92	0.68	0.53	2.37	1.27	2.55
DI Other non-metallic mineral products	3.35	1.39	2.07	1.31	1.31	1.92	1.45
DJ Basic metals and fabricated metal products	0.43	0.93	0.19	1.52	0.31	2.99	0.37
DK Machinery and equipment n.e.c.	0.23	0.54	0.39	0.38	0.96	0.89	0.22
DL Electrical and optical equipment	0.99	0.96	1.00	0.74	0.75	0.53	0.85
DM Transport equipment	1.93	1.85	3.20	1.74	2.94	0.12	3.51
DN Manufacturing n.e.c.	0.21	0.33	0.23	0.16	0.08	0.24	0.14
D Manufacturing	1.00	1.00	1.00	1.00	1.00	1.00	1.00

and hence the role it can perform in facilitating the up-grading of the CEECs industrial structures will actually be performed to different degrees. This is compatible with a picture of differentiated catching-up patterns across the CEECs as pointed out in the previous sections of the report.

b) The distribution of FDI across branches (although this point needs further elaboration which will not be undertaken) indicates that FDI is attracted also to branches which can be classified as medium-/high-tech and thus plays a role in the productivity and quality upgrading process in these branches (for further evidence on the impact of foreign ownership involvement in further productivity improvements and export performance in CEECs, see Hunya [17]).

6.2 *The Role of Educational Attainment*

It is well-known that the large cumulative employment drops in the CEE region since 1989 are reflected in falling labour force participation rates in all CEECs. A comparison between the transition countries covered here and the EU-15 shows that, despite these considerable falls, participation rates are still higher than the EU average (68%) in the Czech Republic, Slovakia and Romania, similar to the EU-15 level in Poland, and lower than in the EU in Hungary and Bulgaria. Employment rates (total number of employed relative to the population aged 15-64) also show a wide range, from close to 70% in Romania and the Czech Republic (in 1998) to 54% in Hungary. A comparison of employment rates in CEECs and the EU in 1998 shows that the average CEE-7 rate stood at 62.7%, slightly higher than the EU average of 61%. Furthermore, the gender gap in employment rates remained smaller in the CEECs compared to most countries in the EU. Unemployment rates amounted to between 9% and 19% in the CEECs by the year 1999 which reflects the development of the labour force (particularly the participation rate) on the one hand and that of employment levels on the other. Unemployment rates across the region have reached a range not dissimilar to the EU in the 1990s.

The labour market structure of the accession countries with respect to skill levels and educational attainment must be seen against the background of these changes in participation rates. A first glance at comparable data across countries reveals high shares of upper secondary education (Table 13).

These data were collected from national labour force surveys and compared to data for European countries reported in European Commission [9]. Although there are methodological difficulties these data provide a rough overview over the structure of educational attainment.

Table 13 shows that most countries have a share of lower upper secondary educational levels in its working-age population of about 30% (lowest in the Czech Republic with 24%) which is at more or less the same level as for the EU-Northern countries. Higher shares are only reported for Bulgaria and Romania with more than 40%. This can be compared to the EU-Southern countries which show a share of almost 60%. With respect to the other aggregates the Central and Eastern European countries have on average higher shares of upper secondary and much lower shares in tertiary education than the EU-Northern and even slightly lower shares in tertiary education than the EU-Southern countries.

However, the shares in the labour force and in employment can differ from that in (working-age) population as participation rates differ across countries and educational levels. Whereas the relative shares between population, labour force and employment across the different educational groups corresponds roughly for the EU-Southern and EU-Northern countries, there are bigger differences in relation to the Central and Eastern European countries. The share of lower upper secondary educational levels in the labour force and in employment is in most cases much below the share in total population which reveals a relatively very low participation rate. Correspondingly the relative shares of people with upper secondary education and tertiary education in the labour force and in employment are relatively higher.

The skill structure of unemployment similarly reflects this picture and also differs from the EU-Northern and EU-Southern

TABLE 13

EDUCATIONAL SHARES
(in %)

	Czech Republic	Hungary	Poland	Slovenia	Slovak Republic	Estonia	Latvia	Lithuania	Bulgaria	Romania	EU-South	EU-North
Population												
Age group 15-64												
by education												
< upper secondary	23.8	38.5	33.1	33.9	28.8	26.2	30.6	31.3	43.9	43.2	58.0	28.6
upper secondary	67.0	50.3	58.3	53.9	63.5	51.3	55.3	36.8	42.7	49.9	29.2	49.5
tertiary	9.1	11.2	8.6	12.1	7.6	22.5	14.1	31.9	13.4	6.9	12.8	21.9
Labour force												
Age group 15+												
by education												
< upper secondary	10.4	18.4	15.8	20.7	9.4	12.4	13.8	12.4	22.9	35.7	54.9	23.5
upper secondary	77.8	65.4	71.9	62.8	80.0	58.5	66.7	44.9	56.8	55.9	28.3	51.6
tertiary	11.8	16.2	12.3	16.5	10.6	29.1	19.4	42.6	20.3	8.4	16.8	24.9
Employment												
Age group 15+												
by education												
< upper secondary	8.8	17.4	14.8	19.9	6.9	10.7	12.7	11.4	19.2	36.8	54.7	22.3
upper secondary	78.7	65.5	71.3	62.8	80.7	57.4	66.3	42.6	57.7	54.4	28.2	51.8
tertiary	12.6	17.1	13.9	17.3	12.4	31.8	21.0	45.9	23.1	8.7	17.1	25.9
Unemployment												
Age group 15+												
by education												
< upper secondary	26.7	32.4	20.8	31.9	19.8	23.9	20.8	18.0	39.0	20.0	56.1	38.0
upper secondary	69.2	64.1	75.0	62.9	77.2	65.1	69.5	57.4	53.0	75.6	29.5	48.7
tertiary	4.1	3.5	4.2	5.3	2.9	11.0	9.8	24.6	7.9	4.4	14.4	13.3

Source: Employment and labour market in CENTRAL EUROPEAN COUNTRIES. EUROPEAN COMMISSION. [10] and own calculations.

countries. People with upper secondary educational levels amount to about 60 to 70% of unemployed compared to 30% in EU-South and 50% in EU-North. On the other hand the share of people with lower upper secondary level is lower (the reason might be the lower participation rate) whereas the share for people with tertiary education is much lower. Unemployment rates are particularly low amongst the persons with tertiary education, even in comparison with the EU Southern and EU Northern countries. This points towards a structural problem, i.e. the lack of highly-skilled workers/employees. However, these data mask further severe deficiencies with respect to particular occupations. E.g. the EBRD [10] reports a lack of skills especially in managerial and other high-skilled employment which corresponds to the relatively low shares in tertiary education.

Although the above definitely requires much more detailed analysis, one can observe strong labour demand pressures for the highly skilled in the transition countries which is compatible with the picture of a catching-up with qualitative up-grading which has been developed in the earlier sections of this paper.

7. - Summary

This paper has attempted to analyse the evolving patterns of industrial specialisation in Central and Eastern Europe. We have shown that a differentiated picture emerges with some countries catching-up relatively fast in technologically more sophisticated branches and also improving their positions in intra-branch product quality. This picture is compatible with an analytical approach in which the potential exists to turn comparative advantages in favour of those areas in which initially bigger gaps (in productivity and product quality) exist. This is an application of the Gerschenkron hypothesis ('advantage of backwardness') at the industrial level. However, the existence of such a potential does not automatically imply its utilisation (a point which Abramovitz emphasised). The approach makes room for a wide diversity of qualitative catching-up patterns and evolving positions of catching-up economies in the international division of labour. This is what we observe with respect to the countries in Central and Eastern Europe where one set of countries got (so far) 'locked in' in a rather traditional pattern of trade and industrial specialisation (in low-skill-, labour-intensive branches), while other CEECs (to varying degrees) show a much more dynamic pattern of integration into the European division of labour.

We have substantiated this picture of diversity in analysing first the broad patterns of structural change in Central and Eastern Europe (Section 2) and then the changes in employment and production structures within manufacturing (Section 3). We then moved towards examining the evidence for a dynamically evolving structure of comparative advantage with a detailed assessment of differential patterns of productivity and unit (labour) cost growth across branches (Section 4) and with an analysis of inter-industry trade specialisation and differential (export) product quality up-grading within industrial branches (Section 5). Finally, we sketched the roles of foreign direct investment and of the existence and utilisation of educational attainment as important factors in determining the positions of individual countries (the analysis could similarly be extended to regions) in the evolving division of labour in the European economy as a whole.

As regards EU Enlargement our analysis shows clearly that different CEECs are in different positions with regard to their achieved levels of catching-up, and this refers not only to overall levels but — probably more importantly — with regard to the qualitative nature of their structural transformations and their positions in cross-European trade structures. We expect such differentiation to have a bearing on how they will cope with the additional adjustments required by the accession process itself and on what footing they will be able to participate in the integrated structures of the Enlarged European economy. This, of course, also has implications for the instruments which will be required to deal with the problems of cohesion which will get further accentuated not only as a result of the accession process itself but as a result of the existence of those other economies which are highly integrated with the EU but will not join in the first round.

APPENDIX

TABLE 14

WIFO TAXONOMIES

	NACE rev. 1	Taxonomy I factor inputs	Taxonomy II labour skills
Meat products	151	4	1
Fish and fish products	152	4	1
Fruits and vegetables	153	4	1
Vegetable and animal oils and fats	154	4	1
Dairy products; ice cream	155	4	1
Grain mill products and starches	156	4	1
Prepared animal feeds	157	4	1
Other food products	158	4	1
Beverages	159	4	1
Tobacco products	160	4	1
Textile fibres	171	3	1
Textile weaving	172	2	1
Made-up textile articles	174	2	1
Other textiles	175	1	1
Knitted and crocheted fabrics	176	1	1
Knitted and crocheted articles	177	1	1
Leather clothes	181	2	1
Other wearing apparel and accessories	182	2	1
Dressing and dyeing of fur; articles of fur	183	2	1

Source: PENEDER M. [24].

	Taxonomy I :	Taxonomy II:
Industry clusters:	1. Mainstream	1. Low-skill industries
	2. Labour-intensive industries	2. Medium-skill/blue-collar workers
	3. Capital-intensive industries	3. Medium-skill/white-collar workers
	4. Marketing-driven industries	4. High-skill industries
	5. Technology-driven industries	

TABLE 14 *(cont)*.

	NACE rev. 1	Taxonomy I factor inputs	Taxonomy II labour skills
Tanning and dressing of leather	191	4	1
Luggage, handbags, saddlery and harness	192	4	1
Footwear	193	4	1
Sawmilling, planing and impregnation of wood	201	2	2
Panels and boards of wood	202	2	2
Builders' carpentry and joinery	203	2	2
Wooden containers	204	2	2
Other products of wood; articles of cork, etc.	205	2	2
Pulp, paper and paperboard	211	3	3
Articles of paper and paperboard	212	1	3
Publishing	221	4	3
Printing	222	4	3
Coke oven products	231		
Refined petroleum and nuclear fuel	232	3	3
Nuclear fuel	233		
Basic chemicals	241	3	3
Pesticides, other agro-chemical products	242	5	3
Paints, coatings, printing ink	243	1	3
Pharmaceuticals	244	5	4
Detergents, cleaning and polishing, perfumes	245	4	3
Other chemical products	246	5	3
Man-made fibres	247	3	3
Rubber products	251	1	1
Plastic products	252	1	1
Glass and glass products	261	1	1
Ceramic goods	262	2	1
Ceramic tiles and flags	263	3	1
Bricks, tiles and construction products	264	2	1
Cement, lime and plaster	265	3	1

TABLE 14 *(cont.)*

	NACE rev. 1	Taxonomy I factor inputs	Taxonomy II labour skills
Articles of concret, plaster and cement	266	1	1
Cutting, shaping, finishing of stone	267	2	1
Other non-metallic mineral products	268	1	1
Basic iron and steel, ferro-alloys (ECSC)	271	3	1
Tubes	272	1	1
Other first processing of iron and steel	273	3	1
Basic precious and non-ferrous metals	274	3	1
Structural metal products	281	2	2
Tanks, reservoirs, central heating radiators and boilers	282	4	2
Steam generators	283	2	2
Cutlery, tools and general hardware	286	4	2
Other fabricated metal products	287	1	2
Machinery for production, use of mech. power	291	1	4
Other general purpose machinery	292	1	4
Agricultural and forestry machinery	293	1	4
Machine-tools	294	2	4
Other special purpose machinery	295	1	4
Weapons and ammunition	296	1	4
Domestic appliances n. e. c.	297	1	3
Office machinery and computers	300	5	4
Electric motors, generators and transformers	311	1	3
Electricity distribution and control apparatus	312	5	3
Isolated wire and cable	313	1	3
Accumulators, primary cells and primary batteries	314	1	3
Lighting equipment and electric lamps	315	1	3
Electrical equipment n. e. c.	316	2	3

TABLE 14 *(cont.)*

	NACE rev. 1	Taxonomy I factor inputs	Taxonomy II labour skills
Electronic valves and tubes, other electronic comp.	321	5	3
TV, and radio transmitters, apparatus for line telephony	322	5	3
TV, radio and recording apparatus	323	5	3
Medical equipment	331	5	3
Instruments for measuring, checking, testing, navigating	332	5	3
Optical instruments and photographic equipment	334	5	3
Watches and clocks	335	4	3
Motor vehicles	341	5	2
Bodies for motor vehicles, trailers	342	2	2
Parts and accessories for motor vehicles	343	3	2
Ships and boats	351	2	2
Railway locomotives and rolling stock	352	2	2
Aircraft and spacecraft	353	5	4
Motorcycles and bicycles	354	1	2
Other transport equipment n.e.c.	355	1	2
Furniture	361	2	2
Jewellery and related articles	362	2	2
Musical instruments	363	4	2
Sports goods	364	4	2
Games and toys	365	4	2
Miscellaneous manufacturing n.e.c.	366	4	2

BIBLIOGRAPHY

[1] AIGINGER K., «The Use of Unit Values to Discriminate Between Price and Quality Competition», *Cambridge Journal of Economics*, vol. 21, 1997, pp. 571-92.

[2] ABRAMOVITZ M., «Catching-up, Forging Ahead and Falling Behind», *Journal of Economic History*, vol. 46, 1986, pp. 385-406.

[3] ATURUPANE C. - DJANKOV S. - HOEKMAN B., «Horizontal and Vertical Intra-Industry Trade Between Eastern Europe and the European Union», *Weltwirtschaftliches Archiv*, vol. 135, 1999, pp. 62-81.

[4] BALDONE S. - SDOGATI F. - TAVOLI L., «Patterns and Determinants of International Fragmentation of Production: Evidence from Outward Processing Trade between the EU and Central Eastern European Countries», *Weltwirtschaftliches Archiv*, vol. 137, n. 1, 2001, pp. 80-104.

[5] BARREL R. - HOLLAND D., «Foreign Direct Investment and Enterprise Restructuring in Central Europe», *Economics of Transition*, vol. 8, n. 2, 2000, pp. 477-504.

[6] BURGSTALLER J. - LANDESMANN M., «Trade Performance of East European Producers on EU Markets: an Assessment of Product Quality», Vienna, The Vienna Institute for International Economic Studies (WIIW), *Research Report*, n. 255, 1999.

[7] EUROPEAN COMMISSION, *European Competitiveness Report 1999*, EC., 1999 (See http://europa.eu.int/comm/enterprise/enterprise_policy/competitiveness/index.htm).

[8] — —, *European Competitiveness Report 2000*, EC, 2000 (See http://europa.eu.int/comm/enterprise/enterprise_policy/competitiveness/index.htm).

[9] — —, *Employment in Europe 2001. Recent Trends and Prospects*, European Commission. DG Employment and Social Affairs, 2001.

[10] EBRD, *Transition Report 2000. Employment, Skills, and Transition*, London, 2001.

[11] FOTAGNÉ L. - FREUDENBERG M., «Intra-Industry Trade: Methodological Issues Reconsidered», Paris, CEPII, *Document de Travail*, n. 97-01, 1997.

[12] GERSCHENKRON A., *Economic Backwardness in Historical Perspective*, Cambridge (Mass.), Harvard University Press, 1962.

[13] GREENAWAY D. - HINE R. - MILNER, C., «Country-specific factors and the pattern of Horizontal and Vertical Intra-Industry Trade in the UK», *Weltwirtschaftliches Archiv*, vol. 130, 1994, pp. 77-100.

[14] GROSSMAN G.M. - HELPMAN E., *Innovation and Growth in the Global Economy*, Cambridge, MIT Press, 1991.

[15] HUNYA G. - Foreign Direct Investment in CEEC Manufacturing, in: LANDESMANN M.A. (ed.), *WIIW Structural Report. Structural Developments in Central and Eastern Europe*, Chapter 5, Vienna, 2000.

[16] — —, *Integration Through Foreign Direct Investment. Making Central European Countries and Industries Competitive*, Cheltenham (UK), Edward Elgar, 2000.

[17] — —, «International Competitiveness: Impact of Foreign Direct Investment in Hungary and Other Central and East European Countries», in MEUSBERGER, P. - JOENS, J. (eds.), *Transformations in Hungary*, Heidelberg, Physica-Verlag, 2001.

[18] JANSEN M. - LANDESMANN M., «European Competitiveness: Quality Rather than

Price», in FAGERBERG J. *et* AL. (eds.), *The Economic Challenge for Europe: Adapting to Innovation-based Growth*, Cheltenham, Edward Elgar, 1999.

[19] KRUGMAN P., A Technology Gap Model of International Trade», in JUNGENFELDT, K. - HAGUE D. (eds.), *Structural Adjustment in Advanced Economies*, New York, Macmillan, 1986.

[20] LANDESMANN M.A., «Structural change in the transition economies, 1989-1999», in *Economic Survey of Europe, United Nations-Economic Commission for Europe*, n. 2000 (2/3), 2000, p. 95-123.

[21] LANDESMANN M.A. - STEHRER, R., «Industrial Specialisation, Catching-up and Labour Market Dynamics», *Metroeconomica*, vol. n. 51, n. 1, 2000, pp. 67-101.

[22] —— - ——, «Convergence Patterns and Switchovers in Comparative Advantage», *Structural Change and Economic Dynamics*, vol. 12, 2001, pp. 399-423.

[23] LANDESMANN M.A. - STEHRER R. - BURGSTALLER J., *Catching-up at the Industrial Level - Prospects for the CEEC's, Structural Developments in Central and Eastern Europe*, Bratislava, 2000.

[24] PENEDER M., *Entrepreneurial Competition and Industrial Location*, Cheltenham (UK), Edward Elgar, 2001.

[25] ROEMISCH R., «Trade in Services in the Central and East European Countries», Vienna, The Vienna Institute for International Economic Studies, WIIW, *Research Report* n. 274, 2001.

[26] STEHRER, R. - LANDESMANN M.A. - BURGSTALLER, J., «Convergence Patterns at the Industrial Level: The Dynamics of Comparative Advantage», Vienna, The Vienna Institute for International Economic Studies, WIIW, *Working Paper*, n. 274, 2001.

[27] STEHRER R. - WÖRZ J., *Technological Convergence and Trade Patterns*, Vienna, The Vienna Institute for International Economic Studies, WIIW, *Working paper*, n. 19, 2001.

[28] TEMPLE, J., «The New Growth Evidence», *Journal of Economic Literature*, vol. XXXVII, 1999, p. 112-56.

[29] UNCTAD, *World Investment Report*, Geneva, United Nations, 2001.

[30] WIIW, «Competitiveness of Industry in CEE Candidate Countries», *Report to the European Commission, DG Enterprise, Final Report*, July 2001 (available on the EU DG Enterprise Web Site).

Central Europe on
the Way to EMU

Daniel Gros*

Centre for European Policy Studies, Brussels

Polonia, Ungheria e Repubblica Ceca (CEE-3) potrebbero oggi situarsi a soli quattro anni dall'ingresso nell'Unione Monetaria Europe. Inoltre, questi paesi sembrano in condizioni più favorevoli per l'ingresso nell'area dell'Euro di quanto non fossero i paesi mediterranei negli anni precedenti il loro ingresso nell'Unione Monetaria, sulla base dei criteri di Maastricht. Tuttavia, non possiamo escludere che, lungo il sentiero della convergenza verso i parametri richiesti, si verifichino attacchi speculativi come accadde per i paesi mediterranei nel 1992-1993. In particolare, occorre prestare attenzione alla dinamica della bilancia dei pagamenti ed alla politica fiscale nei CEE-3.

Poland, Hungary and the Czech Republic (CEE-3) could now be only four years away from joining the euro. Moreover, these countries seem better placed than were some of the current euro area members (Spain, Greece, Italy, Portugal) at a comparable point in time leading up to their accession to EMU. But a smooth convergence cannot be taken for granted. Speculative attacks occurred in the early 1990s, when the process of convergence seemed to have been successfully completed. The CEE-3 share several characteristics of the economies hit by speculative attacks in 1992/95: a weak external position and uncertainty about fiscal policy [JEL Code: F33, F32].

---

* Daniel Gros is Director of the Centre for European Policy Studies in Brussels. Many thanks to Christian Buelens and Alexandr Hobza for excellent research assistance.

N.B., the numbers in square brackets refer to the Bibliography at the end of the paper.

1. - Introduction

In most of Central and Eastern Europe, economic policy is motivated by the desire to join the EU, and eventually also the euro area. There can be little doubt today that these goals will be achieved, but it is difficult to predict how long the process will take and whether the convergence will be smooth. This paper focuses mainly on the economically largest accession candidates, namely Poland, the Czech Republic and Hungary.

These countries are well advanced on the convergence path, but still have some way to go to qualify under the Maastricht criteria. How long will it take them to qualify for EMU membership? The experience of some current euro area members suggests that this could happen sooner, rather than later. It is thus possible that the CEE-3 will have the euro already by 2006, four years from now. Financial markets are discounting this possibility already to a large extent. But financial markets are fickle. The global environment is deteriorating and emerging markets are watched ever more closely for signs that policy might be slipping. The current uncertainty about public finances should thus be taken very seriously.

Experience also suggests that the last stretch of convergence can be very difficult. In early 1992, countries such as Spain and Italy seemed within striking distance of full convergence, but in the middle of the year they were suddenly hit by speculative attacks and forced to abandon their peg to the DM. At the climax of a very volatile period, that lasted over three years, the Italian lira had devalued by over 60% against the DM and long-term interest rates had risen to unprecedented levels[1]. In the end, the Italian and Spanish governments did take the steps necessary to qualify for EMU, exchange rates appreciated and interest rates converged. This chapter thus had a happy ending, but it should serve as a warning that the final stretch of convergence can be the most

---

[1] See GROS D. - THYGESEN N. [4] for a detailed analysis. A financial analyst, writing at this point in one Europe's leading newspapers, likened the bonds of Italian toll motorway companies to toilet paper.

perilous. One might argue that the early 1990s were a particularly difficult period because of the recession and the high real interest rates caused by the German response to unification. But it seems that history is repeating itself: just as the Central and Eastern European Countries (CEEC) are getting ready to converge the international economic environment darkens again. It will thus be more difficult to repeat the experience of Greece, which had a text-book convergence path: initial one-step devaluation, followed by smooth convergence.

The convergence saga is developed in what follows. Section 2 concentrates on the good news that satisfying the Maastricht criteria should not be a major problem, provided the political will to keep fiscal policy under control persists. Section 3 concentrates on the bad news, namely that experience shows that this is not sufficient to protect against trouble in the presence of large current account deficits and potentially overvalued exchange rates. Section 4 then checks whether the current account deficits could be justified by the need to finance domestic investment and Section 5 concludes.

2. - Prospects of Meeting the Maastricht Criteria

Within the EU-15, it is often taken for granted that membership in EMU will come long after accession to the EU because the candidates are supposedly far from meeting the Maastricht criteria. The reason for this assumption is that most assessments of the prospects of the 10 candidate countries from Central and Eastern Europe to meet the Maastricht criteria start from current and past data and thus conclude inevitably that the candidates are a long way from being able to join the euro area. But this approach is misleading, as can be shown by simply asking what one would have concluded for the prospects of the present Southern member countries of EMU if one had used a similar approach in the early 1990s.

What would be the earliest date by which at least some CEECs could aspire to join the euro area? The starting point has to be full EU membership which has now been scheduled for January 2004. The minimum delay between the start of EU membership and joining the euro area is two years of membership in the ERMII (as for Greece and Italy). If advanced member countries join the ERMII immediately upon joining the EU, i.e. in early 2004, they could just join EMU by July 2006. The decision to admit CEE candidates to the euro area could then be taken at a European Council meeting in early 2006, based on data for 2005[2].

A comparison with the start-up of EMU is instructive in this regard. The decision on which countries could form the initial group was taken in 1998 on the basis of 1997 data. Judging the suitability of CEE countries on the basis of 2000/2001 data would thus be similar to having made a prediction about the size of EMU in the early 1990s on the basis of data from 1993 (1995 for Greece). How do the candidates measure up on this yardstick?

Table 1 below shows the main variables that are relevant for the Maastricht criteria: fiscal deficit, government debt, inflation and long-term interest rates. The table is organised in two groups of countries: the CEE-3 and the "Club Med". Within the latter group, the data for Greece are from two years later because this country joined EMU about two years after the others.

Table 1 provides an average for the Club Med. A comparison between the data for the CEE-3 and the corresponding data for the Club Med suggests a clear conclusion: The CEE-3 are definitely much closer to meeting the Maastricht criteria than the Club Med countries were at a comparable time (i.e. 6 years) before the start of EMU. Inflation, although still high is analogous to that of the Club Med in the early 1990s and long-term interest rates are much lower than the corresponding value for the Club Med in 1993. The CEE-3 average fiscal deficit is (at least based on 2001 data) about-half of the Club Med deficit then (average 8.1 % of GDP in 1993). The same observation applies to public debt.

---

[2] A similar procedure was adopted in the case of Greece. A decision taken at a European Council meeting in early 2000 was based on data from 1999, and Greece was then able to join almost immediately.

TABLE 1

MAASTRICHT CRITERIA - CANDIDATE COUNTRIES AND CLUB MED

	Budget deficit (end 2001)	Debt (end 2001)	Inflation	Long-term interest rates
Bulgaria	−1.5	100.0	7.9	5
Czech Republic	−4.5	29.1	4.8	5.4
Estonia	−1.0	5.9	5.9	6.8
Hungary	−3.7	56.7	9.6	6.6
Latvia	−1.4	9.2	3.1	10.2
Lithuania	−1.5	26.1	1.2	6.3
Poland	−5.1	48.4	6.0	8.4
Romania	−3.5	34.1	34.4	49.2
Slovakia	−5.2	45.0	7.5	7.7
Slovenia	−1.2	25.0	8.5	Na
Average	*−2.9*	*38.0*	*8.9*	*11.7*
Average CEE-3	*−4.4*	*44.7*	*6.8*	*6.8*
Maastricht thresholds (2000)	−3.0	60.0	1.4+1.5=2.9	5.4+2=7.4
Club Med - 1993/1995 data				
Portugal	−5.9	61.1	6.9	9.5
Spain	−6.7	58.7	5.3	10.1
Italy	−9.4	118.2	5.5	11.1
Greece	−10.5	108.7	8.9	Na
Average	*−8.1*	*86.7*	*6.7*	*10.23*
Benchmarks				
Germany (1993)	−3.1	47.2	3.7	6.4
Eurozone (2000)	0.4	70.5	1.4	5.4
EU (2000)	1.2	64.6	1.5	5.5

Source: Own calculations based on Commission data (AMECO).

Moreover, in Italy and Spain, the debt to GDP ratio actually *increased* by over 20 percentage points between the early 1990s and the date of accession to EMU, whereas it has fallen over the last five years in most candidate countries.

One might object to the comparison made implicitly in table 1 on the ground that the benchmark today is much stricter. After all, the inflation and the interest criterion are relative to the three best performers in the euro area[3]. Hence one could argue that while in the early 1990s Germany was the benchmark, today it is the Eurozone, whose performance (with exception of public debt) is better than Germany's then, which then had to sustain the cost of unification. However, as the difference is not large such a comparison would give a similar picture.

The data thus suggest clearly that Poland, Hungary and the Czech Republic are already much closer to satisfying the Maastricht criteria than the Southern member states of the EU were in the early to mid 1990s. Moreover, experience has repeatedly shown that a short and sharp adjustment is politically and economically less painful than a protracted, and hence supposedly but erroneously soft one. The case of Greece, which was until the mid 1990s regarded as a lost cause, provides a further illustration of this phenomenon. The relatively small fiscal adjustment that is still required of the candidates could thus come rather quickly and is likely to be politically easier to implement than the slow adjustment of some established member countries. No "strikes against Maastricht", as were called in France, are likely to happen in any of the candidate countries.

The relatively good starting position of the candidate countries in a historical perspective does not mean, of course, that there will be absolutely no problems in meeting the Maastricht criteria. But the problems that remain should be manageable, both for the deficit and debt criteria.

2.1 *Deficits*

Achieving a fiscal deficit below 3% is essentially a question of political will. Until 1999 Poland, the Czech Republic and some other advanced candidates satisfied or were close to this norm. The data for 2000/2001 and the outlook for the next couple of

---

[3] The *Maastricht Treaty* states, that a member states' inflation has to be at most 1.5 percentage points above the average of the three best national performances. For long-term interest rates, the critical value is extended to 2 percentage points. Here we replace the 'best performances' by the Eurozone performance.

years are somewhat less reassuring as deficits have increased under the impact of the global slowdown. While the automatic stabilisers were allowed to work in the EU as well it seems that fiscal deficits are somewhat more variable in transition countries. This reinforces the point that current data are not a useful indicator, and that one should rather look for structural problems that would constitute an insurmountable obstacle in the medium run.

The key question one should ask therefore is: Are there any longer-term factors that could put unbearable pressure on public finances in Poland and other candidate countries? It is often argued that such pressure might arise from the need to build a modern infrastructure in the CEE-3s, plus the pressure on their underdeveloped social system. However, a look at the data again shows that the problems are not worse in the Central part of Europe.

Infrastructure needs? The public infrastructure of the candidates is certainly less developed than that of current EU members. The candidates have fewer motorways and paved roads per inhabitant and square kilometre, fewer fixed telephone lines, etc., but this does not immediately imply that they therefore need more investment in this area. What they have might actually be adequate for their level of development[4]. Poland for example has actually a larger stock of infrastructure than one would expect given its income per capita. It is thus difficult to argue that public infrastructure is the main impediment to growth[5]. Moreover, once

---

[4] See GROS D. - SUHRCKE M. [3], GROS D. - SKEINHERR A. [2].

[5] There are more reasons to doubt the need for large public infrastructure spending: Within the EU one actually does not find any link between public investment and growth in GDP. Ireland, by far the fastest growing economy of the EU over the last decades, has a somewhat below-average ratio of public investment to GDP. Moreover, even if one wanted to give a country of Skoda-drivers the motorways that are appropriate for Mercedes, there is still no need to run large public sector deficits. Given the changes in financial markets that have taken place over the last decade, it is now generally recognised that most infrastructure projects could also be financed and sometimes even operated with substantial private sector involvement. Major projects, such as motorways, are already being undertaken on a mainly private sector basis in the candidates.

the CEEC join the EU they will be eligible for support under the regional policy of the EU, which is designed to finance this type of expenditure.

In the EU it is also often argued that the different candidate countries, have underdeveloped social security systems. It is true that pension expenditures figure prominently in the current debate over the budget crisis in Poland. But the same could be said of most EU countries as well. Indeed, most of the indicators that should signal pressure for spending in the social sphere show little difference between the EU and the CEECs.

For example, there is no significant difference in the age profiles between the EU and most of the candidates. The ageing problem is thus not worse for the new members. Poland actually has somewhat less of a greying problem than the EU. In terms of public spending on health and education (as a percentage of GNP), there is also little difference between the candidates (around 5%) and the EU average (below 6%).

All in all, it thus appears that the pressure on budgets should be manageable over the medium run in all the CEECs, allowing them to achieve the required remaining reductions in deficits.

2.2 Debt

The debt criterion should not constitute a major additional hurdle. With the exception of Bulgaria, all CEEC have debt-to-GDP ratios that are considerably below the euro area average. Furthermore, with an average of 30% (leaving Bulgaria and Romania aside) they are in full conformity with the Maastricht criterion, to which only the value for Hungary (57%) comes close, the Czech Republic (29%) and Poland (48%) are in no near reach yet. In this respect the performance of the Baltic states is also striking with a public debt amounting to only 6% and 9% of GDP for Estonia and Latvia respectively. Debt levels usually change only slowly so that the current data are more informative than for deficits.

But are the data too good to be true? As the Czech case has shown, the process of cleansing the accounts of the banking system can at times lead to large liabilities of the public sector (and a temporary ballooning defict). Debt-to-GDP ratios might thus increase in some candidate countries as they clean-up their banking system. But most of this has already been achieved, and the remainder will be done before accession. Non-performing loans as a percentage of GDP (on the basis of EBRD data) are in the low single digit level in most CEECs. Moreover, the banking systems of the CEECs are now dominated by foreign banks. Further pressure on public finances from this side should thus be limited[6].

Moreover, healthy growth combined with low deficits (say around 3%) should lead to rather strong downward pressures on the debt-to-GDP ratio so that some debt assumption can take place without putting in jeopardy the debt criterion.

3. - Pitfalls During the Final Stretch of Convergence?

The CEE-3 should thus be able to qualify for full EMU membership by early 2006, following a decision by the EU that wraps up the process as early as 2005. But this does not imply automatically that convergence will be smooth. Speculative attacks destroyed the European Monetary System in the early 1990s, exactly when the process of convergence seemed to have been successfully completed.

Why did these attacks come about? Markets developed doubts that the countries concerned would be able to actually carry through the required fiscal adjustment and that some currencies were overvalued. Given the much better starting position of the CEE-3 in terms of fiscal policy, the first reservation might be much less of an issue. But there are certainly signs that some of the CEE-3 currencies are overvalued.

In particular some of the CEE-3 share several characteristics of the economies worst hit by speculative attacks in 1992-1995.

---

[6] See PELKMANS J. *et* AL. [6] for more details.

They have large current account deficits, financed by large, supposedly stable FDI inflows and as a corollary an appreciating real
exchange rate.

On all three counts, the potential dis-equilibrium is larger for
countries such as Poland today, than it was for Spain, Portugal
or Italy then. It will be useful to document this for the three elements separately.

3.1 *Current Account Deficits*

Current account deficits are usually presented as a percentage of GDP, which is useful if one wants to focus on the capacity of a government to service foreign debt. However, if one wants
to have an idea of the exchange rate adjustment required to re-
establish current account equilibrium, one should relate the current account deficit to overall export receipts (goods and services).
Under certain reasonable conditions, one could actually argue that
the deficit as a percent of export receipts gives directly the percent depreciation required to eliminate the current account deficit
without a contraction in domestic demand, i.e. a deficit equivalent to 30% of exports would require a devaluation of about the
same magnitude[7].

On this account, the data diverge slightly between the CEE-
3. (Table 2). The current account deficit of Poland in 2000 amounted to almost 20% of exports which corresponds to the value for
Spain during the early 1990s. (Portugal had only negligible deficits
during this period). This ratio has been much lower in the Czech
Republic, where it has moved around 5% and in Hungary where
it has fallen from 9.5 to 5%.

These data imply that a country such as Poland would require
a large depreciation of around 20%, should it ever need to achieve
a balanced current account quickly. In comparison Hungary and

---

[7] The conditions are that imports are relatively price in-elastic and that the
demand curve for exports has an elasticity of one, which is not far from typical
estimates in the empirical literature.

TABLE 2

CURRENT ACCOUNT DEFICITS
(as % of export receipts)[8]

	1998	1999	2000	2001
Poland	–14.8	–21.1	–19.2	–15.8
Czech Republic	–4.1	–4.7	–6.5	–6.6
Hungary	–9.5	–8.3	–5.2	–5.0

	1990	1991	1992	1993	1994	1995
Portugal	–0.8	–3.3	–0.8	1.0	–8.6	–0.4
Spain	–21.5	–22.2	–21.6	–6.5	–6.4	0.4

Sources: EUROPEAN COMMISSION, IMF and IFS.

the Czech Republic are in a much more stable monetary environment, as their need for devaluation would be much smaller. It is usually argued however, that there will be no need for this because the deficit is financed by stable flows of foreign direct investment. This argument was also frequently used prior to 1992 in the case of Spain and Portugal.

3.2 *Large FDI Inflows*

Table 3 below shows that Portugal and Spain also had rather large inflows of FDI, again measured as a percentage of export receipts. For Spain, FDI flows averaged over 10 % of exports during the pre-crisis period, and for Portugal they were only somewhat smaller.

For Poland today, FDI flows in relation to export receipts are nearly twice as important. During 2000 they amounted to

---

[8] The current account and net FDI values calculated for the Czech Republic and Hungary for the year 2000 are based on a different data base and are overestimated by about 20%.

TABLE 3
NET FDI INFLOWS
(as a percent of export receipts)

	1998	1999	2000
Poland	14.3	17.9	16.9
Czech Republic	11.2	19.1	12.7
Hungary	6.5	6.7	4.7

	1990	1991	1992	1993	1994	1995
Portugal	11.4	9.2	5.0	6.1	3.9	0.0
Spain	12.5	9.0	11.1	5.9	5.1	1.9

Sources: EUROPEAN COMMISSION, IMF and IFS.

over 15 % of exports, financing most of the current account deficit. In Hungary the current account deficit is covered by FDI flows too, though at a smaller magnitude. In the Czech Republic however, FDI flows represent double of the current account.

The key question is thus for how long the CEE-3 can count on inflows of this magnitude. Over the last years, the CEE-3 have experienced rather stable flows, which have on average increased year after year. But can this go on forever? The experience of Spain and Portugal is again instructive in this respect. FDI flows to Spain halved in the year after the first attack (1993) and have then considerably fallen again after the second major attack (1995). By 1997, Spain became a net exporter of FDI, and later Portugal as well (see Graph 1). With swings in external flows of this size it is not surprising that a large adjustment in the real exchange rate of the peseta was needed.

This leads to the third issue: Are the currencies of the CEE-3 overvalued?

GRAPH 1

FOREIGN DIRECT INVESTMENT AS A PERCENTAGE
OF EXPORTS IN PORTUGAL AND SPAIN

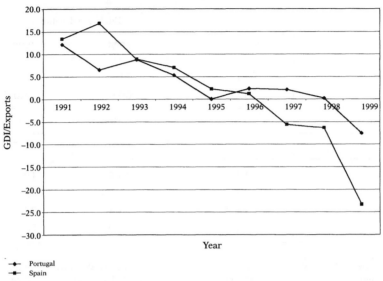

3.3 *Real Overvaluation?*

During the early 1990s, there was a lively discussion whether the Club Med currencies were overvalued. There was no general agreement, because the judgement depended, as usual, on the indicator and the base period used. The two indicators most often used to measure competitiveness are (and were then) the real exchange rate deflated by the CPI and by Unit Labour Costs (ULC). These two usually give different indications. Now, and then (Table 4).

In the case of Spain, it was argued that there was no need for a large exchange rate adjustment because there was no real overvaluation - but only if one used ULC as the competitiveness indicator and 1980 as the base period. Not surprisingly, this was the position taken by the authorities. A similar argument was used in the case of Italy, where there was also a large discrepancy between the ULC- and the CPI-based measures.

Poland today presents a very similar picture. Depending on the base period and the indicator chosen, the zloty could

TABLE 4

APPRECIATING REAL EXCHANGE RATES
(Percent appreciation relative to the indicated base period)

		Early 2001 relative to	
		1996	*1999*
Poland	CPI	21.1	18.1
	ULC	64.4	8.6

Club Med		Relative to End-1991	
		1980	*1987*
Italy	CPI	30.8	10.9
	ULC	−1.0	8.5
Spain	CPI	24.1	25.6
	ULC	1.9	28.0

Sources: GROS D. - THYGESEN N. [4], p. 216 for Club Med relative to Germany. For Poland, real effective exchange rates provided by DB London (weight of EU is 93%).

be seen to be overvalued by any sum between 8% and 64%. For Hungary and the Czech Republic, the potential overvaluation is much smaller across most indicators and base periods.

The argument that the zloty cannot be overvalued because Polish exports keep growing fast was also used in the case of Spain, where exports had actually doubled in dollar terms in the five years prior to the attack of 1992, an even more impressive performance than Poland's. This is typical of countries that have recently opened up to trade, such as the transition countries today or Spain in 1992, when it dismantled its last tariffs within the, then, EC. In such cases both exports and imports tend to grow strongly, whatever the exchange rate, more and more sectors are exposed to international competition[9].

---

[9] For an analysis of the experience of transitions countries see DE BROECK M. - SLEK T. [1], HALPERN L. - WYPLOSZ C. [5].

These data suggest that sooner or later an exchange rate adjustment might be needed. The discussion concentrated on the case of the zloty, where the potential overvaluation is largest because of the recent sharp appreciation. But the other CEE-3 countries might soon face a similar situation. What does this imply for the exchange rate policies pursued by these countries?

Poland and the Czech Republic officially follow a floating exchange rate, accompanied by domestic inflation targets. They are thus in a different situation than Spain and Italy in the early 1990s, which were members of a fixed exchange rate system, the ERM. In theory, an exchange rate adjustment could thus come about gradually and without disruption.

However, experience has shown that large exchange rate adjustments almost always lead to some disruption in financial markets. This was the case even for Spain, which in 1992 had actually a rather large room for manoeuvre under the ERM (Spain had margins of +/- 6%). A sudden large depreciation usually forces the central bank to increase interest rates to limit the domestic inflationary pressures that would otherwise worsen inflation. Moreover, the terms of trade shock (deriving from the depreciation) in combination with higher interest rates might initially lead to a contraction in demand (as in Italy and Spain). This in turn puts pressure on the budget, leading to higher deficits; which then might undermine confidence and thus aggravate the depreciation.

Such a negative spiral does not need to develop. The case of Greece shows that a smooth 'glide path' to EMU is possible. But it would certainly be very dangerous for the CEE-3 countries to enter into an ERM-type arrangement that would tie their currencies to the euro before they have a clearer view of whether the current exchange rate levels are sustainable in the long run. The case of Greece, which engineered successfully a one-step surprise devaluation is instructive in this regard.

4. - Savings and Investment: Capital Mobility in Central Europe

Large current account deficits could be justified if they finance the build up of a strong capital stock, whose returns can then later finance debt service. Unfortunately, this mechanism does not seem to be the main driving force for current accounts in Central and Eastern Europe. This evaluation might appear to be surprising in view of the importance of the flows of foreign direct investment into Central and Eastern Europe. Indeed, for most countries FDI flows are large enough to cover the current account deficit (as already documented for the three largest CEE's above). But the key question is whether FDI is in addition to domestic investment. Here the evidence is rather weak. Across countries there is only a rather weak tendency for countries with higher FDI to have also higher investment rates. Moreover, the countries with the largest current account deficits are not the ones with the highest investment ratios.

Another way to evaluate the driving forces behind the capital flows into the CEEC is to look at the relationship between the changes in current accounts and investment ratios across countries as depicted in Graph 2. It is apparent that countries which recorded large increases in the current account deficits (as % of GDP) were also mostly the ones with highest increase in investment to GDP ratios. Therefore, if one applies the Feldstein-Horioka criterion this suggests that capital mobility is already rather high in Central and Eastern Europe.

How should one evaluate this apparent contradiction? It seems that capital is mobile at the margin (for the CEECs) but enormous differences exist among these countries as to their overall propensity to save. The poorer countries (e.g. Bulgaria and Romania) seem to have the lowest national savings rates (they have low investment rates, but still sizeable current account deficits). The large current account deficits make sense in an inter-temporal context, if one assumes that they help the country to accumulate capital faster than it could if it did rely on national savings alone. But unfortunately the poorer countries do not seem to be the ones that grow faster, which is not surprising in light of their lower investment ratios. This points again to a risk: namely that some countries accumulate large foreign debts that finance an unsustainable rate of consumption. A protracted crisis is likely to result when capital markets discover that the country has difficulties servicing its debt because not enough capital (physical and human) was invested in the tradables sector. Hungary has been in this situation for most of the past decade. It emerged from the over-indebtedness trap only after a long period of belt-tightening which was politically and economically very painful (Poland extricated itself from a similar situation at the end of the 1980s thanks to a combination of large scale debt forgiveness and rapid growth). At present it appears that the CEE-3, are no longer in this situation, but the danger remains for the laggards, i.e. Bulgaria and Romania.

GRAPH 2

RELATIONSHIP BETWEEN CHANGES IN INVESTMENT AND THE
CURRENT ACCOUNT BETWEEN 1995 AND 2000
(as a percentage of GDP)

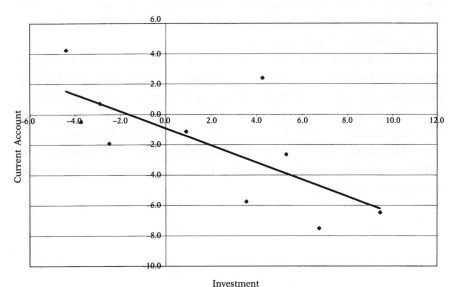

Investment

5. - Concluding Remarks

Poland, the Czech Republic and Hungary seem to be well placed to enter the euro area rapidly once they have acceded to the EU. But experience has shown that the final stretch of convergence can be the most dangerous, especially for countries with a potentially overvalued exchange rate whose level is underpinned by large capital inflows, which cannot be taken for granted forever. The experience of some members of the euro zone is instructive in this regard. There are examples of countries that were able to converge rather smoothly, e.g. Greece, and, to a lesser extent, Portugal. In the cases of Spain and Italy, however, EMU membership was preceded by an extremely volatile period during which time exchange rates depreciated heavily and interest shot up. In both cases financial markets worried not only about over-valued exchange rates, but also weak fiscal policy.

The case of Poland today shows a number of similarities with that of Spain ten years ago: the Spanish economy was also rather dynamic, but characterised by high unemployment and large regional differences; exactly as Poland today. Until the early 1990s fiscal policy in the CEE-3 has been generally under control, resulting in a low debt-to-GDP ratio. But this seemed at risk during the politically and economically turbulent late 1990s and the early years of the new century.

Governments that are really determined to get into EMU can usually withstand the pressure from financial markets. In the case of Spain and Italy, markets calmed down eventually and convergence resumed at a rapid pace. There was a happy ending. But the intervening turbulent times were very costly for these countries. The challenge for policy makers in the CEE-3 will be to avoid similar turbulence while steering their currencies to their final safe harbour, the euro.

BIBLIOGRAPHY

[1] DE BROECK M. - SLEK T., «Interpreting Real Exchange Rate Movements is Transition Countries», Bank of Finland, Institute for Economies in Transition (BOFIT), *Discussion Paper*, n. 7, 2001.

[2] GROS D. - STEINHERR A., *Winds of Change, Economic Transition in Central and Eastern Europe*, London, Addison-Wesley Longman, 1995.

[3] GROS D. - SUHRCKE M., «Ten Years After: What is special about transition countries?», Brussels, CEPS *Working Document*, n. 143, Centre for European Policy Studies, May 2000.

[4] GROS D. - THYGESEN N., *European Monetary Integration from EMS to EMU*, London, Addison-Wesley Longman, 1998.

[5] HALPERN L. - WYPLOSZ C., «Economic Transformation and Real Exchange Rates in the 2000s: The Balassa-Samuelson Connection», *Economic Survey of Europe*, n. 1, 2001, pp. 227-39.

[6] PELKMANS J. - GROS D. - NÚÑEZ FERRER J., «Long-Run Economic Aspects of the European Union's Eastern Enlargement», The Hague, Scientific Council for Government Policy WRR, *Working Document*, n. 109, September 2000.

Accession to the European Union: Real Exchange Rate Dynamics for Candidate Countries

Fabrizio Coricelli - Boštjan Jazbec*

Università di Siena   University of Ljubljana
(Slovenia)

L'allargamento ad Est dell'Unione Europea pone la questione della compatibilità tra il processo di convergenza dei Paesi candidati verso i livelli di reddito dei membri dell'Unione, e l'adozione dell'Euro da parte dei paesi dell'Est. In particolare, si pone il problema della convergenza dei tassi d'inflazione, e quindi della convergenza nominale oltre che reale tra le economie dei Paesi candidati e quelle dell'Unione. In questo articolo, affrontiamo questo tema con particolare attenzione alla dinamica dei tassi di cambio reali e dell'inflazione, con un approfimento sul caso della Slovenia che ha compiuto notevoli progressi sul sentiero della transizione.

Several observers have raised the issue of whether the process of real convergence of candidate countries to income levels of EU members is compatible with the adoption of the Euro, as Maastricht criteria impose strict constraints on nominal variables. In particular, inflation should converge to the best performers in the EU, and thus for candidate countries the process of real convergence should proceed simultaneously with that of nominal convergence. We investigate this issue looking at the dynamics of real exchange rates in candidate countries and the implications for inflation dynamics, with special attention to the case of Slovenia.
[JEL Code: E42, E58, F31, F33].

* Fabrizio Coricelli is Professore Ordinario at the Department of Economics; Central European University Budapest and CEPR Londra. The author is currently an Economic Adviser in the European Commission, ECFIN. Boštjan Jazbec is Teaching Assistant at the Faculty of Economics.

N.B., the numbers in square brackets refer to the Bibliography at the end of the paper.

1. - Introduction

Starting from a very low level of GDP per capita, countries that are in the process of negotiating entry in the European Union (candidate countries from now on) have displayed faster rates of output growth than European Union members. Entrance in the EU should boost growth prospects and with it the process of real convergence. Economic integration and foreign direct investment should lead to a rapid growth of productivity in tradable sectors, creating a gap with productivity growth in the non-tradable sector. Such a process implies that the so-called Balassa-Samuelson effect will operate. This will result in a trend appreciation of the real exchange rate. Several observers have raised the issue of whether the process of real convergence is compatible with EU membership and eventually adoption of the Euro, as Maastricht criteria impose strict constraints on nominal variables. In particular, inflation should converge to the best performers in the EU. In summary, for candidate countries the process of real convergence should proceed simultaneously with that of nominal convergence. In this paper we investigate this issue looking at the dynamics of real exchange rates in candidate countries and the implications for inflation dynamics. We argue that the observed real appreciation of the last few years can be ascribed in most cases to the workings of the Balassa-Samuelson effect. We found also that the trend real appreciation results from higher domestic inflation rather than in a nominal appreciation of the exchange rate. Interestingly, this takes place in a context of in principle flexible exchange rates for most candidate countries. However, a similar pattern is identified for countries with currency board. Thus, inflationary pressures seem to arise irrespective of the exchange rate regime. Accordingly, the paper casts some doubts on the appropriateness of the Maastricht criteria on inflation for candidate countries of Central and Eastern Europe.

The paper proceeds as follows. Section 2 presents a short overview on different interpretations of the real exchange rate appreciation in transition economies. Section 3 describes evidence on the Balassa-Samuelson effect in transition economies. It is argued that structural reforms implemented in transition economies have indeed determined the level of real exchange rate during the transition process. A first-hand examination of the Balassa-Samuelson effect in Slovenia is presented. It is argued that on average one percent increase in productivity differential between labor productivites in industry and services appreciated real exchange rate by almost 1.5% in the period from 1993:1 to 2001:2. These results are used to draw conclusions on the implications for Maastricht criteria and the choice of exchange rate regime in Section 4. Section 5 concludes.

2. - Interpreting the Real Exchange Rate Appreciation in Transition Economies

The real exchange rate can be analytically defined in many different ways. The historical overview on the exchange rate modeling points out the theoretical and empirical problems associated with each approach to the real exchange rate determination. Each of the known approaches to the modeling of the real exchange rate carries its own strengths and weaknesses. Generally, one could abstract from details emerging from different approaches to the empirical testing of the long-run equilibrium real exchange rates and summarize the empirical evidence on different models of real exchange rates in the following two groups of arguments. First, evidence on average suggests that the real exchange rate is not a random walk as evidenced on earlier empirical work may have implied (Meese and Rogoff [17]), and that shocks to the real exchange rate damp out over time, albeit very slowly. In this light, the real exchange rate fluctuates and may exhibit large and sustained deviations from its estimated mean as long as the deviations revert to the mean. The estimated mean is regarded as a purchasing power value, although the estimates may be far from the mean of unity required under purchasing power parity. And second, evidence shows that real exchange rates tend to be lower in rich countries than in poor countries, and that relatively fast growing countries experience real exchange rate appreciation. Historically, technological progress has been higher in the tradable goods production than in the non-traded goods sector. Moreover, the tradable goods productivity bias seems to be more pronounced in high-income countries. An increase in productivity of the tradables production bids up wages in the entire economy. Producers of non-tradables are only able to meet the higher wages if there is an increase in the relative price of the non-tradable goods ensuing a higher general price level since the price of tradable goods is determined in world markets. This phenomenon is best known as the Balassa-Samuelson effect.

Apart from theoretical considerations, the real exchange rate analysis is crucially determined by data availability. It is true that different approaches require different datasets; however, the analysis of the real exchange rate determination in transition economies is greatly affected by available data. Some concepts of the real exchange rate could simply not be developed for transition economies since the structural changes in these economies blurred the perspective on the time horizon needed to determine the equilibrium real exchange rate. In turn, a need to take action in certain aspects of distorted economies at the beginning of the transition process somehow left aside the question of the real exchange rate management. All transition economies have undergone major reforms, all of which have had appreciable consequences for their real exchange rate values. Changes in production and productivity, trade liberalization and removal of state subsidies, restrictive monetary policy accompanied by tax reform, slashing of budget deficits from their initial high levels, underlying process of financial innovations and bank restructuring, are just among the few factors that played an important role in determining the key relative price in transition economies. Moreover, these economies had to choose an exchange rate regime that was appropriate for facilitating the reorientation of their trade toward world market and that was primarily used as a nominal anchor in an attempt to stabilize the economy. Government budget deficits spilled over into current account deficits, which were primarily financed by foreign capital inflows. These inflows, exceeding the surge in imports, required sterilized intervention of varying amounts in some transition economies. All these factors played a major role in establishing an appropriate real exchange rate measure, which helped policymakers to design the optimal policy rules. Additionally, even if one could establish some measures of the real exchange rate in the early days of the transition process, it was virtually impossible to implement econometric analysis, which require long time series in order to discern consistent results. It would, therefore, be expected that real exchange rate development in transition economies varied to a great extent across countries as e result of different policy alternatives faced by policymakers.

However, the early days of transition offered similar real exchange rate paths in all transition economies. In general, transition started with the abrupt depreciation of local currencies that accompanied the end of a command economy and the dismantling of previously prevailing multiple exchange rates. Despite differences in monetary and real shocks that these countries have experienced, real exchange rate movements in all transition economies have followed the same time path. Halpern and Wyplosz [11] offer three explanations for an initial undervaluation of the real exchange rate in transition economies. First, a negligible supply of foreign assets was short of a pent-up demand, which was previously reflected in the black market premium. The undervalued exchange rate in turn allowed for the net acquisition of foreign assets through current account surpluses. Over time, the real exchange rate has been corrected by closing the current account surplus. Second, price liberalization in the presence of monetary overhang was met by a sudden burst in inflation. The process of initial macroeconomic stabilization and price liberalization was associated by the flight from domestic currency. And third, most transition economies were involved with an exchange-rate stabilization program, which required fixing the nominal exchange rate. In light of weak credibility and lack of experience, policymakers were more inclined toward setting the nominal exchange rate at higher levels than necessary. The risk of being unable to sustain convertibility was higher than the possible costs of undervaluation at the beginning of transition. Consequently, the

real exchange rate appreciated in order to correct for the im-
plausible initial devaluation of the nominal exchange rate used as
a nominal anchor in exchange rate based stabilization programs.
However, not all countries have adopted a fixed exchange rate
regime. Rather, they fought inflation by focusing on monetary targets. Slovenia and Latvia are among the most distinguished representatives of the money-based stabilization programs. It would
be expected that the real exchange rate would follow different
transition paths in these two countries. However, that was not the
case; the real exchange rate movement broadly coincided with the
real exchange rate paths in other transition economies, which introduced the fixed exchange rate regime. As Wyplosz [23] concludes, there is not enough evidence to determine whether any
particular exchange rate regime worked better. It is most likely
that exchange rate regimes made little difference in the observed
path of the real exchange rate and were particularly important in
a context of broad stabilization programs with aims to reduce inflation and stabilizing price levels rather than directly influencing
the real exchange rate path (Desai [8]).

Following the initial undervaluation, the real exchange rate
subsequently appreciated. The appreciation of domestic currencies was associated with two phenomena (Roubini and Wachtel
[19]). First, the appreciation was a response to the initial undervaluation of the real exchange rate. And second, the real equilibrium exchange rate itself embarked on a path of trend appreciation mainly explained by the factors, which were already mentioned above. In general, a persistent appreciation of the real exchange rate may not be due to misalignments but rather be caused
by changes in fundamentals. Moreover, it seems that in transition
economies those factors played an even more important role than
is established for other developing countries. Halpern and Wyplosz
[11] and Kraynjak and Zettelmeyer [15] identify six factors as determining the real exchange rate path in transition economies.
First, formerly inefficient production lines responded to market
forces by rapid productivity increases. In turn, income has started to rise again after the initial drop. As suggested by theoretical
work (De Gregorio, Giovannini, and Krueger [6]; De Gregorio, Gio-

vannini, and Wolf [7]), increase in income increases demand for non-tradables and results in appreciation of the real exchange rate. Second, if productivity rises faster in the tradable sector than in the non-tradable sector, then the real exchange rate appreciates as predicted by Balassa [1] and Samuelson [20]. Although one would expect that productivity in the non-tradable sector, which was obviously underrepresented in the previously planned economies, would outperform productivity in the ailing tradable sector, evidence on transition economies refutes this view. The productivity differential between the tradable and non-tradable sectors has been increasing since the early days of transition. One explanation for this development might be found in the overemployed tradable sector before transition, which at the beginning of transition was massively reduced in size and able to adjust to the market. A relatively well-educated labor force caught on to the difference in productivity and let the real exchange rate appreciate. Third, the general price level in transition economies was well below the price levels in countries with comparable PPP-adjusted GDP (Coorey, Mecagni, and Offerdal [3]; Richards and Tersman [18]). Most of the natural resource prices as well as public utility prices in transition economies were administered. The situation was not sustainable and consequently, when prices were liberalized, the real exchange rate appreciated. Fourth, the tax reform in transition economies changed most of the relative prices, which contributed the most to the real exchange rate appreciation. The tax reform was needed since the corporate taxation inherited from central planning had become highly inefficient and tax revenues had quickly shrunk. Fifth, increase in productivity induced an increase in high potential returns on capital. The dynamics of the transition process warranted the potential long-run gains, which attracted foreign capital either in the form of direct investment or as a portfolio investment in emerging stock markets in the region. The surge in capital inflows was comparable to other emerging markets in developing economies. Consequently, capital inflows seem to contribute a lot to the real exchange rate appreciation although the evidence on the relationship between capital flows and the real exchange rate for transition economies is weak and mixed since most transition economies that experienced a surge in capital inflows have engaged in sterilized intervention (Siklos [21]; Calvo, Sahay, and Vegh [2]). And finally, the improved quality of locally produced tradable goods was reflected in better prices obtained in the world market. The terms of trade improved and contributed to the real exchange rate appreciation as predicted by theory (Edwards [9]; De Gregorio and Wolf [7]).

While evidence on the real exchange rate appreciation is not debated despite different measures for the real exchange rate index, there is still an ongoing debate on the causes and effects of this appreciation (Roubini and Wachtel [19]). In one view, the real exchange rate has caused a loss of competitiveness that worsens the current account balance. According to this view — which is rather unfortunately called the *misalignment view*[1] — the real appreciation is the consequence of the choice of the exchange rate regime and the ensuing capital inflows. In general, it represents a loss of real competitiveness. The arguments for this view are based on the reasoning that the real appreciation of the currency is very likely to occur when the exchange rate is pegged and used as a nominal anchor in a stabilization program. While fixing the exchange rate can help to disinflate an economy, pegging the exchange rate will not reduce the inflation rate instantaneously. The reasons why inflation will not come down at the same time can generally be associated with sticky prices and wages in the economy, which disrupt the Law of One Price and consequently the Purchasing Power Parity (PPP). If domestic inflation does not converge immediately to the world level when the exchange rate parity is fixed, a real appreciation will occur over time. This appreciation of the real exchange rate would imply a loss of competitiveness of the domestic economy. Exports become more expensive relative to imported goods, which consequently worsens the

---

[1] In a strict sense of the word, the misalignment view represents situations in which the actual real exchange rate differs significantly from its long-run equilibrium value. What is the long-run equilibrium value, however, remains unclear; or better, different approaches to the long-run equilibrium value of the real exchange rate have emerged over the last two or three decades. The evolution of these issues is provided in WILLIAMSON J. [22] and HINKLE L.E. - MONTIEL P.J. [13].

trade balance and the current account over time. Even small differentials between domestic and foreign inflation can compound rapidly into a substantial appreciation. While a real appreciation is more likely to occur when the currency is pegged to a fixed exchange rate, misalignments of the real exchange rate may also occur under a regime of managed floating exchange rate rules if the central bank does not follow a crawling peg policy of targeting the real exchange rate. The real appreciation under a managed float may occur as a result of large capital inflows (Roubini and Wachtel [19]). If this view were correct, then the large and growing current account imbalances in some transition economies would be caused in part by the real appreciation of the currency. As shown later, this view is widely rejected by empirical studies on the real exchange rate appreciation (Krajnyak and Zettelmeyer [15]), which show that most of the external competitiveness of transition economies is still in line with economic fundamentals underlying the current account imbalances. In the case of Slovenia, Jazbec [14] shows that the misalignment view is generally rejected, as the Bank of Slovenia was successful in implementing sterilization policies during the period 1992-1996. In so doing, the real exchange rate was isolated from the increased capital inflows in that period, although the real exchange rate index continued to appreciate.

On the other hand, the fundamentals view[2] explains the real exchange rate appreciation not as a signal of exchange rate misalignment and competitiveness loss, but as an appreciation of the long-run equilibrium or fundamental real exchange rate. According to this view, the worsening of the current account has not been caused by the real appreciation. It is instead the optimal response to the underlying structural and fundamental changes in the economy. A fundamental real exchange rate appreciation can occur for one of two reasons. First, it represents a correction of

---

[2] The fundamental variables are considered to be associated with real variables in the economy, and not to 'fundamental' variables as the money stock, the interest rates, and the business cycle (DE GRAUWE P. [5]). WILLIAMSON J. [22] considers the terms of trade, tariffs, trade restrictions, and exogenous capital flows as fundamental variables determining the real exchange rate.

earlier depreciation and a return of the real exchange rate to equilibrium levels. And second, the real exchange rate mirrors the shifts in the macroeconomic fundamentals that cause an appreciation. Roubini and Wachtel [19] provide arguments as to why the long-run equilibrium real exchange rate may have appreciated and why the fundamentals approach to the real exchange rate modeling may explain the trend appreciation in transition economies. First, significant increases in productivity growth observed in the region may imply that unit labor costs have not significantly increased in spite of the real appreciation of the currency. While dollar wages have increased in transition economies, the appreciation of the real exchange rate based on relative wages may not imply an appreciation of the real exchange rate measured in terms of unit labor costs. Second, the Balassa-Samuelson approach implies that productivity growth in the production of tradables in the excess of that of non-tradable goods leads to a real appreciation of the CPI-based real exchange rate. The real appreciation is then caused not by a loss of competitiveness, but rather because of the increase in the relative price of non-traded to traded goods caused by the differential productivity growth in the two sectors. And third, structural reforms in transition economies have led to capital inflows that have financed both investment demand for non-tradable factors of production (such as land, real estate, and the service sector labor force) and non-tradable goods and services. Consequently, an increase in the relative price of non-tradable goods to tradables shows up as an appreciation of the CPI-based real exchange rate.

This view is broadly consistent with empirical studies governing the appreciation of the real exchange rate in transition economies (Halpern and Wyplosz [11] [12]; Krajnyak and Zettelmeyer [15]; Richards and Tersman [18]; Coricelli and Jazbec [4]). The fundamentals view corresponds to a broad consensus on the transition process, which states that structural reforms implemented in transition economies have indeed determined the pace of the most important macroeconomic variables among which the real exchange rate plays one of the most important roles. However, in the absence of good measures of the equilibrium exchange rate, it is hard to assess how much of the observed real appreciation is due to misalignments and how much is due to an equilibrium appreciation. Since the real exchange rate appreciated in all transition economies despite different exchange rate regimes, it is argued that the fundamentals view is the most consistent approach to the determination of the real exchange rate in transition economies.

3. - Balassa-Samuelson Effect in Transition Economies

Recent studies on real exchange rate behavior in transition economies support the argument to use the productivity approach to explain the trend appreciation of the real exchange rate in transition economies (especially Halpern and Wyplosz [11] [12]). There is vast potential for gains in productivity in transition economies both through more efficient use of existing resources and technologies and through upgrading technology. However, this approach should also take into account the initial conditions in transition economies at the beginning of reforms, as they significantly determined the macroeconomic policies and structural changes implied by the overall stance of the economies in those times (Coricelli and Jazbec [4]). Decades of central planning have resulted in distorted structures of these economies. Industries had become overwhelming in the composition of output due to the emphasis of central planners on material production, while services were largely neglected. The structure of the economy was reflected in distorted price levels as empirical studies on price development in transition economies indicate. Transition and the introduction of market-determined prices along the other market-enhancing reforms have brought about massive changes in output, employment and, last but not least, in relative prices. To analyze structural changes in transition economies, it is therefore useful to use the approaches that take into account the real changes in the fundamentals rather than models with established patterns of developments in market economies. As such, the productivity approach to the real exchange rate determination serves as a natural candidate for analyzing the real exchange rate in transition economies.

To explain the price differential used to measure the real exchange rate, assume that there is an economy-wide wage that is equal to the marginal product of labor in each sector. To the extent that there are differences in productivity between countries, wages will differ as well. In less-developed countries, productivity is generally lower than in more developed countries. While this applies to both sectors of the economy, there is evidence that the productivity gap is larger for tradables than it is for non-tradables. Also, the scope for productivity gain is more limited in non-tradables than in tradables. Because of this, the price of non-tradables will typically be lower in less-developed countries than in industrial countries. Since the overall price level is a weighted average of the price levels of tradable and non-tradable goods, the general price level will be lower in less-developed countries, with the difference being a function of the proportion of goods that are non-tradable, and the price differential for non-tradables (Richards and Tersman [18]). As an increase in tradable productivity is the main determinant of economic growth — assuming that non-tradable productivity is more or less the same across countries — relatively higher growth is reflected in more appreciated real exchange rate. Graphs 1 and 2 generally confirm this line of argument. Transition economies are classified into three groups: Czech Republic, Hungary, Poland, Slovak Republic, and Slovenia represent Central and Eastern European countries (CEE); Estonia, Latvia, and Lithuania represent Baltic countries; while Bulgaria and Romania are shown separately as they have experienced political difficulties during the transition process and lag behind the implementation of structural reforms. Graph 1 depicts the growth performance in three groups of transition economies in the period from 1995 to 2001. The real appreciation of exchange rate for the same groups of countries is presented in Graph 2.

Generally, countries that have grown faster during the transition process have experienced stronger real exchange rate appreciation. Also, bad performers — in our case Bulgaria and Romania — have experienced strong appreciation due to larger distor-

GRAPH 1

GROWTH IN SELECTED TRANSITION ECONOMIES

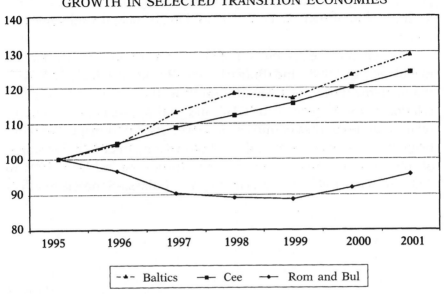

Source: EBRD, *Transition Report*, 2001.

GRAPH 2

REAL EXCHANGE RATE APPRECIATION

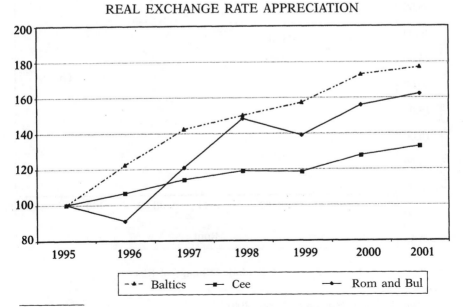

Source: EBRD, *Transition Report*, 2001.

tions and bad initial condition at the beginning of the transition process. Graph 3 presents cumulative change in GDP from 1995 to 2001 plotted against cumulative change in real exchange rate index.

Except for the Czech Republic, which experienced financial turbulence in 1998, and Bulgaria and Romania which lack with the implementation of structural reforms, there exists positive correlation between growth of GDP and real appreciation. The correlation varies across countries, however, its visual inspection confirms the existence of the Balassa-Samuelson effect in latter stages of the transition process as presented for the period from 1995 to 2001. In what follows, the extent of the Balassa-Samuelson effect

GRAPH 3

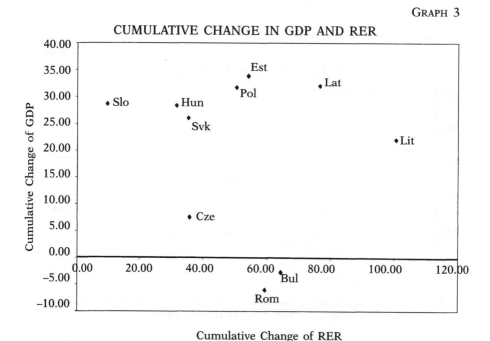

Source: EBRD, *Transition Report*, 2001.

is estimated in a framework which enables one to disentangle the effect of structural reforms at earlier stages of the transition process, and pure Balassa-Samuelson effect in recent years on the level of the real exchange rate in transition economies. The results broadly coincide with other studies on transition economies (Halpern and Wyplosz [11] [12]; Krajnyak and Zettelmeyer [15], various IMF transition country studies) with respect to the existence of a Balassa-Samuelson effect in transition economies. However, the extent of its effect is rather lower than in comparable studies as the effect of structural reforms on the level of the real exhange rate is separated from the pure productivity differential effect. The case of Slovenia is singled out from the analysis in what follows as Slovenia is the most advanced CEE country with respect to GDP per capita and EBRD transition indicators. As such, it is believed that the Slovenian experience with the real exchange rate development is a good indicator for other candidate countries with respect to the fulfillment of Maastricht criteria and implementation of ERM2 mechanism.

3.1 *A Framework to Account for Balassa-Samuelson Effect in Transition Economies*[3]

The real wage is an increasing function of the targeted real wage determined by pre-transition levels, and positive shocks to the demand for labor determined by productivity parameters in both sectors of the economy and government consumption. The more distorted is the pre-transition equilibrium wage (the higher is the equilibrium wage determined by the central plan's objective to produce more of the industrial good relative to services), the higher is the pressure of the union to negotiate for higher wages once transition starts. It is established that the nominal wage is an increasing function of the real wage determined by the pre-transition structural parameter, η, which takes into account a dis-

---

[3] See CORICELLI F. - JAZBEC B. [54] for a full derivation of the model of real exchange rate determination in transition economies.

torted measure of the transition economy, productivity parameters, and government consumption. The nominal wage is, therefore, determined as follows:

(1) $W = W(\omega(\eta), a_T, a_N, G)$

where W is the nominal wage; $\omega(\eta)$ represents the average real wage depending on the structural parameter, η; a_T and a_N represent the technology parameters specific to the production of tradable and non-tradable goods, respectively; and G stands for real government consumption of non-tradable goods.

All variables enter the nominal wage equation with positive signs as expected. The only indeterminacy may arise from the sign of a_N, which can take either a positive or negative value. However, it is assumed that an increase in non-tradable sector productivity in transition economies increases demand for labor to satisfy private sector demand in the tradable and non-tradable sectors by less than the increase in tradable sector productivity. The nominal wage equation is one of the most important equations in this framework since the real economy parameters enter the real exchange rate measure via the nominal wage equation. It is assumed that the price of tradables is determined in the world market and, therefore, is given exogenously to a transition economy. For this reason, the price of tradables could be normalized to 1 in order to provide the following expression for the real exchange rate measure:

(2) $$\frac{1}{P_N} = \frac{\Phi - 1}{\Phi}\left(\frac{a_N}{W(\omega(\eta), a_T, a_N, G)}\right)$$

where P_N is the price index for non-tradable goods and Φ is share of non-tradable goods consumption in total private consumption.

The real exchange rate measured as the relative price of tradables in terms of non-tradable goods, therefore, negatively depends on the productivity differential, the share of non-tradable consumption in total private consumption, and real government consumption. The parameter that measures the extent of structural misalignment inherited from the central plan, η, enters the real exchange rate equation with a positive sign. The regression equation is presented as follows:

$$(3) \qquad \log(P_T/P_N)_{i,t} = \alpha_{oi} - \alpha_1\log(a_T - a_N)_{i,t} + \\ - \alpha_2\text{share}_{i,t} - \alpha_3\text{govreal}_{i,t} + \alpha_4\text{lab}_{i,t} + \varepsilon_{i,t}$$

where $(P_T/P_N)_{i,t}$ is the relative price of tradables in terms of non-tradable goods; $(a_T - a_N)_{i,t}$ is the productivity differential between tradable and non-tradable goods production and is measured in terms of labor productivity in both sectors; $\text{share}_{i,t}$ represents the share of non-tradable consumption in total private consumption; $\text{govreal}_{i,t}$ is the share of government consumption in GDP measured in constant prices; and $\text{lab}_{i,t}$ represents the structural misalignment variable. It is proxied for by the ratio between labor employed in the tradable sector versus labor employed in the non-tradable sector. The sign of all coefficients is negative except the sign on the structural variable, which enters the equation with a positive sign. This constitutes the positive correlation between the real exchange rate and the labor employed in the tradable sector relative to the non-tradable sector. For this reason, the structural variable proxied for by the labor ratio represents the parameter that measures the rigidity of the labor market to structural changes in the economy. As for the rest of the story, this rigidity is assumed to be exogenously determined in the economy and thus independent of all other right-hand side variables in equation *(3)*. This is a relatively stringent assumption on the structure of a transition economy, and its validity can be seriously questioned.

Data used to construct price indices, productivity measures, demand variables, and structural parameters cover 19 transition economies[4]. Each transition economy is observed from the start of its most serious stabilization attempt as defined by Fischer,

---

[4] Armenia, Azerbaijan, Belarus, Bulgaria, Croatia, Czech Republic, Estonia, Hungary, Kazakhstan, Kyrgyzstan, Latvia, Lithuania, Poland, Romania, Russia, Slovak Republic, Slovenia, Ukraine, and Uzbekistan.

Sahay, and Vegh [10]. This implies that the relative price of tradables in terms of non-tradables is set to 1 in the year of the most serious stabilization attempt. The implicit GDP deflator for industry in each country represents the price of tradables. Analogously, the implicit GDP deflator for services defines the price of non-tradables. The criterion for the period of observation was the year after which the relative price of tradables in terms of non-tradables started to consistently decline. However, this criterion has not been followed in all cases[5]. Different periods of observation were examined and compared to each other. For all countries, the period of observation ends in 1998. The longest series runs from 1990 to 1998, while the shortest covers the period from 1995 to 1998. The whole sample includes 122 observations.

In the analysis, two sectors were distinguished: tradable and non-tradable. While theoretical literature on real exchange rates relies upon the division of commodities into tradables and non-tradables, it is almost impossible to construct these two groups of commodities in reality. An obvious benchmark for tradability should be the extent to which the particular good is actually traded. For example, the sector is defined as tradable if more than 10% of total production is exported. In general, one would label manufactures as tradables and services as non-tradables. However, this is quite impossible at this stage in transition economies. In what follows, the tradable sector is represented by the industry sector, which includes manufacturing; gas, electricity, and water; mining and quarrying; and construction. The reason that all other sub-sectors besides manufacturing were included in the measure for the tradable sector was that for some countries sectoral data and data on international trade flows were not available. To ensure consistency, all tradable sectors in different countries include gas, electricity, water, mining and quarrying, and the construction sector although one could doubt their tradabil-

---

[5] Exceptions are Belarus, Romania, and Russia where the relative price of tradables has indeed increased. For these cases, the beginning of the observed period starts after the initial depreciation.

ity. A more substantial problem arises from the inclusion of non-market services into the variable representing the non-tradable sector. However, the reasons for the inclusion of non-market services into the total services sector are the same as for the construction of the tradable sector variable. It is believed that, on average, these complications fade away although in specific cases they could represent the main reason for the different behavior of relative prices, as argued later.

The independent variable is the relative price of tradables in terms of the price of non-tradable goods. The implicit sectoral GDP deflators for industry and services are used to proxy for the price indices in these two sectors. The relative price takes value 1 at the beginning of transition and enters the regressions in logarithms.

Regression equation *(4)* reproduces the results for the full sample of 19 economies, each observed in time since the beginning of the transition process. Coefficient estimates are reported with standard errors adjusted for heteroscedasticiy in parenthesis. Superscript stars indicate their possible insignificance at a 5% level[6] of confidence. Country-specific dummies (not reported) are significant in most of the specifications. The results of the basic equation *(4)* produce the earlier findings that the productivity differential, the share of non-tradable consumption in total private consumption, and real government consumption negatively affect the real exchange rate, thus contributing to the real appreciation. The ratio between labor employed in tradables to labor employed in non-tradable goods production enters the regression with a positive sign as predicted by the model. This suggests that the delay in structural reforms — relatively high values of the labor ratio variable at the beginning of transition relative to its end values — in general tends to act as a restraining force on the real exchange rate.

---

[6] Tests on whether a coefficient differs significantly from zero in the expected direction are based on one tailed *t*-tests and a 5% confidence interval which, for an infinite number of degrees of freedom, involves an absolute value of *t* greater than 1.98.

(4) $\log(P_T/P_N) =$ country dummy $- 0.868 \log(a_T - a_N)^* +$
$$(0.169)$$

$$- 1.656 \text{ share}^* - 0.749 \text{ govreal}^* - 0.644 \text{ lab}^*$$
$$(0.219) \qquad (0.379) \qquad (0.202)$$

$R^2(\text{adj.}) = 0.853$
$N = 122$

The results are fully consistent with the view that structural reforms in transition economies contributed to the real appreciation trend observed in the region from the beginning of transition. Since all regressions[7] are run in transition time, the results indicate that we can still expect further appreciation of the real exchange rate in those economies that started with transition later. As indicated in regression equation *(4)*, the productivity differential used to measure the Balassa-Samuelson effect had a pronounced effect on appreciation of the real exchange rate in transition economies in period prior to 1999. One percent increase in productivity differential has on average contributed to almost 0.9% appreciation of the real exchange rate measured in terms of relative prices. This result is in line according to Balassa-Samuelson effect, which states that prices of tradables are determined in the world market and therefore equalized across countries. Prices of non-tradables are assumed to be determined domestically based on the domestic wage and productivity levels. To the extent that productivity in the two sectors within the country grows at different rates, it is likely that there will be offsetting movements in the relative price of tradables in terms of non-tradables. If the trend growth of productivity in the tradable goods sector exceeds that of the non-tradable goods sector, there will be a tendency for the relative price of tradables to decline over time.

---

[7] Several regressions were run by adding region specific dummies to distinguish possible effects across transition economies included in the sample. Results confirm those presented by equation *(4)*. For the whole description of econometric results see CORICELLI F. - JAZBEC B. [4].

3.2 *The Case of Slovenia*

Econometric results derived from estimation of equation *(4)* can be used to graphically account for development of the real exchange rate in Slovenia presented in Graph 4. Stacked columns represent the level of real exchange rate in each year. The portions of columns correspond to actual contributions that each variable had to the level of the real exchange rate in each year of the transition process. The sum of all portions of a column and country-specific constants add up to the fitted value for the real exchange rate level in the respective year. Nonetheless, it is the dynamics of the contribution of each set of variables that is interesting in explaining the determination of the real exchange rate in Slovenia.

As the effect of demand variables represented by the share of non-tradable consumption in total private consumption and gov-

GRAPH 4

ACCOUNTING FOR REAL EXCHANGE RATE IN SLOVENIA

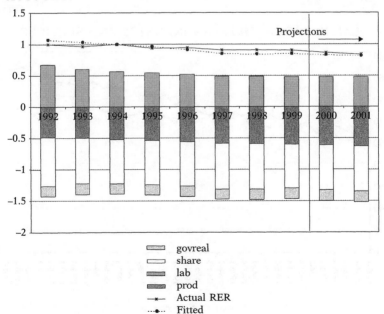

Source: Authors' calculations.

ernment consumption has remained relatively unaltered, the main determinants of the level of real exchange rate in Slovenia were structural changes and productivity differential. In the period from 1992 to 1996, the structural changes proxied by labor shifts from industry to services were the most influential factor determining the level of real exchange rate. From 1996 onwards, the productivity differential between labor productivity in industry and services has started to effect the real exchange rate substantially. The plot of quarterly labor productivity measures in industry and services presented in Graph 5 supports this line of argument.

The structural changes caused the increase of labor productivity in both sectors before 1996. Thereafter labor productivity in industry has been increasing faster than in services. For that reason, the productivity differential believed to cause the real exchange rate appreciation via Balassa-Samuelson effect has started to affect the level of real exchange rate relatively more than

GRAPH 5

LABOR PRODUCTIVITY IN INDUSTRY AND SERVICES

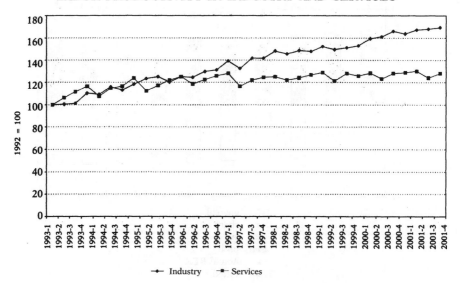

Source: BANK OF SLOVENIA.

the extent of structural reforms which has diminished in recent years.

To test the Balassa-Samuelson effect in the period from the first quarter of 1993 to the second quarter of 2001, bivariate VAR models were tested. Data cover quarterly external real exchange rate calculated as nominal exchange rate for DEM corrected for by German and Slovenian CPI, and quarterly labor productivities in industry and services. Taking into account the concerns regarding data construction, it is assumed that labor productivities are good approximation for total factor productivities in Slovenia. As for the definitions of tradable and non-tradable sectors, the most general approach was considered. In so doing, the industry sector represents tradable sector, and all services — market and non-market services — belong to non-tradable sector.

Tables 1 and 2 reproduce basic econometric results for cointegrated VAR models used to estimate the extent of the Balassa-Samuelson effect in period from 1993:1 to 2001:2. Table 1 presents results of VAR analysis using external real exchange rate and productivity differential. Table 2 presents results for the CPI and productivity differential. In both cases one cointegrating vector was identified. Also specification tests - not shown here - show no sign of model mis-specification. All series were estimated in natural logarithms. Both VAR models were estimated with one lag as identified by specification tests.

Results from Tables 1 and 2 confirm the Balassa-Samuelson effect in Slovenia. The coefficient on the external real exchange rate from Table 1 suggests that one percent increase of productivity differential causes 1.4651% appreciation of external real exchange rate. To test the robustness of the results, cointegrated VAR model for the CPI and productivity differential was estimated. Results in Table 2 show that one percent increase of productivity differential causes 1.7371% increase of the CPI. If the theoretical considerations for the existence of the Balassa-Samuelson effect are correct, than the results for the Slovenian case follow the line of argument usually employed for the transition economies. The estimated Balassa-Samuelson effect for the transition economies is found to be around 2 to 3% per year (Halpern and Wyplosz [12];

TABLE 1

EXTERNAL REAL EXCHANGE RATE
AND PRODUCTIVITY DIFFERENTIAL

Cointegration analysis	Real exchange rate	Productivity differential
β coefficient	1.4651	1.0000
Std. Error	0.31774	0.0000

Choice of Rank

Eigenvalues	Real	Complex	Modulus
	0.9617	0.0000	0.9617
	0.7795	0.0000	0.7795

TABLE 2

CONSUMER PRICE INDEX (CPI)
AND PRODUCTIVITY DIFFERENTIAL

Cointegration analysis	CPI	Productivity differential
β coefficient	−1.7371	1.0000
Std. Error	0.12817	0.0000

Choice of Rank

Eigenvalues	Real	Complex	Modulus
	0.9588	0.0000	0.9588
	0.5392	0.0000	0.5392

Source: Authors' calculations.

several IMF transition country studies). As Slovenia is the most developed transition economy regarding the GDP per capita, and in addition to the conclusions from growth models which state that more developed countries grow at slower pace than less developed counterparts, than the results obtained for the Slovenian case confirm the theoretical framework for the Balassa-Samuelson effect.

However, caution should apply here, especially with respect to data construction and its short interval of observation. First, data aggregation should more strictly follow a tradability approach with respect to the international competitiveness. MacDonald and Ricci [16] present a model with further disaggregation of the economy factoring out a distribution sector. They believe that part of the Balassa-Samuelson effect should be contributed to the size and effectiveness of the distribution sector in the economy. In the case of Slovenia, a high degree of aggregation was used due to lack of sufficient data. For that reason, tradable and non-tradable sectors were represented by industry and services, respectively. Second, instead of labor productivities one should use total factor productivities to estimate the Balassa-Samuelson effect. However, in case of transition economies total factor productivities may be biased due to inappropriate capital valuation. Third, further research activities should focus on the measure of the real exchange rate which would best present the productivity approach to the determination of the real exchange rate. The correct transmission channel from productivity differential to relative price levels has to be identified to fully encompass the Balassa-Samuelson effect. And finally, although no structural breaks and seasonal components were identified in the examined time series their short interval prevents more serious econometric work in order to fully grasp the Balassa-Samuelson effect in transition economies.

4. - Implications for Maastricht Criteria and the Choice of Exchange Rate Regime

Empirical results presented in the paper generally confirm the existence of the Balassa-Samuelson effect in transition economies. In Slovenia in particular, its estimated size is of the order of 1.5% per year based on one percent increase of the productivity differential between labor productivity in industry and services. The size of the effect falls in the bottom of the range estimated in other studies on real exchange rate behavior in transition economies.

Although further work on its estimation is called for, estimation of the Balassa-Samuelson effect in Slovenia could provide a point of reference for the analysis of exchange rate policy in light of the requirements of EU accession and eventually the adoption of the Euro. As an increase in tradable productivity is the main determinant of economic growth — assuming that non-tradable productivity is more or less the same across countries — a rate of growth higher than the average of the EU would necessarily translate into an appreciation of the real exchange rate. The scope for real appreciation arising from one percent higher relative growth should therefore be about 1.5% if our estimated models are well-specified. All the caveats related both to theoretical considerations and data problems should necessarily be taken into account when interpreting this figure. Nonetheless, the case of Slovenia broadly confirms findings in Coricelli and Jazbec [4], where it is shown that the effect of structural reforms diminished over time and disappeared at the fifth or sixth year of the transition process. Based on quarterly data presented in Graph 5, it is shown that the Balassa-Samuelson effect started to take place only in 1996.

Our interpretation of the real exchange rate behavior in the last five years is that the attempt by the Bank of Slovenia to counteract the forces leading to a real appreciation of the exchange rate ended up raising the rate of inflation, that remained at a level of about 8-9%, despite prudent fiscal and monetary policies. The real exchange rate targeting likely contributed to such an outcome, as nominal depreciation of the exchange rate has a strong effect on Slovenian inflation. It should be noted that imported goods account for more than 60% of the total basket making up the CPI.

If one takes the Slovenian experience as a good predictor of how a typical candidate country will operate within the EU prior to EMU membership, one can conclude that maintaining de iure flexibility of the exchange rate does not allow countries to have more freedom in the conduct of monetary policy. In the case of Slovenia, the fear of real appreciation lead to higher inflation.

This scenario may be representative of the likely experience following accession and before adoption of the Euro. Interestingly, if one considers the hypothetical case of an early adoption of the Euro, it turns out that the rate of inflation could be lower, not higher as argued by several observers (including the IMF and the ECB). The issue remains that domestic inflation would remain higher than the average EU. In fact, maintaining the inflation criterion that identifies as reference point the mean of the three best performers, is likely to imply a target inflation rate that is much lower than the one prevailing in the candidate countries. For Slovenia we estimated that a gap of 2% in GDP growth would imply an inflation gap of 3%. As this would be an equilibrium phenomenon, it is the Maastricht criterion on inflation that should be modified. Given that monetary policy is conducted by the ECB, and that fiscal policy is subject to constraints, additional constraints on national inflation appear redundant, unless the constraints on fiscal policy may not be adequate. This poses a more general issue of coordination between ECB policy and fiscal policy in the European Union.

5. - Conclusions

The paper argues that real appreciation of the exchange rate observed in transition countries can be interpreted as a «qualified» equilibrium process. Qualified because it is only after five to six years into transition that the Balassa-Samuelson effect tends to dominate the real exchange rate dynamics. Moreover, using the case of Slovenia as a benchmark case, the presence of real exchange rate targeting may in fact affect real exchange rate dynamics. Based on evidence for Slovenia, the paper concludes that a *de jure* flexible nominal exchange rate is not an insurance for lower domestic inflation. In fact, it is shown that the persistence of high domestic inflation in Slovenia may be largely explained by such an exchange rate policy. This implies that after accession inflation differentials will remain a serious problem, irrespective of the exchange rate regime. In contrast with current wisdom, the paper argued that an early adoption of the Euro may in fact reduce inflation differentials. The working of the Balassa-Samuelson effect would nevertheless imply higher domestic inflation rates in transition economies after accession to the European Union. Thus, transition economies are likely to face problems in meeting the Maastricht criterion on inflation.

BIBLIOGRAPHY

[1] BALASSA B., «The Purchasing Power Parity Doctrine: A Reappraisal», *Journal of Political Economy*, vol. 72, December 1964, pp. 584-96.

[2] CALVO G. - SAHAY R. - VEGH C.A., «Capital Flows in Central and Eastern Europe: Evidence and Policy Options», IMF, *Working Paper*, n. 57, April 1995.

[3] COOREY, S. - MECAGNI M. - OFFERDAL E., «Disinflation in Transition Economies: The Role of Relative Price Adjustment», IMF, *Working Paper*, n. 138, December 1996.

[4] CORICELLI F. - JAZBEC B,, «Real Exchange Rate Dynamics in Transition Economies», London, CEPR, *Discussion Paper*, n. 2869, July 2001.

[5] De Grauwe, Paul, «Exchange Rates in Search of Fundamental Variables», *CEPR Discussion Paper*, n. 1073, December 1994.

[6] DE GREGORIO J. - GIOVANNINI A. - KRUEGER T.H., «The Behavior of Nontradable Goods Prices in Europe: Evidence and Interpretation», IMF, *Working Paper*, n. 45, May 1993.

[7] DE GREGORIO J. - GIOVANNINI A. - WOLF H.C., «International Evidence on Tradables and Nontradables Inflation», IMF, *Working Paper*, n. 33, March 1994.

[8] DESAI P., «Macroeconomic Fragility and Exchange Rate Vulnerability: A Cautionary Record of Transition Economies», *Journal of Comparative Economics*, vol. 26, 1998, pp. 621-41.

[9] EDWARDS S., «Real Exchange Rates in the Developing Countries: Concepts and Measurement», NBER, *Working Paper*, n. 2950, 1989.

[10] FISCHER S. - SAHAY R. - VEGH C.A., «Stabilization and Growth in Transition Economies: The Early Experience», *Journal of Economic Perspectives*, vol. 10, n. 2, Spring 1996, pp. 45-66.

[11] HALPERN L. - WYPLOSZ C., «Equilibrium Exchange Rates in Transition Economies», IMF, *Working Paper*, n. 125, 1996.

[12] ——, *Economic Transformation and Real Exchange Rates in the 2000s: The Balassa-Samuelson Connection*, Mimeo, March 2001.

[13] HINKLE L.E. - MONTIEL P.J. (ed.), *Exchange Rate Misalignment: Concepts and Measurement for Developing Countries*, Oxford, Oxford University Press, 1999.

[14] JAZBEC B., «Oblikovanje Realnega Deviznega Tecǎja. (Real Exchange Rate Determination in Slovenia)», *Slovenska ekonomska revija*, Ljubljana, vol. 49, n. 5, 1998.

[15] KRAJNYAK K. - ZETTELMEYER J., «Competitiveness in Transition Economies: What Scope for Real Appreciation?» IMF, *Staff Papers*, vol. 45, n. 2, June 1998.

[16] MacDONALD R. - RICCI L., «PPP and the Balassa-Samuelson Effect: The Role of the Distribution Sector», IMF, *Working Paper*, n. 38, March 2001.

[17] MEESE A.R. - ROGOFF K., «Empirical Exchange Rate Models of the Seventies», *Journal of International Economics*, n. 14, 1983, pp. 3-24.

[18] RICHARDS A.J. -. TERSMAN G.H.R., «Growth, Nontradables, and Price Convergence in the Baltics», *Journal of Comparative Economics*, vol. 23, 1996, pp. 121-45.

[19] ROUBINI N. - WACHTEL P., «Current Account Sustainability in Transition Economies», NBER, *Working Paper*, n. 6468, 1998.

[20] SAMUELSON P.A., «Theoretical Notes on Trade Problems», *Review of Economics and Statistics*, vol. 46, March 1964, pp. 145-54.

[21] Siklos L., «Capital Flows in a Transitional Economy and the Sterilization Dilemma: The Hungarian Case», IMF, *Working Paper*, n. 86, 1996.

[22] Williamson J., *Estimating Equilibrium Exchange Rates*, Washington, Institute for International Economics, 1994.

[23] Wyplosz C., *Ten Years of Transformation: Macroeconomic Lessons*, Paper presented at the World Bank Annual Bank Conference on Development, Washington, April 1999.

Varieties, Jobs and EU Enlargement

Tito Boeri - Joaquim Oliveira Martins[1]

Università «Bocconi», Milano   OECD, Paris

Una economia aperta può crescere velocemente senza incorrere in problemi di bilancia dei pagamenti, a condizione che riesca a produrre un crescente numero di varietà di beni.

Un aumento della varietà di beni differenziati prodotti in Europa Centro-Orientale richiede una riallocazione della forza lavoro, che è ancora relativamente concentrata in settori che producono beni omogenei ed a elevate economie di scala, ed un aumento della numerosità delle imprese, che è bassa secondo standard europei. I sussidi di disoccupazione possono favorire questo processo alimentando la mobilità in uscita, ma non devono essere troppo elevati per non inibire la ricerca di nuova occupazione.

Small open economies can grow faster than their neighbours without running into a balance of payment crises if they succeed in increasing the number of differentiated goods produced domestically. A further increase in the number of varieties produced in Central and Eastern Europe will require more worker and job reallocation as production is still largely concentrated in homogeneous good and scale-intensive industries and enterprise density is significantly lower than in Western Europe. Unemployment benefits can support this process by providing seed capital for self-employment choices. But they should be neither too low nor too high. Otherwise, they would prevent restructuring or discourage job search. [JEL Code: F12, L11, P21].

---

[1]Tito Boeri, Professor of Economics and Joaquim Oliveira Martins Senior Economist, wish to thank Riccardo Faini and Stefano Manzocchi for useful comments on the previous versions of this paper. Anne Legendre provided excellent statistical assistance. The views expressed are those of the authors, and do not necessarily reflect those of the OECD or its Member countries.

N.B., the numbers in square brackets refer to the Bibliography at the end of the paper.

1. - Introduction

Two key factors that have so far allowed fast growing economies of central and eastern Europe to cope with their external constraint have been *(i)* the presence of relatively low unit labour costs and *(ii)* the initial under-valuation of the exchange rate. The accession to the EU will inevitably reduce both sources of competitiveness of eastern European exports. Real wages are likely to catch-up western European levels and current EU members are pushing these countries to enforce labour market and social regulations that will increase labour costs. Moreover, stability of the exchange rate will be pursued as these countries wish to qualify for the EMU.

Small open economies can grow faster than their neighbours without running into a balance of payment crises if they succeed in increasing the number of differentiated goods produced domestically. The multiplication of the number of varieties in these countries after trade liberalisation is an unambiguous sign that consumers coming from the empty shelves of the pre-transition era have a strong taste for varieties, and hence that new varieties can create their own demand. This link between growth, trade and product variety has been highlighted in theoretical and empirical literature (Krugman [14]; Oliveira Martins [19]; Funke et Ruhwedel [11]). The increase in the number of varieties will also involve a furthering of the worker reallocation process as production is still largely concentrated in homogeneous good and scale-intensive industries and enterprise density is significantly lower than in Western Europe.

This major re-orientation of consumption away from the previous homogeneous goods towards the type of differentiated goods existing in western markets has often been neglected by the literature on transition economics (Boeri [4]). Indeed, there was a formidable lack of varieties in the pre-transition period, which prevented the socialist-autarkic equilibrium to be jointly determined from the demand and supply side: consumers were strongly rationed in the purchase of varieties (Matsuyama [16]). Accordingly, we argue in this paper that the "variety effect" can contribute to explain the pattern of trade flows during the transition process.

Notably, it could explain why trade did not collapse in line with output and the major geographical re-orientation of trade with an increased demand for goods produced in the West. It also enables to understand why persistent trade specialisation of these countries in traditional industries.

This paper starts by reviewing the changing profile and orientation of trade in transitional economies of central and eastern Europe. Next, developments in enterprise density and the performance of greenfield vs. state and privatised firms are reviewed in an attempt to assess barriers to the entry and growth of small business. Finally, numerical simulations with the model are developed which enable to assess the likely impact on employment, unemployment and gross worker flows of reductions in start-up costs.

2. - The Patterns of Trade Flows During the Transition

This Section documents the stylised facts about the pattern of trade flows during the transition. For the sake of statistical comparability, the focus will be on the group of Visegrad countries, Romania and Slovenia.

2.1 *Trade Did Not Collapse in Line With Output*

All transition countries experienced after 1989 one of the most marked depressions ever observed in recent economic history. Between 1989 and 1991, GDP declined in Eastern Europe by as much as 30% in countries such as Bulgaria and Romania (Graph 1). Different causes for the output declines have been discussed in the literature[2]. While this transitional depression is a well known and

---

[2]For example, a disorganisation effect of the previous production and distribution networks (BLANCHARD O. - KREMER M., [3]; ROLAND G. - VERDIER T., [21]) or the loss of CMEA markets. Nevertheless, the country-by-country patterns suggest that the output fall can be partly explained by taking into account the level of pre-

documented fact in the literature, the fact that trade volumes did not collapse in line with output has received much less attention. These countries were experiencing a deep economic depression whereas imports were rather buoyant (Graph 2) throughout the region, with the only exception of Bulgaria and Romania. The asymmetries in output and trade dynamics point to supply-side determinants of GDP falls in transitional economies.

GRAPH 1

GDP DECLINE 1990=100

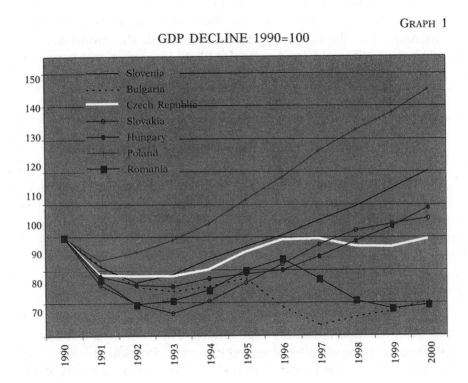

Source: CEPII, Chelem database

---

transition distortions and the management of the reform process. For example, in the most advanced transition countries, such as Hungary or Slovenia, a more de-centralised decision-making process was already in place before the transition. Some countries also adopted reforms more quickly and fully, thus reinforcing their favourable position. Overall, the larger output declines and late bottoming-out can be found in countries which had the largest pre-transition distortions and have accumulated delays in implementing reforms, such as Romania and Bulgaria.

GRAPH 2

IMPORTS IN US$ 1990=100

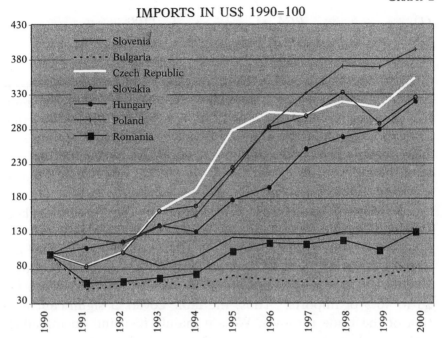

Source: CEPII, Chelem database

2.2 *The Persistent Specialisation in Traditional Goods*

A well known feature of trade patterns in Central Eastern Europe was the collapse of the CMEA and unexpectedly rapid re-orientation of trade flows towards developed market economies (mainly the European Union). By 1995, the latter accounted for nearly 70% of both exports and imports of Central and Eastern Europe. However, a perhaps less well understood feature of trade patterns has been the persistent trade specialisation of transitional economies in heavy energy-intensive industries and low-skilled segments of the manufacturing sector, in spite of a rather well-educated labour force with lower cost of labour relative to their western counterparts. In order to document this fact, we computed the following revealed comparative advantage (RCA) indicator proposed by Neven [17]:

$$(1) \qquad RCA_i = \left(\frac{X_i}{\sum X_k} - \frac{M_i}{\sum M_k} \right).100$$

where X_i and M_i are, respectively, the exports and imports of product i. This indicator is bounded between 100 and (-100). The lower and upper limits of the index can be attained only in the (theoretical) case when there is a complete trade specialisation and there are only two goods. Under real world circumstances, the value of the index rarely exceed 10 (in modules). The higher the value of the index, the stronger trade specialisation[3].

We selected according to this criterion the top-10 and the bottom-10 RCAs for manufacturing products[4], for all countries for which data were available (Table 1). The products are ranked according to the RCAs in 1999. In that year, these top-ten products account for 40% and above of exports, whilst the bottom-ten for 25 to 40% of imports. Thus, the table covers a significant portion of the trade turnover. We are mainly focusing on manufacturing products for two reasons. First, agricultural products tend to be highly distorted by strong trade barriers in European markets which affect our measure of comparative advantage. Second, the product variety effects discussed in this paper are mainly related to manufactured products.

By mid-1990s, most transition countries were still characterised by a persistent specialisation in homogeneous goods produced by heavy industries. In the Czech Republic the main revealed comparative advantages were in heavy industries and intermediate products such as coals, non-metallic mineral manu-

---

[3]The RCA index can be interpreted as a "normalised" trade balance (i.e. given that the sum of the RCA indicator across sectors is equal to zero, the comparative advantages are in this way measured under the theoretical condition of a balanced trade). The value of this indicator is also related to the intensity of intra-industry trade. The stronger two-way trade, the lower specialisation, the closer to zero the index (OECD [19]).

[4]As can be seen from Table 1, the value of the RCA index decreases (in modules) rather quickly, hence there is no loss of information in confining the list to the top-seven and bottom-seven products. More detailed results are, in any event, available from the authors upon request.

TABLE 1

MANUFACTURED PRODUCT SPECIALISATION IN EASTERN EUROPE

		RCAs[1]			Export share 1999			RCAs[1]			Import share 1999
		1993	1996	1999				1993	1996	1999	
Bulgaria											
DB	Clothing	4.84	5.67	9.32	10.37	FU	Commercial vehicles	-1.41	-2.18	-1.50	1.82
CC	Non ferrous metals	4.15	6.25	6.59	8.15	FC	Engines	-1.58	-1.46	-1.51	2.44
CA	Iron steel	5.65	6.06	5.44	7.11	KF	Sugar	-1.17	-0.82	-1.52	1.94
DC	Knitwear	1.47	1.33	3.00	5.51	IA	Coals	-3.86	-4.19	-1.91	2.24
JB	Other edible agricultural prod.	2.65	1.51	2.77	4.17	FT	Cars and cycles	-2.99	-1.43	-2.06	2.12
KH	Beverages	2.42	3.24	2.73	3.31	FG	Specialized machines	-1.61	-1.70	-2.19	2.80
IH	Refined petroleum products	4.54	3.82	1.75	4.07	FN	Telecommunic. equipment	-0.59	-0.84	-2.36	2.58
KI	Manifactured tobaccos	2.44	2.91	1.68	1.95	DA	Yarns fabrics	-1.25	-2.82	-5.20	7.05
GB	Fertilizers	3.30	5.23	1.59	2.16	IC	Natural gas	-8.07	-8.25	-7.34	7.35
DE	Leather	1.39	0.97	1.33	3.20	IB	Crude oil	-14.41	-14.10	-10.44	10.44
		32.85	37.01	36.20	50.01			-36.93	-37.79	-36.03	40.79
Czech Republic											
FT	Cars and cycles	1.32	0.23	6.32	9.14	GE	Toiletries	-0.84	-0.55	-0.91	2.10
BC	Glass	2.59	2.12	2.08	2.70	FI	Precision instruments	-2.06	-1.32	-1.06	1.99
EB	Furniture	0.71	1.41	1.63	2.97	CC	Non ferrous metals	-0.85	-0.98	-1.23	2.24
FS	Vehicles components	-0.50	0.47	1.41	5.41	IH	Refined petroleum products	-0.83	-0.35	-1.32	2.15
FR	Electical apparatus	-1.37	-0.51	1.27	8.46	FO	Computer equipment	-3.32	-1.62	-1.73	2.75
IA	Coals	2.72	2.21	1.11	1.23	GH	Plastic articles	-0.81	-0.82	-1.85	5.13
FA	Metallic structures	0.31	0.65	1.00	1.63	GF	Pharmaceuticals	-1.15	-1.54	-1.90	-2.67
GC	Basic organic chemicals	1.22	1.50	0.98	1.87	IC	Natural gas	-2.74	-2.59	-1.99	2.01
GI	Rubber articles (incl. tyres)	0.33	0.53	0.98	2.25	FN	Telecommunic. equipment	-1.51	-2.01	-2.01	2.64
FB	Miscellaneous hardware	0.36	1.26	0.88	6.71	IB	Crude oil	-3.66	-3.53	-2.21	2.27
		7.70	9.87	17.65	42.35			-17.78	-15.31	-16.23	25.95

[1]RCA indicator correspondes to $(Xi/SMi - Mi/SMi)*100$, see text.
Source: CEPII, Chelem database

TABLE 1 *(cont.)*

MANUFACTURED PRODUCT SPECIALISATION IN EASTERN EUROPE

		RCAs[1]			Export share				RCAs[1]			Import share
		1993	1996	1999	1999			1993	1996	1999	1999
Hungary												
FO	Computer equipment	-2.04	0.29	9.22	16.21	EC	Paper	-1.97	-1.93	-1.30	2.58
FC	Engines	-0.27	2.67	6.47	11.60	EE	Miscellaneous manuf. artic.	-0.83	-0.90	-1.42	2.29
FM	Consumer electronics	0.05	1.56	5.31	6.02	FL	Electronic components	-0.73	-1.12	-1.99	2.40
FT	Cars and cycles	-5.43	-0.87	2.10	5.48	IC	Natural gas	-3.09	-4.02	-2.04	2.09
KC	Meat	4.17	3.40	1.82	1.95	FB	Miscellaneous hardware	-0.20	-1.11	-2.12	4.92
DB	Clothing	5.35	3.26	1.74	2.63	FG	Specialized machines	-2.53	-1.90	-2.32	2.99
FR	Electrical apparatus	2.26	2.82	1.29	7.80	FN	Telecommunic. equipment	-0.37	-1.80	-2.37	4.17
JA	Cereals	0.83	0.83	1.00	1.12	DA	Yarns fabrics	-3.13	-3.54	-2.44	3.35
DC	Knitwear	1.74	1.20	0.90	2.02	IB	Crude oil	-4.19	-3.61	-2.50	2.50
JB	Other edible agricultural prod.	2.85	2.04	0.68	1.63	NV	N.e.s. products	-3.69	-0.01	-6.59	7.21
		9.51	17.20	30.53	56.46			-20.74	-19.94	-25.08	34.50
Poland												
EB	Furniture	3.92	6.06	6.68	7.57	IC	Natural gas	-1.42	-1.51	-1.32	1.33
DB	Clothing	8.34	6.91	5.27	6.37	FS	Vehicles components	-1.31	-2.56	-1.78	3.99
IA	Coals	7.45	4.99	2.94	3.11	FC	Engines	-1.65	-2.00	-1.87	4.11
CC	Non ferrous metals	4.14	3.68	2.81	4.20	GF	Pharmaceuticals	-1.66	-1.62	-2.50	3.02
EA	Wood articles	1.93	2.26	2.71	3.30	FN	Telecommunic. equipment	-1.91	-1.79	-2.81	3.48
FV	Ships	3.31	1.86	2.67	2.71	GH	Plastic articles	-2.60	-2.91	-2.90	5.37
FM	Consumer electronics	-0.69	-0.12	1.29	2.24	FO	Computer equipment	-1.79	-1.54	-2.95	3.15
FR	Electrical apparatus	0.54	0.84	1.22	5.14	FG	Specialized machines	-3.48	-3.23	-3.13	4.18
KE	Preserved fruits	0.28	0.70	1.12	2.01	DA	Yarns fabrics	-5.48	-4.98	-3.76	5.04
CA	Iron steel	5.21	3.72	1.08	3.14	IB	Crude oil	-8.05	-4.99	-3.99	4.15
		34.43	30.88	27.79	39.79			-29.37	-27.15	-27.02	37.82

TABLE 1 (*cont.*)

MANUFACTURED PRODUCT SPECIALISATION IN EASTERN EUROPE

Code	Product	RCAS¹ 1993	RCAS¹ 1996	RCAS¹ 1999	Export share 1999	Code	Product	RCAS¹ 1993	RCAS¹ 1996	RCAS¹ 1999	Import share 1999
Romania											
DB	Clothing	11.67	13.87	16.62	19.82	FI	Precision instruments	-1.19	-1.09	-1.37	1.61
DC	Knitwear	2.36	2.43	4.51	6.69	FT	Cars and cycles	0.81	-3.20	-1.38	1.49
EB	Furniture	7.32	4.95	4.28	4.84	GE	Toiletries	-1.00	-1.57	-1.64	1.97
JC	Non-edible agricultural prod.	0.61	1.39	3.91	4.62	GH	Plastic articles	-0.06	-0.65	-1.78	3.22
CA	Iron steel	10.63	6.24	3.76	5.94	IC	Natural gas	-5.59	-5.23	-1.92	1.96
DE	Leather	1.93	2.48	3.57	8.89	GF	Pharmaceuticals	-0.69	-1.01	-2.16	2.40
CC	Non ferrous metals	0.98	2.15	2.12	2.84	FN	Telecommunic. equipment	-1.73	-1.50	-2.85	3.27
FV	Ships	0.90	1.31	2.04	2.13	IB	Crude oil	-11.60	-7.23	-3.84	3.85
IH	Refined petroleum products	3.11	1.50	1.17	3.13	FG	Specialized machines	-3.67	-4.32	-4.12	4.64
CB	Tubes	1.11	1.68	0.94	1.49	DA	Yarns fabrics	-5.47	-7.75	-11.77	12.78
		40.61	38.01	42.93	60.40			-30.20	-33.56	-32.84	37.20
Slovak Republic											
FT	Cars and cycles	-1.37	0.13	13.78	16.83	FI	Precision instruments	-0.26	-0.58	-1.06	1.61
CA	Iron steel	10.23	7.77	6.03	8.06	DA	Yarns fabrics	-0.29	-0.23	-1.29	3.79
IH	Refined petroleum products	3.41	3.51	3.01	4.25	IC	Natural gas	-6.46	-1.80	-1.59	1.63
DB	Clothing	3.48	3.24	2.90	3.54	GF	Pharmaceuticals	-0.29	-0.95	-1.71	2.64
JC	Non-edible agricultural prod.	1.45	1.10	0.98	1.96	IA	Coals	-4.17	-2.54	-1.80	1.83
BA	Cement	1.31	1.05	0.91	1.09	FG	Specialized machines	-3.69	-1.99	-1.86	3.14
GI	Rubber articles (incl. tyres)	2.20	1.74	0.90	1.94	FC	Engines	-2.19	-1.92	-3.63	5.20
DE	Leather	1.02	0.89	0.86	2.54	NV	N.e.s. products	-0.05	-3.06	-3.67	4.65
EC	Paper	1.84	1.72	0.85	3.51	FS	Vehicles components	1.17	-0.13	-3.72	7.69
FP	Domestic electrical appliances	1.15	0.57	0.84	1.61	IB	Crude oil	-7.32	-6.51	-5.93	5.95
		24.71	21.71	31.04	45.32			-23.55	-19.73	-26.26	38.13

TABLE 1 *(cont.)*

MANUFACTURED PRODUCT SPECIALISATION IN EASTERN EUROPE

		RCAs[1]			Export share 1999
		1993	1996	1999	1999
Slovenia					
EB	Furniture	4.08	3.72	6.45	7.97
FP	Domestic electrical appliances	3.86	4.50	4.67	5.68
DB	Clothing	5.40	4.03	2.66	3.92
GF	Pharmaceuticals	2.12	2.72	2.52	4.53
FT	Cars and cycles	-2.30	0.72	2.37	9.28
EA	Wood articles	2.47	2.22	1.58	2.41
FQ	Electrical equipment	1.30	1.45	1.52	2.40
FB	Miscellaneous hardware	1.54	1.55	1.27	5.95
GI	Rubber articles (incl. tyres)	1.76	1.42	1.22	2.32
EC	Paper	1.49	1.32	1.02	3.93
		21.72	23.63	25.26	48.39

		RCAS[1]			Import share 1999
		1993	1996	1999	1999
NV	N.e.s. products	-0.15	-0.70	-1.21	1.43
JB	Other edible agricult. prod.	-1.35	-1.85	-1.24	1.55
FC	Engines	-1.27	-1.34	-1.26	3.99
GH	Plastic articles	-2.03	-2.09	-1.36	4.26
FS	Vehicles components	-2.65	-1.74	-1.42	3.93
FN	Telecommunic. equipment	0.01	-0.32	-1.49	2.26
FG	Specialized machines	-1.96	-1.63	-1.87	3.02
FO	Computer equipment	-1.36	-1.08	-1.88	2.16
DA	Yarns fabrics	-3.73	-2.59	-2.11	4.60
IH	Refined petroleum products	-2.97	-4.64	-3.40	3.64
		-17.45	-17.98	-17.25	30.84

factures (e.g. glass), metal products, or base chemicals. The only final consumption product represented among the top-7 was road vehicles. All these industries were the core of the former industrial structure. In Slovakia, the bias towards heavy industries was even more marked with the iron and steel sector having an RCA above 10 and accounting, by itself, for 17% of total exports. In contrast, the comparative disadvantages are observed in consumer goods or highly differentiated industries, that is, sectors characterised by a large number of varieties, such as office machines, telecommunications, machinery or pharmaceutical products.

Poland appeared relatively more specialised in light industries, such as articles of apparel and clothing, furniture or transport equipment. However, it should be noted that these exports are the result of an intense subcontracting with western firms[5]. Product specification and design (i.e. the activities most relevant for product differentiation) are mainly realised by the contractors rather than by the local firms. The same applied to Romania and Bulgaria.

Only Hungary and Slovenia display the main comparative advantages on light industries and are also able to be significant net exporters in industries such as Electrical machinery or pharmaceutical products. This is a clear sign of a more advanced stage of the transition.

A important fact is that towards the end of the 1990s the specialisation seems indeed to be evolving towards a different pattern in all countries, notably with more product diversification and differentiation. But, at it will be discussed below, the pace of this transition is not uniform across countries and can be associated with structural features of the supply in each economy. For example, in Hungary, computer equipment products or engines displayed a negative RCA in 1993 whereas by 1999 they were amongst the strongest comparative advantages and together accounted for over 25% of exports. In Poland, the weight of iron & steel or coal products declined in the export structure, while

---

[5]See HOEKMAN B. - DJANKOV S. [13] for evidence on the role of outward processing trade in the trade relations between the EU and Eastern Europe.

the role of light industries (such as furniture) increased. The case with automobile industry in Slovakia and the Czech Republic is also an example of this diversification towards less traditional exports. There is also evidence that there has been some 'quality upgrading' in the export structure of transition countries, although this aspect of product differentiation is beyond the scope of this paper (Aiginger [2], Landesmann and Stehrer [15]).

To summarise, trade did not collapse in line with output, its geographical orientation changed dramatically, while the sectoral specialisation of transitional economies showed a strong resilience to traditional exports. Moreover, there are signals that the most advanced transition countries are moving towards less traditional exports. The model developed in the next section accounts for these facts and enables to make predictions as to the future course of events.

3. - Product Variety and the Transition: A Simple Model

Surprisingly enough, the literature on transitional economies has somewhat overlooked a crucial dimension of structural change, namely the shift from "homogeneous" goods to more differentiated goods and, in particular, to many different product varieties. Why were varieties lacking before the start of transition? Under central planning, resources were systematically diverted away from final consumption goods, and countries maintained very limited trade relations with western countries, which were confined to exports of raw material or intermediate goods. Moreover, the increase in the number of varieties available to consumers generally requires a multiplication in the number of firms and there were practically insurmountable entry barriers to enterprise creation in these countries[6]. A characteristic of the socialist firms was also a high degree of vertical integration which

---

[6] Hungary is a partial exception in this context. Entry was allowed, but only for relatively large firms.

naturally (even under a market system) does not favour the development of product varieties[7].

One of the first steps of the transition towards a market economy was the opening-up to trade, and hence the lifting of restrictions to the purchase of differentiated goods by domestic consumers. Put another way, demand started to matter in the determination of the equilibrium. Accordingly, a large number of varieties were imported. Domestic production of varieties also begun, but gradually. The build-up of a network of variety producers is, after all, a time consuming and costly process. Insofar as this requires new business start-ups, there are large sunk entry costs to be afforded and high failure rates. Entry barriers were particularly high in Eastern Europe because of a lack of market institutions, entrepreneurship, and financial intermediaries channelling resources to new enterprise creation. The stronger entry barriers, the less business start-ups, the slower the development of new varieties.

3.1 *Consumption Technologies*

The effects of the development of varieties on trade and domestic production can be highlighted within a very simple model. The demand plays a major role in our results. Thus, it is useful to start by characterising consumption technologies.

We are mainly interested here in isolating the effects of the increase in the number of products. Hence, we will *not* assume changes over time in consumers' tastes (e.g., intervening at the start of transition) or asymmetries in tastes between the transitional economy (the East) and the rest of the world (the West). We assume, for the sake of simplicity, that there are only two goods — an homogeneous product (H) and a differentiated good (D). The homogeneous good assembles the characteristics of va-

---

[7]See FEENSTRA R. *et* AL. [10] for evidence of this effect in the case of the exports of Korea and Taiwan.

rieties into a lower quality homogenous good. Preferences of the representative consumer[8] are of the standard, CES-type:

$$U = \left[\alpha H^\rho + (1-\alpha)D^\rho\right]^{1/\rho}$$

(2) where: $\quad D = \left(\sum_{n \in M} x_i^\theta\right)^{1/\theta}, 0 < \alpha < \frac{1}{2}, \theta < 1, -1 < \rho < \infty$

This specification of the utility function has the advantage of summarising all the relevant information on consumers' preferences in three basic parameters. The parameter ρ characterises the degree of substitutability between homogeneous and differentiated goods, whilst α is a "distributional" parameter, affecting the allocation of the consumer's budget between the two bundles of goods. We assume that consumers prefer varieties to the homogeneous good, and hence we restrict the parameter α to be lower than 0.5. Finally, the parameter θ summarises the extent of "love for varieties" of consumers: the lower θ, the stronger the welfare change associated to the multiplication of varieties available to consumers. As is apparent from *(2)*, the sub-utility function over the differentiated good is also modelled as a CES function, following the standard Dixit-Stiglitz [6] model. Out of a very large potential number of varieties *(M)*, only *n* goods are produced and are available to consumers.

The utility maximisation problem can, as usual, be split in two stages. At first, the representative consumer decides how to allocate her/his budget between the homogeneous and the composite differentiated good. At the second stage, the consumer decides how to allocate her expenditure over the available varieties.

As customary in the product variety literature, we assume that production technologies allow for increasing returns in both variety and homogeneous good productions. This requires that firms

---

[8] We allow only for horizontal product differentiation. Thus, there is no problem in modelling the economy as populated by a single consumer.

have some degree of monopoly power in order to be profitable. We assume further that the extent of increasing returns is larger in homogeneous good production than in the production of varieties, insofar as the latter involves higher fixed costs[9].

We will also keep the standard assumption that each variety can be produced by only one (atomistic) firm[10]. Since everything is symmetric in this model, at the equilibrium all varieties will be equally priced. Define this identical price of each variety as **p**. Given the utility function, the consumer will spread her consumption uniformly over varieties, demanding the same amount (say *x*) of each brand. We can therefore rewrite the (relative) demand for the homogenous good as follows:

$$(3) \qquad \frac{H}{D} = \left[\frac{p}{P_H n^{\frac{1-\theta}{\theta}}} \frac{\alpha}{1-\alpha} \right]^{\sigma}$$

where $\sigma = 1/(1-\rho)$ is the elasticity of substitution between the homogeneous *(H)* and the composite good *(D)*. This shows that increases in the number of varieties *(n)* produced involve reductions in the consumption of the homogenous good. Put another way, when a large number of varieties becomes available to consumers, the relative price of P_H must decline in order to sell any given supply of the homogeneous good.

The fact that the demand of the composite good increases with *n* does not mean that the demand for each variety increases as well. Insofar as the elasticity of substitution across varieties

---

[9]Define by a^i and a^i_l respectively, overhead and unit input requirements in the production of variety *i*. For symmetry we impose that $a^i = a$ and $a^i_l = a_l$ for all *i*. The homogenised good has a stronger degree of economy of scale than varieties because $a^H > a$ and $a^H_l \leq a_l$.

[10]A convincing rationale for this assumption is that imitation involves sunk costs and that firms may engage in ex-post price competition. Under these conditions, imitators would never be able to recoup the sunk-costs at entry. We also rule out the (remote) possibility of having more varieties of the same type being produced prior to the opening to trade. This is because, prior to transition, there are virtually no varieties produced domestically (see below).

(σ_x) is higher than σ (i.e., inasmuch as $\theta > \rho$) the demand for each variety will actually decline with n. We will assume henceforth that this is the case. This is quite natural an assumption as typically the degree of substitutability is larger within than between composite goods.

3.2 *Comparing Equilibria Before and After Trade Liberalisation*

We use the above static framework simply to characterise the impact effect of trade liberalisation. Prior to transition only the homogeneous good is produced domestically (e.g., there is only one type of shirts, soft drinks or cars) and consumers have no access to imported varieties. Such an outcome (the fact that only the homogeneous good is produced) can be pursued by a (non-benevolent) central planner maximising output along with the Marxian primary accumulation ideology[11]. Thus initially consumers can only have access to H.

At the outset of transition, trade is liberalised. This involves a sudden increase in the number of varieties available to eastern residents. Now they can finally spread their consumption over the large number of varieties (n^w) produced in the West. As domestic and foreign consumers have identical preferences, the country is small relative to the West and there are no asymmetries in production technologies[12], varieties can only have the same price[13] at the equilibrium, namely the price initially pre-

---

[11] The problem of the planner can be written as follows:

$$\underset{n,H}{\text{Max}}\left(n \cdot x + H\right)$$

s.t. i)$n \geq 0$ and ii)$n \cdot (a + a_I x) + a^H + a_I^H H \leq L$

where L is the total amount iof labour resources in the economy (work is considered as a duty, so that the planner can freely dispose of L). This is a two-stage linear programming problem with corner solution at $n=0$.

[12] The case where domestic producers of varieties are less efficient than their western counterparts is not treated herein for the sake of simplicity. Under asymmetric technologies, we would expect to have deficits in the trade balance even at the long-run equilibrium.

[13] As in standard monopolistic competition models, this common price of varieties, p, will embody a mark-up over operating costs, which is inversely related

vailing in western markets[14] (p^w). Denote by x the demand for varieties of the representative consumer; x is decreasing in p^w and – as discussed above – in the total number of variety producers (n^w). Trade equilibrium at the start of transition will therefore be given by:

$$(4) \qquad p^w \cdot x\!\left(p^w, n^w\right) \cdot n^w = H_x^e$$

where H_x^e denotes net eastern exports of the homogeneous good. In other words, the eastern country must be initially a net exporter of the homogeneous good in order to finance imports of varieties. Insofar as varieties start being produced domestically, then also varieties can be exported as trade becomes increasingly of the (horizontal) intra-industry type. But entry of variety is a long process, as discussed below. Meanwhile, coping with the external constraint forces transitional countries to sell low-price homogeneous goods abroad.

The second event marking the start of transition is the free entry of variety producers. According to the standard Dixit-Stiglitz monopolistic competition model, the optimal number of varieties produced in the East in the long-run will (n^e) depend on the size of the market, the degree of substitutability across varieties and the sunk costs *(F)* associated with the creation of new firms. Let L^e and L^w denote the eastern and western populations, respectively. We have then that:

$$(5) \qquad n^e = \frac{L^e}{\sigma_x \cdot F}$$

As is apparent from *(5)* and the symmetry in technologies and preferences, trade in varieties is balanced only when enterprise

---

to the elasticity of demand for varieties, hence to the total number of variety producers.

[14]If n^w is sufficiently large, the opening to trade with the East (the appearance of a new variety) does not alter the equilibrium price of varieties.

density in the East converges to the levels prevailing in the West, that is:

$$(6) \qquad\qquad \frac{n^e}{L^e} = \frac{n^w}{L^w}$$

Insofar as enterprise density in the East is lower than in the West, the country is bound to export the homogeneous product. The full characterisation of the pre-transition and long-run post-transition equilibrium is provided in Appendix 1.

Summarising, this simple static model predicts that transitional economies initially experience a large trade deficit in differentiated goods, financed via large exports of the homogeneous good, and, in the long-run, only trade of the intra-industry type[15].

In order to fully characterise trade equilibrium after the transition, we still have to mention what happens to the terms of trade. As variations in p^w associated to the entry of firms in the East are of a second-order magnitude (L^w is large relative to L^e), changes in the terms of trade can only be associated to variations in the production of the homogeneous good[16]. The impact effect of trade liberalisation is, as we have shown, a marked decline in P_H. The terms of trade improve only gradually for the transitional economy insofar as an increasing number of varieties is produced domestically. This involves less production, hence higher prices, of the homogeneous good.

---

[15]A possible extension of our model is to assume that the (total) factor productivity in the production of varieties increases with the number of intermediate inputs available to enterprises. We do not pursue this route herein although - when interpreted in terms of intermediate goods — the shift towards increasing varieties movement can also be interpreted as a shift from energy-intensive and homogeneous products to light and diversified productions.

[16]As it can be derived from the CES dual price price index for the composite good, the change in the price of the composite good from the initial and the long-run equilibria is given by:

$$P_D^0 - P_D^* = p^w \left[\left(\frac{1}{n^w} \right)^{\frac{1-\theta}{\theta}} - \left(\frac{1}{n^e + n^w} \right)^{\frac{1-\theta}{\theta}} \right]$$

3.3 *The Transition*

Increasing the number of firms is a time-consuming process and, especially in manufacturing, may involve significant sunk costs. Moreover, the probability of failure is high. In EU countries failure rates among entrants are as high as 50% after five years of business (Eurostat, [7]. Failure rates in transitional economies may be even larger given a lack of entrepreneurship, bad infrastructures to support new business creation, a banking system unable to provide venture capital for new business because highly inefficient and often interlocked with large (and heavily indebted) corporations, and potentially large co-ordination failures. Thus, it seems to be more realistic to model the development of varieties as a lengthy process, involving high sunk costs and many episodes of failure.

The above features of the entry process can be framed in a very parsimonious fashion in a Harris-Todaro type dynamic model, involving labour reallocation from the homogeneous good producer to firms producing varieties. A model of this kind is sketched in Appendix 2 and provides the support for the numerical simulations discussed below. Workers can move from one sector to the other experiencing intervening non-employment spells. Thus, the decision to leave the homogeneous good firm involves some risks. Workers can only be induced to take such risks if there is an insurance providing them income support while not having a job and probabilities of success are not too low. An alternative way to read this reallocation process is to consider that homogeneous good producers behave as monopolists, reacting to changes in the demand for the homogeneous product with cuts in production capacity. However, measures to "buy-out" the workers are required to shed labour, given the power of the workers' councils to appoint and dismiss managers. Models of this kind, embodying political economy barriers to staff reductions, are frequent in the optimal speed of transition literature (Boeri, [4]).

The production of a new variety is modelled as a self-employment choice. This is consistent with the observation in these countries of very large increases in self-employment rates at the outset of transition. The startup of such new activities, involves significant sunk costs, F, which can be financed by investing the unemployment benefits. Many transitional countries have in place startup loans involving the provision of residual unemployment benefit claims as lump-sums to the workers wishing to take their chance. The workers who succeed in the startup, enjoy the rents associated with the production of varieties (the rents are due to the presence of sunk costs) until they fail. There is indeed an exogenous probability of failure after entry, λ, for all variety producers. Those workers who do not succeed in starting up a new activity, lose their previous period unemployment benefits, but may take once more their chance next period, clearly paying again the sunk costs.

Unemployment benefits are financed via taxes on labour, notably on rents in the production of varieties. Hence they play a twofold role in this model. On the one hand, they induce workers to change jobs (or, equivalently, allow homogeneous good producers to restructure their firms). On the other hand, they make for non-employment created in the transition to exert a negative "fiscal externality" on the development of varieties.

There were many gaps in the provision of varieties to be filled at the outset. Many gaps meant easier entry at the outset, although not necessarily easier survival after entry. Thus we model the probability of success as decreasing[17] in the number of varieties produced (in the size of the self-employment pool). In particular, the probability of success is increasing in the deviation of the initial density of firms from its long-run equilibrium *(6)*. Denoting by V the *(ex-ante)* value of producing a variety, and by e the number of firms paying the sunk entry costs, we have the free-entry condition:

(7
$$\begin{cases} -F + \delta\pi(n*-n_t)V = 0 & \text{if } e_t > 0 \\ -F + \delta\pi(n*-n_t)V < 0 & \text{if } e_t = 0 \end{cases}$$

---

[17]The probability decreases less than proportionally with n as there may be critical mass effects related to the creation of a mittelstand of variety producers.

where π denotes the probability of success, and δ the discount factor $(\delta=1/1+r)$[18]. Insofar as the stream of profits attainable by entrants declines with n, all apprentice businessmen will leave the homogeneous good firm immediately after trade liberalisation. There is evidence of a veritable explosion in the number of registered entrepreneurs and private entities just after the first systemic reforms (OECD [18], Table 6.4). As is apparent from *(7)*, the number of newly registered private entrepreneurs will be larger, the greater n^* and the lower F.

Graph 3 displays numerical simulations of the model. In the baseline scenario (continuous lines), unemployment benefits are set to replace 35% of wages in the homogeneous good production. This is broadly in line with the levels currently prevailing in the Visegrad countries. Sunk entry costs match exactly this amount so that those trying to startup their own business can just use the benefit for this purpose. As shown by the top panel, (self)employment in varieties increases soon after the start of transition; the growth continues afterwards at a slower pace and reaches in five years about 50% of the working age population. From being inexistent at the outset, non-employment also jumps immediately, as workers leave (or are laid-off from) the homogeneous good producers; then non-employment declines in line with the growth in the number of varieties, which are the engine to job creation. It increases again at later years insofar as the startup of new activities is made more difficult by the filling of most market niches while employment continues to steadily decline in the homogeneous good sector. Output follows the U-shaped pattern characterised in the first section of this paper. Output falls originate from two factors: the first is the impact of trade liberalisation on the price of the homogeneous good; the second is the decline of employment in H which, in presence of increasing returns to scale, involves more than proportional declines in output.

---

[18]The literature on product variety often makes a number of assumptions which essentially reduce consumption choices to a static decision problem (GROSSMAN G. - HELPMAN E. [12]). Following this convention — which may actually be more justified when modelling transitional economies rather than OECD countries — we therefore assume that the pure rate of time preference of consumers equals the market interest rate. This implies that (nominal) spending is constant over time.

GRAPH 3

GDP DECLINE 1990=100

Employment in Variety Production

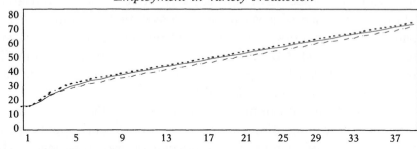

——— Baseline
- — - — Lower Unemployment Benefits
- - - - - - Lower Unemployment Benefits and Entry Costs

Non Employment

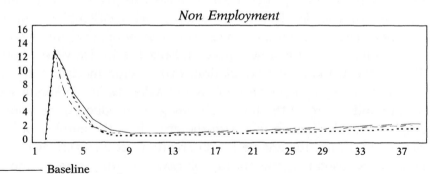

——— Baseline
- — - — Lower Unemployment Benefits
- - - - - Lower Unemployment Benefits and Entry Costs

Output
$(t_0 = 100)$

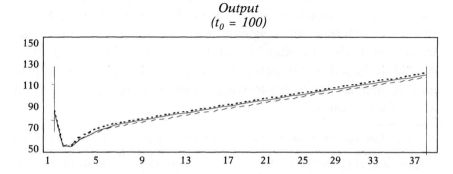

——— Baseline
- — - — Lower Unemployment Benefits
- - - - - - Lower Unemployment Benefits and Entry Costs

Two simple experiments are carried out with this model. The first involves a decline in the sunk costs at entry. This causes non-employment to rise (and output to decline) more at the outset than in the baseline insofar more workers are induced to leave the homogeneous good production for self-employment. However, lower entry costs induce faster growth of self-employment (and less non-employment) later on. The second experiment consists of declines in non-employment benefits. In this case we have just the opposite result. Employment falls less at the outset than in the baseline, but later is also slower to recover. This is because lower unemployment benefits discourage self-employment choices, hence the type of structural change required to foster the growth of varieties.

4. - Coping With the Facts

The model(*s*) sketched in the previous section accounts for the three stylised facts of transition inspiring this paper.

4.1 *Supply-Side Determinants of the Output Collapse*

The model generates steep output declines at the outset of transition as a result of trade liberalisation and structural change. The opening to trade reduces the (relative) price of the homogeneous good. Structural reallocation causes labour to move away from the *H* sector and output falls even more than employment, due to the presence of increasing returns to scale[19].

---

[19]Rather than ruling out other explanations for the *U*-shaped output dynamics in these countries, the story behind our model is consistent – if not complementary – with the work of two additional factors, which may have magnified output losses. First, as suggested by DAIANU D. [5], the large change in relative prices induced by the transition (e.g., the change in relative prices between homogeneous and differentiated goods induced by the explosion of *n*) cannot be easily absorbed in a short period. Neither changes in relative prices can be accommodated via exchange rate adjustments. Therefore, the transitional economy is put under a "strain" taking its short-run equilibrium further away from the production frontier. Second, the traditional sectors producing homogeneous goods were typically composed of large and

Both effects are larger when the country starts with a very low enterprise density. This is because the price change associated to trade liberalisation is larger in this case and the scope of labour reallocation is larger: there are more gaps in the provision of varieties to be filled.

Hence, not only this model accounts for the coexistence of output falls and increasing trade with the West, but also predicts that output falls should be larger in the countries having at the outset the lowest enterprise densities. It also suggests that countries with low unemployment benefits (or high entry costs) should experience lower output (and, above all, employment) losses at the outset, but also slow, if any, recovery afterwards. This seems to fit well with the asymmetries in the patterns of employment and output adjustment in the Visegrad countries *vis-à-vis* Bulgaria, Romania and the CIS countries.

While our focus is here mainly on the output collapse, this model can also mimic the GDP decline registered in transitional economies at the beginning of the 1990s. The latter stems from the increase in the price of varieties associated with trade liberalisation and failure of national accounts (CPI indexes) to properly measure the variety effect. The latter is typically obtained as a simple weighted (by the consumption shares) average of the prices of the various goods, that is, in our model the (national accounts) consumer price index before trade liberalisation is given by:

(8) $$CPI = \alpha \cdot P_H + (1 - \alpha) \cdot p$$

and considering that by definition P_H is taken as numeraire ($P_H = 1$), the recorded change in CPI is:

(9) $$\Delta CPI = (p^w - p)(1 - \alpha)$$

whereas the change in the "true" CPI index, that is, the index which properly takes into account the increase in the number of varieties is:

extremely integrated firms. This created different sorts of indivisibilities that magnified output losses associated with the shift of resources from the production of homogeneous goods towards the differentiated good sector.

$$(10) \qquad \Delta CPI^* = \left[\alpha \cdot + (1-\alpha) \cdot \left(n^w\right)^{\frac{1}{1-\sigma}} \cdot p^w \right]^{\frac{1}{1-\sigma}} - \alpha - (1-\alpha)p$$

Equation *(10)* shows that consumer prices may actually decline after trade liberalisation insofar as the effect on the increasing number of varieties available to consumers offsets the increase in the price of each single variety. Table 2 provides a numerical illustration of how the variety effect can produce rather different pictures of the impact on GDP of trade liberalisation. Assuming the counterfactual parameters of our simulation, if one uses *(9)* real GDP collapses whilst applying *(10)* a slight increase of the true GDP measure is actually observed. This variety effect is a bias in the measurement in the consumer price index, which has recently been analysed and measured in the context of the US economy (ACSCPI [1]). In the case of transition countries, for the reasons discussed in this paper, this bias is likely to be particularly large.

TABLE 2

SIMULATION OF THE IMPACT OF
LIBERATISATION WITH DIFFERENT CPI MEASURES

	Variables	Pre transition	After liberalisation	Rate of change (%)
Variety price	p	1.00	1.50	50
Homogeneous good price	P_H	1.00	1.00	0
Aggregate elasticity of substitution	σ	1.50	1.50	0
Elasticity of substitution between varieties	σ_x	10	10	0
Number of varieties	n	1	50	4900
preference coefficient betwen H and D	α	0.50	0.50	0
Wage rate	w	1.00	1.00	0
Population	L	1000.00	1000.00	0
Price for the composite good	P_D	1.00	0.97	-3
CPI as weighted average of H and p [1]	CPI	1.00	1.25	25
CPI incorporating the variety effect [1]	CPI*	1.00	0.99	-1
real GDP using CPI [2]	GDP	1000.00	800.00	-20
real GDP using CPI* [2]	GDP	1000.00	1014.76	1

[1] See text.
[2] Computed as $w.L / CPI$

4.2 *The "Perverse" Trade Specialisation*

As shown above, the balance of trade for varieties is initially in deficit and improves with the increase in the number of varieties produced domestically. Therefore a transitional country is initially a net exporter of H even if in the long-run equilibrium the country increases its specialisation in the differentiated good. The issue is that H has to be exported until a critical mass of domestic variety producers is reached. As an aside, the collapse of CMEA and trade reorientation can also be explained in this context. Indeed, trade within the CMEA mainly involved final "homogenised" goods (apart from the imports of energy and raw-materials from the former USSR). After trade liberalisation none of the former CMEA partners had the supply potential to satisfy the demand for differentiated products.

5. - Back to the Evidence

According to our model, the transitional depression is related to shifts in the structure of consumption rewarding differentiated products and inertia of the previous supply structure to adapt to this shock. This explanation of a supply-driven depression is consistent with two facts documented above, namely: *(i)* aggregate investment fell less than output[20], and ii) while GDP and industrial production were collapsing, imports did not fall in the same fashion and actually grew very rapidly after the early transition phase. An important feature of our model is that the demand shift occurs without (exogenous) changes in the preferences.

Our story is also consistent with the increase in enterprise density registered since 1990 in all transitional economies. Table 3 drawn from Eurostat [8] shows that enterprise density rapidly

---

[20]In a demand-driven depression the investment would be expected to fall in line with output. This was not observed in the transition countries where a revival of investment occurred before the output bottomed-out (see on this ROSTOWSKI J. [22]). It should also be stressed that investment in business startups is poorly recorded by national accounts.

increased in central and Eastern Europe, but was below the levels prevailing in EU countries.

TABLE 3

COMPARISON OF ENTERPRISE DENSITY
(NUMBER OF ENTERPRISES PER 1,000)

	EU	Central and Eastern Europe[1]
Inhabitants	43	31
Active population	95	64
Non farming population	113	83

Source: EUROSTAT [8].
[1]Albania, Bulgaria, Czech Republic, Estonia, Hungary, Latvia, Lithuania, Poland, Romania, Slovakia and Slovenia.

Graph 4 shows that the relation between the enterprise density[21] (corrected for the dormant or dead firms) and the levels of real income per capita (GDP at PPP rates) holds reasonably well on a cross-country including both the transition and the western European countries. The countries more advanced in the transition as the Czech Republic, Hungary and Slovenia are also the countries with the highest GDP per capita and enterprise density. Moreover, the countries where enterprise density was higher from the start (hence, according to our model, the countries that were initially producing more varieties) displayed lower and less protracted declines in output. For example, output fell more in Romania than in Hungary. This is also consistent with the predictions of our model.

Another piece of evidence that is coherent with the predictions of our model can be drawn by computing the Feenstra [9] product variety indicator for the transition countries (Graph 5)[22]. The indicator suggests consistently that the product variety of imports was higher than export. It also shows that there is an in-

---

[21] This data comprises all non agricultural enterprises.
[22] We thank Professor Michael Funke for having extended the measures of product variety put forward in FUNKE M. - RUHDEWEL R. [11] to a selected group of transition countries and having made these results available to us.

GRAPH 4

ENTERPRISE DENSITY[1] AND GDP PER CAPITA, 1995.

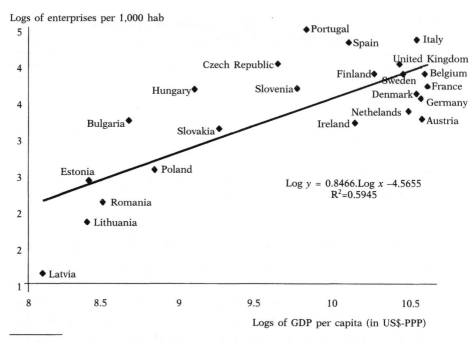

Source: EUROSTAT [8] and author's calculations.
[1]Not including agriculture and adjusted for the non-active

creasing trend of export product variety. Finally, the indicator also suggests that the variety gap was bigger in the less advanced transition countries, such as Romania and Bulgaria, than in Poland, Hungary or Slovenia.

The soaring trade deficits that appeared in the early stages of transition and re-appeared again in 1996 and 1997 are also in line with the implications of our model. Insofar as the number of domestic variety producers is far from its long-run equilibrium, increases in real wages (e.g., associated to catch-up effects) translate into increased demand for varieties that, for a large part, are imported. In our model labour supply fixed, but these unit labour cost effects can be modelled as exogenous changes in marginal

GRAPH 5

FEENSTRA PRODUCT VARIETY INDEX
FOR EXPORTS AND IMPORTS[1]

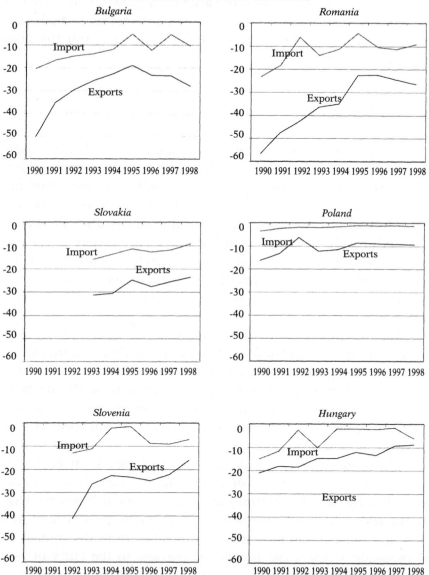

Source: Calculations provided by MICHAEL FUNKE

[1]The indicator is the Log of the relative product variety in a given country compared with the US. For more details on the indicator, see FEENSTRA R. [9] and an application for OECD countries can be found in FUNKE M. - RUHWEDEL R. [11].

costs of H making it more difficult for the country to finance its variety gap. Overall, the only way to sustain real wage growth over the long-run is in the growth of varieties, a growth which creates its own demand. By favouring economic integration of both capital and trade flows the EU enlargement could accelerate this convergence process.

6. - Final Remarks

The purpose of this paper was to show that a better understanding of the transition mechanics can be gained by considering a dimension of structural change which has been, thus far, fairly neglected by the literature. We refer to the "shelf-shock" occurred in all transitional economies immediately after the fall of the Berlin wall. A simple model framing this variety effect can contribute to explaining several stylised facts of transition. It also has some relevant implications for the design of policies accommodating economic transformation and for the EU enlargement process.

The bottoming-up of the transition recession has been in many countries associated to demand from OECD countries of homogeneous goods produced in the East. However, our model suggests that durable growth can only come from the development of many specialised small units in the manufacturing sector, that is, growth in the long-run needs to be supported by an increase in enterprise density.

Although entry is the driving force of long-term economic growth, in the short-run it diverts away resources from production, thereby inducing output losses. These initial losses are larger, the wider the gap between the inherited enterprise density and that prevailing in the long-run. The recovery from the transitional recession is lower the higher the barriers to the entry of new firms. Measures reducing such barriers are likely to significantly speed-up the transition and reduce its costs in terms of forgone output.

After the initial explosion of new business startups, the pace of creation of new firms is slowing down considerably and these countries are still far from reaching enterprise densities comparable to those of OECD countries. Most of the development of a "new private sector" has occurred in "gap-filling" service activities rather than in manufacturing. The environment is still unfavourable to the development of small firms in manufacturing: there are high real interest rates, lack of venture capital, interlocking of banks and large corporations, and an absence of infrastructures for small firms development. EU enlargement and access to EU Structural Funds may improve matters, but it will take time before the effects of public investment materialise.

Trade liberalisation has been a major shock for these countries, and one which has been associated with dramatic output falls and a rise of non-employment. This does not imply trade should have been liberalised only gradually. Opening to trade played a crucial role in paving the way to the entry of new firms, and promoted subcontracting in some sectors (e.g. machinery and apparel), which hopefully will be followed by the transfer of know-how and learning and the creation of a critical mass of SMEs sufficiently dynamic and innovative. But much remains to be done in order to reduce barriers to the entry and survival of new firms in transitional economies.

The success of transition, notably of those countries that entering the European Union will likely face increasing pressures for real wage convergence with the EU, will very much depend on how fast is the reallocation of labour from homogeneous to diversified good producers.

From an historical perspective, we have shown in this paper that high cost of entry had to be accompanied with rather generous unemployment benefits in order to start the reallocation process on a sufficiently large scale. Non-employment benefits, however, ended-up increasing the social security burden on the active population and things can only get worse in this respect with the entry in the EU as pressures to increase social spending will be stronger. A better way to start the process would have been to reduce the obstacles to the startup of new activities and, conditional on that, have lower non-employment benefits in place.

Although it is easy to be wise after the events, these lessons are still useful for the countries lagging behind the transition process.

1. - Pre - and Post - Transition Equilibrium

Assume that all residents supply one unit of labour. Then, under full employment, individuals' income will always equal one unit of the homogeneous good. Denote the equilibrium before the transition with the superscript "O". Given the symmetry of production and consumption technologies, demand for each variety at the initial and final equilibria will, respectively, be given by:

$$(11) \qquad \frac{(1-\alpha)}{p^0} \cdot L^e \quad \text{and} \quad x_i = \frac{(1-\alpha) \cdot p^{-\sigma_x}}{\sum_i p_i^{(1-\sigma_x)}} \cdot \left(L^e + L^w\right) \quad \forall i$$

The price of varieties before the start of transition is equal to average costs, that is:

$$(12) \qquad p^0 = \frac{a}{x^0} + a_l$$

where: $0 < a < (1 - \alpha)$, whilst profit maximising (under monopolistic competition) price setting when the perceived demand is x_i implies:

$$(13) \qquad p_i = a_l \left(1 + \frac{1}{|\varepsilon_x|}\right) = a_l \left(1 + \xi(n)\right) \quad \forall i$$

where ξ is the mark-up over marginal costs and ε_x is the demand-price elasticity,

$$|\varepsilon_x| = \sigma_x + \cdot \frac{1}{\sum_j p_j^{(1-\sigma_x)}} \cdot \left(1 - \sigma_x\right)$$

At the symmetric equilibrium with $(n^e + n^*)$ large, we will have:

(14)
$$\xi\left(\sigma_x, n^e + n^*\right) \approx \frac{1}{\sigma_x}$$

The market clearing conditions for varieties are therefore:

(15)
$$x^0 = \frac{(1-\alpha)-a}{a_l} \quad \text{and} \quad x = \frac{(1-\alpha)}{na_l(1+\xi(n))} \cdot (L^e + L^w)$$

Domestic demand for the homogeneous good is both prior and after the transition given by:

(16)
$$H^0 = \alpha L^e$$

Domestic output of H will then be given residually by the overall resource constraint:

(17)
$$x^0 = H^0_s = L^e - (a + a_l x^0) \quad \text{and} \quad H_s = L^e - n^e(a + a_l \cdot x)$$

Hence, substituting *(15)* into *(17)*, exports of H (H_x) will be given by:

(18)
$$H^0_x = (1-\alpha)(L^e - 1) \quad \text{and} \quad H_x = (1-\alpha)(L^e - \frac{n^e}{n}\frac{L}{(1+\xi n)}) - n^e a$$

using the long-run entry equilibrium condition *(6)* and after some manipulation, the post-transition equilibrium exports of the homogeneous good can also be rewritten as:

(19)
$$H_x = n^e[(1-\alpha)d\frac{\xi(n)}{1+\xi(n)} - a]$$

where: d is the (inverse) long-run enterprise density and the mark-up tends to a constant for large n. This completes our characterisation of the pre-transition and long-run post-transition equilibria.

The equilibrium prevailing under the transition phase is obtained simply by subtracting the term $n^e a$ from the RHS of *(18)*.

2. - Transitional Dynamics

The purpose of this Appendix is to illustrate the dynamic model used to simulate the transition from the autarckic equilibrium under central planning to the long-run equilibrium with free trade, which have been characterised in the static model presented in the third section of the paper.

As in the static model, we have two sectors, an homogenised good sector inherited from the previous regime and a new variety sector.

Workers are heterogeneous. First of all, they have different reservation utilities (productivity in home production). Secondly, they have different skills. Thus, there is a non-trivial matching process involved by the start-up of new activities, which is modelled as a self-employment choice: workers should find activities corresponding to their specific skills.

Individuals can either be employed in one of the two sectors or non-employed. The total population is normalised to one unit. The reservation utility, u is distributed uniformly along the unit interval.

The asset value of being employed in the homogenised good sector is:

$$(20) \qquad W_H = w + \delta\{(1-\lambda)W_H + \lambda W_u\}$$

where λ is the (exogenous) layoff rate, W_u is the asset value of non-employment. The value of being self-employed in the new sector is:

$$(21) \qquad W_n = S + \delta\{(1-\lambda_n)W_n + \lambda_n W_u\}$$

where $S > w$ is the positional rent enjoyed by new posts relative to those located in the old sector and λ_n is the probability of failure in the new sector.

Non-employed individuals can be actively seeking a job (whishing to start-up their own activity) or not searching. If they are seeking a job, they do not enjoy their reservation utility and pay the start-up costs, having a probability π_u of success. If they are not seeking, they receive the non-employment benefit and, on the top of that, they can draw their own reservation utility (or productivity in the subsistence sector). Hence, the value of being non-employed for an individual with reservation utility u is

$$(22) \quad W_u(b) = b + \max \left\{ -F + \delta(\pi_u W_n + (1 - \pi_u)W_u(u)), u + \delta W_u(u) \right\}$$

where: $0 < c < b < 1$ and F is the (sunk) entry cost.

The above equations define a cut-off reservation utility level, $\tilde{u}$, at which the non-employed are indifferent between being active and inactive. In particular, $\tilde{u}$ is defined by:

$$(23) \qquad \tilde{u} = \delta\pi_u \left(W_n - W_u(u) \right) - F$$

Clearly, the cut-off reservation utility is decreasing in the entry cost, while it is increasing in W_n and the discount factor. The probability of success is given by:

$$(24) \qquad \pi_u = m\left(n^* - n, \mu(\tilde{u}) \right)$$

where $\mu(\tilde{u})$ is a measure of the non-employed with reservation utility lower or equal to $\tilde{u}$ and $m(.)$ is a matching function increasing in both arguments.

The 'free-entry condition' is then:

$$(25) \qquad \delta m\left(n^* - n, \mu(\tilde{u}) \right) W_n = F$$

Dynamics are induced by matching technologies (which are function of the past realisations of the state variables). In the numerical simulations displayed in the paper, the following system of difference equations is used:

(26) $$E_H^{t+1} = (1-\lambda)E_H^t$$

(27) $$n^{t+1} = (1-\lambda_n)n^t + \pi_u^t\mu(\tilde{u}_t)$$

(28) $$N^{t+1} = N^t - \pi_u^t\ \mu(\tilde{u}_t) + \lambda_n n^t + \lambda E_H^t$$

where E_H, and N denote, respectively, employment in the homogenised good sector and non-employment.

We specify matching technologies as Cobb-Douglas and we let $0 < \alpha < 1$ denote the elasticity of matching with respect to the number of gaps yet to be filled (the distance from the long-run enterprise density, n^*). As customary, we assume that there are constant-returns to scale in matching technologies. Hence, (1- α) is the elasticity of matching with respect to the pool of apprentice entrepreneurs.

The numerical simulations commented in the paper include a 'fiscal externality' effect. This involves adding a government budget constraint to the model, related to the payment of non-employment benefits out of payroll taxation.

In particular, payroll taxes have at each point in time to satisfy the (static) social security budget constraint:

(29) $$bN_t = \tau_n(pn_t + wE_H^t)$$

where τ denotes the statutory contributions rates, which adjusts at each point in time to clear the social security budget, i.e.:

(30) $$\tau = \frac{bN_t}{pn_t + wE_H^t}$$

As is apparent from above, insofar as $w < p$, an increased employment share in varieties (per given N), involves lower statutory contribution rates.

BIBLIOGRAPHY

[1] ACSCPI (ADVISORY COMMISSION TO STUDY THE CONSUMER PRICE INDEX),«Towards a More Accurate Measure of the Cost of Living», *Final Report to the Senate Finance Committee*, Washington (D.C.), December 4, 1996.

[2] AIGINGER K., «Qualitative Competitiveness» Y. WOLFMAYR-SCHNITZER (ed.), in *The Competitiveness of Transition Countries*, Vienna, WIFO, 1997.

[3] BLANCHARD O. - KREMER M., «Disorganization», *Quarterly Journal of Economics, November 1997*, pp. 1091-126.

[4] BOERI T., *Structural Change, Welfare Systems and Labour Reallocation*, Oxford, Oxford University Press, 2000.

[5] DAIANU D., «Stabilization and Exchange Rate Policy in Romania», *Economics of Transition*, vol. 4, n. 1, 1996; pp. 229-48.

[6] DIXIT A. - STIGLITZ J., «Monopolistic Competition and Optimal Product Diversity», *American Economic Review*, n. 67, 1977, pp. 297-308.

[7] EUROSTAT, *Enterprises in Europe, Fourth Report*, Luxembourg, 1996.

[8] – –, *Enterprises in Central and Eastern Europe*, Luxembourg, 1996.

[9] FEENSTRA R., «New Product Varieties and the Measurement of International Prices», *American Economic Review*, vol. 84, n. 1, 1994, pp. 157-77.

[10] FEENSTRA R. - HUANG D. - G. HAMILTON, «Business groups and trade in East Asia: Part 2, Product Variety», *NBER, Working Papers*, n. 5887, January 1997.

[11] FUNKE M. - RUHWEDEL R., «Product Variety and Economic Growth: Empirical Evidence for the OECD countries», *IMF, Staff Papers*, vol. 48, n. 2, December 2001.

[12] GROSSMAN G. - HELPMAN E., *Innovation and Growth in the Global Economy*, MIT Press, Cambridge (MA) and London (UK), MIT, Press, 1991.

[13] HOEKMAN B. - DJANKOV S., «Intra-Industry Trade, Foreign Direct Investment and the Reorientation of East European Exports», CEPR, *Working Papers* n. 1377, April, 1996.

[14] KRUGMAN P., «Differences in Income Elasticities and Trends in Exchange Rates», *European Economic Review*, n. 5, 1989.

[15] LANDESMANN M. - STEHER R., «Trade structures, Quality Differentiation and Technical Barriers in CEE-EU Trade», WIIW, *Research Papers* n. 282, January, 2002.

[16] MATSUYAMA K., «New Goods, Market Formations, and Pitfalls of System Design», *Journal of the Japanese and International Economies*, n. 9, 1995, pp. 376-402.

[17] NEVEN D., «Trade Liberalisation with Eastern Nations: How sensitive?», in Faini R. - Portes R. (eds.) *European Trade with Eastern Europe: Adjustment and Opportunities*, London, CEPR, 1995.

[18] OECD, *Employment Outlook*, Paris, 1992.

[19] – –, *Economic Survey of the Slovak Republic*, Paris, 1996.

[20] OLIVEIRA MARTINS J., «Export Behaviour with Differentiated Products: Exports of Korea, Taiwan and Japan to the US domestic market», in DAGENAIS M. - MUET P. (eds.) *International Trade Modelling*, London and New York, Chapman & Hall, 1992, pp. 37-52.

[21] ROLAND G. - VERDIER, T, «Transition and the Output Fall» *Economics of Transition*, vol. 7, n. 1, 1999, pp. 1-28.

[22] ROSTOWSKI J., «Comparing two Great Depressions: 1929-33 and 1989-93» in S. ZECCHINI (ed.), *Lessons from Economic Transition: Central and Eastern Europe in the 1990s*, Notwell (MASS), Kluwer Academic Pulishers, 1997.

On the Welfare Costs of Exclusion: the Case of Central Eastern Europe

Cinzia Alcidi - Stefano Manzocchi - Gianmarco I.P. Ottaviano*

Università di Perugia   Università «Bocconi», Milano

Nel decennio passato, l'Unione Europea ha proceduto lungo il sentiero dell'integrazione con il completamento del Mercato Interno e l'Unione monetaria, mentre i paesi dell'Europa Centro-Orientale (ECO) non hanno partecipato a questo processo. In questo lavoro ci chiediamo quali siano state le conseguenze, in termini di benessere sociale, dell'esclusione dell'ECO dalle dinamiche dell'integrazione europea. Le nostre simulazioni, condotte sulla base di un modello di geografia economica con agglomerazione e crescita basata sugli spillover tecnologici, sembrano indicare che i costi dell'esclusione non sono stati compensati dai benefici della transizione.

In the past decade, we observed an acceleration of Western European integration, while the transition countries of Central Eastern Europe (CEE) have not become members of the EU. In this paper, we conduct numerical simulations on the consequences of such a kind of differential integration within the European economic region by a spatial model of endogenous growth. Special attention is paid to the welfare effects on insiders and outsiders, from a dynamic viewpoint (that is, accounting for different growth regimes and transition). The main finding is that successful transition does not seem to counterbalance the costs of exclusion for CEE. [JEL Code: F15, F21, F31, P31, P2, R13]

* Cinzia Alcidi, Ph. D. Candidate at the Department of Statistics, Stefano Manzocchi and Gianmarco I. P. Ottaviano, Professors of Economics in their Departments of Economics, are grateful to Paul Brenton and to the participants in seminars held at Ceps (Brussels) and Politecnico di Milano, for useful comments on early drafts of the paper.

N.B., the numbers in square brackets refer to the Bibliography at the end of the paper.

1. - Introduction

In the past decade, Western Europe has undergone a wave of so-called "deep" integration, while the transition countries of Central Eastern Europe have remained outside of an ever more integrated European Union (EU). A natural question to ask is whether the process leading, first, to the Internal Market and second, to the Economic and Monetary Union (EMU) has yielded an increase or a fall in inequality between the insiders and the outsiders (in our case, the countries of Central Eastern Europe (CEE)). A related issue is whether a successful transition process in CEE can provide relief against the possible costs of exclusion for the outsiders.

To answer these questions, we use a spatial model of endogenous growth and run numerical simulations on the consequences of such differential integration within the European economic area. Two aspects are analysed: first, we simulate the welfare effects of inclusion and exclusion for insiders and outsiders from a dynamic viewpoint (that is, accounting for different growth regimes associated with local or global R&D spillovers). Second, we analyse the impact of transition – modelled as an improvement in labour productivity – in this context. Transition can act as a counterbalancing effect, insofar as it provides the outsider with a larger domestic market.

We adopt a dynamic set-up where income and welfare measures can be sensibly defined (over an infinite horizon). This allows us to calculate real per capita income and welfare under several scenarios implying different rates of agglomeration and intertemporal preference, as well as different costs of innovation. We then look at the welfare impact of transition for both outsiders and insiders, providing a joint evaluation of the consequences of differential integration and successful economic reform. "Transition" is modelled as an improvement in overall productivity and, although the adopted definition of the reform process in CEE is perhaps naive, the simulations yield a number of interesting results. Transition always improves the relative welfare performance of the outsider *vis-a-vis* the insiders, while as far as absolute welfare changes are concerned, the outsider clearly benefits under global R&D spillovers. Under local spillovers the outsider only gains when the growth effects on welfare, which are negative in this case as transition leads to less agglomeration, are limited. However, transition can be detrimental for the integrated area (the EU) as long as CEE remains excluded: fully-fledged enlargement is a necessary – though perhaps not sufficient – condition for sharing the benefits of economic reform across all regions.

The paper is organised as follows. Section 2 briefly describes the analytical structure underlying the simulations, which is derived with a number of variations from a model by Manzocchi and Ottaviano [16]. This is a stylised model that does not claim to provide an adequate description of the complexity of actual economies; rather, it must be viewed as a heuristic device that can shed light on basic connections among economic variables. Within this framework, numerical simulations are useful to clarify some of the qualitative implications of policy changes, especially when we move towards a more complex model featuring asymmetry across regions and the process of transition in CEE. Section 3 presents selected simulations run within a three-region framework. The exercises concern income and welfare comparisons under alternative parameter sets and growth regimes, as well as the impact of transition on agglomeration and welfare. Section 4 provides concluding remarks with an eye on other strands of the literature on current European developments.

2. - The Underlying Analytical Structure: A Brief Description

The model is derived, with some variations, from Manzocchi and Ottaviano [16]. It relates to the literature on "new economic geography" (Krugman [13], [14]) which formalises the intuitive argument that, as frictional trade barriers due to the existence of protected national markets go down, one should expect firms in increasing-returns-to-scale sectors to relocate in the biggest national markets. Most results in this literature are derived in a simple setting in which firms can choose where to locate between two countries only.

Manzocchi and Ottaviano [16] address this issue in different terms. First, a three-country framework is adopted to study the effects of preferential integration on the international allocation of resources. Second, there is a step towards a dynamic setting in which resources are endogenously accumulated, rather than given forever: this is relevant when making welfare comparisons both for insiders and outsiders. Two main departures from the framework of Manzocchi and Ottaviano [16] are shown here, which in our view add more reality to the model although at the price of more complexity. First, we perform numerical simulations of the welfare impact of integration starting from an initial asymmetric situation, where two regions are already more integrated relative to the third one: this is different from Manzocchi and Ottaviano [16] where the effects of a process of preferential integration are evaluated starting from an initial symmetric situation. Second, we explicitely model the impact of "transition" on productivity, localisation and welfare, and perform a numerical analysis of the consequences of transition on discounted income levels in insiders and outsiders.

The model by Manzocchi and Ottaviano [16] consists of two sectors, three countries (or regions) and two factors, internationally immobile labour and freely mobile capital, which is employed where its return is higher. The general result is that, when regional integration occurs, returns to capital become higher within the integrated area with respect to the isolated country (the 'outsider'). This will cause capital to leave the outsider to be invested in the insiders. This flow of investment will increase (reduce) the number of factories in the insiders (outsider). The outsider will therefore suffer from 'delocalisation'. In the presence of local (or national) technological spillovers, this short-term location effect can also have relevant effects on the long-run rate of growth (as well as on welfare).

Here is a list of other main assumptions (see the Appendix for a more detailed exposition): *a)* there exist only two sectors, characterised respectively by perfect and monopolistic competition; *b)* trade costs and frictions only pertain to the monopolistic sector; *c)* capital only enters the production of the monopolistic sector, while the competitive good only requires labour; *d)* analytical results are derived under the assumption of initially symmetric countries, though this is clearly irrealistic in the case of West-East European relations; *e)* preferences are nested, with a higher Cobb-Douglas function incorporating a lower Dixit-Stiglitz function; *f)* capital accumulation is driven by the decision of firms to invest in innovation and the production of new blueprints (new varieties of the monopolistic good).

Concerning the geographical allocation of production factors, Manzocchi and Ottaviano [16] assume three identical countries with the same endowments of labour *(L)* and capital *(N/3)*. Labour supply is fixed, while the process of capital accumulation is briefly reviewed in Section 2.3 and in the Appendix. The supply side consists of two highly stylised sectors, where entry and exit are free.

2.1 The "Traditional" Sector

The first sector produces a homogeneous 'traditional' good with constant returns to scale (CRS) and perfect competition, using labor as the only input with a unit labor requirement equal to one. Furthermore, for analytical convenience, we assume no transaction costs of international trade in the traditional sector. This is clearly an oversimplification, but one that is commonly adopted in economic geography models; moreover, introducing trade costs in the traditional sector does not generally lead to qualitative different results provided they are lower than in the advanced sector (Fujita *et* AL. [9], Chapters 5 and 7).

Under these assumptions the traditional good will be priced at marginal cost. Given that only labor is used in its production and the unit input requirement is one, in each country the traditional good price will be equal to local wages. However free trade will ensure that the price of the traditional good, hence the wage rate, will be the same across countries as long as each country produces the traditional good. This will be the case if global demand of the traditional good cannot be satisfied by a single country alone which is henceforth assumed. Finally, by choosing the traditional good as the numeraire, the price of the traditional good and the wage will be equal to one in every country.

Of course, the last result is generally counterfactual and removes one of the relevant factors affecting firms' location choices (wage differentials across regions). However, this simplification is useful in order to focus on other factors, namely transaction costs and economies of scale, that seem more relevant in those capital-intensive industries that attract the bulk of international direct investment.

2.2 The "Advanced" Sector

The second sector supplies a horizontally differentiated 'advanced' good with increasing returns to scale (IRS) and monopolistic competition, using both labor and capital. Each variety of the differentiated good has a linear cost function (for further details, see Martin and Ottaviano [17], p.285): variable costs are paid in terms of labor with a unit input requirement equal to β. Fixed costs are paid in terms of capital whose unit input requirement is set to one so that the number of active firms in a given location is equal to the capital endowment. Since a unit of capital is required to produce each variety, but the scale of production is determined by the input of labor, we have increasing returns to scale in the production of each variety. Assuming zero costs of product differentiation is enough to ensure a one-to-one relation between varieties and firms (hence capital) in each country, namely all scale effects work through the number of available varieties as in most of the 'new geography' models (see for instance Fujita et AL. [9], p. 52).

International trade costs in the 'advanced' sector are modelled following Samuelson [21] as 'iceberg' costs: to sell a unit of the differentiated good from one country to another more than one unit have to be sent. This 'erosion' is due to the resources absorbed by tariffs, transport and other transaction costs (for instance, insurance and foreign exchange costs). Let $\tau > 1$ be the number of units to be sent for one unit to arrive from one insider to the other, and

$\tau' > 1$ from (to) a insider to (from) the outsider. It is as if $\tau-1$ ($\tau'-1$) units of the good melt away because of frictions: this is equivalent to assume that trade costs are paid in terms of the transported good.

2.3 *Localisation, Growth and Welfare: a Non-Technical Exposition*

Consumers in each of the three regions behave identically and devote constant shares of their expenditures to the traditional and the advanced good. Moreover, their utility is enhanced if they consume the largest possible number of varieties of the IRS good. Over time, capital accumulation is driven by the introduction of new varieties of the differentiated good, invented in a R&D sector. R&D is a costly, perfectly competitive activity that produces new capital using labour as the only input: as there exists a one-to-one correspondence between the units of capital and number of available varieties of the differentiated good, capital accumulation and innovation coincide. The unit cost of innovation depends on a constant (η) but is decreasing in the number of existing varieties in the whole economy (global spillovers) or in each region (local spillovers). As the total cost of innovation must be equal to the discounted flow of operating profits from the introduction of new varieties, operating profits in equilibrium are proportional to η, but also to the share of capital in the innovating regions under local spillovers. Welfare is defined as discounted per capita income, in real terms. Nominal per capita income consists of labour income and dividends due to the ownership of capital (all operating profits are distributed): as we will see, what is relevant in the model is the evolution of the deflator of nominal income in the different regions (the "exact" price index), which crucially depends on the localisation of advanced firms and the associated configuration of trade costs.

The working of the model is centered on the idea of preferential, or discriminatory, integration. This means that two of the three regions (the insiders) unilaterally decide to lower the trade costs (τ) between them (including tariffs, non-tariff barriers, foreign exchange costs, and others) while the costs of trading from the excluded to the integrated area, or viceversa, (τ') remain constant or decline less than τ. In our view this simple parameter adjustment summarises, although in a rough way, the developments in the European region during the last decade, when the integration process between the Northern and Southern members of the European Union has deepened with the completion of the Internal Market and the creation of the Monetary Union, while the transition countries of Central Eastern Europe have been excluded.

The consequences of preferential integration are far-reaching in this model. First, the localisation of advanced firms is affected: recall that trade costs only pertain to the advanced good, which is an extreme assumption but captures the idea that trade in oligopolistic, capital– and R&D-intensive sectors is overall more affected by trade barriers than trade in traditional manufactures (we neglect agricultural goods). When trade costs between two regions decrease (at least in relative terms), it becomes more convenient for advanced enterprises to locate there because the costs of exporting to any of the two declines while the cost of exporting to the excluded region (the outsider) stay constant (or decline to a lesser extent). This amounts to say that returns to capital will be higher in the integrating regions, as capital is only employed in the advanced sector; it is also internationally mobile at zero cost, hence capital will flow out of the outsider towards the insiders, and a new geographical distribution of the advanced firms will prevail with a higher share of firms in the insiders than before. As we will see, however, there are limits to this process of agglomeration, as part of the output of the advanced sector must be sold in the outsider's market (recall that workers are immobile, hence nominal income and demand stay constant in the three areas) hence it will be convenient for a number of firms to remain located there.

How does this affect the process of capital accumulation and welfare? Capital accumulation is unaffected if spillovers are global, as in this case the cost of innovation is invariant with the geographical distribution of advanced firms. On the contrary, if spillovers are local the cost of innovation declines in the insiders, all R&D activities move there (just a simplifying assumption) and capital accumulation and growth are fostered. As for welfare, one has to distinguish between residents in different regions. Residents in the insiders are positively affected in static terms, as their trade costs are reduced for two reasons: they pay less for their imports from the integration partner, and they import a larger share of the advanced goods from it as more firms have relocated there. For this last reason, the outsider is damaged (it imports more than before more from the insiders, and we assume for simplicity that τ' stays constant). The dynamic effects on welfare are the same for residents in each region: if spillovers are local, there is a negative effect on the value of outstanding capital and a positive effect on the rate of growth. With global spillovers, no dynamic effect of localisation on welfare occurs. Hence, welfare variations always benefit the insiders in relative terms: they either gain more or lose less than the outsider. Note that this amount to divergence in real per capita discounted income between insiders and outsiders.

How can transition affect these findings? If successful transition is modelled as a "neutral" increase in labour productivity across sectors, it amounts to an increase in the efficiency units associated with the labour force of the outsider. This has two effects. First, welfare rises in the outsider because workers are becoming more productive. Second, the dimension of the outsider's domestic market rises along the transition path, hence some of the re-localisation effect described above work in the opposite direction as more firms will find it convenient to move to the excluded region. If one combines the impact of transition with that of exclusion, the number of possible outcomes increases, and even more so if one distinguishes between global and local R&D spillovers. In the first case, transition has no effect on the growth rate though the re-localisation process; in the second case, the specific impact of transition on the growth rate is negative as the cost of innovation increases when part of the advanced sector moves into the outsider. Hence, transition has a twofold effect on welfare in the outsider: in static terms, it unambiguously increases per capita real income as import costs decrease, and in this sense the outsider gains in relative terms with respect to the insiders.

In dynamic terms, however, transition may either leave the growth rate unaffected (global spillovers) or lower it (local spillovers).

3. - Exclusion, Transition and Welfare: Simulation Results

A complete set of simulations concerning the impact of differential integration on the localisation of advanced firms, trade flows and foreign direct investment is presented in Alcidi and Manzocchi [21]. Here we focus on the welfare consequences for Central Eastern Europe of exclusion (from the EU) and transition towards a market economy. The parameter values adopted in this Section are chosen according to two criteria, to preserve the general balance of the simulations and to keep some parameters within a "realistic" range.

First, with one exception, we show the welfare simulations relative to initial asymmetric scenarios, as this is more realistic compared to the European situation at the beginning of the 1990s (relatively lower trade barriers within the EU). We ensure that the interplay of the parameter values yields: *a)* a realistic value of the real growth rate, ranging from zero to seven per cent under local R&D spillovers; *b)* a consistent ratio between the shares of national income accruing to wages and operating profits (the simulations yield a ratio of about five to one, but once the returns to human capital – not explicitly modelled – are included in the wage share); *c)* γ, the proportion of firms localised in each of the two insiders, less or equal to 0.5.

The elasticity of substitution among varieties of the differentiated good ranges from 2.5 to about 3, a value associated with strong market power but needed to keep the profit share reasonably high. A consumption share, α, of about 0.3 for the IRS good is often suggested in the "new economic geography" literature (see for instance Fujita *et* AL. [9]). Moreover, $\alpha \leq 1/3$ is a sufficient condition to avoid complete specialisation in the advanced sector of any of the three regions. This is a useful parameterisation to adopt, as complete specialisation in the advanced sector would mean that the wage rate in the specialising region is no longer tied to its level in the traditional sector (which is fixed and set equal to one for simplicity).

The rate of intertemporal preference (ρ) ranges between 0.06 and 0.15. A value of 0.06 is considered a benchmark reference both in the growth literature (Barro and Sala-i-Martin [3]) and in the literature on the welfare consequences of transition in Eastern Europe (see, for instance, Piazolo [20]), while the upper bound of 0.15 can be considered realistic especially for transition countries starting from low levels of per capita income. Exchange costs range from 15 to 45% of the f.o.b. value of the merchandise traded and are slightly biased towards the upper bound of the range reported in the literature (Fujita *et* AL. [9]; Martin and Ottaviano [17]), although recent surveys of trade costs are not inconsistent with such figures (Overman *et* AL. [19]). More information on trade costs in different industries can be found for instance in Forslid *et* AL. [8]. All we need to assume here is that labour intensive CRS industries are associated with lower trade barriers than capital intensive IRS sectors, where "barriers" include both tariff and non-tariff constraints (technical regulations being an important item under the last heading: see Brenton *et* AL. [4]). As far as the values of η, the cost of innovation, and L are concerned we found no clear references in the literature; hence, they are set in order to obtain a balanced outcome from the simulations. In particular, η ranges from 12 to 18 (approximately, as in Martin and Ottaviano [17]) and L from 8 to 11.

Table 1 reports the key findings of our welfare and growth simulations. We believe that the asymmetric case is the most interesting and realistic to investigate, as it corresponds to an initial condition in which the degree of integration of Central and Eastern Europe with the EU was much lower than the degree of integration within the EU. The first row of Table 1 provides the baseline asymmetric case for the six parameters, plus an identical value for the labour force in both the insiders (L) and the outsider (L^{TE}). Other columns provide the simulation model's outcome for the initial share of IRS industries in each insider (γ), global operating profits ($N\pi$), and the initial growth rate under local spillovers (g). The sum of labour incomes in the three regions is given by ($2L + L^{TE}$).

TABLE 1

WELFARE SIMULATIONS WITH OR WITHOUT TRANSITION EFFECTS

τ	τ'	σ	α	η	ρ	L	L^{TE}	γ	$N\pi$	g	dV	dV^*	dV/dV^*	dVL^{TE}	$dV{*}L^{TE}$	$dVL^{TE}/dv{*}L^{TE}$	$Diff$
1.25	1.45	2.5	0.32	20	0.1	11	11	0.445	4.7989	0.00	3.0796	-0.6625	–	2.9352	-0.5521	–	2.4994
–	–	–	–	15	–	–	–	0.445	4.6552	0.038	4.3204	0.5783	7.4709	4.0832	0.6163	6.6253	3.3325
–	–	–	–	–	0.15	–	–	0.445	4.8708	0	1.7428	-0.7519	–	1.6698	-0.6597	–	1.4811
–	–	–	–	–	0.06	9	9	0.445	3.7147	0.05	9.8446	3.6078	2.6766	9.1198	3.5031	2.6033	7.5740
–	–	2.9	–	10	–	–	–	0.411	3.1401	0.07	6.7909	2.5836	2.6285	6.1809	2.4980	2.4743	8.2005
1.4	–	–	–	15	–	–	–	0.354	3.2699	0.017	5.6484	0.4541	12.439	5.2986	0.5380	9.8490	3.2600
1.15	1.15	–	–	–	–	–	–	0.333	3.2772	0.013	27.058	15.0213	1.8013	26.317	14.7073	1.7894	6.1947
–	1.5	–	–	–	–	11	–	0.500	3.620	0.06	3.7973	0.0	–	3.4033	0.1924	17.7333	5.3257

Four measures of welfare change are provided, namely dV and dV^* in the case of preferential integration without transition, dVL^{TE} and dV^*L^{TE} in the case of joint preferential integration and transition. All these measures are computed under the assumption of local R&D spillovers; the associated equations are discussed in the *Appendix* and reported in Table 2. The measures dV and dV^* are the derivatives of welfare (that is, logarithmic real discounted income) with respect to a decrease in trade costs within the integrated area, for the insiders and the outsider respectively[1].

In the first row of Table 1 we can see that the initial growth rate associated with the particular parameter configuration is zero, hence there are no positive dynamic welfare effects associated with initial asymmetry. As trade barriers are further lowered across insiders, static effects tend to prevail and welfare changes are positive for the insiders and negative for the outsider. As we move one row down, we observe that a lower value for the cost of innovation ($\eta = 15$) raises the growth rate to almost 4%, and this has favourable welfare consequences in all regions. In this case, both insiders and outsiders gain from further integration in, say, Western Europe, and this means that dynamic gains outweigh static losses in the excluded area. Nevertheless, the outsider loses in relative terms, as the ratio of dV to dV^* is much larger than one: hence, we observe real income divergence as a consequence of preferential integration. A higher rate of intertemporal preference (ρ equal to 15% in row three of the Table) reduces the growth rate, as *ceteris paribus* less resources are devoted to innovation: again, the outsider loses in absolute terms from discriminatory integration. A much lower ρ (6%), by contrast, generates a growth rate of 5% and considerably reduces the gap between dV and dV^* (from about seven to two and a half times)[2].

If we move to a slightly more competitive scenario for the "advanced" industry (row five of the Table), which is associated

---

[1] The complete expressions for the welfare measures are provided in Table 2 in the Appendix.

[2] Adopting L equal to 9 instead of 11 does not significantly affect the simulation results.

with a higher elasticity of substitution among varieties (σ) and lower innovation costs ($\eta = 10$), the growth rate rises to 7%, as less agglomeration (represented by a smaller γ) is more than compensated by the decrease in the costs of innovation. Due to the fall in the value of existing capital, welfare gains are reduced in both regions, but their ratio is barely changed at about 2.6. Larger initial trade costs within the integrated area (from 25 to 40% of the *f.o.b.* value of merchandise trade: see row six of the Table) yield a lower γ and this has a negative impact on the initial growth rate (which is reinforced by higher innovation costs). In this case, lower barriers to trade across the insiders have a strong impact on re-localisation, and this severely damages the outsider, as the ratio of dV to dV^* rises to more than 12 times.

In general, our simulations show that welfare is promoted in the outsider, and divergence with the insiders is limited, when the conditions for higher growth are fulfilled. This is non-trivial if we consider that they include lower trade costs within the integrated area and less competitive conditions in the IRS sector. The final simulation runs explore two extreme cases: row seven of the Table shows a symmetric initial situation where trade costs are low enough that even a small growth rate of about 1% generates enough dynamic gains to outweigh the static losses for the outsider (recall that these losses are due to an increase in the volume of import upon which tariff and other border costs are imposed). As a consequence, the welfare derivative ratio is rather small (less than two). Finally, in row eight of the Table we impose a two-fold asymmetry (both in trade costs and economic size L) and get an extreme value for γ, which corresponds to the complete agglomeration of the "advanced" sector in the integrated area. In this case, a reduction in trade costs between the insiders leads to static benefits for them, due to lower "iceberg" costs, but does not affect the outsider.

Let us now move to the columns headed with dVL^{TE} and dV^*L^{TE}, which show the sum of the derivatives of welfare with respect to a decrease in trade costs within the integrated area and a simultaneous rise in labour productivity in the outsider, respectively for the insiders and the outsider (still with the assumption of local R&D spillovers). Recall that, under our definition of "transition", a rise in labour productivity in the outsider has two effects. First, it directly affects income and welfare in the outsider. Here we assume that "transition" is also associated with a catching-up effect that raises the growth rate in the excluded region. Second, successful economic reform leads to an enlargement of the domestic market in the excluded area[3]. However, the second channel might have a negative impact on welfare under local R&D spillovers, since it leads to a reduction in γ, and hence ceteris paribus a fall in the growth rate.

Our simulations show that welfare changes in the insiders are always lower under the joint assumption of preferential integration and transition compared to the simple integration case (compare dV and dVL^{TE} under all parameter sets). This is not surprising, as transition brings no direct benefits to the insiders while it subtracts a share of advanced firms from their territory. As for the outsider, in five out of eight cases transition has a positive impact on welfare relative to the case of just integration (compare dV^* and dV^*L^{TE}). This is interesting, as it shows that in the area excluded from regional integration, the static benefits of enhanced labour productivity and of a larger share of advanced industries located in the outsider's territory, plus the catching-up effect, tend to prevail over the dynamic costs of lower agglomeration.

Finally, one has to recall that the trade-off between static benefits and dynamic costs of transition only occurs under local R&D spillovers. Under global spillovers, the rates of innovation and growth do not depend on γ, hence the growth rate does not change with agglomeration or transition. Moreover, the model predicts that the growth rate is always larger under global R&D spillovers (see the Appendix). The last column of Table 1 (labelled Diff.) provides the positive differential in welfare levels which has to be added to the discounted utility of both insiders (V) and outsiders (V^*) in the case of global spillovers, and which is invariant with respect to the hypotheses of deeper integration and transition. Of

---

[3] The complete expressions for these welfare measures are provided in the Appendix.

course the question of whether local or global R&D spillovers are a better approximation to reality is highly debated (Overman *et* AL., 2001, for a recent update).

We have seen that transition may offer the outsider (CEE, in our case) a partial antidote against exclusion from the integrated area (the EU). This is always the case under global spillovers and occurs rather frequently under local spillovers. However, in our simulations the absolute size of the welfare benefits associated with transition appears limited with respect to the impact of preferential integration, whilst the relative gains of the outsider (the fall in the extent of divergence, compare dVL^{TE}/dV^*L^{TE} with dV/dV^*) rely more on the reduction in dVL^{TE} *vis-a-vis* dV. In other words, transition slightly improves the outcome for the outsider, in terms of the localisation of advanced firms and welfare, but at the price of an income loss for the insiders. This situation is clearly inefficient, as one can check that the "transition loss" incurred by the insiders (dV minus dVL^{TE}) is always equal to or larger than the "transition gain" of the outsiders (dV^*L^{TE} minus dV^*). In other words, the model seems to suggest that the EU should not support transition (under local spillovers), due to the negative consequences of de-localisation and rising trade costs.

This sounds odd, as one would expect the EU to support transition in the excluded regions of Central and Eastern Europe. The reason why the opposite may hold in this model is that the exclusion of CEE from deeper integration in the EU generates a sort of "anti-transition" incentives in Western Europe. This result provides a further economic motivation for the decision of the EU of implementing a asymmetric phasing-out of tariff barriers *vis-a-vis* CEE during the 1990s, that is in the period when deeper integration in Western Europe was under way. More precisely, the *Europe Agreements* signed by the EU and the candidate countries in the first half of the 1990s established that the EU would have unilaterally lowered its tariffs *vis-a-vis* CEE (except in some sensitive sectors such as agricolture and textiles), so that the trade costs τ' would have partly followed the decreasing trend displayed by τ favouring localisation in Central Eastern Europe.

A superior solution for the outsider's welfare would have clearly been to fully enter the preferential trade agreement (Single Market included), which would have substantially reduced its trade costs and enhanced its welfare especially under global spillovers. Notice that – under global innovation spillovers – EU enlargement can be a better strategy for the insiders as well: in this case, a reduction in trade costs τ' to the same level of τ slightly increases welfare in the insiders while substantially improving the former outsider's condition. Under global spillovers, trade costs *vis-a-vis* CEE would be reduced in the EU, while CEE would gain both from lower trade costs and from re-localisation of firms[4]. In order to accomplish this, however, fully-fledged EU enlargement and global spillovers are required. If only partial integration of CEE with the EU is implemented (τ' smaller but still larger than τ), we could find that re-localisation to CEE and the rise in the import volume of advanced goods in the EU increase global trade costs in Western Europe, thus undermining its support for an extension of the integrated area. Once fully-fledged EU enlargement is accomplished, moreover, there are no reasons why the EU should not encourage transition in CEE as economic reform in these countries would bring about a larger domestic market, and consumers in each of the three integrated regions would benefit from a wider product variety, regardless of where advanced firms were located[5].

4. - Concluding Remarks

Using numerical simulations, we analyse the impact of preferential integration and transition on the localisation of economic activities, trade specialisation, capital flows and welfare in those regions included in, and those excluded from, a trade and monetary agreement. As Europe has undergone a decade of intense in-

---

[4] Under local spillovers, however, *re*-localisation to CEE would lower the global growth rate hence welfare calculations must take into account such dynamic effects as well.

[5] Again, this occurs under global spillovers.

tegration on its Western side, while at the same time the Central Eastern transition economies have remained excluded from the EU, a natural question to ask is whether these phenomena have led to more or less regional inequality.

Following Manzocchi and Ottaviano [16], we find that preferential integration leads to a re-location of advanced enterprises and of capital from the outsider region (Central Eastern Europe) to the EU, and that trade specialisation in the excluded area shifts towards "traditional" CRS products that are relatively labour intensive. Larger import volumes of the advanced good have negative welfare consequences for the outsider, as its trade costs increase (static welfare effect). In the presence of local innovation spillovers, agglomeration is however conducive to economic growth, and this raises welfare in both regions. Adding up the static and dynamic effects, welfare is likely to increase in CEE as a consequence of EU integration, although we provide some simulations where the opposite happens.

Notice however that, even if it gains in absolute welfare terms from the creation of an integrated area, the outsider often loses in relative terms with respect to the members of the economic and monetary union. This is true in real-income terms, and has potentially heavy consequences as it suggests that piece-wise integration generates divergence between insiders and outsiders. This in turn makes the future accession of an outsider more problematic, as further enlargements could involve large redistributions of income and welfare between old insiders and newcomers.

We also look at the rate of growth implicit in the different scenarios, and at the impact of "transition" – modelled as an improvement in overall productivity – on localisation, trade and investment. Although the adopted definition of the transition process is naive, the simulations yield interesting results, for instance that the outsider reduces its relative welfare gap *vis-a-vis* the insiders. However, in our simulations the absolute size of the welfare benefits associated with transition appears limited with respect to the impact of preferential integration, while the relative gains of the outsider rely more on the welfare loss of the insiders. Thus, transition slightly improves the outsider's condition in terms of localisation of advanced firms and welfare, but at the price of an income loss for the insiders.

The lack of Western European support for transition in this model is related to the exclusion of CEE from the EU, which may generates "anti-transition" incentives in Western Europe. EU enlargement could allow for better strategies and outcomes for the outsider, but also for the insiders under some circumstances. For instance, under global innovation spillovers, a harmonisation of trade costs (τ' the same as τ) slightly increases welfare in the insiders while substantially improving the former outsider's condition. However, partial integration (τ' smaller but still larger than τ), could lead to firm re-location to CEE, a rise in the import volume of advanced goods in the EU and an increase global trade costs in Western Europe, thus undermining its support for an extension of the integrated area. With fully-fledged EU enlargement there is no reason why the EU should not encourage transition in CEE, since a larger regional market would be to the benefit of all.

Being focused on the consequences of "exclusion" from the EU, our contribution differs from the descriptive literature on the transition progress in CEE (see for instance Stern [22]; Nsouli [18]; EBRD [6]; Ferragina [7]) or the path towards EU accession (Temprano-Arroyo and Feldman [23]), and from analytical studies on the consequences of the Eastern enlargement. There are, however, analogies between some of these papers and our work. Baldwin *et* AL [2], Forslid *et* AL [8] and Lejour *et* AL [15] quantify the impact of a wider EU and agree that the economic benefits of enlargement would be much stronger in CEE than in Western Europe, something our model also suggests when τ' is reduced to the same level of τ. Forslid *et* AL [8] also calibrate the impact of economic reform in CEE, and find that the growth effects of transition are strong in Eastern Europe but modest in the West, thus providing a motivation for our catching-up assumption. Other interesting findings of Forslid *et* AL [8] are that transition draws resources out of the competitive sectors (including agriculture in their model), and that IRS industries are more than proportionally affected by a Hicks-neutral increase in productivity, something that our model also suggests. Most important, perhaps, they also conclude that integration in the EU and improved market access are key prerequisites for a successful transition.

Lejour *et* AL [15] find that industrial relocation is the main engine of gains from trade in an enlarged Europe, while Piazolo [20], in the context of Polish accession to the EU, highlights the negative implications of large discount rates for welfare in a transition economy (something we stress in Section 3). Lejour *et* AL [15] and Forslid *et* AL [8] calibrate multi-sector CGE models, while we use a two-sector simulation model of spatial endogenous growth, to draw some insights on the consequences of exclusion and successful transition for the countries of Central and Eastern Europe. We also suggest that welfare analysis — based on economic models of localisation, trade and growth — can be used to supplement more traditional political-economy approaches to EU enlargement (see for instance Heinemann [11]) in order to clarify potential obstacles, and solutions, along the path towards accession. For instance, we underline the costs of exclusion for CEE in terms of income divergence from the EU, hence the potential dangers of a delayed (or "sequential") enlargement process associated with relative income redistributions among the Western and Central-Eastern European regions. Furthermore we argue that, although successful transition can provide a partial remedy against the exclusion of CEE from the EU, it can damage the existing members of the European Union if enlargement is not accomplished, and that — under global innovation spillovers — fully-fledged enlargement looks a better strategy for both the outsider and the insiders.

1. - Preferences, Pricing and the Equilibrium Location of Firms

Consumers' instantaneous utility is of the nested-C.E.S. type (Dixit and Stiglitz [5]):

(1)

$$U = \log D^\alpha Y^{(1-\alpha)} \qquad D = \left[\sum_{i=1}^{N(t)} D_i^{\frac{\sigma-1}{\sigma}} \right]^{\frac{\sigma}{\sigma-1}}$$

where $\sigma > 1$ is the elasticity of substitution between any two varieties and the elasticity of demand for each variety of the advanced good, D_i is the consumption of the ith variety, D is the C.E.S. quantity index or aggregator, Y is the consumption of the traditional good and $0 < \alpha < 1$ is the share of expenditure devoted to the differentiated good.

Because of monopolistic competition the varieties of the differentiated good will be priced according to the standard mark-up rule over marginal costs (Helpman and Krugman [12]:

(2)

$$p = \frac{\beta\sigma}{\sigma - 1}$$

where p is the domestic price of any variety and we have used the fact that, as stated in the main text, the price of the traditional good (and, thus, the wage rate) is constant and equal to one in each country. With free entry and exit, profits have to be zero in equilibrium. Together with free international capital mobility, this determines the worldwide return to capital, say π, as the residual value of sales after labour costs (i.e. operating profits):

(3)

$$\pi = \frac{\beta x}{\sigma - 1}$$

where x is the scale of production, i.e., the output of each variety, which is therefore the same for all firms no matter where they are located.

In equilibrium the supply of each variety must equal its demand (inclusive of trade costs). For an insider this means:

(4)
$$x = \frac{\alpha(\sigma-1)}{\beta\sigma N}\left[\frac{(1+\delta)EL}{(1+\delta)\gamma+\delta'(1-2\gamma)}+\frac{\delta'EL}{2\delta'\gamma+(1-2\gamma)}\right]$$

where the two terms inside the brackets come respectively from insiders' and outsider's demand, $\delta \equiv \tau^{1-\sigma}$ and $\delta' = \tau'^{(1-\sigma)}$ are inverse functions of the trade costs, and $\gamma \equiv n/N$ is the share of advanced firms located in one of the identical insider countries. A similar condition holds for the outsider:

(4)'
$$x = \frac{\alpha(\sigma-1)}{\beta\sigma N}\left[\frac{2\delta'EL}{(1+\delta)\gamma+\delta'(1-2\gamma)}+\frac{EL}{2\delta'\gamma+(1-2\gamma)}\right]$$

Equations *(4)* and *(4)'* can be solved together for x and γ to find their equilibrium values. As to the scale of production (x), this yields:

(5)
$$x = \alpha L\frac{\sigma-1}{\beta\sigma}\frac{3E}{N}$$

which, given *(2)*, shows that global 'advanced' revenues (Npx) equal the 'advanced' share, α, of total world expenditures, $3LE$: that is $Npx=3\alpha LE$. Moreover, given *(3)*, it implies that the world rate of return on capital is $\pi = 3\alpha LE/(\sigma N)$. As to the equilibrium location of firms, the analytical solution of equations *(4)* and *(4')* yields:

(6)
$$\gamma = \frac{(1-2\delta'+\delta)-\delta'(1-\delta')}{3(1-2\delta'+\delta)(1-\delta')}$$

2. - Growth Regimes, Welfare and Transition

To analyse the implications for long-run growth, the analytical framework must be enriched to allow for ongoing capital accumulation. Manzocchi and Ottaviano [16] assume that the typical consumer maximises an intertemporal utility function, which is equal to the discounted flow of instantaneous utility *(1)*:

(7)

$$U = \int_0^\infty \log D(t)^\alpha Y(t)^{1-\alpha} e^{-\rho t} dt \qquad D(t) = \left[\sum_{i=1}^{N(t)} D_i(t)^{\frac{\sigma-1}{\sigma}} \right]^{\frac{\sigma}{\sigma-1}}$$

where, apart from the introduction of the time variable t and the rate of time preference ρ, the definitions of the other variables and parameters are the same as before.

Drawing on Grossman and Helpman [10], accumulation of capital is assumed to take place through R&D modelled as a costly, perfectly competitive activity that produces new capital using labour as the only input. Entry and exit are free in the R&D sector. The labour unit input requirement in R&D is η divided by N in the case of global spillovers, or divided by γN in the case of local spillovers.

This specification of the mechanics of accumulation does not affect the instantaneous ('short-run') dimension of the model hence all the above results apply. As to the solution of the dynamics, it can be noticed that this model is essentially a so-called *AK-model* and therefore jumps immediately to a steady growth path. Along this equilibrium path, both the global and the national capital stocks grow at a constant rate (g) and location (γ) does not change. Since all the future of this economy is embedded in the initial value of a unit of capital (v_0), to find g one has to solve the following system under the assumption of a constant growth rate of N:

(8)

$$v_0 = \int_0^\infty \pi e^{-\rho t} dt$$

(9)
$$v_0 = \frac{\eta}{\gamma N_0}$$

(10)
$$3EL = 3L + \frac{\rho\eta}{\gamma}$$

The first equation states that the value of a unit of capital is equal to the discounted flow of the operating profits of the corresponding firm. The second is the zero-profit condition in the R&D sector: the returns from and the cost of R&D have to be equal in equilibrium. The third equation states that total expenditure is equal to total factor permanent income. Together with *(3)* and *(5)*, these three equations imply that the equilibrium rate of growth of *N* is:

(11)
$$g = \frac{3L}{\eta}\frac{\alpha}{\sigma}\gamma - \left(\frac{\sigma - \alpha}{\sigma}\right)\rho$$

where γ is the equilibrium location of firms (see equation *(6)*). Note that equations *(9)*, *(10)* and *(11)* hold under local spillovers, while one has to set γ equal to 1 under global spillovers.

Equation *(11)* re-states a standard result (Grossman and Helpman [10]) according to which the equilibrium growth rate is increasing in the world stock of labour (3L), the expenditure share of the differentiated good (α) and the degree of increasing returns to scale (a negative function of σ as already argued), while it is decreasing in the cost of innovation (η) and the rate of time preference ρ.

As far as welfare analysis is concerned, the chosen welfare measure is the present value of indirect utility flows in an insider (*V*) or in the outsider (*V**). In steady state, instantaneous utility is equal to the logarithm of permanent factor incomes divided by the relevant ('exact') price indexes that correspond to the instantaneous utility function (equation *(1)*) (more on this in Manzocchi and Ottaviano [16]). Under local spillovers, if we differentiate V and V^* with respect to δ only, or to δ and L^{TE} jointly, four equations for the welfare changes in insiders *(13)* and *(13')* and outsiders *(14)* and *(14')* can be obtained (Table 2)[6].

The four terms on the right hand side of *(13)* are respectively: *(i)* the 'firm's value effect' by which relocation to the insiders in the presence of spillovers negatively affects the value of the initial stock of capital; *(ii)* a positive 'relocation effect' by which, for given prices, integration shifts firms towards the insiders decreasing their price indexes (while increasing that of the outsider); *(iii)* the 'growth effect' by which integration through relocation affects the speed of invention; and *(iv)* the (direct) 'trade cost effect' by which integration reduces the prices of imported varieties from the insider for a given spatial distribution of firms. The four terms have the same meaning in equation *(13')*, but as "transition" has a negative effect on agglomeration, the derivatives of γ with respect to preferential integration and to economic transition have opposite signs hence their sum can be positive or negative. By contrast, the (direct) 'trade cost effect' is identical to that in equation *(13)*.

In equation *(14)*, showing the welfare effects of exclusion for the outsider, the terms are respectively: *(i)* the firm's value effect; *(ii)* a negative relocation (or 'delocalisation') effect; (iii) the growth effect. The outsider is not directly affected by a transaction-cost reduction occurring between the insiders. The first three terms in equation *(14')* are the same as in equation *(14)*, provided one recalls that the derivatives of γ with respect to preferential integration and to economic transition have opposite signs hence their sum can be positive or negative. The fourth term in *(14')* is a catching-up effect that stems directly from economic transition in the outsider: as workers become more productive under successful reform, we assume the excluded region benefits from a positive growth edge *vis-a-vis* the insiders.

Finally, equation *(15)* provides the differential impact on wel-

---

[6] Equations *(13)* through *(14')* have been used to run the simulations reported in Table 1.

fare of the shift from local to global innovation spillovers: as g is larger under global spillovers, welfare is positively affected in the insiders as well as in the outsider. Besides, further integration, transition or enlargement have no consequences on the growth rate through γ.

TABLE 2

WELFARE DERIVATIVES

Insider
Integration effect under local spillovers:

(13)

$$dV = \frac{1}{\rho}\left\{ \frac{-\rho\eta}{(3L\gamma + \rho\eta)\gamma} \cdot \frac{\partial\gamma}{\partial\delta} + \frac{\alpha}{\sigma-1} \cdot \frac{(1+\delta-2\delta')}{(1+\delta-2\delta')\gamma + \delta'} \cdot \frac{\partial\gamma}{\partial\delta} + \right.$$

$$\left. + \frac{\alpha^2(2L+L^{TE})}{\rho\sigma\eta(\sigma-1)} \cdot \frac{\partial\gamma}{\partial\delta} + \frac{\alpha}{(\sigma-1)} \cdot \frac{\gamma}{\left[(1+\delta-2\delta')\gamma + \delta'\right]} \right\}$$

Integration and transition effects under local spillovers:

(13')

$$dVL_{TE} = \frac{1}{\rho}\left\{ \frac{-\rho\eta}{(3L\gamma + \rho\eta)\gamma} \cdot \left(\frac{\partial\gamma}{\partial\delta} + \frac{\partial\gamma}{\partial L^{TE}}\right) + \frac{\alpha}{\sigma-1} \cdot \frac{(1+\delta-2\delta')}{(1+\delta-2\delta')\gamma + \delta'} \cdot \right.$$

$$\left. \cdot \left(\frac{\partial\gamma}{\partial\delta} + \frac{\partial\gamma}{\partial L^{TE}}\right) + \frac{\alpha^2}{\rho(\sigma-1)} \cdot \frac{(2L+L^{TE})}{\sigma\eta} \cdot \left(\frac{\partial\gamma}{\partial\delta} + \frac{\partial\gamma}{\partial L^{TE}}\right) + \frac{\alpha}{(\sigma-1)} \cdot \frac{\gamma}{\left[(1+\delta-2\delta')\gamma + \delta'\right]} \right\}$$

Outsider
Exclusion effect under local spillovers:

(14)

$$dV^* = \frac{1}{\rho}\left\{ \frac{-\rho\eta}{(3L^{TE}\gamma + \rho\eta)\gamma} \cdot \frac{\partial\gamma}{\partial\delta} - \frac{\alpha}{\sigma-1} \cdot \frac{2(1-\delta')}{2(\delta'-1)\gamma+1} \cdot \frac{\partial\gamma}{\partial\delta} + \right.$$

$$\left. + \frac{\alpha^2}{\rho(\sigma-1)} \cdot \frac{(2L+L^{TE})}{\sigma\eta} \cdot \frac{\partial\gamma}{\partial\delta} \right\}$$

TABLE 2 *(cont.)*

WELFARE DERIVATIVES

Integration and transition effects under local spillovers:

(14')

$$dV * L_{\text{TE}} = \frac{1}{\rho} \left\{ \frac{-\rho\eta}{\left(3L^{TE}\gamma + \rho\eta\right)\gamma} \cdot \left(\frac{\partial\gamma}{\partial\delta} + \frac{\partial\gamma}{\partial L^{TE}}\right) - \frac{\alpha}{\sigma-1} \cdot \frac{2(1-\delta')}{2(\delta'-1)\gamma+1} \cdot \left(\frac{\partial\gamma}{\partial\delta} + \frac{\partial\gamma}{\partial L^{TE}}\right) + \right.$$

$$\left. + \frac{\alpha^2}{\rho(\sigma-1)} \cdot \frac{\left(2L + L^{TE}\right)}{\sigma\eta} \cdot \left(\frac{\partial\gamma}{\partial\delta} + \frac{\partial\gamma}{\partial L^{TE}}\right) + \frac{\alpha^2}{(\sigma-1)} \cdot \frac{\gamma}{\rho\sigma\eta} \right\}$$

Welfare Differential Moving from Local to Global Innovation Spillovers

(15)

$$Diff = \frac{1}{\rho} \cdot \frac{\alpha}{\rho(\sigma-1)} \left[\frac{\left(2L + L^{TE}\right)}{\eta} \cdot \frac{\alpha}{\sigma} \cdot (1-\gamma) \right]$$

BIBLIOGRAPHY

[1] ALCIDI C. - MANZOCCHI S., «Transition without Accession: The Effects of Differential Integration on Trade and Welfare in Europe», in BRENTON P. - MANZOCCHI S. (eds.), *Enlargement, Trade and Investment*, Cheltenham (UK), Edward Elgar, forthcoming, 2002.

[2] BALDWIN R. E. - FRANCOIS J. F. - PORTES R., «The Costs and Benefits of Eastern Enlargement: The Impact on the EU and Central Europe», *Economic Policy*, n. 24, 1997, pp. 127-170.

[3] BARRO R. – SALA-I-MARTIN X., *Economic Growth*, New York, McGraw-Hill, 1995.

[4] BRENTON P. - SHEEHY J. - VANCAUTEREN M., «Technical Barriers to Trade in the EU: Data, trends and Implications for Accession Countries», *Journal of Common Market Studies*, n. 30, 2001, pp. 143-156.

[5] DIXIT A. - STIGLITZ J., «Monopolistic Competition and Optimum Product Diversity», *American Economic Review*, vol. 67, n. 2, 1977, pp. 297-308.

[6] EBRD, *Transition Report 1999. Ten Years of Transition*, London, EBRD, 1999.

[7] FERRAGINA A., «Price vs. Quality Competition in Italy's Trade with CEECs», Roma, Università «Roma tre», *Working Paper*, n. 15, 2000.

[8] FORSLID R. - HAALAND J. - KNARVIK K.H.M. - MAESTAD O., «Integration and Transition. Scenarios for Location of Production and Trade in Europe», Foundation for Research in Economics and Business, Oslo, *Discussion Paper*, n. 13/99.

[9] FUJITA M. - KRUGMAN P. - VENABLES A., *The Spatial Economy: Cities, Regions and International Trade*, Cambridge (MA), MIT Press, 1999.

[10] GROSSMAN G. - HELPMAN E., *Innovation and Growth in the World Economy*, Cambridge (MA), MIT Press, 1991.

[11] HEINEMANN F., *The Political Economy of EU Enlargement and the Treaty of Nice*, mimeo, Mannheim, ZEW, 2000.

[12] HELPMAN E. - KRUGMAN P., *Market Structure and Foreign Trade*, Cambridge (MA), MIT Press, 1985.

[13] KRUGMAN P., *Geography and Trade*, Cambridge (MA), MIT Press, 1991.

[14] — —, «Increasing Returns and Economic Geography», *Journal of Political Economy*, n. 99, 1991, pp. 483-99.

[15] LEJOUR A. - DE MOOIJ R. - NAHUIS R., «EU Enlargement: Economic Implications for Countries and Industries», The Hague, CPB, *Document*, n. 11, 2001.

[16] MANZOCCHI S. – OTTAVIANO G.I.P., «Outsiders in Economic Integration: The case of a Transition Economy», *Economics of Transition*, n. 9, 2001, pp. 229-49.

[17] MARTIN P. – OTTAVIANO G.I.P., «Growing Location: Industry Location in Models of Endogenous Growth». *European Economic Review*, n. 43, 1999, pp. 281-302.

[18] NSOULI S.M., «A Decade of Transition: An Overview of the Achievements and Challengers», IMF, *Finance and Development*, Vol. 36, n. 2, 1999.

[19] OVERMAN H. - REDDING S. - VENABLES A., «The Economic Geography of Trade, Production and Income: A Survey of Empirics», Centre for Economic Policy Research, London, *Discussion Paper*, n. 2978, 2001.

[20] PIAZOLO D., «Welfare Effects versus Income Effects of Poland's Integration into the European Union», *Kiel Working Paper*, n. 940, 1999.

[21] SAMUELSON P., «The Transfer Problem and Transport Costs, II: Analysis of Effects of Trade Impediments», *Economic Journal*, n. 64, 1954, pp. 264-89.

[22] STERN N., «The Future of the Transition», EBRD, *Working Paper, n.* 30, 1998.

[23] TEMPRANO-ARROYO H. - FELDMAN R.A., «Selected Transition and Mediterranean Countries: an Institutional Primer on EMU and EU Accession», *Economics of Transition*, Vol. 7, n. 3, 1999, pp. 741-806.

Moving to Central-Eastern Europe: Fragmentation of Production and Competitiveness of the European Textile and Apparel Industry*

Salvatore Baldone - Fabio Sdogati - Lucia Tajoli[1]

Politecnico di Milano

La frammentazione internazionale della produzione verso paesi a basso costo del lavoro è la strategia seguita dai paesi industrializzati in risposta alla crescente pressione competitiva esercitata nei settori tradizionali dai paesi emergenti. Noi stimiamo l'entità della riduzione dei costi di produzione di cui le imprese Ue del settore tessile-abbigliamento beneficiano grazie a questa pratica. Confrontando i prezzi dell'abbigliamento prodotto attraverso il perfezionamento in Europa centro-orientale con quelli dell'abbigliamento proveniente dai produttori di aree emergenti, concludiamo che è proprio attraverso la frammentazione internazionale della produzione verso i Paesi dell'Europa Centro-Orientale che le imprese Ue di un settore tradizionale possono mantenere le proprie posizioni competitive sui mercati internazionali.

International fragmentation of production towards some low labor-cost countries is the strategy followed by industrialized countries to counter the growing competitive pressures from other low

---

* A preliminary version of this paper was presented at the 2nd Annual Conference of the European Trade Study Group, Glasgow, 15-17 September 2000. The authors gratefully acknowledge financial support from the MURST (Cofinanziamento al programma di ricerca scientifica di rilevante interesse nazionale *L'allargamento dell'Unione Europea ai Paesi dell'Europa Centro-Orientale: specializzazione commerciale, delocalizzazione produttiva e loro effetti sulle economie dell'Unione*, 1999).
[1] Salvatore Baldone is Professor of Economics, Fabio Sdogati is Associate Professor of Economics and Lucia Tajoli is Associate Professor of Economics.

N.B., the numbers in square brackets refer to the Bibliography at the end of the paper.

labor-cost countries. Using custom data on Outward Processing Trade by EU textile and apparel firms we estimate the cost saving associated with Outward Processing in the Central and Eastern European countries relative to a counterfactual scenario in which firms do not take advantage of such practice. The process will continue at an increasing pace, it possibly being, along with product-quality upgrading, the only way for the EU apparel industry to stay competitive on world markets. [JEL Code: F14, F15]

1. - Introduction

There appears to be a widespread consensus in the economic profession about «emerging» countries gradually displacing industrialized countries on their own markets as suppliers of labor-intensive goods. The dynamics of market shares in the US and in Europe is claimed to support such beliefs, leading to the conclusion that "traditional" industrial countries are slowly but surely losing their comparative advantage in the production of such goods.

In this paper we take a different stand on both theoretical and empirical grounds. On the theoretical level our hypothesis is that the growing competitive pressure typically coming from low labor-cost countries in South-East Asia has certainly eroded long-established comparative advantages in the production of final goods. This competition forced industrialized countries to re-design modes and patterns of production and international sales of labor-intensive goods through a strategy combining a relatively higher productivity at home with lower labor costs abroad, that is by fragmenting production internationally, which is generating increasingly large trade flows among countries. Because of the relevance of such peculiar trade flows, on the empirical level we claim that aggregate trade data (combining final trade flows and flows of goods to be processed abroad) used to support the loss-of-comparative-advantage thesis are misleading, in that aggregate data hide the true, new nature of large shares of world trade especially in labor-intensive goods.

International fragmentation of production, defined as the spreading of a production process over production sites located in different countries, will replace an integrated technology, where all production segments take place within the same location, if this allows producers to take advantage of differences in technologies and factor prices among countries, thereby obtaining a reduction in costs by setting up an international production network (Jones and Kierzkowski [9]). Cost savings arise as long as countries' differences are large enough to offset any additional cost incurred with fragmentation such as transport costs, or additional co-ordination costs. In this paper we look for evidence supporting the hypothesis that international fragmentation of production is a cost-saving technology with respect to integrated production. More formally, we seek to estimate the size of the cost savings associated with international fragmentation of production, that is, the gain in cost competitiveness due to fragmentation.

Of course, a cost-reducing strategy may lead to different ways in which international delocalization of production takes place. In the apparel industry, for instance, pre-assembling phases of the production process are skill intensive or have become relatively capital intensive due to growing automation, whereas the assembling ones, which contribute most to overall value added, are relatively labor intensive. Such differential features of the production process make it both technically and economically convenient to delocalize abroad the assembling segments of the production process only, under the condition that the final consumer perceives that the firm originating the process still retains control of the final-product quality, to be granted for instance through the persistence of the original national trademark. It is for these reasons that international delocalization of apparel production takes «naturally» on the form of international fragmentation of the production process in terms of Outward Processing (OP)[2]. *Viceversa*, the textile industry, being characterized by high levels of production automation in most segments of the production process, will

---

[2] Which does not imply that other forms of international delocalization of production are not observed and relevant. For example, one is foreign direct investment. Through proprietary control of the foreign subsidiary, this form allows for a better monitoring of the organization and actual carrying-out of the production process, aiming at adequately high qualitative standards of the finished product.

show a «natural» tendency to delocalize abroad the entire production process: foreign direct investment and international subcontracting appear to be more convenient ways to delocalize the
activities of this industry.

Whatever their forms, it is questionable whether it was «the
market» to supply such strategies. For instance, the European
Union (EU) began long ago to offer incentives, especially to firms
in the textile and apparel (TA) industry, to adopt such strategies,
stating very explicitly that the reason for such regulations was to
restore the competitiveness of the TA industry in the Union[3]. This
was accomplished by making even more favorable the already existing regulations on Outward Processing Trade (OPT)[4] when they
are applied to trade of textiles and apparel. It is for all these reasons that we chose to produce our estimates for the textile and
apparel industry.

A growing body of literature is pointing out that Central-Eastern European Countries (CEECs)[5] have become a preferred location by manufacturers of most EU member countries that wish to
delocalize production activities outside the boundaries of the
Union. Prominent among the industries most and longest affected by such process is TA, an industry heavily subject to the growing competitive pressures coming from low labor-cost countries.
There are several reasons that qualify the CEECs as a particularly appealing area toward which re-localize TA production activities (Graziani [7]). First comes the large labor-cost differential between EU and CEECs, a differential we will show to be not en-

---

[3] In the foreword to European Community Regulation no. 3036/94 issued by
the EU Council on December 8, 1994, which institutes the economic regime of
outward processing for some textile and apparel products re-imported into the EU
after being processed abroad, it is indeed stated that this Regulation was adopted considering that «the policy followed by the Community is intended in particular to enable the textile and clothing industry to adapt to the conditions of international competition; whereas these new outward processing arrangements
must fit in with efforts to increase the competitiveness of Community industry...».

[4] OPT is nothing other than international shipments for the purpose of processing abroad and consequent re-import. The two related flows of trade, exports
of commodities to be processed abroad and subsequent imports of the processed
goods, are called temporary exports and re-imports, respectively.

[5] For the purposes of this paper we identify as CEECs Bulgaria, Czech Republic, Hungary, Poland, Romania and Slovakia.

tirely offset by productivity differentials. Indeed, EU member countries with the longest and most intense tradition of recourse to the practice of international fragmentation of production are those with traditionally higher labor costs[6]. Secondly, geographic and cultural proximity with the EU allows for low transportation costs and quick turnovers of materials and finished products. Thirdly, there exists in Central-Eastern Europe in general, and in Hungary and Poland in particular, a long-standing tradition in the production of clothing, as there is one in the production of textiles in the case of the former Czechoslovakia. Such tradition contributes to make locally available productive capacity and skilled labor. Finally, EU manufacturers can reasonably look at the CEECs as potentially interesting markets.

In this paper we supply an estimate of the overall cost savings accruing to EU firms delocalizing segments of their production processes to the CEECs. To the best of our knowledge there have been as yet no specific attempt to estimate the overall cost savings obtained through outward processing relative to the alternative hypothesis that all phases of the production process were to be kept «in house». Yet, a measure of such savings is crucial if one is to gauge the gain accruing to EU firms in terms of price competitiveness *vis-à-vis* the competitors from low-wage countries, especially from Asia. To compute such estimate[7], we follow these steps: *a)* from the value of apparel re-imports from the CEECs to the EU we subtract temporary exports of textile and apparel from the EU to the CEECs, obtaining an estimate of value added in the CEECs; *b)* we assume that all value added in the CEECs is due to labor, as very small amounts of capital or material value are embodied in the good apart from those originally shipped from the EU; *c)* dividing by productivity levels in the CEECs and in the EU gives the number of workers needed to produce that value added in the

---

[6] Within the EU, these are mostly the German mark-area countries, which did not seek to offset the loss in cost competitiveness through nominal exchange rate realignments.

[7] To conduct this exercise, we use data on outward processing trade provided by Eurostat (Comext database), which is the only official EU source on EU outward processing.

two areas respectively; *d)* we use wage rates for the CEECs and the EU to determine how much more it would have cost to EU producers to produce in-house the relevant value added. Through this methodology we can compare actual TA prices of EU firms to those obtained from a counterfactual scenario where costs are those incurred by firms were they not to take advantage of legislation allowing them to internationally delocalize at least the labor-intensive phases of their production process.

The paper is organized as follows. In Section 2 we supply general, quantitative evidence about the size of international fragmentation, to show the importance and the characteristics of this production strategy. The aim of Section 3 is to show that OPT with the CEECs involves not only low-quality garments, as can be argued on the basis of export prices for Germany and Italy. Sections 4 and 5 are the core of the paper. In Section 4 we produce estimates of labor costs and productivity differentials among all the countries in our sample, the goal being to determine the extent to which labor cost differentials may be offset by productivity differentials. The methodology adopted is reported in Appendix 3. Estimated factor price and productivity differentials are then used in Section 5 to estimate the cost saving associated with fragmentation; this result is then used as a basis to further estimate the price competitiveness gain associated with the practice *vis-à-vis* Asian and other low-labor cost competitors. The final Section supplies some concluding remarks.

2. - European Union's OPT and the Roles of Germany and Italy

Data reported in Table 1 show that, beginning in 1989 and until 1996 at least, the TA industry has been absorbing a growing share of the OPT originated within the EU and directed to the rest of the world[8]. Indeed, while OPT grew in the aggregate at a dou-

---

[8] Data on OPT are collected at a very high level of merchandise disaggregation since 1988 at the EU member country level, the reason for data collection about this special type of trade being that goods re-imported after processing abroad are subject to customs treatment particularly advantageous relative to final imports. The

ble-digit Average Annual Growth Rate (AAGR)[9], the share of the TA industry grew from 29% in 1989 to 35% in 1996 when measured through temporary exports and from 34% to 47% when measured through re-imports. One can notice the prevailing weight of textiles among the temporary exports, though it has fallen over time from a ratio of five to one in 1989 to a ratio of four to one in 1996. Data for 1997 would appear to show a turning point relative to the pattern just identified, given that for the first time in that year temporary exports of TA and their share fall at the same time that the annual rate of growth of TA re-imports, already declining in 1996, falls to slightly more than zero in 1997. Actually, though it may well be that the rate of growth of OPT fell in 1997, this occurrence is largely due to a substantial shrinking of this type of trade as a statistical, rather than economic, phenomenon[10].

---

data set thus assembled allows for the monitoring of the international sequel of the production process, because the re-imported goods must clearly contain the goods originally shipped abroad for processing if they are to be admitted to the customs preferential treatment. Being collected to register a very specific type of international trade of goods, OPT data necessarily underestimate the extent of international fragmentation of production in its general definition (see footnote 2). Yet, we believe that it is primarily using this type of data that one can pinpoint features and extent of that phenomenon, for what OPT data capture is the extent to which previously in-house held production processes are disintegrated internationally in a manner that allows the originator of the outward trade to control the whole production process according to its own specifications. Due to the intensity and the rapid growth of the phenomenon, OPT data have recently been the object of careful monitoring and analysis, especially with respect to TA data. See, for instance, NAUJKOS P. - SCHMIDT K.D. [10] and BALDONE S., SDOGATI F. - ZUCCHETTI A. [3] about OPT in general and OETH [12], UNECE [14], GRAZIANI G. [7], and BALDONE S. - SDOGATI F. - TAJOLI L. [1] about the TA industry especially. Their general aim being to seek evidence of patterns of production and trade specialization of the countries involved, such studies have been generally confined to the dimensional and structural characteristics of the phenomenon. Nonetheless, they have shown that OPT represents the preponderant share of total TA trade flows between the EU and the CEECs. Here we only report evidence on extra-EU Outward Processing Trade since data on intra-EU OPT are no longer collected since 1 January 1993.

[9] The Annual Average Growth Rate g is computed as the constant rate of growth coherent with the two extremes of the time series, that is: $V_{1997} = V_{1988}(1+g)^9$.

[10] Indeed, beginning January 1, 1997 most of the tariff and trade restrictions imposed by the EU on final imports from the CEECs are no longer into effect. Since it was the presence of such trade restriction that made it profitable for EU firms to have their imports registered as re-imports (after temporary exports for reason of processing), the removal of such barriers has made unnecessarily costly for them to access the regime. It follows that data on OPT are no longer a proxy for a substantial part of outward processing originating from EU firms. For more empirical evidence and a detailed discussion of it see BALDONE S. - SDOGATI F. - TAJOLI L. [1].

TABLE 1

EU-12 OPT WITH EXTRA-EU COUNTRIES (MLN ECU)

	1988	1989	1990	1991	1992	1993	1994	1995	1996	1997	aagr
TEMPORARY EXPORTS											
Extra-EU countries											
Textile and apparel	1273.66	1581.43	1890.46	2256.24	2626.38	3248.17	3693.21	4188.10	4552.77	4490.57	0.15
Textiles	1081.11	1348.52	1605.73	1882.66	2196.62	2690.27	2987.96	3384.31	3601.73	3528.80	0.14
Apparel	192.55	232.92	284.73	373.58	429.76	557.90	705.23	803.79	951.04	961.77	0.20
Total	3864.61	5364.61	5936.21	7484.63	8292.23	9628.52	11032.21	12069.61	13009.82	14035.55	0.15
TA share	0.33	0.29	0.32	0.30	0.32	0.34	0.33	0.35	0.35	0.32	0.00
CEECs											
Textile and Apparel	463.35	547.87	739.19	1056.99	1450.03	1904.53	2237.61	2599.45	2855.05	2702.01	0.22
Textiles	389.68	462.41	619.42	864.39	1185.57	1547.36	1798.92	2062.32	2215.07	2064.88	0.20
Apparel	73.67	85.47	119.78	192.60	264.46	357.17	438.69	537.13	639.98	637.13	0.27
Total	647.39	787.68	1077.51	1631.74	2389.58	3016.36	3683.57	4171.97	4644.16	4695.12	0.25
TA share	0.72	0.70	0.69	0.65	0.61	0.63	0.61	0.62	0.61	0.58	-0.02
Textiles: share over final exports	1.16	1.15	1.60	1.73	1.83	1.96	1.70	1.57	1.53	0.94	-0.02
Apparel: share over final exports	1.21	0.81	0.82	0.90	1.07	1.27	1.22	1.33	1.32	0.93	-0.03
CEECs/extra-EU in TA temp. exp.	0.36	0.35	0.39	0.47	0.55	0.59	0.61	0.62	0.63	0.60	0.06
RE-IMPORTS											
Extra-EU countries											
Textile and Apparel	1762.95	2173.47	2664.62	3241.48	3616.55	4243.69	5074.00	5745.17	6206.67	6219.00	0.15
Textiles	30.13	35.80	48.88	57.61	67.65	92.60	130.98	160.60	174.35	150.43	0.20
Apparel	1732.82	2137.67	2615.74	3183.86	3548.90	4151.09	4943.02	5584.58	6032.32	6068.57	0.15
Total	4593.40	6330.12	7118.87	8604.02	9488.78	10019.04	11949.56	12675.47	13338.83	14677.13	0.14
TA share	0.38	0.34	0.37	0.38	0.38	0.42	0.42	0.45	0.47	0.42	0.01
CEECs											
Textile and apparel	658.77	779.39	989.87	1437.88	1916.62	2456.39	3078.77	3568.53	3866.54	3606.98	0.21
Textiles	2.10	3.84	15.15	23.14	32.45	47.31	80.92	100.04	127.68	94.60	0.53
Apparel	656.67	775.55	974.73	1414.74	1884.18	2409.07	2997.84	3468.49	3738.86	3512.39	0.20
Total	1034.64	1248.61	1541.72	2182.07	2997.97	3597.11	4425.18	4932.79	5368.38	5328.28	0.20
TA share	0.64	0.62	0.64	0.66	0.64	0.68	0.70	0.72	0.72	0.68	0.01
Textiles: share over final imports	0.01	0.01	0.05	0.07	0.08	0.12	0.15	0.17	0.25	0.12	0.36
Apparel: share over final imports	1.50	1.75	2.01	2.43	2.42	2.81	3.52	3.97	4.06	2.04	0.03
CEECs/extra-EU in TA re-imports	0.37	0.36	0.37	0.44	0.53	0.58	0.61	0.62	0.62	0.58	0.05

Source: EUROSTAT, COMEXT.

Data on EU-CEECs trade, reported in the lower part of Table 1, bear witness to the growing importance of the CEECs as processing countries for goods originated in the EU in general[11], and for the TA industry in particular. When measured through the value of re-imports, the share of the industry's products processed in the CEECs over products processed in the rest of the world increased from 36% in 1989 to 62% in 1996, with a sudden acceleration in 1991 and later slowing-down. Temporary exports exhibit a similar dynamic pattern, with the CEECs share growing from 35% in 1989 to a 63% in 1996[12].

Finally, Table 1 allows for an estimate of the importance of processing trade for the CEECs: EU re-imports of apparel, that is, the single most important component of trade, amounted to about four times the value of final imports in 1996, and to two times in 1997.

Data in Table 2 show that OPT originating from Germany, Italy, France and the Netherlands sum up to roughly 90% of overall OPT between the EU-12[13] and the CEECs. Striking are: first, that the share of Germany-based firms over the total has been systematically above 70%, with a hint to decrease only in the last two years of the sample; and second, the fast-rising role of Italy-based firms, whose share over total re-imports grows from about 2% in 1991 to 15% in 1997, a path leading Italy to be among the largest EU-12 originators of processing trade, second only to Germany. It is also worth noting that Italy is the only country exhibiting a positive growth rate for both temporary exports ant re-imports even in 1997[14].

But, how relevant is OPT relative to domestic production in the originating countries? Evidence from Table 3 shows that countries such as Germany and the Netherlands exhibit a larger use of OPT relative to national production than countries that attempted to re-

---

[11] The average annual growth rate of total EU re-imports from the CEECs outgrows the twin rate calculated for re-imports from the rest of the world by more than six percentage points.

[12] In 1997, the ratio falls to 58% for temporary exports and to 60% for re-imports due to reasons discussed in footnote 10.

[13] Our sample covers only EU-12 countries in order to have homogenous time series for the entire period.

[14] See Section 2.2 for a possible explanation of the phenomenon.

TABLE 2

TA OPT BETWEEN SELECTED EU-12 COUNTRIES AND THE CEECs

	1988	1989	1990	1991	1992	1993	1994	1995	1996	1997
Value (mln ECU)										
Temporary exports										
Germany	332.51	385.06	526.38	756.31	1017.41	1351.70	1601.99	1824.29	1877.99	1691.09
Italy	2.76	8.21	13.69	38.78	92.53	153.19	214.29	271.51	358.05	411.80
France	57.93	73.01	89.19	108.14	114.88	125.00	152.86	174.64	194.03	189.69
The Netherlands	39.58	42.46	52.96	66.96	94.05	112.06	63.30	117.51	169.51	119.74
Total	432.78	508.74	682.22	970.19	1318.86	1741.95	2032.43	2387.94	2599.57	2412.31
EU 12	463.35	547.87	739.19	1056.99	1450.03	1904.53	2237.61	2599.45	2855.05	2702.01
Re-imports										
Germany	486.02	569.38	736.51	1059.50	1329.94	1724.53	2137.55	2350.42	2437.33	2222.96
Italy	2.78	7.20	8.68	32.62	90.48	156.25	256.51	325.72	467.40	516.40
France	46.96	65.52	75.34	109.09	158.15	168.57	201.74	238.87	265.25	264.48
The Netherlands	60.72	72.83	87.08	107.30	149.58	202.01	229.48	283.73	273.96	226.73
Total	596.48	714.93	907.60	1308.52	1728.15	2251.36	2825.29	3198.74	3443.94	3230.57
EU 12	658.77	779.39	989.87	1437.88	1916.62	2456.39	3078.77	3568.53	3866.54	3606.98

TABLE 2 *(cont.)*

	1988	1989	1990	1991	1992	1993	1994	1995	1996	1997
Shares										
Temporary exports										
Germany	0.72	0.70	0.71	0.72	0.70	0.71	0.72	0.70	0.66	0.63
Italy	0.01	0.01	0.02	0.04	0.06	0.08	0.10	0.10	0.13	0.15
France	0.13	0.13	0.12	0.10	0.08	0.07	0.07	0.07	0.07	0.07
The Netherlands	0.09	0.08	0.07	0.06	0.06	0.06	0.03	0.05	0.06	0.04
Total	0.93	0.93	0.92	0.92	0.91	0.91	0.91	0.92	0.91	0.89
EU 12	1.00	1.00	1.00	1.00	1.00	1.00	1.00	1.00	1.00	1.00
Re-imports										
Germany	0.74	0.73	0.74	0.74	0.69	0.70	0.69	0.66	0.63	0.62
Italy	0.00	0.01	0.01	0.02	0.05	0.06	0.08	0.09	0.12	0.14
France	0.07	0.08	0.08	0.08	0.08	0.07	0.07	0.07	0.07	0.07
The Netherlands	0.09	0.09	0.09	0.07	0.08	0.08	0.07	0.08	0.07	0.06
Total	0.91	0.92	0.92	0.91	0.90	0.92	0.92	0.90	0.89	0.90
EU 12	1.00	1.00	1.00	1.00	1.00	1.00	1.00	1.00	1.00	1.00

Source: EUROSTAT, COMEXT.

TABLE 3

VALUES OF TA OPT AND SHARES OF TA OPT TO DOMESTIC PRODUCTION FOR SELECTED EU-12 COUNTRIES

		1988	1989	1990	1991	1992	1993	1994	1995	1996	1997
Values (mln ECU)											
Temporary exports											
Germany	textiles	797.18	941.44	1143.76	1373.44	1548.38	1900.36	2155.78	2392.09	2400.63	2267.10
	apparel	122.49	135.09	168.40	217.95	223.34	288.48	336.48	379.62	413.59	365.84
Italy	textiles	7.47	18.57	23.57	44.97	82.59	142.52	200.66	250.51	311.54	346.05
	apparel	2.37	4.29	4.86	12.39	32.62	48.68	87.36	123.33	190.51	236.42
France	textiles	129.00	187.89	186.50	165.72	197.67	238.31	243.45	257.41	258.03	253.51
	apparel	46.28	62.29	63.81	69.51	74.13	80.63	116.65	133.23	133.21	138.83
The Netherlands	textiles	97.84	113.45	135.73	149.52	165.97	183.21	124.12	221.98	307.62	252.56
	apparel	13.68	17.40	20.28	27.05	31.13	35.73	26.66	40.92	57.92	43.72
Re-imports											
Germany	textiles	18.10	20.16	31.94	42.57	46.89	63.85	87.43	108.25	116.60	90.75
	apparel	1253.93	1496.00	1847.12	2325.27	2434.58	2877.60	3354.59	3575.56	3716.97	3665.07
Italy	textiles	0.90	1.42	1.44	1.51	3.01	7.32	21.87	29.91	35.55	35.52
	apparel	7.41	25.17	26.75	61.00	117.79	192.42	317.61	418.02	617.09	697.32
France	textiles	9.54	10.80	10.51	7.62	7.81	7.13	6.79	7.36	9.56	10.17
	apparel	201.90	307.46	348.93	322.01	400.77	446.67	474.62	515.03	503.10	512.79
The Netherlands	textiles	0.32	0.21	0.35	0.43	0.37	1.18	1.28	1.56	3.06	7.96
	apparel	160.63	177.44	209.31	237.21	281.64	314.26	371.00	469.95	453.45	383.09

TABLE 3 (*cont.*)

		1988	1989	1990	1991	1992	1993	1994	1995	1996	1997
Shares to domestic production											
Temporary exports											
Germany	textiles	0.000	0.000		0.065	0.076	0.099	0.117	0.138	0.147	0.140
	apparel	0.000	0.000		0.015	0.017	0.022	0.027	0.031	0.036	0.032
Italy	textiles			0.001	0.001	0.002	0.004	0.006	0.007	0.008	0.008
	apparel			0.000	0.000	0.001	0.002	0.004	0.005	0.008	0.010
France	textiles	0.008	0.012	0.011	00.010	0.012	0.015	0.015	0.016	0.016	0.016
	apparel	0.004	0.005	0.005	0.005	0.005	0.006	0.009	0.010	0.011	0.012
The Netherlands	textiles	0.042	0.047	0.053	0.058	0.065	0.067	0.046	0.077	0.101	
	apparel	0.017	0.019	0.021	0.027	0.032	0.035	0.026	0.041	0.056	
Re-imports											
Germany	textiles				0.002	0.002	0.003	0.005	0.006	0.007	0.006
	apparel				0.164	0.180	0.216	0.265	0.289	0.320	0.319
Italy	textiles	0.000	0.000	0.000	0.000	0.000	0.000	0.001	0.001	0.001	0.001
	apparel	0.000	0.001	0.001	0.002	0.005	0.008	0.014	0.019	0.026	0.029
France	textiles	0.001	0.001	0.001	0.000	0.000	0.000	0.000	0.000	0.001	0.001
	apparel	0.016	0.023	0.026	0.024	0.030	0.034	0.037	0.039	0.040	0.043
The Netherlands	textiles	0.000	0.000	0.000	0.000	0.000	0.000	0.000	0.001	0.001	
	apparel	0.203	0.197	0.212	0.238	0.290	0.311	0.359	0.475	0.441	

Source: EUROSTAT, COMEXT, OECD, STAN, DATABASE 2001, for Germany, Italy and France; OECD, STAN DATABASE 2000, for the Netherlands; our calculations.

gain price competitiveness through exchange rate devaluations[15]. As for apparel, Germany's OPT/production ratio grows from 16% in 1991 to 32% in 1996, and for the Netherlands from 24% to 44%, which are obviously very substantial shares. On the other hand, ratios for France and Italy take on much lower, though growing, values. It is interesting to notice that the ratio of apparel to textile national production is generally lower for those countries exhibiting a more substantial access to OPT, and that sudden accelerations in the recourse to the practice are correlated with falls in the level of national production, which hints to some degree of substitutability between national and off-shore production[16].

The analysis that follows focuses on Germany and Italy, by far the two most important EU-12 countries in terms of OPT with the CEECs. The choice of countries is also dictated by the differences in their history of access to the OP practice[17]: German firms in the industry began very early such practice, and originate a very large share of OPT toward the CEECs; Italian firms, on the other hand, have begun just around 1992 to access the practice to a sizable extent, but they expanded their share at a very fast rate. It is for this reason that, though data are available since 1988, the time span of the analysis covers only the period 1993-1997, that is, a period for which both countries exhibit sizeable volumes of trade.

Although the basic features of textiles and apparel trade with the CEECs are rather similar for Germany and Italy, the two countries exhibit some non-negligible differences in terms of merchandise composition, even at the two-digit level of the Combined Nomenclature — that is, the «chapter» level. Some important differences can also be observed when comparing the composition of final and OPT flows between the two EU countries and the CEECs. A visual presentation of the underlying data is reported in Graphs 1 and 2.

---

[15] See also footnote 6.

[16] A possible causal explanation of such correlation is that growing competition from low labor-cost countries puts downward pressure on world demand for domestic production and forces domestic EU producers to access CEECs production facilities to reduce overall average production costs as a way to hold on to pre-existing market shares. Some evidences about this point are supplied in Section 5.

[17] See BALDONE S. - SDOGATI F. - TAJOLI L. [1] for a detailed comparative analysis of the countries' practice of OP.

GRAPH 1

STRUCTURE OF GERMAN TRADE WITH THE CEECs
BY CHAPTERS OF THE CN

1. *Final Exports*

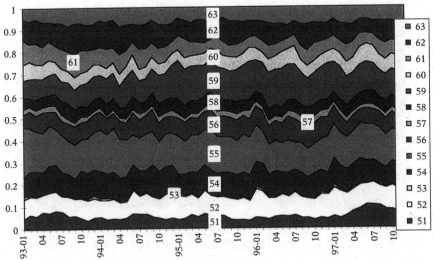

2. *Temporary Exports*

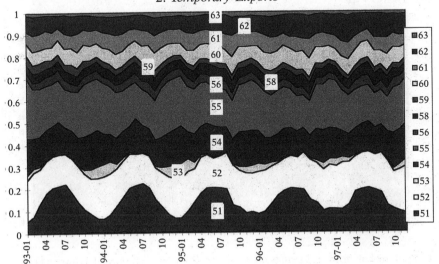

Source: EUROSTAT, COMEXT.

GRAPH 1 *(cont.)*

STRUCTURE OF GERMAN TRADE WITH THE CEECs
BY CHAPTERS OF THE CN

3. *Final Imports*

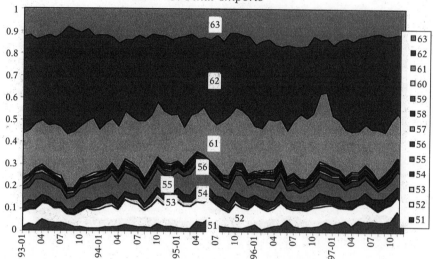

4. *Re-Imports*

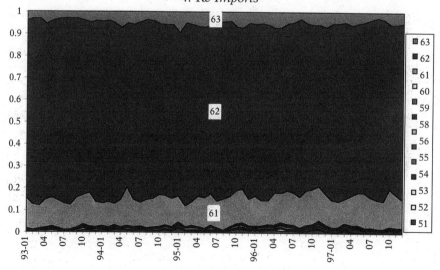

Source: EUROSTAT, COMEXT.

GRAPH 2

STRUCTURE OF ITALIAN TRADE WITH THE CEECs
BY CHAPTERS OF THE CN

1. *Final Exports*

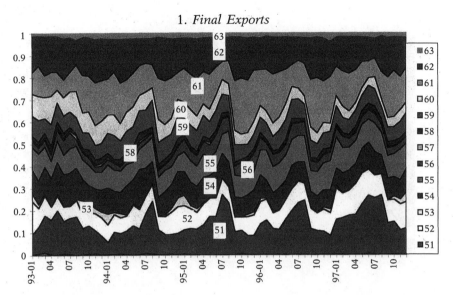

2. *Temporary Exports*

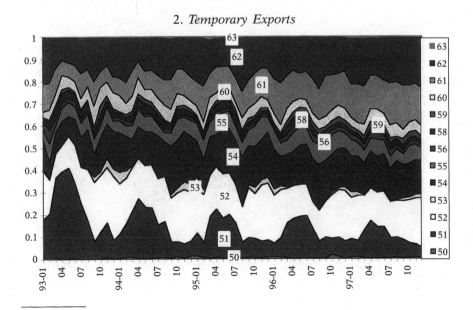

Source: EUROSTAT, COMEXT.

GRAPH 2 *(cont.)*

STRUCTURE OF ITALIAN TRADE WITH THE CEECs
BY CHAPTERS OF THE CN

3. *Final Imports*

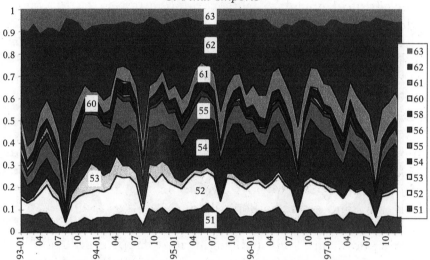

4. *Re-Imports*

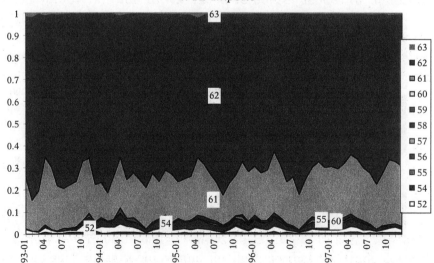

Source: EUROSTAT, COMEXT.

Data show that merchandise composition of trade is remarkably stable for both countries, save for oscillations of a seasonal nature.

By looking at German trade with the CEECs, one can immediately observe that German exports are mainly made up by textiles, while imports are mostly made up by apparel goods. Textiles range from 73% in 1993 to 79% in 1997 of the TA industry's final exports and from 85% to 83% of the industry's temporary exports. Apparel goods constitute the largest share of imports under both regimes, but there are significant differences between the composition of final imports and the composition of re-imports. While the share of apparel in TA final imports ranges between 70% and 75%, re-imports consist almost entirely of apparel goods, which indicates that the processing activity in the CEECs is concentrated in this sector. Furthermore, the composition of apparel imports differs between the two regimes: chapters 61, 62 and 63 constitute 14%, 81% and 5% respectively of apparel re-imports, while the share of the same chapters is 30%, 52% and 18% in final imports.

Trade data show that the structure of Italian trade with the CEECs is more subject to seasonal fluctuations than the German one and that, especially as far as temporary exports are concerned, Italian trade composition evolves over time more than the German one. The share of textiles in the Italian TA exports is smaller than for Germany: in the last three years of the sample, the textiles account on average for about two-thirds of both temporary and final exports, with a falling pattern for the former. The higher share of apparel delocalized by Italian firms relative to Germany's is a clear indicator that Italian firms tend, on average, to delocalize productive segments more concentrated in the final stage of the production process.

Italian final imports in the industry are traditionally characterized by a share of textile products which is noticeably larger than the German one: in the central years of the sample their share reaches a staggering 60% to decline in the following years to about 46%. Instead, nearly all re-imports by Italy are classified within Chapters 61 (articles of apparel, knitted or crocheted) and

62 (articles of apparel, not knitted or crocheted) of the apparel industry: between 1993 and 1997 the former's share grows from 21% to 25%, while the latter's fall from 75% to 69%. Thus, Italy appears to be processing abroad relatively more knitted or crocheted apparel than Germany, while the opposite is true for Chapter 63, which includes especially linen, curtains and articles for interior furnishing.

3. - Prices and Quality of Goods Subject to Outward Processing

3.1 *Prices of Goods Traded Between Germany and the CEECs*

One might expect that products originating in the EU and subject to further processing in the CEECs result in a final product of medium-to-low quality relative to the goods produced top-to-bottom in the EU. Justifications put forward for such hypothesis are not entirely unfounded: on the one hand, goods being processed outside the EU could be in the low-quality range, as these are most subject to competitive pressures from low labor-cost countries; on the other, medium-to-low quality products might be best suited to processing in the CEECs, because of the possible lack of skills adequate to the processing of high-quality products in those countries. Still, such hypothesis does not find any strong support in empirical evidence. In Graph 3, the unit value of Germany's temporary exports of textiles to the CEECs for reason of processing is systematically higher that the corresponding unit value for final exports[18]. We interpret this evidence as an indication of the fact that German textiles processed in the

---

[18] These are Laspeyres prices constructed on the basis of unit export values computed at the 4-digit level of the CN. They are computed with weights first given by the average annual shares of the 4-digit aggregates over total temporary trade (imports and exports), and then with weights given by the same shares over final trade. In both cases weights are those for 1993. Only monthly series with no more than three missing observations were used. In these instances missing observations were replaced by the average of the two observations next to them. In this context, an observation is «missing» whenever the relevant trade in the relevant months was nil.

GRAPH 3

PRICES OF GERMAN FINAL AND OP TRADE WITH THE CEECs[*]

1. *Chapters 50-60 (Textiles) Temporary and Final Exports*

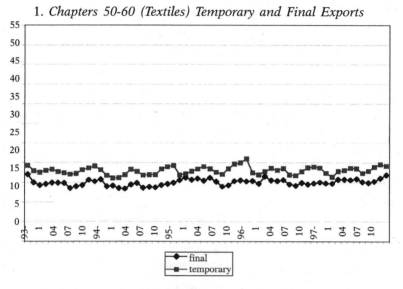

2. *Chapters 50-60 (Textiles) Re-Imports and Final Imports*

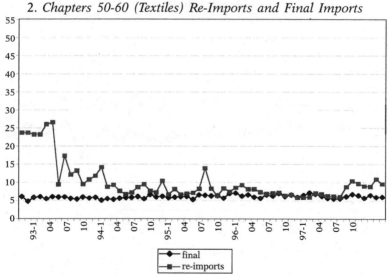

[*] Elementary prices of exports are aggregated using as weights the 4digit average composition of 1993 temporary exports; weights for elementary prices of imports are the corresponding composition of 1993 re-imports.
Source: EUROSTAT, COMEXT.

GRAPH 3 *(cont.)*

PRICES OF GERMAN FINAL AND OP TRADE WITH THE CEECs[*]

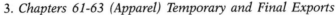

3. *Chapters 61-63 (Apparel) Temporary and Final Exports*

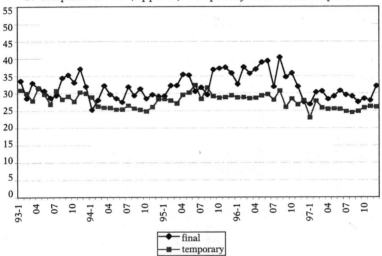

4. *Chapters 61-63 (Textiles) Re-Imports and Final Imports*

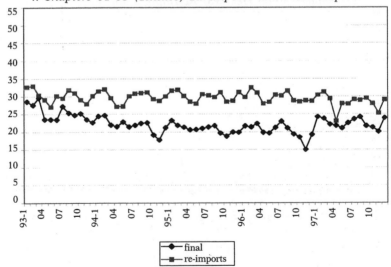

---

[*] Elementary prices of exports are aggregated using as weights the 4digit average composition of 1993 temporary exports; weights for elementary prices of imports are the corresponding composition of 1993 re-imports.
Source: EUROSTAT, COMEXT.

GRAPH 3 *(cont.)*

PRICES OF GERMAN FINAL AND OP TRADE WITH THE CEECs[*]

5. *Chapters 61 Temporary and Final Exports*

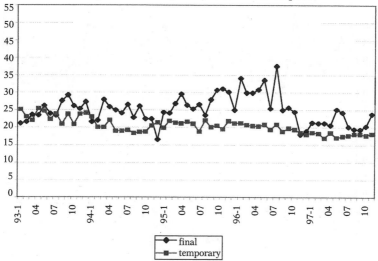

6. *Chapters 61 Re-Imports and Final Imports*

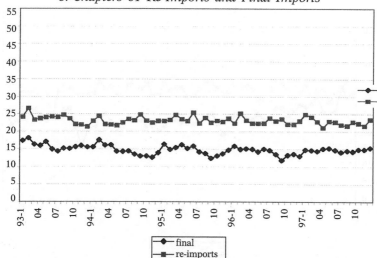

[*] Elementary prices of exports are aggregated using as weights the 4digit average composition of 1993 temporary exports; weights for elementary prices of imports are the corresponding composition of 1993 re-imports.
Source: EUROSTAT, COMEXT.

GRAPH 3 *(cont.)*

PRICES OF GERMAN FINAL AND OP TRADE WITH THE CEECs[*]

7. *Chapters 50-60 (Textiles) Temporary and Final Exports*

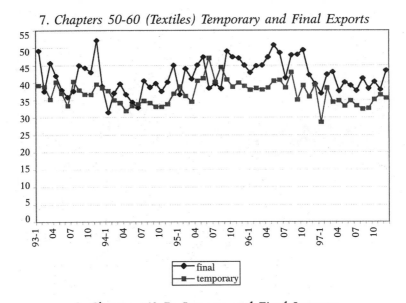

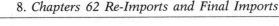

8. *Chapters 62 Re-Imports and Final Imports*

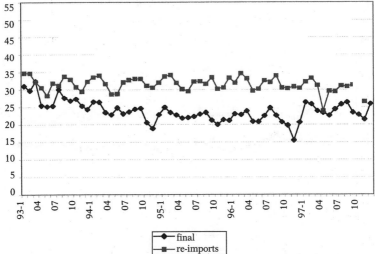

---

[*] Elementary prices of exports are aggregated using as weights the 4digit average composition of 1993 temporary exports; weights for elementary prices of imports are the corresponding composition of 1993 re-imports.
Source: EUROSTAT, COMEXT.

CEECs may be of relatively high quality,[19] and that German producers export temporarily to the CEECs much more than «junk garments» to be processed.

Comparing final export prices and temporary export prices for commodities of Chapter 61 (articles of apparel, knitted or crocheted) and of Chapter 62 (articles of apparel, not knitted or crocheted) would appear to lend support to the hypothesis that goods processed in the CEECs are of a relatively lower quality. Yet, such a direct comparison is misleading. Though classified under the same merchandise headings, goods exported temporarily are intermediate products still to be subjected to further labor-intensive — thus, particularly expensive — processing before they become "as finished as" final exports. It follows that it is not surprising that the price of final exports is higher than the price of temporary exports.

To correctly compare prices of products at a similar stage of processing we have to look at Germany's imports. Graph 3 show that the price of Germany's re-imports from the CEECs registered in Chapters 61 and 62 of the CN, that is, goods that represent the overwhelming majority of Germany's re-imports, is substantially higher than that of the corresponding final imports. In particular, the price difference for imports of articles of apparel (knitted or crocheted) grew from 45% to nearly 70% between 1993 and 1996, to end up at 50% in 1997; the price difference for articles of apparel (not knitted or crocheted), which accounts for about 80% of Germany's re-imports from the CEECs, has been growing from 15% in 1993 to 45% in 1996, to 23% in 1997.

The fall of the differential between temporary trade prices and final trade prices in 1997 could be a direct consequence of the fi-

---

[19] Inferring differences in quality from differences in prices of the same kind of goods is a very questionable procedure, especially when commodities come from different countries or are sold in different markets. Among other things, the price gap may reflect differences in production costs or pricing-to-market strategies. This is not our case because commodities come from one country and are directed to the «same» market. In Section 3.2, where prices of Italian temporary exports are compared to prices of German temporary exports toward the CEECs, differences in production costs are explicitely taken into account to explain differences in prices.

nal dismantling of tariff and non-tariff barriers by the EU *vis-à-vis* the CEECs. Such liberalization reduced or even canceled the economic advantage stemming from the use of the OP regime to process goods abroad, and since 1997 a larger share of goods to be processed has been recorded as final trade. Thus, the absence of tariffs and quotas makes price differences tend to zero over time because it leads to a statistical increase of the share of final over total trade[20].

3.2 *Prices of Goods Traded Between Italy and the CEECs*

Comparing data reported in Graph 3 and Graph 4, it is evident that prices of Germany and Italy's temporary exports to the CEECs show similar patterns. Though with sizeable seasonal flows and ebbs, the price of temporary exports of textiles exceeds that of final exports by about 40% in 1993 to about 50% in 1997. Furthermore, just as it has been observed for Germany, Italy's final export prices also exceed prices of temporary export of apparel products, but the same argument put forward for Germany should hold here.

On the import side, though, one does not observe the same large price differentials between temporary and final trade we have documented on the export side in the case of Germany. The price of re-imports of articles of apparel (knitted or crocheted) moves right along with the price of final imports, whereas the price of re-imports of articles of apparel (not knitted or crocheted), estimated to be about 30% higher than final imports in 1993, falls throughout the sample period to end up below the latter in 1997.

Thus, the mixed evidence so far analyzed requires that some further qualifications be discussed before one can reject the hypothesis that the quality of Italian goods processed abroad is higher than that of goods imported under the «final imports» regime. First, prices of final imports of apparel by Italy grew steadily in the second half of the sample period, to reach those of Germany's

---

[20] See footnote 10.

GRAPH 4

PRICES OF ITALIAN FINAL AND OP TRADE WITH THE CEECs[*]

1. *Chapters 50-60 (Textiles) Temporary and Final Exports*

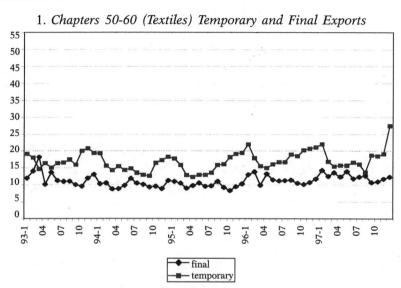

2. *Chapters 50-60 (Textiles) Re-Imports and Final Imports*

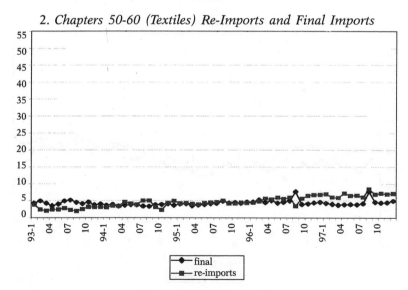

[*] Elementary prices of exports are aggregated using as weights the 4digit average composition of 1993 temporary exports; weights for elementary prices of imports are the corresponding composition of 1993 re-imports.
Source: EUROSTAT, COMEXT our calculations.

Graph 4 *(cont.)*

PRICES OF ITALIAN FINAL AND OP TRADE WITH THE CEECs[*]

3. *Chapters 61-63 (Apparel) Temporary and Final Exports*

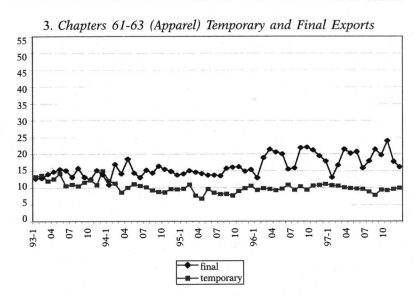

4. *Chapters 61-63 (Apparel) Re-Imports and Final Imports*

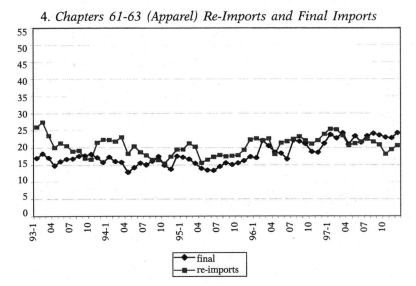

[*] Elementary prices of exports are aggregated using as weights the 4digit average composition of 1993 temporary exports; weights for elementary prices of imports are the corresponding composition of 1993 re-imports.
Source: EUROSTAT, COMEXT our calculations.

GRAPH 4 *(cont.)*

PRICES OF ITALIAN FINAL AND OP TRADE WITH THE CEECs*

5. *Chapters 61 Temporary and Final Exports*

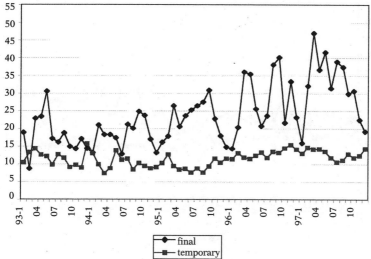

6. *Chapters 61 Re-Imports and Final Imports*

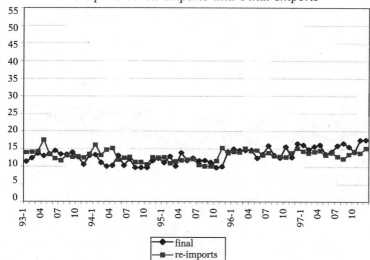

---

* Elementary prices of exports are aggregated using as weights the 4digit average composition of 1993 temporary exports; weights for elementary prices of imports are the corresponding composition of 1993 re-imports.
Source: EUROSTAT, COMEXT.

Graph 4 *(cont.)*

PRICES OF ITALIAN FINAL AND OP TRADE WITH THE CEECs[*]

7. *Chapters 62 Temporary and Final Export*

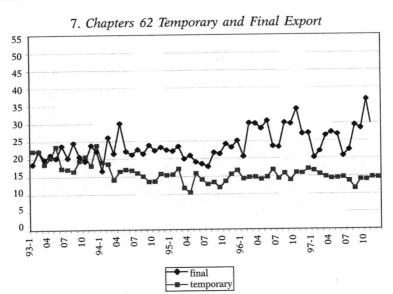

8. *Chapters 62 Re-Imports and Final Imports*

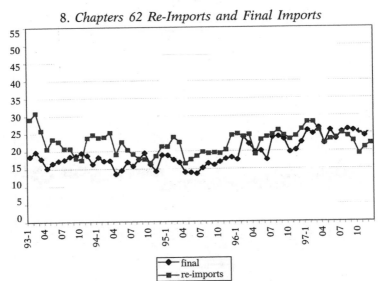

[*] Elementary prices of exports are aggregated using as weights the 4digit average composition of 1993 temporary exports; weights for elementary prices of imports are the corresponding composition of 1993 re-imports.
Source: EUROSTAT, COMEXT.

final imports: this is shown by Graph 5, which reports the ratio of German to Italian prices for all types of trade. Keeping aside the issue of the possible effects on these ratios of differences in merchandise composition between German and Italian trade even for any specific type of flow, it seems appropriate to conclude that German and Italian final imports in those industries are, at least in the second half of the sample period, of a similar quality.

Secondly, prices of temporary exports from Italy are systematically and sizably lower than those of comparable bundles of goods temporarily exported from Germany, though the difference appears to close somewhat in the latter part of the sample period for at least some of the bundles[21]. Overall, the relative price of German temporary exports exhibit an upward trend up to the second quarter of 1995, it falls steadily in the second part of that year and the first semester of 1996, and it appears to stabilize in 1997. Such dynamics is largely due to the dynamics of the exchange rates of German Mark and Italian Lira against the ECU, the unit of account used to compute both countries' prices[22]. Finally, it is to be emphasized that

---

[21] In particular, price difference is the smallest for textile products, falling from 10% to 5%; it falls from an average of about 100% in the first three years in the sample to about 40%-50% in the last two years for knitted articles of apparel; and it settles to about 130% after a peak at 150% in 1995 for not knitted articles of apparel. Also, the relative price of German textiles exhibits an important seasonal component: it is sizably higher than unity over the Spring-Summer, and it falls under one in the Fall-Winter. Such pattern in prices is likely due to the seasonality of clothing processing: the price of German textiles is higher when they are used for winter products, to be processed in the Spring-Summer, and lower when they are used for clothing to be worn in Spring-Summer, whose production takes place in the Fall-Winter.

[22] The dynamics of the nominal exchange rates German Mark/ECU and Lira/ECU over the period is reported in the graph below:

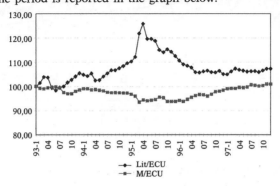

GRAPH 5

RATIOS OF GERMAN TO ITALIAN PRICES OF TRADE WITH THE CEECs

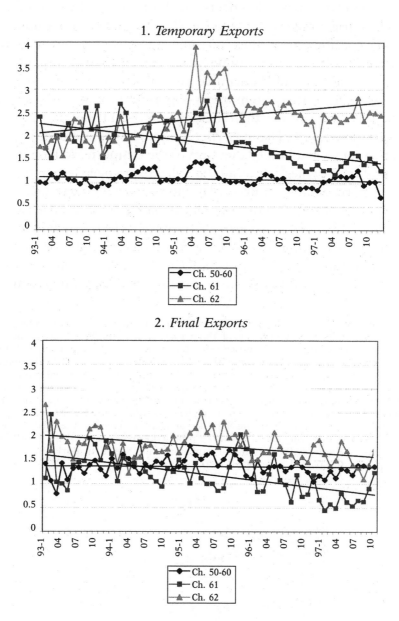

1. *Temporary Exports*

2. *Final Exports*

Source: EUROSTAT, COMEXT our calculations.

GRAPH 5 *(cont.)*

RATIOS OF GERMAN TO ITALIAN PRICES OF TRADE WITH CEECs

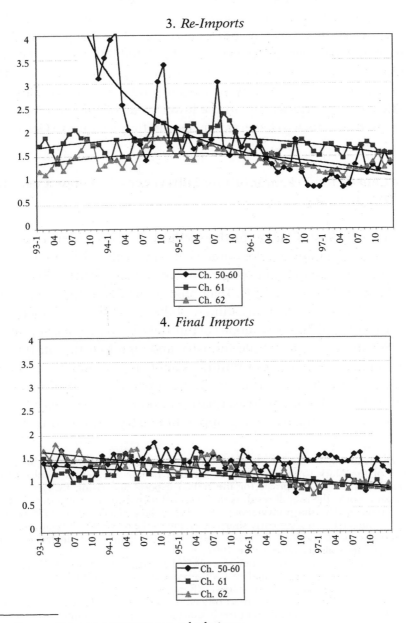

3. *Re-Imports*

4. *Final Imports*

Source: EUROSTAT, COMEXT our calculations.

the higher average unit value of German temporary exports *vis-à-vis* Italian ones is largely due to labor-cost differentials between the two countries and observed in both industries[23].

Issues of merchandise composition aside, on the basis of what has been said here, we conclude that the existence of a positive price differential between temporary and final Italian imports, not exhibited to such an extent by German prices, is not necessarily the indicator of a lower quality of Italian products processed by the CEECs, but it is rather due to the lower value of Italian temporary exports, due in turn to lower labor costs in Italy relative to Germany.

4. - Causes for Fragmentation: Differences in Labor Cost and Productivity

The low cost of labor, further deflated in some countries by recurring devaluations and/or somewhat long-lasting depreciations, is the single most important competitive advantage of the CEECs *vis-à-vis* the economies of the EU. Data reported in Table 4, though to be taken with caution, offer an estimate of the size of the phenomenon[24].

In 1996-1997 hourly labor cost in Italy is on average sevenfold the Polish one in the textile industry and eightfold that in the apparel industry. Even higher multiples apply to Germany: over ten in the textile industry, over thirteen in the apparel industry. From 1993 to 1997 Polish labor cost rises relative to both Italy and Germany in the textile industry, but in the apparel industry it grows only in the

---

The tendency of the Lira to depreciate and the parallel, though slighter, tendency of the Mark to appreciate over the first half of the period result, *ceteris paribus*, in falling ECU prices for the Italian exports and rising ECU prices for German exports: the overall result is the observed increasing relative prices of German products. The sharp inversion of the cycle taking place in May 1995 results, a few months later, in a similarly sharp inversion in the dynamics of relative prices. The relative price stability discussed above finds its counterpart in the nominal exchange rate stability observed in 1997.

[23] A simple econometric exercise reported in Appendix 2 shows that three-quarters of the price differential in textile products and close to 70% in apparel products are «explained» by labor-costs differentials.

[24] Even though we use data from official sources, reasons for caution abound, as data are collected with different methodologies in different countries and at different points in time for a given national economy.

TABLE 4

LABOR COST PER HOUR IN THE TEXTILE
AND APPAREL INDUSTRIES

	1993	1994	1995	1996	1997
Textiles (ISIC 3-D 17) ($)					
Poland	1.61	1.71	2.16	2.37	2.43
Czech Rep.	1.65	1.86	2.32	2.62	2.41
Slovakia	1.55	1.63	1.99	2.07	2.14
Hungary	2.53	2.69	2.68	2.51	2.41
Romania	062	0.66	0.82	0.86	0.71
Bulgaria	0.71	0.60	0.75	0.60	0.61
Germany	22.10	23.14	27.18	26.90	23.72
Italy	15.54	15.73	16.22	17.44	16.32
Apparel (ISIC 3-D 18) ($)					
Poland	1.41	1.39	1.68	1.75	1.80
Czech Rep.	1.56	1.76	2.18	2.28	2.26
Slovakia	1.45	1.61	1.86	1.84	1.96
Hungary	2.18	2.25	2.24	2.14	2.09
Romania	0.60	0.67	0.79	0.84	0.76
Bulgaria	0.59	0.50	0.62	0.43	0.44
Germany	18.72	19.69	23.34	24.80	21.88
Italy	13.29	13.47	13.60	14.90	13.97
Relative cost in the textile industry (Poland = 1.00)					
Poland	1.00	1.00	1.00	1.00	1.00
Czech Rep.	1.02	1.09	1.07	1.11	0.99
Slovakia	0.96	0.96	0.92	0.88	0.88
Hungary	1.58	1.58	1.24	1.06	0.99
Romania	0.39	0.39	0.38	0.37	0.29
Bulgaria	0.44	0.35	0.35	0.26	0.25
Germany	13.74	13.57	12.56	11.37	9.75
Italy	9.66	9.23	7.49	7.37	6.71
Relative cost in the apparel industry (Poland = 1.00)					
Poland	1.00	1.00	1.00	1.00	1.00
Czech Rep.	1.11	1.27	1.30	1.30	1.25
Slovakia	1.03	1.16	1.11	1.05	1.09
Hungary	1.55	1.62	1.34	1.22	1.16
Romania	0.43	0.48	0.47	0.48	0.42
Bulgaria	0.42	0.36	0.37	0.24	0.25
Germany	13.31	14.18	13.90	14.14	12.12
Italy	9.45	9.70	8.10	8.49	7.74

Source: ILO, US BLS and UNIDO data; our calculations.

last three years of the sample relative to Italy and only in 1997 relative to Germany. As to relative labor cost between Germany and Italy, the disadvantage suffered by the former in 1992 (+16%)[25] grows to more than 40% in 1993 and to nearly 70% in 1995 mostly due to the large Lira devaluation in 1992 and subsequent depreciations. It is interesting that such differential decreases only partially in 1996, when the Italian Lira experiences a sizeable appreciation, and approaches again the 1993 level only in 1997.

Labor cost differentials are present among the CEECs themselves: on the one hand are Czech Republic, Hungary, Poland and Slovakia, the more industrialized countries and those exhibiting the higher cost of labor. By 1996, US Dollar labor costs in the textile industry tend to be very similar across these countries, whereas systematic differences exist in the apparel industry: in 1997 Czech Republic and Hungary exhibit a cost of labor in the industry higher than Poland's by 25% and 16% respectively.

In the second group of countries, Bulgaria and Romania, labor costs are much lower in both industries, especially in Bulgaria. Over the last two years in the sample labor costs in Romania and Bulgaria are respectively at about one third of and one fourth that of Poland in the textile industry; in the apparel industry they are at about 45% and 25% respectively.

But, of course, wage costs differentials cannot be evaluated independently of labor productivity, for a low level of the latter may offset the competitive advantages stemming from the former. In Tables 5 and 6 we report our estimates of labor productivity in the industries of the countries of interest[26].

---

[25] Data not reported in Table 4.

[26] Measuring relative productivity gives rise both to conceptual and computational problems. On the conceptual level, «productivity» is not just an issue of units of output per unit of labor. Especially in the clothing industry, it is also a matter of «qualitative gap», which can be defined in terms of texture, cut, refinements, etc. of the finished product as well as in terms of marketing, packaging, delivery time, consumer services, etc., that is, a whole array of aspects of the production process which are likely to be rather relevant for goods entirely produced and marketed by CEECs producers. Unfortunately, lacking any reliable measure of quality gaps, output differentials per person engaged cannot be corrected accordingly. In this context, this problem may be less serious in that outward processing may help reduce substantially such qualitative gap to the extent that the processing firm receives from the assigning firm accurate and detailed blueprints

TABLE 5

LABOR PRODUCTIVITY IN THE TEXTILE INDUSTRY[a]

	1993	1994	1995	1996
Output per person engaged ($ at PPP for GDP)				
Poland	26621	31864	32791	32998
Czech rep.			54371	54038
Slovakia	26311	27227	28096	35488
Hungary	27185	29506	36558	42048
Romania	21813	21810	26797	33519
Bulgaria	20620	24343	23514	27838
Germany	94118	100019	107412	113939
Italy	129607	151388	166725	158991
Value added per person engaged ($ at PPP for GDP)				
Poland	10187	11642	11709	12859
Czech rep.			13893	14713
Slovakia	9885	9365	8792	8776
Hungary	8860	9954	12648	15973
Romania	6966	7631	8800	10130
Bulgaria	7126	6885	7275	6882
Germany	32386	34118	34150	36717
Italy	43392	48325	52017	48015
Relative productivity Output per person engaged (Poland = 1.00)				
Poland	1.00	1.00	1.00	1.00
Czech rep.			1.66	1.64
Slovakia	0.99	0.85	0.86	1.08
Hungary	1.02	0.93	1.11	1.27
Romania	0.82	0.68	0.82	1.02
Bulgaria	0.77	0.76	0.72	0.84
Germany	3.54	3.14	3.28	3.45
Italy	4.87	4.75	5.08	4.82

TABLE 5 *(cont.)*

	1993	1994	1995	1996
Value added per person engaged (Poland = 1.00)				
Poland	1.00	1.00	1.00	1.00
Czech rep.			1.19	1.14
Slovakia	0.97	0.80	0.75	0.68
Hungary	0.87	0.86	1.08	1.24
Romania	0.68	0.66	0.75	0.79
Bulgaria	0.70	0.59	0.62	0.54
Germany	3.18	2.93	2.92	2.86
Italy	4.26	4.15	4.44	3.73
Output per person engaged (Italy = 1.00)				
Poland	0.21	0.21	0.20	0.21
Czech rep.			0.33	0.34
Slovakia	0.20	0.18	0.17	0.22
Hungary	0.21	0.19	0.22	0.26
Romania	0.17	0.14	0.16	0.21
Bulgaria	0.16	0.16	0.14	0.18
Germany	0.73	0.66	0.64	0.72
Italy	1.00	1.00	1.00	1.00
Value added per person engaged (Italy = 1.00)				
Poland	0.23	0.24	0.23	0.27
Czech rep.			0.27	0.31
Slovakia	0.23	0.19	0.17	0.18
Hungary	0.20	0.21	0.24	0.33
Romania	0.16	0.16	0.17	0.21
Bulgaria	0.16	0.14	0.14	0.14
Germany	0.75	0.71	0.66	0.76
Italy	1.00	1.00	1.00	1.00

Source: UNIDO, ISTAT, SB and WIIW data; our calculations.
[a] ISIC3 for Poland, Czech Republic, Slovakia, Hungary, Romania, Germany and Italy; ISIC2 for Bulgaria.

TABLE 6

LABOR PRODUCTIVITY IN THE APPAREL INDUSTRY[a]

	1993	1994	1995	1996
Output per person engaged ($ at PPP for GDP)				
Poland	23092	23101	19533	18922
Czech Rep.			27226	26677
Slovakia	20646	19432	17991	21967
Hungary	20286	21184	19830	22089
Romania	13549	19531	24102	25737
Bulgaria	14389	13549	13613	16496
Germany	94005	103510	110378	120238
Italy	94936	110647	122386	114528
Value added per person engaged ($ at PPP for GDP)				
Poland	11362	10274	9943	9408
Czech Rep.			12074	9741
Slovakia	10470	10244	9340	9235
Hungary	11699	12828	10492	12740
Romania	6524	10959	12890	13181
Bulgaria	8341	6588	6798	8498
Germany	28236	30523	30938	32865
Italy	30266	33798	36764	35390
Relative productivity Output per person engaged (Poland = 1.00)				
Poland	1.00	1.00	1.00	1.00
Czech Rep.			1.39	1.41
Slovakia	0.89	0.84	0.92	1.16
Hungary	0.88	0.92	1.02	1.17
Romania	0.59	0.85	1.23	1.36
Bulgaria	0.62	0.59	0.70	0.87
Germany	4.07	4.48	5.65	6.35
Italy	4.11	4.79	6.27	6.05

Source: UNIDO, ISTAT, SB and WIIW data; our calculations.
[a] ISIC3 for Poland, Czech Republic, Slovakia, Hungary, Romania, Germany and Italy; ISIC2 for Bulgaria.

TABLE 6 *(cont.)*

	1993	1994	1995	1996
Value added per person engaged (Poland = 1.00)				
Poland	1.00	1.00	1.00	1.00
Czech Rep.			1.21	1.04
Slovakia	0.92	1.00	0.94	0.98
Hungary	1.03	1.25	1.06	1.35
Romania	0.57	1.07	1.30	1.40
Bulgaria	0.73	0.64	0.68	0.90
Germany	2.48	2.97	3.11	3.49
Italy	2.66	3.29	3.70	3.76
Output per person engaged (Italy = 1.00)				
Poland	0.24	0.21	0.16	0.17
Czech Rep.			0.22	0.23
Slovakia	0.22	0.18	0.15	0.19
Hungary	0.21	0.19	0.16	0.19
Romania	0.14	0.18	0.20	0.22
Bulgaria	0.15	0.12	0.11	0.14
Germany	0.99	0.94	0.90	1.05
Italy	1.00	1.00	1.00	1.00
Value added per person engaged (Italy = 1.00)				
Poland	0.38	0.30	0.27	0.27
Czech Rep.			0.33	0.28
Slovakia	0.35	0.30	0.25	0.26
Hungary	0.39	0.38	0.29	0.36
Romania	0.22	0.32	0.35	0.37
Bulgaria	0.28	0.19	0.18	0.24
Germany	0.93	0.90	0.84	0.93
Italy	1.00	1.00	1.00	1.00

Labor productivity in the textile industry in Poland, measured by output per person engaged (Table 5), turns out to be one fifth of Italy's and slightly less than one third of Germany's; among the CEECs, the Czech Republic exhibits a productivity 60% higher than Poland's; Hungary's roughly compares to Poland's in the first half of the sample whereas it shows a remarkable increase in the last two years; Slovakia's is between 85% and 100%; last come Bulgaria and Romania, whose productivity is on average about 80% of the benchmark. When productivity is measured as value added per person engaged the ranking among countries is unchanged, though Poland's productivity grows from one fifth to one fourth of Italy's and over one third of Germany's; the Czech Republic's shrinks from 60% to 16% above the Polish productivity.

In the apparel industry, the one heavily affected by outward processing, productivity levels in different countries turn out to be rather different according to the type of indicator used. In particular, using Italy as a benchmark, relative productivity levels turn out to be systematically higher when measured as value added per person engaged than when measured as output per person engaged[27]. For instance, over the period 1993-1995 Poland's productivity relative to Italy is one fifth when measured in term of output per person engaged and it is one third when measured in terms of value added[28].

The change of pattern observed in the case of apparel spills over to the textile industry as well: while productivity levels are of the same order of magnitude when measured as output per person en-

---

and substantial assistance in the conduct and overseeing of the production process. On the computational level, problems arise because information is incomplete and non-homogeneous across countries. Furthermore, the problem of the impact of different national price levels for the products of the industry has been "solved" by using US Dollar prices according to purchasing power parity for the entire GDP. Further computational details can be found in Appendix 3.

[27] The same phenomenon arises partly in the textile industry as well in the case of Poland and Hungary, whereas for the Czech Republic the opposite happens. It is worth noting that these are the three largest processing countries of EU textiles.

[28] It is to be noted that the increase of labor productivity in the Italian clothing industry relative to most of the CEECs' is likely to be due to a strong temporary component due to the devaluation of the Italian Lira between 1992 and 1995 and the subsequent large increase in both production and exports by the industry.

gaged, when measured as value added per person engaged productivity in apparel is sizably greater than in textiles. It is reasonable to postulate that the reason for such differences among productivity measures is that a substantial part of CEECs clothing production capacity is employed in the processing of intermediate products supplied by EU firms. Assuming, as it is reasonable for the reasons already discussed, that the value of intermediate inputs added locally to those imported temporarily is very limited, it follows that the value of the local domestic production amounts to the value added by local processing. If, furthermore, account is taken of the fact that most EU producers, and German ones especially, delocalize all the segments of the production process leading from the textile input to the final apparel product, it follows that the correct measure of productivity in terms of number of units of apparel per person engaged should account for both value added in production and value of textile intermediate inputs[29].

One way to construct a proxy for such measure of productivity is to add the value of that part of temporary exports of textiles from the EU going to be incorporated into the re-imports of final apparel goods to the production value for each of the CEECs[30]. Data thus obtained are reported in Table 7.

Comparison of data in Table 7 with those in Table 6 show that productivity measured by output per person engaged obtained through the correction method just described are remarkably close to those obtained when value added per person engaged is used. The remaining excess of the latter is due to the fact that a non-negligible part of temporary exports of clothing is subject to processing to an extent comparable to that to which textiles are subjects. We conclude that we find legitimate to adopt value added per person engaged as the better measure of productivity, that is, the one measure that best captures the «real efficiency» of the CEECs in the apparel industry.

---

[29] The largest part of incoming intermediate products to be processed origins in the EU.

[30] To account for the (though slight) outward processing within the textile industry, the value of temporary exports of textiles has been reduced, for each Chapter of the CN, by a factor given by the ratio of volumes of re-imports over the corresponding temporary exports.

TABLE 7

OUTPUT PER PERSON ENGAGED IN THE APPAREL INDUSTRY:
ADJUSTED VALUES*

	1993	1994	1995	1996
Output per person engaged ($ at PPP for GDP)				
Poland	31100	31465	27635	26853
Czech Rep.			35030	34252
Slovakia	32530	32031	30604	37850
Hungary	29992	30689	32200	34889
Romania	20812	28228	36686	39783
Bulgaria	21919	22464	24246	33236
Germany	94005	103510	110378	120238
Italy	94936	110647	122386	114528
Relative productivity (Poland = 1.00)				
Poland	1.00	1.00	1.00	1.00
Czech Rep.			1.27	1.28
Slovakia	1.05	1.02	1.11	1.41
Hungary	0.96	0.98	1.17	1.30
Romania	0.67	0.90	1.33	1.48
Bulgaria	0.70	0.71	0.88	1.24
Germany	3.02	3.29	3.99	4.48
Italy	3.05	3.52	4.43	4.26
Relative productivity (Italy = 1.00)				
Poland	0.33	0.28	0.23	0.23
Czech Rep.			0.29	0.30
Slovakia	0.34	0.29	0.25	0.33
Hungary	0.32	0.28	0.26	0.30
Romania	0.22	0.26	0.30	0.35
Bulgaria	0.23	0.20	0.20	0.29
Germany	0.99	0.94	0.90	1.05
Italy	1.00	1.00	1.00	1.00

Source: UNIDO, ISTAT, SB, WIIW and Eurostat data; our calculations.
* ISIC3 for Poland, Czech Republic, Slovakia, Hungary, Romania and Italy; ISIC2 for Bulgaria.

If anything, our estimates of cost saving due to fragmentation underestimate actual savings. This is so because our measures reflect labor productivity in the overall apparel industry in the CEECs, whereas we are interested in labor productivity only in the delocalized segments, which are labor-intensive relative to the whole process and capital required is negligible. Even when delocalized phases of production require a more sophisticated processing, employees in the CEECs are often equipped with tools supplied by the EU firms themselves[31]. Therefore, it is likely enough that differences in labor productivity in the delocalized segments only are less remarkable than they are for the whole production process.

Table 8 reports the final values of our measures of labor costs and productivity in the apparel industry in Germany and Italy. Estimates are supplied for both situations, i.e., production taking place entirely at home (Germany and Italy), and production being at least partially delocalized to the CEECs.

Between 1993 and 1996, hourly labor cost in the CEE area[32] for German producers was 7-8% of domestic labor cost, while for Italian producers Eastern European labor cost was about 10% of the domestic one. This labor cost differential does not reflect the productivity gap we calculated: in terms of value added per person engaged, productivity for German productions taking place in the CEECs falls from 39% to 33% of domestic productivity whereas the same ratio for Italian productions is stable at about 1/3.

Taking into account data presented in Table 7, and assuming that relative productivity in the apparel sector for Germany and Italy is the one presented in Table 6, we obtain for both EU countries the ratio between domestic unit labor cost and unit labor cost in the CEECs.

It can be observed from Table 9 that labor cost differences are remarkable even taking into account the lower productivity of

---

[31] For evidence on this see PELLEGRIN J. [13].

[32] Labor cost and productivity for the area were obtained as a weighted average of the corresponding CEECs' data, using as weights the share of each country in German and Italian re-imports. We replaced missing productivity data for the Czech Republic with estimates based on the productivity differential with Poland in 1995.

TABLE 8

LABOR COST AND PRODUCTIVITY: DOMESTIC - AND OUTWARD - PROCESSING FOR GERMAN AND ITALIAN APPAREL INDUSTRY

		1993	1994	1995	1996
Labor cost per hour ($)					
Germany	in the CEECs	1.40	1.44	1.64	1.65
	domestic	18.72	19.69	23.34	24.80
Italy	in the CEECs	1.42	1.30	1.35	1.31
	domestic	13.29	13.47	13.60	14.90
Value added per person engaged ($ at PPP for GDP)					
Germany	in the CEECs	10795	10994	10707	10609
	domestic	28236	30523	30938	32865
Italy	in the CEECs	9879	11126	11218	11953
	domestic	30266	33798	36764	35390
Relative cost per hour (Italy = 1.00)					
Germany	in the CEECs	0.11	0.11	0.12	0.11
	domestic	1.41	1.46	1.72	1.66
Italy	in the CEECs	0.11	0.10	0.10	0.09
	domestic	1.00	1.00	1.00	1.00
Relative productivity (Italy = 1.00)					
Germany	in the CEECs	0.36	0.33	0.29	0.30
	domestic	0.93	0.90	0.84	0.93
Italy	in the CEECs	0.33	0.33	0.31	0.34
	domestic	1.00	1.00	1.00	1.00

Source: ILO, UNIDO, ISTAT, WIIW data; our calculations.

TABLE 9

RATIO BETWEEN LABOR COST PER UNIT OF OUTPUT AT HOME AND IN THE CEECs

	1993	1994	1995	1996
Germany	5.10	4.94	4.92	4.85
Italy	3.05	3.41	3.08	3.85

Source: Our calculations.

the CEECs. In terms of labor, domestic processing costs German producers over four times as much as processing a good in the CEECs, while Italian producers who do not delocalize phases of production triple their processing costs. The difference is so large that it is very likely than even taking into account transport and monitoring costs, international fragmentation of production allows for sizable savings.

5. - Effects of International Fragmentation of Production

5.1 *Size of Cost Savings*

In this Section we use estimates from Section 4 to assess overall cost differences due to fragmentation relative to a no-fragmentation counterfactual scenario. The crucial point in building the counterfactual rests with the estimation of the value added generated in the CEECs. Given that we define "value added in the CEECs" to be the difference between the value of the flow of temporary exports and the value of the corresponding flow of re-imports after processing, we need to identify the correct time lag between the two flows.

Since apparel production does not generate sizeable amounts of discarded intermediate inputs, and since it is unlikely that the processing firms in the CEECs add substantial amounts of components to the intermediate inputs supplied by EU firms, the weight of products re-imported after processing should amount roughly to the weight of temporarily exported intermediate inputs[33]. Such being the case, the weight of temporary exports

---

[33] This statement is true in the absence of triangulation, that is, the procedure through which processed goods are re-imported through customs points located in member countries other than the one they were originally exported temporarily from. Under the conditions spelled out in the text, such (perfectly legal) procedure could generate an apparent statistical discrepancy between the volume of temporarily exported intermediate inputs and the volume of re-imported goods for any given country. Of course, such problem would not arise at the aggregate EU level, at which all such discrepancies would net out entirely.

should be a very good indicator of the weight of potential re-imports. The average length of time that processing operations and transportation require can therefore be easily estimated by finding out the time lag between the weight of re-imports and the weight of temporary exports that gives the greatest correlation between the two time series[34]. A two-month lag between the two flows of trade emerges from computation both for Germany and Italy, as shown in Graph 6.

The dynamics of value added on a monthly basis is reported in Graph 7 and in Graph 8. Data confirm that the two-month lag estimated between temporary exports and subsequent re-imports is an appropriate one, and that value added to temporary exports in the CEECs tends to be basically stable[35].

Value added in the CEECs as a percentage of temporary exports shows for Germany a slightly downward trend, going from about 35% at the beginning of the period to about 30% average over the last three years. The large dispersion around the mean of the distribution, as witnessed by Graph 7.2, is largely due to high seasonality in both volumes and composition of trade; use of de-seasonalized data[36] allow for a clearer representation of such trend (Graph 7.4).

Data plotted in Graph 8 highlight an important feature of

---

[34] This problem of synchronization is particularly relevant when flows of trade exhibit high variance over time, which may lead to see the weight of temporary exports greater than the weight of re-imports in a given time period. Since the phenomenon is more markedly apparent the lower the frequency at which observations is taken, we work with monthly data, the highest frequency at which data are published. However, the high variance of monthly data series require smoothing, which we accomplished filtering the series through a three-month moving average. See Appendix 3 for further computational details.

[35] Monthly values of processing trade reported in Graph 7 and Graph 8 witness to all three features already discussed earlier on the basis of yearly data: the higher values of Germany's trade relative to Italy's; the fast growth of Italy's trade between 1993 and 1996; the slowing down and the reduction of trade beginning around the middle of 1997.

[36] Data were de-seasonalized using a twelve-month moving average centered on the month of June. Data availability up to 1998 allowed computing the moving average to obtain de-seasonalized data until December 1997. The series could not be completed backward to the beginning of 1993, using 1992 data, because of the thinness of the Italian trade in that period.

GRAPH 6

WEIGHT OF GERMAN AND ITALIAN OPT WITH THE CEECs
(METRIC TONS)

1. *Germany: Historical Data*

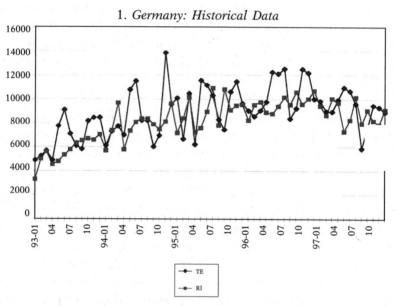

2. *Germany: Filtered and Synchronized Data*

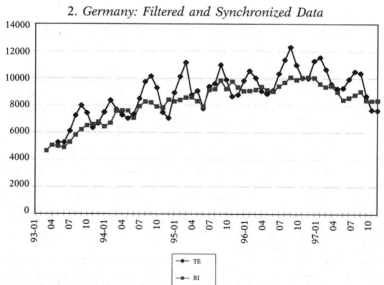

Source: EUROSTAT, COMEXT our calculations.

GRAPH 6 *(cont.)*

WEIGHT OF GERMAN AND ITALIAN OPT WITH THE CEECs
(METRIC TONS)

3. *Italy: Historical Data*

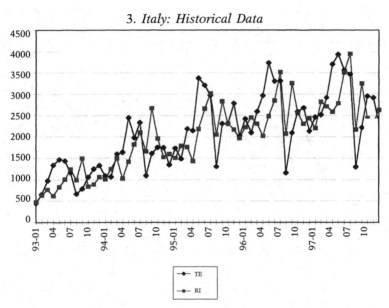

4. *Italy: Filtered and Synchronized Data*

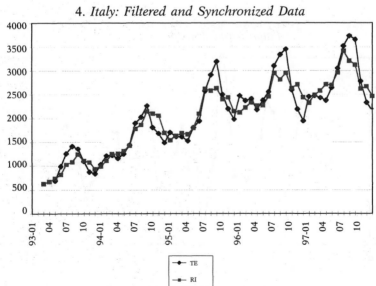

Source: EUROSTAT, COMEXT our calculations.

GRAPH 7

VALUES OF GERMAN OPT WITH THE CEECs AND RATIO OF
THE CORRESPONDING VALUE ADDED OVER TEMPORARY EXPORTS

1. *OPT Value: Filtered and Synchronize Data (Min ECU)*

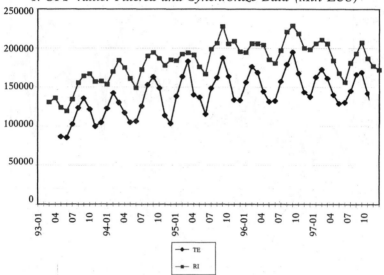

2. *Ratio of Value Added Over Temporary Export:*
Filtered and Synchronized Data

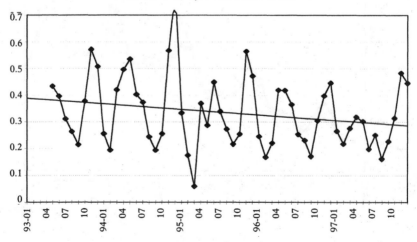

Source: EUROSTAT, COMEXT our calculations.

GRAPH 7 *(cont.)*

VALUES OF GERMAN OPT WITH THE CEECs AND RATIO OF
THE CORRESPONDING VALUE ADDED OVER TEMPORARY EXPORTS

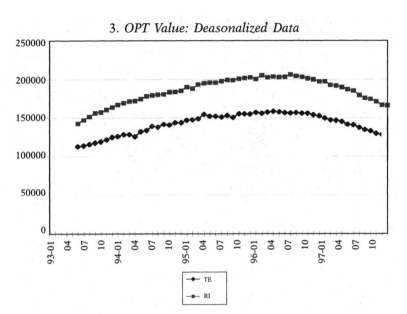

3. *OPT Value: Deasonalized Data*

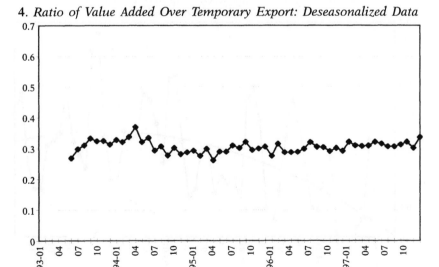

4. *Ratio of Value Added Over Temporary Export: Deseasonalized Data*

Source: EUROSTAT, COMEXT our calculations.

GRAPH 8

VALUES OF ITALIAN OPT WITH THE CEECs AND RATIO OF THE CORRESPONDING VALUE ADDED OVER TEMPORARY EXPORTS

1. *OPT Value: Filtered and Synchronize Data*

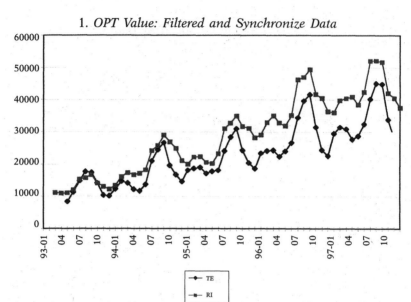

2. *Ratio of Value Added Over Temporary Export: Filtered and Synchronized Data*

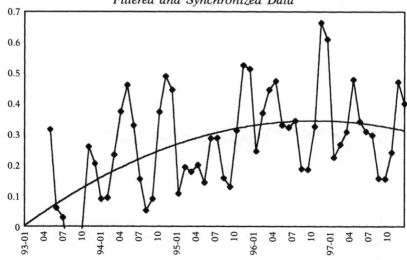

Source: EUROSTAT, COMEXT our calculations.

GRAPH 8 *(cont.)*

VALUES OF ITALIAN OPT WITH THE CEECs AND RATIO OF THE CORRESPONDING VALUE ADDED OVER TEMPORARY EXPORTS

3. *OPT Value: Deasonalized Data*

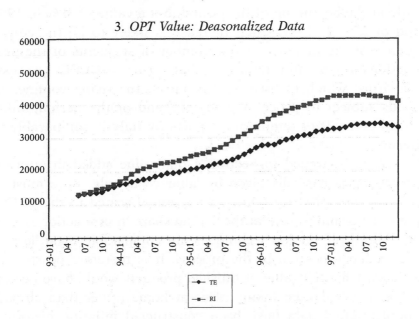

4. *Ratio of Value Added Over Temporary Export: Deseasonalized Data*

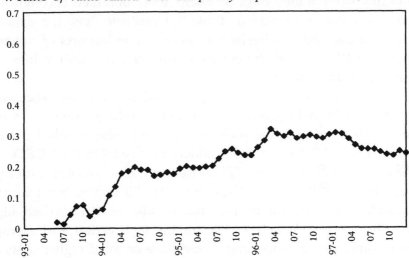

Source: EUROSTAT, COMEXT our calculations.

Italian processing trade, namely a large increase in the value added as a percentage of temporary exports: both raw and de-seasonalized data lead to estimate a very low value for this ratio at the beginning of the period, but a value of 30% in 1996 and of 25% in 1997. Such increase is likely to be the consequence of the increase in the number of segments of the production process allocated by Italian firms to CEECs processing firms, which in turn is also due to the rising volumes of goods subject to processing. By the end of the period, value added per unit of temporary exports by Italy is comparable to Germany's.

We have argued in Section 4 that value added in outward processing is basically given by labor costs only, since most of the segments of the production process allocated to the CEECs are so labor intensive that the capital share in production is negligible and production techniques are comparable regardless of geographical location of the process. It is therefore possible to estimate what the value of finished products would have been if processing had been taking place at home rather than abroad. Counterfactual data have been constructed inflating historical monthly value added data by coefficients obtained through linear interpolation of data in Table 9. Graphs 9 show the dynamics of actual and counterfactual values of re-imports of apparel from the CEECs and the corresponding average unit values for both Germany and Italy.

The size of cost reduction generated by outward processing in the CEECs is impressive: if German products were to be entirely processed at home their average unit value would be more than twice that of the same products processed in the CEECs. In the case of Italy the estimated cost advantage associated with outward processing is not as large but it is still impressive: with the exception of a period around the middle of 1993, when high volatility of trade is responsible for the high variance of average unit values, home processing would have entailed higher costs of about 70% until the Autumn of 1995, and around 100% over the last two years in the sample.

GRAPH 9

ACTUAL AND COUNTER-FACTUAL VALUES OF
GERMAN AND ITALIAN APPAREL RE-IMPORTS FROM THE CEECs

1. *German Re-Imports (min ECU)*

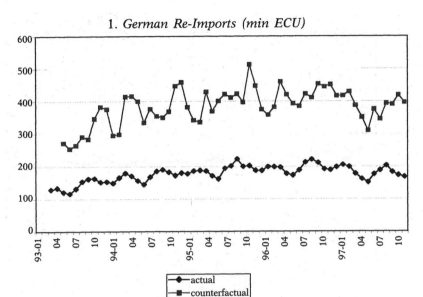

2. *Italian Re-Imports (min ECU)*

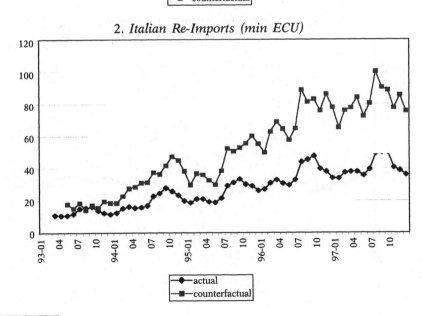

Source: EUROSTAT, COMEXT our calculations.

GRAPH 9 *(cont.)*

ACTUAL AND COUNTER-FACTUAL VALUES OF
GERMAN AND ITALIAN APPAREL RE-IMPORTS FROM THE CEECs

3. *AUV of German Re-Imports (ECU/Kg)*

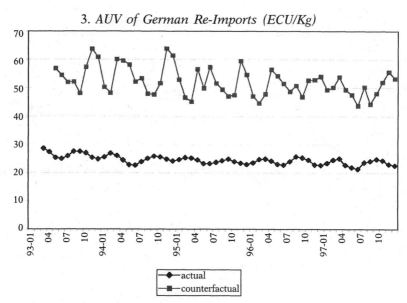

4. *AUV of Italian Re-Imports (ECU/Kg)*

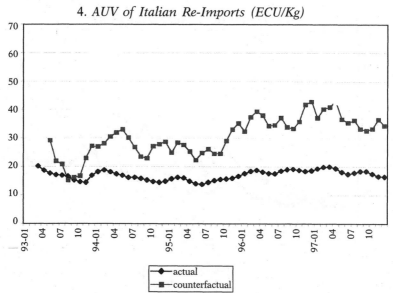

Source: EUROSTAT, COMEXT our calculations.

5.2 *Size of Competitiveness Recovery*

The efficacy of delocalization of production to the CEECs as a strategy by the European TA industry to contain competitive pressure from low labor-cost countries is documented in Graph 10. There we report both actual and counterfactual average unit values of re-imports from the CEECs and average unit values of final imports by Germany and Italy of the same bundles of finished goods[37] from the most competitive areas of the world[38].

Observation of Graph 10.1 reveals that average unit values of German products processed in the CEECs are basically aligned to those imported from the Mediterranean Basin, China and the NICs. In the case of products imported from East Asian countries, and even more so for those imported from the Indian Basin, the average unit value differential is still in favor of the latter areas, even though it is likely that the lower average unit value is associated with a lower standard of quality. Anyway, it is entirely clear that German goods would be entirely non-competitive *vis-à-vis* similar imported goods if the production process were to be carried out entirely at home.

---

[37] In order to compare average unit values (AUV) of re-imports from the CEECs with AUV of final imports from each of the competing areas, we assumed that the merchandise composition of German and Italian final imports were identical to the composition of re-imports from the CEECs. With this assumption we removed from the calculated AUV the effect of the different composition of trade flows, which is indeed relevant. In the case of Germany, AUV calculated in this way appear to be significantly higher than the actual average unit values of imports from the Mediterranean Basin, from the Indian Basin and from China, while they are close to the actual values in the case of imports from East Asian countries and the NICs. With respect to Italy, AUV calculated keeping a constant merchandise composition are higher than actual AUV from every area, even if this difference fades out toward the end of the period especially for East Asian countries and the NICs. These results lend further support to the view that the flow of goods processed in the CEECs includes high quality segments. Due to missing data in the German import price series, the aggregated AUV for Germany is underestimated. Missing data and lack of stability in the merchandise composition of re-imports from the CEECs, especially in the early years of our sample, are the causes of the higher volatility observed for the Italian AUV.

[38] We considered the following areas: Mediterranean Basin (Malta, Cyprus, Turkey, Morocco, Algeria, Tunisia, Libya, Egypt, Israel, West Bank/Gaza, Lebanon, Syria, Jordan), Indian Basin (India, Pakistan, Bangladesh, Sri Lanka, Maldives, Nepal, Bhutan, Mauritius), East Asian countries (Myanmar, Thailand, Laos, Vietnam, Cambodia, Indonesia, Malaysia, Brunei, Philippines), NICs (Singapore, South Korea, Taiwan, Hong Kong), China (China, North Korea, Macao). These areas originate nearly 91% of German final imports of textiles and clothing from non-EU countries, and almost 89% of Italian final imports. Excluding the NICs, these are all low-wage countries.

GRAPH 10

AVERAGE UNIT VALUE OF GERMAN AND ITALIAN APPAREL IMPORTS FROM EXTRA-EUROPEAN AREAS COMPARED TO AVERAGE UNIT VALUE OF RE-IMPORTS FROM THE CEECs (ECU/KG)

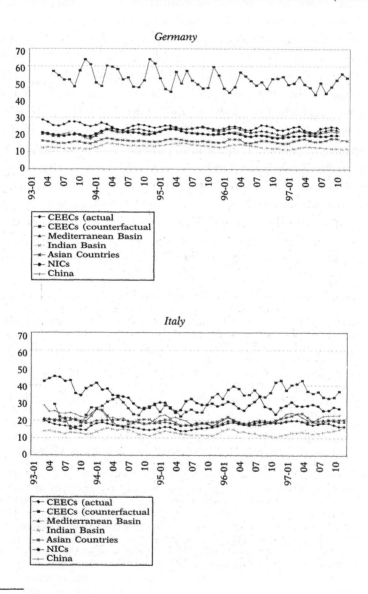

Source: Our calculations.

Delocalization of processing to the CEECs as a strategy to contain competitive pressures from other low labor-cost countries appears to be even more effective for Italy, which shows average unit values of re-imports systematically lower than Germany's and generally lower than those of apparel imported from all competitive areas, with the only exception of the Indian basin. Unlike Germany's, Italy's final imports from the NICs exhibit average unit values higher than those of goods processed in the CEECs, and beginning in 1994 they are even aligned to the estimated counterfactual one[39].

When talking about competitive pressure on the European apparel industry one thinks immediately about Southeast Asian producers. Yet, a sizeable share of German and Italian imports from outside of the EU come from the Mediterranean Basin. This can be seen from Graph 11 reporting, for each of the two countries, the geographic composition of final and total imports[40] respectively from non-EU areas[41].

This should not come as a surprise, for the Mediterranean Basin ranks as one among the very first areas toward which the European apparel industry began de-localizing production, and the most important one until it became possible to access production facilities in Central-Eastern Europe on a sizeable scale. It is therefore reasonable to postulate that a large share of EU imports from the Mediterranean Basin represents a measure of the degree to which European countries counter competitive pressure from South-East Asian countries much the same way they do through delocalization of production to the CEECs. In this light, the German firms' strategy to delocalize abroad more or less extended segments of the production process is turning out to be effective. The same is true, on a smaller but growing scale, for Italian firms. This hypothesis is supported by the sizeable reduction of the share of total imports coming from South-East Asia, as reported in Figure 11: between December 1993 and December

---

[39] This can explain the small weight of this area in Italian apparel imports from extra-EU countries.

[40] Total imports are the sum of final imports and re-imports.

[41] Shares were calculated using monthly import data, de-seasonalized using a 12-period moving average.

GRAPH 11

GEOGRAPHIC-STRUCTURE OF GERMAN AND ITALIAN APPAREL IMPORTS FROM *EXTRA*-EU AREAS

1. *German Final Imports (De-Seasonalized Data)*

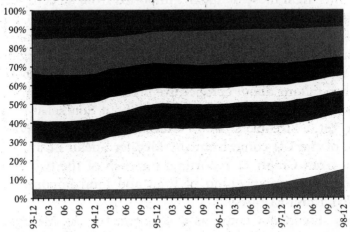

■CEECs □Medit. Basin■Indian Basin□Asian Countries■NICs ■China ■Other Countries

2. *Italian Final Imports (De-Seasonalized Data)*

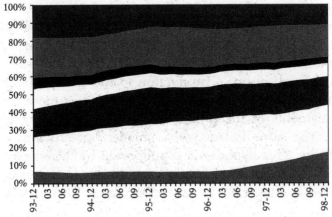

■CEECs □Medit. Basin■Indian Basin□Asian Countries■NICs ■China ■Other Countries

Source: EUROSTAT, COMEXT our calculations.

GRAPH 11 *(cont.)*

GEOGRAPHIC-STRUCTURE OF GERMAN AND ITALIAN APPAREL IMPORTS FROM *EXTRA*-EU AREAS

3. *German Total Imports (De-Seasonalized Data)*

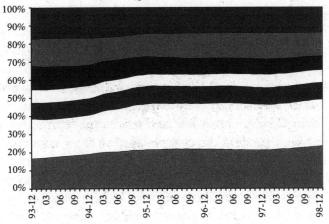

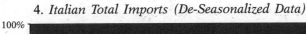

■CEECs □Medit. Basin■Indian Basin□Asian Countries■NICs ▨China ■Other Countries

4. *Italian Total Imports (De-Seasonalized Data)*

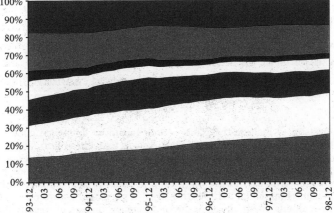

■CEECs □Medit. Basin■Indian Basin□Asian Countries■NICs ▨China ■Other Countries

Source: EUROSTAT, COMEXT our calculations.

1998 the share of German imports coming from the area fell from 44% to 37% and Italy's from 51% to 37%[42]. At the same time, Germany's imports from the Mediterranean Basin grew from 22% to 26%, and Italy's from 18% to 23%, while the CEECs' grew from 17% to 23% in Germany and from 14% to 26% in Italy.

There are two reasons why we extended the length of the sample to December 1998 for the purpose of the latest comparisons. On the one hand, this was deemed necessary to offer a «longer» time perspective to trends emerging from our analysis; on the other, to emphasize the phenomenon already mentioned in the closing part of Section 3.1, that is, the fact that outward processing trade with the CEECs will be captured by statistics less and less in the future. Indeed, comparison between geographic composition of final imports and total imports in Graph 11 shows that, while total imports follow the trend observed in previous years, starting in 1997 there is a sharp increase in final imports for both Germany and Italy. As already mentioned, this sudden increase is due to the removal of barriers to trade between the EU and the CEECs, which reduced or even nullified the economic convenience to ship goods to be processed abroad using the special OPT regime. Therefore, beginning in 1997, a larger share of the goods to be processed has been recorded together with final trade. It is also possible that, as the CEECs advance in their transition as market economies, a growing number of EU firms is shifting to delocalize completely their production activities in Eastern Europe through direct investments in those countries, taking advantage of the knowledge accumulated in ten years of technical and commercial relations.

---

[42] The reason to include the NICs — not any more low-wage countries — together with other countries of South-East Asia is that the region, when considering the textile and clothing industry, appears to be an integrated economic area, organized in a hierarchical structure according to the different phases of production. Within this structure, in the upgrading process of their apparel industry, the NICs — Taiwan, Hong Kong and South Korea in particular — are playing the leading role, delocalizing themselves the labor intensive phases of production toward lower labor-cost countries. Therefore, Western firms that are outsourcing from the NICs, actually have their goods processed in truly low-wage countries, from where the goods are shipped back. Each NIC has its favorite location to delocalize production. Hong Kong and Taiwan delocalize especially in China, South Korea favors Indonesia and North Korea, while firms from Singapore concentrate in Malaysia and Indonesia (GEREFFI G. [6]).

6. Conclusions

Three results arising from the analyzed evidence are worth mentioning. First, the extent of outward processing in the CEECs undertaken by German and Italian firms in the textile and apparel industry is shown to be relevant both in terms of quantity and quality. Secondly, we estimated the cost saving due to international fragmentation of production to be relevant as well, in the order of more than 50% for Germany and between 40% and 50% for Italy. The cost reduction obtained in comparison to a totally autarkic production is due to the labor cost differential in favor of the CEECs, which is not counterbalanced by the productivity gap penalizing these countries. Finally, by comparing the average unit values of apparel imports from the main competing areas in Asia with the average unit values arising through the process of delocalization, it emerges that outward processing allows German and Italian producers to keep their production costs in line with their main competitors.

Outward processing trade with the CEECs seems to be an effective strategy — possibly not only for apparel producers — in response to the competitive pressure arising from low wage countries, especially in the most labor-intensive segments. Like other forms of internationalization and fragmentation of production, OPT allows producers in advanced countries that still own a strong competitive advantage in many segments of the production chain — design, input supply, distribution to final customers — to profitably exploit what would be a disadvantage, if firms were forced to keep the organization of production integrated and unchanged.

Over time, the effectiveness of this particular form of delocalization depends crucially upon two elements. First, unit labor costs in the CEECs must stay constant relative to the costs of the competitors of Germany and Italy. Second, the upgrading of apparel firms in the CEECs should not allow them to develop an autonomous and sufficient degree of competitiveness in international markets. Taking into account that complete integration of the CEECs within the EU will take place in the near future, it seems unlikely that the current wage differential will be maintained, and only a corresponding increase in productivity could keep labor cost per unit of output at the present level. With full membership in the EU, also the exchange rate will no longer be viable as a means to regain competitiveness. Signals of a change in the delocalization pattern away from the CEECs with relatively higher wages (Poland, Hungary, Czech Republic) and toward countries with relatively lower wages (Bulgaria, Romania) have already been observed (Baldone *et* AL. [2]). Plans aiming at increasing minimum wages, such as the one considered in Hungary, could accelerate this process and push OPT away from Central Europe toward the Balkans, Ukraine, or the Confederation of Independent States. We could witness a sequence of migrations of the most labor-intensive segments of production toward the countries that maintain the lowest wages, similarly to what happened in Southeast Asia.

An important issue is that of the role played by OPT in the process of upgrading of the textile and apparel industry in the CEECs. Certainly, through fragmentation of the production process OPT has allowed for the emergence of comparative advantages in specific segments of the process, thus allowing for the survival of local firms by slowing down the fall of domestic demand during the transition years. Beyond all that, however, OPT is the means through which domestic producers become acquainted with more modern design, better products, and qualitative standards higher than those they were accustomed to. There is little doubt that some firms were able to improve their technology without having to find ways to finance sizeable investments, for it is often the case that firms delocalizing production also supply modern machinery in order to increase qualitative standards and reduce waste. Having said all that, it remains true that simply assembling components supplied by the foreign firm seldom allows the local producers to establish that network with a number of suppliers and customers which is crucial if the firm is to acquire an autonomous position on the market. Furthermore, the dependence from Western-European firms ends up destroying the previous network of relations with the local textile firms, given that local apparel firms were forced to work for foreign suppliers of textile and intermediate products (Comisso [5]).

Is delocalizing production toward the CEECs likely to generate negative effects on EU countries? Even assuming that delocalization of the most labor-intensive segments allowed re-gaining the lost EU price competitiveness, it is quite likely that the direct impact of this process on domestic employment will be negative. Yet, it must be enphasized that this would not be the appropriate measure to use to estimate the social cost of delocalization. In fact, the job loss due to delocalization should be compared with the job loss that would have occurred without delocalization, thus accounting for the loss of competitiveness of EU firms and the subsequent fall in production. In such perspective, international fragmentation of production is a convenient solution, allowing production in traditional sectors to continue taking place in advanced, high labor-cost countries, rather than moving entirely to emerging countries, as one would expect to occur following the logic of the product-cycle model. It is also possible that advanced countries' firms, by concentrating production in the most skill-intensive segments of the production process such as design, outsourcing and marketing, may be able to generate higher-than-expected levels of demand for skilled labor in those segments. The size of this positive employment effect will depend crucially on the degree of industrial upgrading realized as measured by the ability to set-up and manage economic and commercial networks between suppliers and customers. Were EU firms capable of successfully establishing and managing such networks, they could conceivably carry out the entire material production process in low labor-cost areas, while focusing their activity on the more immaterial segments of production such as co-ordination and management of the producer-customer network. Such a development would greatly resemble that already well established by the NICs and by Hong Kong especially[43].

---

[43] On the concept of "industrial upgrading" and the role of the NICs in Asia in the textile and apparel sector, see GEREFFI G. [6]. This phenomenon concerns many industrial sectors besides textiles and apparel that are involved in segmentation of production processes. On this, see NG F. - YEATS A. [11]. On the role played by Hong Kong as a commercial intermediary between China and the rest of the world and on the domestic and foreign employment effects of such practice see CHENG L.K. - QIU L.K. - TAN G. [4].

1. Textile and Apparel Chapters of the Combined Nomenclature (2 digits)

50 Silk
51 Wool; fine or coarse animal hair; horsehair yarn
52 Cotton
53 Other vegetable textile fibres; paper yarn woven fabric
54 Man-made filaments
55 Man made staple fibres
56 Wadding; felt and nonwovens; special yarns; twine; cords
57 Carpets and other textile floor coverings
58 Special woven fabrics; tufted textile fabrics; lace; tapestry
59 Impregnated, coated, covered or laminated textile fabrics
60 Knitted or crocheted fabrics
61 Articles of apparel and clothing accessories, knitted or crocheted
62 Articles of apparel and clothing accessories, nor knitted or crocheted
63 Other made-up textile articles; worn clothing and worn textile

2. The Role of Labor Costs in Determining TA Prices

Throughout this paper, a key assumption is that labor costs are crucial for overall production costs and competitiveness of the TA industry. To support this assumption, and in particular to support our hypothesis that differences in temporary export prices between Germany and Italy reflect differences in the domestic production costs, because of higher cost of labor in Germany, we computed the correlation between the ratio of the average unit values (AUV) of German and Italian temporary exports and the relative cost of labor in the two countries. Results of this test for the textile and the apparel industries are reported in Table 10.

It can be seen that the correlation is remarkably high, and in the very simple pooled regression run to estimate the overall correlation, relative labor costs alone explain a large part of AUV fluctuations in both industries. The significance of the relative labor cost variable is robust to different specifications, supporting our view of the key role played by this variable.

TABLE 10

CORRELATION BETWEEN RELATIVE (GERMAN/ITALIAN) LABOR
COST AND RELATIVE AUV OF TEMPORARY EXPORTS

Toward:	Textiles	Apparel
Hungary	0.99	0.35
Poland	0.84	0.71
Romania	0.95	0.81

Textiles
Annual data 1989-1997
Panel estimates with fixed effects
Dependent variable: relative (German/italian) AUV of temporary exports
Relative labor cost coefficient 2.22 (*t*-stat. 8.29)
$R^2 = 0.78$

Apparel
Annual data 1992-1997
Panel estimates with fixed effects
Dependent variable: relative (German/italian) AUV of temporary exports
Relative labor cost coefficient 0.81 (t-stat. 3.23)
$R^2 = 0.69$

3. - Some Problems With the Computation of the Competitiveness Gain

In order to build the counterfactual average unit values of the German and Italian TA goods presented, it is necessary to estimate the amount of production cost of the final good attributable to production taking place in the home country and in the CEECs. In this Section, we present some details on the methodological procedure used.

3.1 *Size and Synchronization of Processing Trade*

As explained in Section 5.1 of the text, to calculate the amount of value added produced by the CEEC firms processing EU goods, we need to estimate the amount of time required for processing operations and transportation. To assess the length of that time lag appropriately, we computed the correlation coefficient between the filtered time series of outgoing and returning traffic in volume, lagging the former relative to the latter for a maximum of four months (plus the within-month correlation). Estimated coefficients at different time lags lead to choose two months as the appropriate one.

Time lag (months)	Correlation coefficient	
	Germany	Italy
0	0.761	0.831
1	0.806	0.892
2	0.838	0.939
3	0.819	0.906
4	0.766	0.832

The lower degree of correlation between the two components of Germany's processing trade is basically due to two reasons.

First, Germany exhibits shorter time lags between temporary exports and re-imports than Italy, due to shorter distances from the processing firms located in the CEECs and to the higher degree of integration between the German economy and those of the CEECs. Breaking down trade data for Germany by processing country allows to see that re-imports of processed goods from the Czech Republic, the country closest geographically and most integrated economically, take place within a month of temporary exports; the lag extends to two months for processing in Bulgaria and Romania; and it takes on an intermediate value of between one and two months in the case of Poland.

The second reason is that German firms do appear to practice "triangulation" with bordering countries (the Netherlands, Denmark, Belgium, and Austria) and the United Kingdom, especially as far as trade with Hungary and Poland is concerned. Indeed, when the correlation coefficient between temporary exports and re-imports lagged two months is computed not for Germany but for the whole area identified in the text, it grows to 0.8666 as against 0.8384 for Germany alone and 0.8803 for the EU as a whole.

3.2 *Measuring Productivity*

In the available international statistics, productivity is usually measured in terms of output per capita, or value added per capita. The first problem that emerges when comparing this measure across countries is the number of workers that should be included: number of employees only or the total number of people engaged in this activity? If the percentage of autonomous workers (working proprietors, active business partners and unpaid family workers, according to the UNIDO definition) in the industry is the same in each country, the comparison across different countries will not be distorted by either of the definitions used. But this is not our case. Given the peculiar structure of the TA industry in Italy, where very small firms play a key role and the number of autonomous workers is relatively high, especially in the apparel sector, a measure of productivity for this country using only the number of employees will over-estimate the true productivity level. Therefore we chose to compute productivity in terms of the number of people engaged. This gives a more realistic measure of productivity as all participants to the productive activity are included, and it allows for a more correct comparison between Italy and Germany. For the CEECs we had to use the number of employees, as these were the only available data. This should not introduce a major distortion, as the number of autonomous workers in this group of countries is probably still negligible.

TABLE 11

RELATIVE PRODUCTIVITY IN TEXTILE AND
APPAREL INDUSTRY (POLAND = 1,00)

	1993	1994	1995	1996
Output per Person Engaged ($ at PPP for GDP)				
Poland	1.00	1.00	1.00	1.00
Czech Rep.			1.80	1.81
Slovakia	0.96	0.87	0.91	1.15
Hungary	0.95	0.93	1.11	1.25
Romania	0.74	0.77	1.04	1.22
Bulgaria	0.74	0.73	0.78	0.96
Germany	3.82	3.79	4.43	4.82
Italy	4.62	4.98	6.00	5.80
Value Added per Person Engaged ($ at PPP for GDP)				
Poland	1.00	1.00	1.00	1.00
Czech Rep.			1.24	1.20
Slovakia	0.93	0.90	0.86	0.85
Hungary	0.96	1.07	1.08	1.32
Romania	0.62	0.85	1.02	1.10
Bulgaria	0.70	0.62	0.67	0.71
Germany	2.82	3.01	3.10	3.29
Italy	3.44	3.86	4.27	4.00

The second problem is to choose between output and value added. If two countries adopt similar production technologies, relative productivity of labor should be similar independently of the measure used. As discussed in Section 5 of the text, this is not the case for the CEECs' productivity relative to Germany and Italy, and therefore the computation of this measure requires special care.

Further problems arise from the technological differences between the textile and the apparel industries. In the CEECs, productivity in apparel is far larger than in textiles when measured in terms of value added per employee. It follows that productivity measures computed for the aggregate TA industry would lead to underestimate the efficiency of the CEECs in the apparel industry, that is, the one industry in which most of the processing of foreign intermediate inputs takes place. The same data used to derive results presented in Tables 6 and 7 would generate the estimates for the TA industry as a whole reported in Table 11.

To underscore the difficulties associated with constructing productivity estimates we report relative productivity measures expressed as output per employee for the five most important CEECs, which are computed on the basis of data supplied by Havlik [8] for the year 1993:

Poland	1.00
Czech Rep.	1.35
Slovakia	1.00
Hungary	0.64
Romania	0.49

Havlik used raw data published by UNIDO as well as data from national accounts. Aside from the missing measure for the Czech Republic, it is striking that our measure of relative productivity for Hungary and Romania are about one third higher than those computed by Havlik [8]. A reason for such discrepancy could be that UNIDO data for Hungary only cover firms employing at least 100 employees, or 300 Mln. Forint of sales, or firms worth at least 150 Mln. Forint. For Romania, firms in the sample are only those under State control, which represent both about 80% of firms and manufacturing production. A similar problem arises for Italy, for UNIDO data only refer to firms with at least twenty employees. Complementing such data with data from firms with less than twenty employees we found that productivity falls by 25% when measured as output per employee and by 23% when measured as value added per employee (average over the period 1993-1996 and for the TA industry as a whole). Given the costs associated with search and monitoring of processing firms in the CEECs, and given that such firms should have some "visibility" and reliability of their own before a contractual relationship is set up with a EU firm, it is likely that the process affects mostly firms of non-trivial dimensions. We conclude that productivity data for the larger firms are the more appropriate ones to use, along with labor costs, to assess the degree of profitability associated with the form of international delocalization of production we are interested in.

4. - Data Sources

Trade Flows, Final and Processing Trade:	Eurostat, Comext CD-Rom, *Intra- and Extra-EU trade* (various issues).
Industrial Production:	OECD, *STAN Database for Industrial Analysis*, vol. 2000 and 2001.
Labor Cost:	International Labor Organization (Laborsta website) and U.S. Bureau of Labor Statistics website.
Employment, Output, Value added:	UNIDO, *International Yearbook of Industrial Statistics* (various issues); Istat, *Conti Economici delle Imprese* (various issues); Statistisches Bundesamt, Produzierendes Gewerbe, Fachserie 4, Reihe 4.3, *Kostenstruktur der Unternehmen des Verarbeitenden Gewerbes sowie des Bergbaus und der Gewinnung von Steinen und Erden* (various issues).
Purchasing Power Parity Exchange Rates:	WIIW database for the CEECs; OECD, *Main Economic Indicators* for the EU countries.

BIBLIOGRAPHY

[1] BALDONE S. - SDOGATI F.- TAJOLI L., *Il traffico di perfezionamento passivo con i paesi dell'Europa Centrale e Orientale nel comparto tessile-abbigliamento: un'analisi strutturale per i principali committenti dell'Unione Europea*, Mimeo, Politecnico di Milano, Dipartimento di Economia e Produzione, 1999.

[2] — - — - —, «Patterns and Determinants of International Fragmentation of Production: Evidence from Outward Processing Trade Between the EU and Central Eastern European Countries», *Weltwirtschaftliches Archiv*, vol. 137, 2001, pp. 80-104.

[3] BALDONE S. - SDOGATI F. - ZUCCHETTI A., «From Integration Through Trade in Goods to Integration Through Trade in Production Process? Evidence from EU OPT Statistics», in BALDONE S. - SDOGATI F. (eds), *EU-CEECs Integration: Policies and Markets at Work*, Milano, F. Angeli, 1997, pp. 247-90.

[4] CHENG L.K. - QIU L.D. - TAN G., «Foreign Direct Investment and International Fragmentation of Production», in ARNDT S.W. - KIERZKOWSKI H. (eds), *Fragmentation, New Production Patterns in the World Economy*, Oxford, Oxford University Press, 2001, pp. 165-86.

[5] COMISSO E., «'Implicit' Development Strategies in Central East Europe and Cross-National Production Networks», BRIE, *Working Papers Series* n. 129, 1998.

[6] GEREFFI G., «International Trade and Industrial Upgrading in the Apparel Commodity Chain», *Journal of International Economics*, vol. 48, 1999, pp. 37-70.

[7] GRAZIANI G., «Globalization of Production in the Textile and Clothing Industries: The Case of Italian Foreign Direct Investment and Outward Processing in Eastern Europe», in ZYSMAN J. - SCHWARTZ A. (eds), *Enlarging Europe: The Industrial Foundations of a New Political Reality*, University of California, International and Area Studies, *Research Series*, n. 99, 1998.

[8] HAVLIK P., «Labour Cost Competitiveness of Central and Eastern Europe», in OECD, *The Competitiveness of Transition Economies*, Proceedings, 1998, pp. 159-77.

[9] JONES R. - KIERZKOWSKI H., «A Framework for Fragmentation», in ARNDT S. - KIERZKOWSKI H. (eds), *Fragmentation, New Production Patterns in the World Economy*, Oxford, Oxford University Press, 2001, pp. 17-34.

[10] NAUJOKS P. - SCHMIDT K.D., «Outward Processing in Central and East European Transition Countries: Issues and Results from German Statistics», Kiel, Institute of World Economics, *Working Paper*, n. 631, 1994.

[11] NG F. - YEATS A., *Production Sharing in East Asia: Who Does What for Whom and Why?*, Mimeo, Washington, The World Bank, 1999.

[12] OETH, *The EU Textile and Clothing Industry 1993/94*, Brussels, 1994.

[13] PELLEGRIN J., «Linking up with Western European Firms: on the Prospects of Outward Processing Traffic», in BALDONE S. - SDOGATI F. (eds), *EU-CEECs Integration: Policies and Markets at Work*, Milano, F. Angeli, 1997, pp. 291-315.

[14] UNECE, «Outward Processing Trade Between the European Union and the Associated Countries of Eastern Europe: The Case of Textile and Clothing», *Economic Bulletin for Europe*, no. 47, Ch. 5, 1995.

Not Only EU Enlargement: the Need of Changing the Community Regional Policy

Giuseppe Mele*

Confindustria, Roma

Tra i rilevanti problemi dell'allargamento dell'UE, quello sul futuro della politica regionale e di coesione sembra diventare il più discusso. I contenuti di questo dibattito non sono finora soddisfacenti, poiché eccessivamente focalizzati sulle posizioni allocative e contributive degli Stati membri rispetto al bilancio UE. Le prime analisi svolte in questo articolo evidenziano numerosi aspetti critici nell'impostazione adottata e nei risultati ottenuti, e suggeriscono un percorso inverso all'attuale dibattito: prima la valutazione, poi la sostenibilità. In questo modo si evidenziano diversi aspetti contraddittori, da cui derivano le reali esigenze di riforma di questa politica comunitaria, soprattutto la sua capacità di integrare le politiche nazionali di sviluppo regionale, per affrontare efficacemente i rilevanti divari territoriali nella futura Unione.

The future of the regional and cohesion policy seems to have become the most discussed issue among the remarkable ones regarding the EU enlargement. The contents of this debate are so far not satisfactory, since the debate itself is excessively focused on the allocative and contributory member states' positions towards the EU budget. The preliminary analysis developed in this article highlights many critical points concerning the formulation so far adopted and the outcomes achieved; it also suggests a reverse debate method: appraisal first and then sustainability. Thus, several contradictory aspects emerge, from which the real reform needs, as special regards to its capability of integrating the national regional policies, can derive in order to face in an efficient way the considerable territorial gaps in the future Union. [JEL Code: R58, R11, O23]

* The author, Director for Territorial Policies, is particularly grateful to Alessandro Terzulli and Piera Magnatti for their accurate review. The paper reflects solely the point of view of the author, to which any remaining imperfection is attributable.

N.B., the numbers in square brackets refer to the Bibliography at the end of the paper.

1. - Introduction

The current enlargement process is the widest and most substantial that EU has ever planned. This process, compared with the past ones, may even interests the basis of the EU, since its size makes any solution founded on simple adaptations of the current Community set-up insufficient. This applies not only to the EU as a whole but also to its most important institutional profiles, among which the cohesion and regional policy (CRP); the implications the EU enlargement process contains are such they may overturn its methodological, financial and operational order, that is, according to the current formulation, the ground of its most important intervention tools: the Structural Funds (SFs) and the Cohesion Fund (CF).

These consequences seemed to be just perceivable right after the Luxembourg European Council in December 1997, after which the margins to the enlargement to the countries of Central, Eastern and Mediterranean Europe were set. The end of the negotiation on *Agenda 2000* in Berlin in March 1999 (CEC [14]) gave then a predominant political and bureaucratic formulation to the process; above all it faced every more immediate and evident financial implication, by allocating an endowment of specific resources up to 2006, to be used for the pre-accession and the accession of the Candidate countries (CCs). At the end of 2001 a more concrete enlargement size was reached (European Council [25]), by the decision (CEC [18]) regarding the entry in the EU of 10 Official Candidate countries (OCCs) by 2004[1].

This decision should widen and push the debate between the states and the Commission, especially on very delicate EU inter-

---

[1] The EU Enlargement was originally oriented on 13 countries: Bulgaria, Cyprus, the Czech Republic, Estonia, Hungary, Latvia, Lithuania, Malta, Poland, Romania, the Slovak Republic, Slovenia and Turkey. The accession process started in March 1998 by including all these countries but Turkey, and the accession negotiations with Cyprus, Czech Republic, Estonia, Hungary, Poland and Slovenia started right after. In December 2001 the Council of Laeken approved an enlargement to 10 new member states (excluding Turkey and, until 2006, Bulgaria and Romania) by the end of 2004.

nal equilibrium subjects such as the CRP. For some decades, this policy has been given an essential role for the removal of the existing structural imbalances across the European regions and for the promotion of economic equity in the integration process, on one side, and even for the political cohesion among the member states, on the other one.

At present, the debate still being very open, the actors (Commission and single states, both members and candidates) are even playing in an instrumental way, with the goal of taking-up the enlargement's costs and benefits sharing to a large extent. The debate does not seem (at least so far) to be focusing on an open and critical way on the model of the CRP carried out, starting from the results ensued and the validity of the followed approach. The application of the latter one to the actual 15 member states has already shown several limits and its applicability to a 25/27 EU member states has not been proved yet.

A large number of studies and researches about the enlargement has been already undertaken, but the profile of the in-depth analysis is still incomplete and that is even more evident when these studies and researches are also extended to the CRP. It seems in fact that the wanted results are excessively addressed to the aim of predisposing a political counter-balance to the doubts concerning the possible impacts on the Community and national budgets equilibria. These equilibria represent the most controversial aspect of the enlargement, especially for the Community budget's net contributor Partners, but also for those which take a higher benefit out of it.

There has been a lack of analysis on the appraisal of the enlargement impact on a regional basis for quite a certain period of time. The hope is it will sensitively increase as the CCs accession will approach, at least for a better understanding of the risks and the opportunities that can come up at a regional level. But even when the studies and analysis framework on the enlargement's territorial impact will have sufficiently progressed, there will still be however an important question to answer: at what conditions and objectives and according to what criteria regional development and cohesion Community policy will have to be kept and rein-

forced, if necessary? At that point it is to be hoped that both analysts and politicians will concentrate on the viable regional policy model at the Community level and try to give a consistent answer.

A reasonable and fair analytical approach should try *a)* to
evaluate the achieved results first, *b)* to compare with the old
unsolved needs and the new ones to be faced in the future then,
and finally *c)* to reason on the possible changes, without for-
getting this approach has to be related to the economic sound-
ness and the financial and political sustainability of the choices
that have to be made. This proposal could be easily accused of
being barely realist; it anyway appears like a very logical one,
but also essential for the effectiveness of the mission and its
results and for the convergence and re-balancing of development
levels and competitiveness conditions among the current and
future EU regions.

The conclusions this paper aims to reach cannot anyway be
definitive; the disposable data and analysis do not succeed in finding the necessary framework for the knowledge requirements and
so they produce problematic results. The attempt is therefore the
one of reconstructing a preliminary framework of internal and external references to the current CRP and of defining more consistently the Community action's reform needs for the future enlarged EU regional development and cohesion.

2. - The Evolution of CRP and its Outcomes

2.1 *The Foundations of the Current CRP*

They are three the basic motivations on which the premise to
the current CRP is founded: *A)* the reduction of disparity across
regions; *B)* the worsening of disparity depending on the economic European integration; *C)* the direct and indirect effects on the
ability of national economic policies to reduce the structural delays compared with the other EU member states. This evolution
scheme of the CRP was completed when the European monetary

union (EMU) was born; until that moment these motivations had come up one by one. The *Agenda 2000* (CEC [14] and [15]) however, the last action project for the years 2000-2006, *D*) should have reviewed this scheme, as regards to the weight of the last two motivations. Strangely, the basic scheme of the CRP has only suffered marginal changes, in spite of the adoption of a new target: the EU enlargement and its organization.

A) Among the three basic motivations of the CRP, the first one hasn't been for a long time considered sufficient to justify a regional development Community policy (Mele [35]), until a stronger justification has come along: the «non territorial neutrality» of the European economic integration process. This general concept was founded on the progressive and always more evident arising of economic and structural competitiveness gaps for the weakest regions, with the risk of emphasising the territorial imbalances in the development level and welfare. This assumption was only indirectly inferable from the principles included in the initial EEC Treaty (1957), as regards to the «harmonious development» and the «improvement of the less developed regions». But the assumption itself was however used to justify — even though with difficulty (Holland [29]) — the beginning of a primitive form of CRP, by the creation (1975) of the European regional development fund (ERDF).

The formulation which followed was the one of facing EU regional gaps, especially through a contribution to national policies, without particular Community orientations, but that to provide a support from the EU budget to national interventions in favour of regional development theoretically consistent with the *Treaty's* goals[2].

B) A more definite position on the regional divergences em-

---

[2] The «non territorial neutrality» of the integration process, more evident then, could be especially found in the tariffs abatement policy (not easily appraisable at territorial level, because gradually managed and hardly perceivable as real asymmetrical shocks), and also in the Common Agricultural Policy (CAP), to which a preponderant financial allocation of the EU budget resources was linked. This way, the new ERDF was rather easily identified as a limited attempt to a less unbalanced redistribution of the EU budget resources among states (through the regions).

phasis induced by the economic integration was achieved by the completion of the internal market project, defined by the *White Paper* in 1985 (CEC [9]) and sanctioned then by the *European Single Act* in 1987. The birth of the CRP was actually enacted through the introduction of a Title on the «Economic and Social Cohesion» in the *EEC Treaty*[3].

Generally, the analysis developed then on the regional impacts of the internal market did not exclude that the higher growth of European economy (CEC [10]) would have even been able to help the development perspectives of the economically weakest areas[4]. Anyway, the outcomes distribution across countries and regions was not very clear, thus there was concern about the effects of the Single Market integration process on the increase in economic and territorial differences and the concentration of the negative ones in the weakest areas[5]. The opinion shared by almost all the studies focused on the risk of an inevitable and progressive rejection of peripheral areas with a development delay. The last ones had the problem of overcoming their disadvantage in terms of external economies of the strong areas and the need of recovering from

---

[3] Some of the project recommendations recalled the attention on possible regional imbalances. Even though not quantified, the *Cecchini Report* (CEC [8]) identified the social and regional potential imbalances deriving from a «not correct and loyal redistribution of the benefits» produced by the abatement of non-tariff barriers. This is why a higher territorial concentration in the use of the SFs was recommended.

[4] The theory of international commerce, adopted in several studies, could not fully highlight the impact induced by the development of international economic exchanges, since it assumes that comparative advantages are given, whereas in a dynamic framework they can be modified by the firms' answer strategies, the individual behaviour and the policies adopted by national and supranational institutions.

[5] The many studies made in those years (BALDWIN R. [3]; NEVEN D. and ROELLER L. [37]; NEVEN D. [39]; SMITH A. and VENABLES A. [47]) however converged towards an univocal conclusion on the impact of the Single Market: such process would have induced more developed areas to exploit their relevant economies of scale (even though this basis assumption was not shared by all the analysts, as NEVEN D. [39]). For the less developed European areas the strategy should have been founded mainly on the exploitation of comparative advantages, first, and on the increase in their specialization in labour intensive sectors, then. Such a strategy would have anyway implied some risks for the latter areas, exposed to the raising competitive pressure of developing countries (and already since then Eastern Europe) with a lower labour cost (NEVEN D. and ROELLER L. [38]). The competitive reaction should have even led to a gradual productive specialization in capital intensive sectors.

their own structural weakness and also their considerable territorial and physical disadvantages[6].

This conclusion implied a reconsideration, in an expansive
and more incisive way, of the regional policy (national and Community) actions, addressed towards the abatement of the natural barriers; a process, this one neither easy nor rapid nor ob-
tainable in completely sharp terms. The counter-balancing of the
asymmetrical effects of the internal market completion, with evident repercussions on the planning orientations, was the prevailing ratio. In any case, a «moral duty», induced by the risks
of further regional gaps amplification implicit in the integration
process, was given to the EEC for the strengthening of the CRP
in the period 1989-1993. There obviously were contrary opinions
towards any kind of «interventionism», founded on the traditional neo-classical approach on market clearing and limited
state involvement, especially at a Community level; in this last
case, serious doubts were even based on the fact that a regional development policy organised by the Community was not more
efficient than the national ones from the political and economic point of view (Armstrong and Taylor [1]).

C) The current basic scheme of the CRP was completed by
the subsequent phase regarding the planning period 1994-1999.
The EU action was addressed to the territorial effects of the
EMU, which represented the most relevant conclusive aspect of
the internal market completion, since the last economic barrier

---

[6] Other authors (KRUGMAN P. and VENABLES A. [31]) indeed believed that the
elimination of non-tariff barriers could not be comprehensive of all trade costs,
which include natural barriers (distances, transport costs, cultural differences, ...)
too. An only partial reduction of trade costs (for all the European areas), through
interaction with economies of scale (concentrated in the prosperous areas), would
have therefore limited, in a strong way, the possible relocation of productions, as
suggested by a strategy (for the weak areas) based only on the compared advantages of cost. In brief, capital and labour mobility could have led to a levelling of
regional per capita incomes only in the extreme and unreal for certain aspects,
conditions as the absence of economies of scale or specific geographical factors
able to influence investment decisions (SARCINELLI M. [44]). In order to avoid the
risk of concentration in the most developed regions, suitable measures were found
for the readjustment of regional imbalances inside the Community, by the promotion of investment and employment conditions in the lagging areas comparable to those of more developed ones (PADOA-SCHIOPPA T. [41]).

to the free circulation of people, goods and capital had been eliminated. This way, the subject of the asymmetrical effects on a territorial basis came out again, even though with some important implications which potentially led to a subsequent widening of the role of the CRP. At the base of the EMU there was (and there still is) a sensitive constraint to the intervention capacity of member states, to acquire and/or maintain the required macroeconomic convergence (McCrone [34]); the states' intervention on a territorial level could have suffered the effects of a limited redistribution of the national fiscal policies, both in general terms (but certainly with more negative effects for the less developed regions) and in specific terms (in case a member State already had its own regional policy, additional to the standard fiscal redistribution).

For the weakest regions, the EMU could have therefore represented not only the final emerging of the problems caused by a stronger economic and territorial competitiveness, but, in some cases, also a considerable limitation to the intervention opportunities for the restraint of its effects on regional development. Also in this phase of the European integration process the choice was the one of widening the support of the CRP, together with the addition of a new and conspicuous financial instrument, the CF created by the *EU Treaty* (1992) and defined by a special protocol. The CF should have been an answer to several needs; from the operational point of view it should have favoured the carrying out of the infrastructure development for the less developed member states' (and indirectly the regions') competitiveness; from the financial point of view it should have preserved the great public investments level on these states' budgets. Moreover, this financial tool should have helped in neutralizing the additional tensions that EMU could have generated on the recipient countries' national budgets (Spain, Greece, Portugal and Ireland) in terms of predetermined constraints on public deficit and debt.

From the theoretical point of view, as regards to EMU also, less «interventionist» market solutions were proposed; these proposals were definitely rejected (Delors [21]), because of regionalist motivations too[7].

D) Agenda 2000, both the revision project of the Community policies and the EU current budget, is the political framework in which the CRP was reformulated for the subsequent period 2000-2006. Its definitive approval represented an important step for the CRP; it was the first time, after many years, this policy, as a tool for the equilibrium of the general Community action, suffered a financial downsizing[8], without a revision of its formulation, in spite of the intervened relevant changes[9].

This time, a strengthening of the CRP would have met more resistance than in the past. The Single Market completion should have substantially been concluded and the EMU achieved, even though the change-over still had to be done; but the tensions produced by the EMU itself on national public finances were not certainly over, they rather were in a critical phase. This is probably the main reason which pushed the member states to confirm the scheme of the CRP.

---

[7] The limited national capabilities of direct intervention (with possible repercussions on the growth and employment for the weakest regions) could have been compensated by a higher factors mobility, labour above all. This higher mobility would have certainly damaged the weak regions' development perspectives, the competitive realignment of which could have been achieved by migrations within (towards the stronger national regions) and across (towards the strongest European regions) states. In the first case, capital and labour mobility would have subsequently been detrimental for the weak regions, while in the second one, they, strongly limited by cultural and language differences, could have mainly favoured the concentration of (European and foreign) capital in the EU strongest territorial core, notoriously included in a radius of 500 km around Luxembourg (CEC [11] and [12]).

[8] The initial proposal for Agenda 2000 (CEC [14]) included a general fund of 792.7 milliards of Euros at 1999 prices for the period 2000-2006, according to following allocation: 42.7% to the CAP, 30.2% to the CRP, 2.8% to the pre-accession, 7.1% to the enlargement and 17.2% to other functions. By its definitive approval in Berlin (CEC [15]), the general fund was reduced to 702.8 milliards of Euros (-11.3%), unchanging the funds for the pre-accession and the enlargement and reducing those for the CAP (-12.1%), for the CRP (-11%) and for the other functions (-16.5%).

[9] The important changes for the CRP are not only those induced by the European integration, analysed more in detail in these pages, but they should also be the ones generated by the World economy's evolution (LUCAS R.E. JR. [33]); e.g., from a long term point of view, how "globalisation" and "new economy" could contribute to extend the convergence process both among and within countries.

The real political priority of *Agenda 2000* is the enlargement, in reference to which the EU budget has identified the way for a specific support. This priority change is not a weakening sign of the CRP, since the attention given to pre-accession and enlargement is actually based on the extension of the CRP to the CCs. Indeed, it could be stated that by *Agenda 2000* the CRP is being assigned to the CCs, which are going through the same phases of the integration already faced before by current member states and regions.

In such a logic framework the confirmation of the scheme of the CRP for the current member states includes some differentiating or (better) amplifying aspects of some of its characteristics. It seems nearly perceivable an initial step of general *phasing out* of the CRP (already introduced by the intervention regarding the regions and the areas on their way out of the regional development priority objectives) or a transformation of the CRP, from an action founded on the combination of the structural realignment objective and the one of their reinforcement, justified by the integration, to another action mostly focused on the first objective.

The repercussions of such a (although implicit) review of the CRP can also be caught by other signs, not only the ones concerning the financial allocation, which it may be worth investigating. According to this preliminary analysis, *Agenda 2000* has consolidated the formulation of the CRP and its intervention tools, instead of favouring its wide revision. In short, if the enlargement had to be the EU political priority starting from 2000 and the CRP its main support element, the reform of the latter one, at least in its fundamental aspects, should have been done in Berlin instead of being postponed to 2004-2005. Overall, a critical analysis should have been developed on the outcomes of the CRP in order to avoid the prosecution of the several contradictions of its intervention scheme.

2.2 *The Outcomes Achieved by the CRP: a Synthesis*

The economic disparity trend is a traditional synthetic key of the economic territorial performance; this analysis can help in understanding the effectiveness of the economic policy tools as the CRP and the national regional policies, even though it should be integrated by other elements. However, especially for the CRP, territorial economic disparity represents an important factor in comparison with the considerable resources allocated by the EU[10].

In the current EU 15 a pretty fast disparity reduction across member states is taking place; this is one of the most relevant effects of the economic integration and unification process. On the contrary, there is a general low regional disparity reduction trend. This phenomenon can be noticed by the Commission as regards both to the farthest in time (CEC [17]) and to the most recent past (CEC [19]).

In the whole period 1995-1999, in fact, the gap significantly decrease across EU states (Graph 1), while the disparity was substantially unchanged across regions, even though intermediate data show for some years a worsening. According to these results, the CRP seems to have developed a prevailing «defensive» function so preventing a comprehensive disparity amplification somewhat, without favouring a disparity reduction[11].

---

[10] The reference index (V_w) here used for the definition of disparity is the one proposed by WILLIAMSON [50]:

$$V_w = \frac{\sqrt{\sum_i (y_i - \bar{y})^2 \frac{f_i}{n}}}{\bar{y}},$$

where f_i is the population of the i region, n is the national (or supranational) population, y_i is the per capita income of the i region and y is the national (or supranational) per capita income. The calculations have been processed by using the most recent Eurostat available data for the period 1995-1999 (statistically homogeneous, ESA 95, not comparable with the previous ones yet, ESA 79). Anyway, the conclusion is unchanged when considering the data covering only the previous period (CEC [19]).

[11] This conclusion seems to be supported even though in terms intuitively counter-factual by an analysis of disparities across CCs, in which there are not cohesion and regional development interventions; in these countries relatively helped by the pre-accession funds, a wider divergence between the very few strong (the urban areas of the capital cities) regions and weak ones emerges (MELE G. [36]). By a more detailed analysis, this phenomenon would seem emerge also in the Objective 1 regions and in the CF countries of the current EU, even though in a more modest size measure, but in remarkable terms.

GRAPH 1

NATIONAL AND REGIONAL DISPARITY:
THE EU 15 AND ENLARGED EU 25

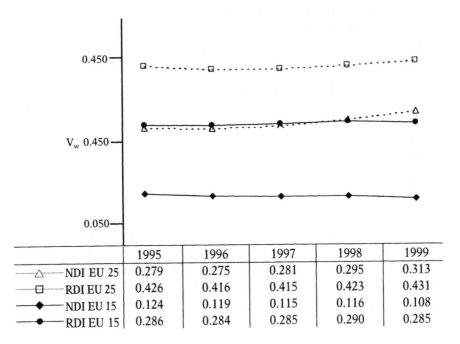

	1995	1996	1997	1998	1999
△ NDI EU 25	0.279	0.275	0.281	0.295	0.313
▫ RDI EU 25	0.426	0.416	0.415	0.423	0.431
◆ NDI EU 15	0.124	0.119	0.115	0.116	0.108
● RDI EU 15	0.286	0.284	0.285	0.290	0.285

Legenda: NDI: National disparity index.
               RDI: Regional disparity index.
Source: Own calculations on EUROSTAT data.

On a national level the situations are rather diversified and discordant (Graph 2). First of all a general interruption of the decreasing trend and a considerable disparity amplification, in some countries have to be noticed. Countries, mainly interested by the CRP like Spain and Portugal, have suffered a notable worsening, which was lower in Germany and Ireland; in counter-tendency it is the modest recent reduction of regional disparity in Italy (IS-TAT [30]) and in Greece, higher in the former than in the latter one.

Italy is the country with the highest regional disparity level, very close to the one calculated for the Community (see RDI,

GRAPH 2

REGIONAL DISPARITY ON A NATIONAL LEVEL IN THE EU 15

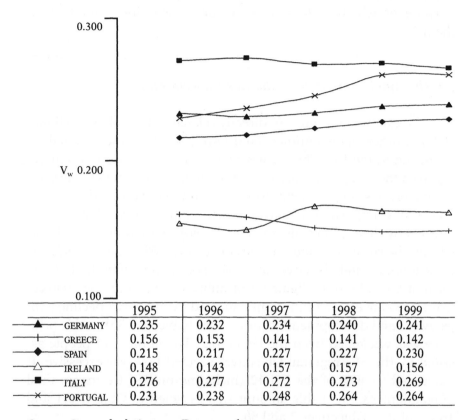

	1995	1996	1997	1998	1999
▲ GERMANY	0.235	0.232	0.234	0.240	0.241
+ GREECE	0.156	0.153	0.141	0.141	0.142
◆ SPAIN	0.215	0.217	0.227	0.227	0.230
△ IRELAND	0.148	0.143	0.157	0.157	0.156
■ ITALY	0.276	0.277	0.272	0.273	0.269
× PORTUGAL	0.231	0.238	0.248	0.264	0.264

Source: Own calculations on EUROSTAT data.

Graph 1), but followed at a certain distance by Portugal, Germany and, at an even lower level, by Spain. Internal disparities are clearly low in Ireland and in Greece compared with the other EU countries, even though in progressive worsening.

It is unexpected that the «cohesion countries» group itself (that benefits from the CF, in addition to the SFs) achieved so modest outcomes in terms of inside re-balancing. Disparities within countries grew sensitively, because of the emerging of a frac-ture between strong and weak regions. This is not such a big surprise, since territorial competitiveness tends to favour strong urban polarities, but not without a regional policy, the fundamental purpose of which is to reduce regional disparities, not to feed them[12].

2.3 *The Ambiguous Role of the SFs Concentration*

The examined trends are directly related to the role that (financial and other) interventions could have played for the regional rebalancing in the EU. The studies and the recommendations emerging from the completion project of the Single Market had focused on a principle of strong concentration of the interventions and resources on the most important regional problems and the areas that were interested by them (especially the less developed areas and, in a limited way, the rural ones and the ones in decline). With the definition of three fundamental objectives of regional development in the 1988 reform of the CRP — realignment of underdeveloped regions (Objective 1), re-conversion of the zones affected by industrial decline (Objective 2) and development of rural zones (Objective 5b) — this principle was weakened from the beginning. The number of people assisted by the SFs regional Objectives seemed however excessive. It amounted to 40% of the EU 12 (including unified Germany) total population; 23.3% of this amount was assigned to Objective 1 and 16.7% of it to Objectives 2 and 5b.

In the revision which followed for the period 1994-1999 there was an increase up to 43.9% in the regional objectives percentage of recipient population (out of the EU 15 total, after the 1995 enlargement to Austria, Finland and Sweden); this result was produced by the «creation» of Objective 6 (interventions in the poorly populated

---

[12] Among the weak EU regions the ones with the most important urban areas normally grow more than the other ones or, at least, they do not grow less (CEC [17]); this is true for Ireland (Southern and Eastern region, where Dublin is, grew more than the rest of the country), Portugal (Lisboa and Vale do Tejo) and Spain (Comunidad de Madrid, Cataluña, Pais Vasco). Development concentration phenomena are less stressed in Greece, even though the Attiki region stays as the one where most of the national economic activity is located.

zones of Sweden and Finland, representing the 0.3% of the EU population) and by an increase in the population coverage in the already assisted areas under all the other regional objectives (to 24.4% for Objective 1 and to 19.1% for Objectives 2 and 5*b*).

As regards to the period 2000-2006 there was an attempt to simplify the priority regional objectives of the SFs which substantially led to an inclusion of Objective 6 (in Objective 1) and of Objective 5*b* (in Objective 2). As a matter of fact, such unification did not actually focus on the most relevant regional problems, since the eliminated objectives were absorbed by the two priority regional objectives left. Moreover, with the exception of some *phasing out* areas (that is the zones previously included in the Objectives 1, 2 and 5b and excluded from the new Objectives 1 and 2), the recipient population of the SFs was reduced by about 9 millions of people, with a decrease in the less developed regions' share (down to 21.6% of EU population, net of former Objective 6) and a lower decrease in the new Objective 2 share (down to 18.3%).

This lack of concentration did not only regard the most important problems and interested areas, but also the resources distribution. The considerable news of the 1988 SFs reform surely was the «doubling» of their allocations in real terms to be achieved by the end of the period 1987-1993[13]. Actually, the Objective 1 got only about 64% of them (rather than 70%, even though the only ERDF should have got 80% about); this share was reduced to 61.7% in the period 1994-1999 and only for the period 2000-2006 was brought again to the previous share (65.7%). Besides the resources concentration problem in terms of intervention consistency was even more important. It has to be in fact reminded that a large part of the intervention zones in decline or in rural development (the current Objective 2) has always showed higher development levels than the Objective 1 ones.

---

[13] This choice was carried out by an integrated use of the ERDF, the European Social Fund (ESF), the *section guidance* of the Agricultural Fund (EAGGF), the intervention of the European Investments Bank (EIB) and other financial tools. At least for the ERDF, the doubling in real terms would have meant a small change in the growth trend constantly recorded since 1975. Such an operation, even though in a slow and progressive way, would have at least triggered a re-balancing process of the EU budget, especially in terms of total weight of the SFs in comparison with the CAP (MELE G. [35]).

In some cases, these relatively developed zones included important urban areas; even though affected by temporary phases of decline, the CRP assistance has not been very clear (except some cases, not easily identifiable in the adopted selection criteria, particularly sensitive to the completion of the internal market or characterised by a persistent economic and social decline).

Other potential distorting elements can be found in the interventions of the SFs by non-regional objectives (with 13-15% share of the general allocations of the CRP in the different planning periods for the human resources policies and the agricultural and fishing policy) or for those directly managed by the European Commission (by the so-called Community Initiatives regarding even the zones out of the regional Objectives to which a 5-10% share of resources of the SFs was ascribed). Another critical aspect regards of the CRP the resources allocation methods at both national and regional level, especially for the Objective 1[14]. The strong weight the political negotiation was given has generated not entirely consistent, with the regional re-balancing finalities, effects. By the enlargement, the confirmation of such mechanisms could imply even more remarkable disequilibria, because the gap in development levels between CCs and the Community ones is too high.

---

[14] In the first period of planning (1989-1993), Greece, Ireland and Portugal received too high resources in comparison with their development level. In the second (1994-1999) and third period (2000-2006), these three member states, with the addition of Spain, maintained this favourable treatment. A better understanding of this can be obtained through an estimation based on the comparison between the Objective 1 resources really allocated and theoretically allocable with the Community allocation-development level average ratio; in the period 2000-2006, Portugal will receive the 61% of additional resources, while it should have received (according to its regional level of disparity) only 11% more than the Objective 1 average; the same is for Greece (with an additional 32%, compared with the 1% less it should have received), Spain (additional 9% instead of 1% more) and Ireland (11% less instead of 19% less). Among the less favoured countries as regards to the resources allocation for Objective 1, the most impressive cases are: United Kingdom (33% less instead of 8% less), Austria and Italy (respectively, 37% and 24% less, instead of the Community average ratio). These results derive from a formulation followed by the Commission which gives an excessive weight to the development level of the member State as a whole (as a matter of fact, the four favoured countries are also the recipient of the CF) and a lower one to the other considered variables (regional prosperity and unemployment). The results which emerge are only partially acceptable and the general comments about the used methodology's fitness can be shared (BARBIERI G. and PELLEGRINI G. [5]).

TABLE 1

THE CONCENTRATION OF SFs RESOURCES AND AREAS: SYNTHESIS FOR THE 1989-1993, 1994-1999 AND 2000-2006 PERIODS

Final destinations	1989-1993 Allocations Total (millions of UCE)	1989-1993 Yearly average	1989-1993 Population (.000 - in % of the EU)	1994-1999 Allocations Total (millions of UCE)	1994-1999 Yearly average	1994-1999 Population (.000 - in % of the EU)	2000-2006 Allocations Total (millions of Euros)	2000-2006 Yearly average	2000-2006 Population (.000 - in % of the EU)
Objective 1	43,818	8,763.6	84,814.1	93,991	15,665	90,375.9	127,543	18,220.4	81,508.1
Objective 6				697	116	1,290.1			(1,528.0)
Objective 2	6,130	1,226.0	56,994.0	15,352	2,559	61,189.3	19,733	2,819.0	68,941.9
Objective 5b	2,232	446.4	3,990.5	6,860	1,143	9,674.8			
Total regional Objectives	52,180	10,436.0	145,798.5	116,900	19,483	162,530.1	158,408	22,629.7	151,978.0
Phasing out Objective 1							8,411	1,201.6	
Phasing out Objective 2							2,721	388.7	
Other Objectives	10,771	2,154.2		21,339	3,557		25,156	3,593.7	
Community Initiatives	5,285	1,057.0		14,021	2,337		10,442	1,491.7	
Grand total	68,236	13,647.2		152,260	25,377		194,006	27,715.1	

Distribution (%)

Final destinations	1989-1993 Total	1989-1993 Population	1994-1999 Total	1994-1999 Population	2000-2006 Total	2000-2006 Population
Objective 1	64.2	23.3	61.7	24.4	65.7	21.6
Objective 6			0.5	0.3		(0.4)
Objective 2	9.0	15.6	10.0	16.5	10.2	18.3
Objective 5b	3.3	1.1	4.5	2.6		
Total regional Objectives	76.5	40.0	76.8	43.9	81.7	40.3
Phasing out Objective 1					4.3	
Phasing out Objective 2					1.4	
Other Objectives	15.8		14.0		13.0	
Community Initiatives	7.7		9.2		5.4	
Grand total	100.0		100.0		100.0	

Source: Own calculations on COMMISSION OF THE EUROPEAN COMMUNITY data.

The distributional function of the CRP was very clear since the beginning; this policy's size has often required a wide and shared political consent among the Partners, not always consistent with the regional development finalities though. This ambiguity of the CRP was even more evident in its revision after the EMU was born. The outcomes of the regional re-balancing process have disappointed the implicit expectations of the orientations of the CRP for 1994-1999, although they offered undeniable advantages to some countries (Greece, Ireland, Portugal and Spain) through the CF[15].

The Commission and member states conclusion was, in theory, much stronger than the 1988 reform of the CRP, also because the *EU Treaty* stipulation (1992) set the objectives of the economic and social cohesion in the more urgent terms of productivity and income convergence levels, with particular attention to the support to the least favoured regions. This also induced to a strengthening of the action of the SFs the total allocations of which was significantly increased (+60%) for the period 1994-1999.

The formulation for the 2000-2006 planning period was substantially maintained, although this period was characterised by important events for the European integration process: the adoption of the Single Currency and the greatest enlargement in the EU history. The maintenance of the CF for the same countries was instead contradictory and inconsistent with the premises on which it was founded and the changes in the meantime intervened. At the moment of the *Agenda 2000* definitive approval (1999), only Greece did not make the EMU, while Spain, Ireland and Portugal joined the Union by having perfectly fulfilled all the macroeconomic convergence criteria. The fundamental mission of the

---

[15] The CF was openly given an integrative role of national public finance. As regards to the development gaps relevant problems, the risk not to make the EMU was very high for some countries. Nevertheless, there also were tensions in other countries' national public finance as in Italy and, after the reunification, Germany; these were anyway excluded according to the selection criteria (per capita GDP higher than the 90% of the EU average). Both mentioned countries kept their important regional development national policies, with notable difficulties before and after the birth of the EMU. CF countries instead kept also on being the main recipients of the SFs, but they are now having problems in respecting the convergence criteria (e.g. the case of Portugal).

NATIONAL ALLOCATIONS OF THE CF IN THE 1993-1999
AND 2000-2006 PERIODS (MILLIONS OF EUROS)

Allocations	Greece	Ireland	Portugal	Spain	Total
			1993-1999		
Total (millions of Euros)	2,998.2	1,495.2	3,005.4	9,251.1	16,749.9
Environment	1,463.7	746.9	1,559.4	4,654.2	8,424.2
Transport	1,534.5	748.3	1,446.0	4,596.9	8,325.7
Yearly average					
Total (millions of Euros)	428.3	213.6	429.3	1,321.6	2,392.8
Per capita (Euros)	41.4	59.9	43.5	33.8	38.1
			2000-2006		
Total yearly average					
Minimum	411.4	51.4	411.4	1,568.6	2,571.4
Maximum	462.9	154.3	462.9	1,632.9	2,571.4
Annual average (Euros per capita)					
Minimum	39.1	13.7	41.2	39.8	40.4
Maximum	44.0	41.2	46.4	41.4	40.4

Source: Own calculations on COMMISSION OF THE EUROPEAN COMMUNITY data.

CF could be considered almost fully achieved; its role could therefore be revised.

Another and more evident revision need should have derived from the signs of internal divergence in the CF countries. From the regional policy point of view, these results show strong doubts regarding the expected effectiveness of the general action of the CRP. The possibility that a member state as a whole may benefit from the SFs should not only be addressed to the growth of every region, but also to the reduction of the existing disparities across them; this need was not sufficiently taken into account. The joined operational mechanisms of the SFs and the CF in a country includes some potential distorting elements which need to be considered, because the intervention of the SFs in the weakest regions could be counterbalanced or crowded-out by an inconsistent intervention of the CF in the most developed ones. This occurrence must not be undervalued, because the persistence of the internal gaps within member states represents a relevant in progress phenomenon which could be fed by this ambiguous formulation of the CRP. A similar conclusion can also be attained as regards to the intervention mechanisms of the SFs. A priority has certainly to be given to the Objective 1 lagging regions, but the (not well calculated and limited) resources allocation — to Objective 2 or even to areas not included in the regional Objectives — can favour the growth of disparity or its persistence[16]. As regards to the reform of the CRP subsequent to the enlargement, this should induce to finally give more attention to the resources planning within member states and their effects on the internal disparities.

2.4 *The Difficult Relation between the Community and National Regional Policies towards the Operational Set-Up of the CRP*

The potential implicit CRP's distortion on the regional re-balancing finalities introduces another important leading issue, regarding the complementary role that the CRP should have on the regional development national policies. This role may have a double aspect: the planning of the intervention tools of the CRP and the co-ordination of this ones with the regional development national economic policies.

The intervention tools planning of the CRP makes emerge in particular the cases of recipient areas including single regions (within the same member state) or whole member states. In the first case, the action complementarity of the SFs would presuppose (or induce to) the existence of a national regional policy; whereas in the second one the distinction between this policy and the national economic one would be difficult to highlight. In both cases the control function has to check that the intervention of the SFs may not substitute the regional re-balancing national public finance. The adoption of weak criteria for the additionality of the SFs to the national public finance (art. 9, *Reg. EEC* n. 4253/88, afterwards modified by the subsequent *Regulations* of the *CRP*) would have generated the risk for any EU regional development

---

[16] Even the *competition policy* may produce similar distortions, since the rules and orientations on regional finality State aids allow, according *t* the *EC Treaty* (art. 87, par. 3, letters *a* and *c*), derogations both for the less developed regions and for the zones with economic difficulties.

action to become a simple quantitative reallocation towards the national budgets of the resources financing the same action. Such situations can create further distortions of the CRP, deriving from the national regional policies weakening (or neutralization), maybe also induced by the pressure on the public budgets.

In reference to this regard, another relevant problem comes out, the one of «true» and «apparent» national regional policies. For a long time, only a few recipient countries of the SFs have had a true regional policy. These countries have wanted to keep their own national policy — in co-ordination with the CRP, but independent from the operational and financial point of view — also to integrate the excesses or deficiencies of the CRP itself (e.g. in order to strengthen the infrastructural intervention or re-balance the action for the lagging regions in comparison with those in decline). The strengthening of the CRP has also pushed other countries to promote regional development national policies (at least for the co-financing requested by the *Regulations*). In these cases, there could be a homologation between the CRP and the national policies which may favour a real substitution, especially from the financial point of view. The additionality principle does not seem to be able to guarantee a more balanced resources and interventions regional allocation consistent with regional development finalities; and that is easier for the member states fully covered by the SFs (and by the CF too). This way, member states can be the simple regional development «interpreters» instead of its «co-authors»[17].

The national regional policies homologation (*lato sensu*) may also have been favoured by a particular application of the partnership (between Commission and member states) principle; according to it, the programmes were substantially negotiated under the strong Commission power, which has often dictated the intervention choices; according to the subsidiarity principle then, the member states should have had the most important role.

---

[17] The most evident effects of the prominent role developed by the Commission for the choices of the member states regional policy are also shown by the high homogenisation level; this is of course a positive aspect for the improvements achieved in the planning feasibility more than in the contents one, which is usually addressed to the direct and indirect support of productive activity (YUILL D. and McMASTER I. [51]).

The Commission *modus operandi* has also favoured even the intervention strategies formulation of the SFs, affected by an endogenous development approach for long time; this choice was not shareable because of the big differences among the territorial realities covered by the CRP; from the effectiveness point of view, such theories have better fitted to the decline situations rather than the underdevelopment's ones (Armstrong [2]). Since the *Single Act* was approved, the CRP should have concentrated on a variable mix of actions, however predominantly based on external economies (Smith and Venables [47]) less on the direct and indirect interventions for the firms and on a local basis.

This approach was strengthened by the 1994-1999 revision (CEC [13]) and reduced for the 2000-2006 period (CEC [17]). In the first case, the strengthening can also be seen as a natural consequence of the regional convergence in income levels; as an answer to the heavy criticisms for the scarce past results, this convergence had to be perceived (if possible) in the short-medium term too. Nevertheless, the increase of actions addressed to the basic externalities and the transport costs reduction in lagging areas could have been more efficient. The productivity and income effects on the convergence could have been obtained in the long term, but the external investments attraction could be more effective than the one deriving from a temporary external costs reduction, more suitable to consolidate pre-existing investments[18]. The approach's reduction, jointly with a great attention for the external economies and the territory, brought an appreciable change, although not imposed, in the intervention choices[19], even in terms of an effective subsidiarity principle.

---

[18] The intention is not to raise issues on the approach followed (and substantially favoured) by the Commission for many years, but there is enough literature on the regional development experiences to understand that there can be many different ways; what appeared excessive then (and still today) it was the choice of a specific way of development which could turn out effective in every situation. Obviously, in formulating a regional policy, the leading orientations derive from the resources allocation mix; that is the CRP, even though giving a great attention to the factors, had not certainly neglected the increase of externalities and the reduction of «peripherality»; nevertheless, the smaller relative weight given to the latter ones because of the Commission strategic preferences for the lagging regions was not irrelevant for their development perspectives.

[19] This change is also due to the '90s theoretical debate about the regional eco-

This principle has often been related to the regional and local institutions involvement or responsibility. If this interpretation is broadly (but not always) reasonable as regards to the modest financial size of interventions in the declining areas, it could be less effective in the lagging regions, the development of which can be more consistent with the relevant interregional interventions, planned by the national administrations or, if necessary, by the Commission itself (e.g. for the *Trans-European Networks*). The strong decentralization would limit this need, since the programmes could show themselves as a micro-interventions aggregate; certainly important, more for the local economies needs and less for their marginality problems. Subsidiarity doesn't only mean making the administrative decisional responsibility closer to the people, but also more effective; the administrative level of the CRP does not always match with local institution, because it may reduce the necessary strategic and systemic profiles of a Community policy. This formulation may have caused a less effective and efficient resources allocation on an excessive number of zones, programmes and interventions.

A last but not least issue regards the current set-up of the CRP operational procedures, which have been more incisively based on the programmes starting from the 1988 reform of the CRP (while before, especially in the beginning of the ERDF, they were predominantly found on specific projects). The reformulation for the 1994-1999 period substantially confirmed the planning method together with a strengthening of the evaluation role. Such an approach is basically shareable, but the bureaucratic be-

---

nomic development space determinants (KRUGMAN P. [32]), on which the *New Economic Geography* studies have been based. By starting from this aprroach, different perspectives, focused on the "net economy" role (VENABLES A. [49]) as well, were opened to the regional development orientations; these changes were partially included in the most recent CRP's planning options, thanks to the EU greater attention to the opportunities offered by the "information technology". Generally, the slow and difficult merging of the theoretical debate in the planning options is not caused only by the lower *subsidiarity* of the CRP or the limite "s" attention of the national regional policies; even the economists should still increase research on some interesting approaches, e.g. on the growth and income "residual determinants", such as technology, human capital, externalities, etc. (EASTERLY W. and LEVINE R. [24]) and on the "social capital" overall perpectives on a regional basis (BEUGELSDIJK S. and VAN SCHAIK T. [6]).

haviour of the Commission has favoured the programmes proliferation, especially of small size ones, keeping on applying the strict
bookkeeping formalities and financial management rules. The effort in the definition and the carrying-out of the whole planning
of the CRP has implied considerable difficulties for the Commission and, above all, for the member states. These ones had to use
relevant and specific human and technical resources, especially in
the adjustment of their own management systems to the Community model.

Agenda 2000 had taken into account this fundamental simplification need of the SFs, through the assignment of a great
management responsibility to both the national and the regional institutions in charge of the programmes accomplishment. The
timing and the conflicts between national administrations and
the Commission have actually significantly increased and the
contradictions regarding the ambiguous respect of the subsidiarity principle have not disappeared. The operational conditions were not absolutely decisive for the success of the CRP on
the actual EU, but they could be one of the problems which
caused the very little outcomes so far achieved. Besides, the administrative impact issue does not seem to be adequately considered in the management of the resources of the SFs and the
CF for the CCs. In this case also, it seems that the complicated
administrative EU model is being imposed, without any proposal for a new, simpler and valid model, for both actual and future member states. The real risk is that the 10 OCCs will not
succeed in fully using the conspicuous flow of resources already
allocated to them for the 2004-2006 period[20], with the result of
spending a large part of their time and energies for the necessary management adjustment.

---

[20] This occurrence is even considered by the Commission itself to justify the
sufficiency of the pre-accession and the enlargement resources (SCHREYER M. [45];
CEC [18]).

3. - Enlargement and Cohesion

3.1 *The Changes in the Territorial Development*

The need of changing the contents and the operational set-up of the CRP is evident independently from the EU enlargement. Even a political need comes out. If the EU regional finalities are still the basis for the unification process, a Community co-ordination duty is at least necessary. Is a direct intervention also necessary? In answering this question it is useful to refer to the basic scheme of the CRP and its applicability in the future EU.

The first motivation of the CRP, founded on regional disparities, is still relevant and greater and more than the past. The 25 EU members defined by the Council of Laeken would cover a territory of almost 4 millions of kms and a population (1999 data) of 451,6 millions of people (with an increase respectively of 22.7% and 19.9%, in comparison with the current EU 15). The general GDP would increase only by 8.8% (1999 data), from around 8 milliards in *Purchasing Power Parities (PPP)* to around 8.7.

Compared with previous EU enlargements (CEC [16] and [17]), the most important aspect of the next one is, therefore, given by the deep development gaps existing between the two areas, showed by the level of per capita GDP in *PPP* for the OCCs 10, which equals 59.2% of the EU 25 average. In this group of countries, the most developed one (except for Cyprus, with a per capita GDP equalling 93.5% of the EU average) is Slovenia, the level of per capita GDP of which almost equals the one for the less developed EU 15 countries (Greece, 75.2% of the EU average)[21].

The national and regional disparities are even more emphasised by the opposite dynamics in the OCCs 10, that is by an higher and growing level in comparison with the reduction of the na-

---

[21] This paper focuses overall on the CCs economic distance from EU, because this is the most relevant aspect of existing disparities, even of social and territorial ones (MELE G. [36]); another interesting approach is based on a «multidimensional» perspective (FISHER S., SAHAY R. and VÉGH C.A. [26]), inclusive of time, physical and institutional distances from EU.

tional and the rigidity of the regional disparities in the EU 15 (see Graph. 1). If regional disparities within the EU 15 are still rigid, in general terms the enlargement to the OCCs may significantly increase them: it may leave, however, unsolved the pre-existing gaps. This is also confirmed by the regional disparities size, absolutely considerable in the OCCs and certainly not less important in the EU 15.

As regards to the economic and social cohesion in the EU 25 (CEC [17] and [19]), the data confirm that the largest territorial disparities concentrate in the underdeveloped regions, characterised by a low income, a poor and a low employment population. These problems are linked to a strong territorial marginality, since these regions are mostly located at the EU borders and they have a low accessibility, not only because of the distance from the important economic centres, but also for the low infrastructure availability.

The enlargement should therefore modulate the economic and territorial marginality of the Union area, with interruptions located in some great urban areas of the OCCs capital cities. From the territorial point of view, the EU 25 socio-economic problems can also be interpreted according to some stereotypes (CEC [17]), that for decades have represented the structure of the CRP (urban areas, rural and industrial re-conversion zones and border regions, etc.). But the most relevant issue remains the one of lagging regions, also after the EU 25 enlargement and even more after the EU 27 one. Thus, the enlargement imposes again a concentration strengthening in order to stop the objectives and the intervention lines proliferation and the resources dispersion.

3.2 The (Hypothetical) Impacts at a Regional Level

If the analysis on the regional disparity confirms the need of keeping the first basic motivation of the CRP, this need is not so evident for the other motivations. The subject tends to separate the different situations between the OCCs 10 and the EU 15.

The CCs economic integration process is going through a

phase which could almost be defined «post-accession», since the formal attainment of the Community *acquis* is rather advanced, even though with strong differences across Countries. In reference to the economic effects both at the EU and at a single member state level the conclusions are generally positive[22], even though strongly varying for the second territorial analysis level. The same attention has not been given to the sub-national level yet; at this level in fact the repercussions could also be negative (but limited), especially in some South Europe territorial situations. In these regions the effects that can be generated in some productive, particularly sensitive to the process of enlargement, branches have to be checked more carefully.

The European Commission itself (CEC [17]) has underlined these regions' high «vulnerability» to competition shocks, which could emerge even without the accomplishment of such an enlargement process; this one could though favour it in a more direct and meaningful way. Nevertheless, given the modest economic role of CCs, the enlargement's regional effects can however be very moderate. Moreover, these effects can already be partially absorbed, since the mobility barriers to goods and capital have been removed a long time ago; the production and marketing adjustments to the EU standards would take place very slow in time.

By the way, a great attention to competition between CCs and

---

[22] In the last years, the progressive opening of exchanges has important effects, even though variable between EU and CCs, as regards to some objective factors (culture, language, distance, etc.). The outcome is that the economic integration is by now in a very advanced phase; many of the economic and commercial patterns have already been defined between the two groups of countries, thanks also to the high CCs adjustment degree to the internal market rules (PELKMANS J., GROS D. and NùÑEZ FERRER J. [42]). In the years to come before the CCs' final accession there should not be substantial or sudden changes, so the analysts' evaluations should be confirmed (BALDWIN R. E., FRANCOIS J. F. and PORTES R. [4]). According to these evaluations, the general enlargement effects will be (definitely and clearly) positive for both groups of countries (HALLET M. [27]; DAE [22]). In this adjustment and transition period to the accession, a competitive pressure is expectable; it should be relatively higher for the CCs labour intensive sectors in lack of a competitive re-positioning of the actual Partners. Nevertheless, the CCs economic size doesn't seem to be able to cause real shocks (NEVEN D. [40]). This is the substantial conclusion to which the European Commission above all gets (CEC [16]) in reference to a non gradual enlargement, as instead assumed in the past (SENIOR NELLO S. and SMITH K.E. [46]).

EU weak areas is understandable, in order to appraise both the previous and the predictable effects in the pre-accession phase first and in the accession one then. The CCs modest economic and industrial size would not actually be able to generate competitive pressures on the EU strong areas; rather for some aspects, the prevailing characteristics of the CCs economic-productive systems (strong specialisation in the traditional and labour intensive sectors) is complementary to the economic structure of the EU strong areas and thus in competition with the one of EU weak areas. For other reasons (professional qualification, labour costs, etc.), also the higher technological and innovative sectors content could find mostly convenient the location in the CCs particular regions, at least for some years.

Besides, the accession process may open new market opportunities for the production and the consumption of goods and services, also in alternative terms to the different existing options within the actual EU; anyway, the enlargement could induce, from the economic point of view, an increase in the goods and investment flows from the strongest EU countries and regions to the CCs as well, rather than the EU weakest areas. In comparison with the previous single market experiences (Krugman and Venables [31]), it does not seem that the physical barriers are excessively limiting the investment flows even as regards to some particularly peripheral CCs (as Romania and Bulgaria, temporarily excluded from the 2004 enlargement) or they are only under certain conditions[23.]

This is an aspect not to underestimate, because in the enlargement process the most remarkable territorial elements are normally other ones, that are engraving and will continue to engrave on the economic integration and on the flows of goods, in-

---

[23] This is particularly evident for the considerable growth of investment and commercial interchange between Italy and these countries. This case makes think about the competitiveness among alternative localisation areas within the EU, as those of the Mezzogiorno. These regions have some aspects similar to those of CCs (high availability of skilled labour supply, short infrastructure and services availability, etc.), and other ones different from them (higher labour cost and a relative greater incidence of administrative and fiscal costs). These aspects are evidently considered by a lot of firms more incisive than the higher territorial marginality of Romania and Bulgaria (MELE G. [36]).

vestments and people. The «proximity» and the «accessibility» (CEC [17]) would play a decisive role and the accession should subsequently consolidate what is already happening in the economic relationships between some EU countries and some CCs[24].

Nevertheless, a contingent integration need exists, as regards to the union between the EU countries and the CCs, the last ones being required a higher public investment expense not easily affordable through their weak financial conditions. Moreover, the possible impacts of the adjustments on the CCs cannot be excluded; in particular, actual EU most peripheral regions could react to the enlargement process and the increased competitive pressure on them generated by it. For the lagging South Europe regions, from a territorial point of view the answer could favour a great polarization. This could require the CCs to reduce (or to keep low) fiscal pressure, with evident impacts on their public finance (Darrigues and Montaud [20]). This aspect would have immediate repercussions on the CCs financial equilibria in relation to their structural adjustment needs, to which the action of the CRP should mainly be addressed by the CF, at least according to its current mission.

From the theoretical point of view, the enlargement process possible effects at a territorial level cannot therefore be ignored, because already induced by a high competitive «vulnerability» and a more considerable territorial «marginality» characterising both the actual and the future EU. Even though they seem to be very modest for the EU 15 regions compared to the CCs lower economic size, the enlargement process probable impacts on a territorial basis should be however considered with more attention; these effects should be geographically circumscribed and not simultaneously and immediately perceivable, because of the progressive technical adjustments which will derive from the new Partners' accession (Mele

---

[24] This is the case for Austria and, especially, Germany; another border case is the one regarding Italy and Slovenia, even though in a more limited way (PREPARITY [43]). FDIs, commercial exchanges, joint ventures and, in perspective, also immigration (in reference to the progress in the people's mobility regulation) flows between these countries could subsequently grow stronger. This would explain why the most peripheral economic relations are strengthening, as a consequence of the CCs markets saturation effects relatively to the closest ones as well (see previous footnote).

[36]). The enlargement territorial impact could at the moment assume a certain importance only for some of the EU local specificities, the most sensitive ones to the possible CCs competition; further elements are though necessary to such an assumption which seems to be the most substantial in an intuitive way.

The mentioned effects must be altogether considered in order to persuasively pursue the enlargement process and acquire the necessary consent by a larger number of the game actors (Heinemann [28]). This analysis is also very useful to better understand how to manage the future formulation of the CRP and the action of its tools.

4. - More «Sensitive» Enlargement Profiles

It is, at least for now, evident that integration effects motivations induce to extend to CCs, in particular, the intervention of the CF; this one as regards to the EU 15 has perhaps to be limited only to the completion of the necessary investments in order to make some of these countries' areas less peripheral and more integrated in the European territory. In reference to the intervention of the SFs, their correct motivation remains the one of reducing regional disparities, both in the EU 15 and the CCs. The enlargement to the CCs does not eliminate the large pre-existing regional disparities in the EU 15 which put further and more evident socio-economic and territorial imbalance in between the underdeveloped regions and the other ones. This problem cannot be hidden by the statistic changes induced by the decrease in the future EU 25 average development level.

This should lead to a more careful reflection on the current operational mechanisms' reformulation needs regarding the territorial development policy intervention tools of the Community. In comparison with the current structure of the CRP, the enlargement process considerably widens the lagging regions problem (the SFs Objective 1). From a simulation based on the hold application of the current selection criteria for these areas in the EU 25, it emerges an increase in the recipient population to around 116 millions of people, including about 70 millions of the OCCs 10 inhabitants, which equals about 93% of this group of countries' resident population. In this case a notable downsizing would occur for the EU 15 Objective 1 regions, the population of which would reduce from 83.1 (for the 2000-2006 period) to 46 millions of people (-43.6%), from 21.6% to 12.2% of the actual member countries' population.

In reference to the EU 15 only, the enlargement would produce a significant statistical effect, without which the EU 15 lagging regions would count almost 72 millions of people, that is 19.1% of the total population[25]. A statistical effect between 19.1% and 12.2% of the recipient population would not be so acceptable and should draw attention on the adjustments of the CRP for after 2006[26].

For the CF, the keeping of the admissibility threshold of 90% of the EU average per capita GDP in *PPP* would imply a reduction in the number of recipient member states from 4 (Greece, Spain, Portugal and Ireland) to 3 (the 4 but Ireland); the covered population would decrease from 63.6 to 59.9 millions of people[27]. The OCCs 10, but Cyprus, would all be admitted to the CF by making increase the total recipient population up to 134.2 millions of people (29.7% of the EU 25 total one).

As regards to the intervention finalities and the reformulation of the CRP for the future EU 25, a very considerable CF and SFs assisted areas overlapping comes out. This aspect has to be firmly faced, and this not only for the EU and the member states financial equilibria's problems, because the risk of mutual «crowding out» among the intervention tools of the Community and between these and the national (regional development and/or territorial re-balancing) policies would be higher.

---

[25] In order to follow the «as if now» selection criteria of the CRP, it was necessary to define the Objective 1 regions, which correspond to level 2 *Nomenclature of Territorial Units for Statistics (NUTS)* regions with a development level below 75% of the EU average per capita GDP level in PPP for the 1997-1999 period. This simulation excludes the reservation for the «outermost regions» (French Overseas Departments, Azores, Canary Islands and Madeira) and for the Sweden and Finland low demographic density regions (the old Objective 6 for the 1994-1999 period).

[26] The attention of the countries which would be damaged the most (as Spain) by these enlargement induced changes, under the same conditions of the CRP, is focusing on the statistical effect complete neutralisation issue, which would have to be considered as preliminary.

[27] A reduction should however occur for the EU 15 in 2003, according to the regulation of the CF; as a matter of fact in that year there will be an intermediate check on the recipient countries admissibility. The enlargment could even exclude Spain, now very close to the admissibility threshold.

TABLE 3

POPULATION IN NUTS 2 REGIONS WITH PER CAPITA
GDP LOWER THAN 75% OF THE EU AVERAGE, 1997-1999

| Member Sate | Objective 1 Regions in the EU 25 | | | Objective 1 regions in the EU 15 | | |
| | Population (.000) | Distribution (%) | | Population (.000) | Distribution (%) | |
		EU	National		EU	National
Belgium				1,280.4	1.8	12.5
Denmark						
Germany	2,213.7	1.9	2.7	12,917.2	17.9	15.7
Greece	4,338.9	3.8	41.2	9,587.8	13.3	91.1
Spain	13,947.4	12.1	35.4	17,497.5	24.3	44.4
France	1,662.1	1.4	2.8	1,662.1	2.3	2.8
Ireland						
Italy	17,041.9	14.7	29.6	17,649.8	24.5	30.6
Luxembourg						
Netherlands						
Austria				277.6	0.4	3.4
Portugal	6,304.2	5.4	63.2	6,652.9	9.2	66.7
Finland				691.3	1.0	13.4
Sweden						
United Kingdom	492.5	0.4	0.8	3,766.4	5.2	6.3
EU 15	46,000.7	39.8	12.2	71,983.0	100.0	19.1
Cyprus						
Czech Republic	9,093.0	7.9	88.4			
Estonia	1,442.0	1.2	100.0			
Hungary	7,216.0	6.2	71.7			
Lithuania	3,700.0	3.2	100.0			
Latvia	2,432.0	2.1	100.0			
Malta	387.2	0.3	100.0			
Poland	38,655.0	33.4	100.0			
Slovenia	1,986.0	1.7	100.0			
Slovak Republic	4,778.0	4.1	88.6			
OCC 10	69,689.2	60.2	92.9			
EU 25	115,689.9	100.0	25.6			

Source: Own calculations on EUROSTAT data.

It is not surprising the EU budget resources is the cohesion and enlargement's most followed subject at the moment. A lot of simulations have been carried out on this subject, leading to univocal conclusions: the statistical effect will exclude many of the EU 15 regions and, if the lagging regions have to maintain their priority, the other issues faced in these years by the CRP will suffer a drastic downgrading, unless the member states do not decide (this is very improbable though) to change the EU budget financing actual limits. As for the EU budget's «own resources»' quantity (a maximum of 1.27% of the EU GDP), for the financial resources allocated to the CRP some quantitative criteria have been defined as well; the most important of them regards the resources *plafond*, which can reach up to the 0.45% of the EU GDP. The «structural operations» resources (Heading 2 of the EU budget) fall within this ambit, including the fundamental tools of the CRP, SFs and CF. Another criterion concerns the value of the financial transfers to the member states that cannot exceed 4% of national GDP. By comparing the last two criteria with the OCCs 10 GDP (equal to 3.75% of the EU 25 GDP in 1999), the maximum of resources these countries could absorb would be equal to 0.15% of the EU 25 GDP, that is 1/3 of the 0.45% allocated to the CRP, of course under the hypothesis such criteria stay unchanged[28].

In short, could the 2/3 around of resources of the CRP satisfy the actual EU 15 intervention needs after the enlargement? The total allocations could be not modest (including resources for pre-accession and enlargement of/to CCs left and other countries which would like to join the EU), but a change of the current formulation is needed. And this is not unfortunately all, because the allocations' reduction for the actual 15 Partners would imply a worsening of the EU budget contribution/allocation positions (together with the downsizing of the recipient areas) of single member states.

This is just an estimation exclusively based on a current EU budget «conservative» hypothesis. By starting from an «expansive» hypothesis, based on the inclusion of all regions and countries currently covered by the CRP at the same conditions, other estimations (Dresdner Bank [23]) highlight instead a raising of the current «own resources» criterion. The intervention levels maintenance for all the tools and finalities currently pursued (SFs, CF,

---

[28] With reference to the GDP in Euros 1999, the yearly allocations of the CRP would amount to 37.5 milliards of Euros, thus the maximum OCCs 10 resources share would be 12.5 milliards of Euros. In the case in which Romania and Bulgaria were added to the OCCs 10, the maximum amount of resources to the CCs would increase to 0.17% of the EU 27 GDP, that is 14.2 milliards of Euros.

Objectives priority and other intervention lines) would obviously imply a possible worsening of the contribution/allocation position of actual EU member states (by cleaning in this case the statistical effect of the intervention areas selection criteria off).

In between these two extreme solutions, the confrontation on the CRP among member states is now beginning. It has to be confirmed though that this issue cannot be faced without a preventive reflection on the intervention needs consequent to the enlargement, if an effective reform is really wanted; it would otherwise be consistent reflecting, from a financial point of view, on more drastic reduction (or even dismantling) solutions.

5. - Conclusions

The role the CRP is asked to develop cannot be the one of «attracting» new Partners (Boldrin and Canova [7]) and sustaining the level of «political cohesion» already achieved by the old ones. Its role is that of contributing to solve a fundamental problem: how to reduce at the same time the development and welfare territorial gaps, which limit the weakest areas' share of benefits that the process of economic integration can produce (and on this point there are not contrary opinions), but they can also distribute in an unbalanced way, so stressing the development territorial gaps.

This question must also be answered for the sake of the Union's political needs, because the next enlargement will bring about an even stronger demand for cohesion.

In this perspective, the real question posed by the enlargement on the CRP cannot be that one of whether facing or not a need which has become too big and difficult to sustain, but the one of whether an «European regional issue» still exists, first and how it can be solved, then.

In the analysis here developed, the non-definitive conclusions about these matters lead to identify a fundamental aspect of the current CRP that has never been faced or sufficiently made clear before; this aspect regards the member states and the Commission roles towards the regional development problems in an European context; if this essential issue is not solved, it is well founded the fear that the CRP can only get to modest results, less significant for the reasons (for which) it has been created and should be maintained. This leading explanation need would much help in giving the theme of the EU budget financial equilibria a more correct dimension.

Besides, the debate on the future CRP should try to develop at least three main aspects, the lack of which is noticed.

The first one concerns the effectiveness of the CRP and «if» and in «what measure» it has attained its assignments, starting from the achieved results and the expected effectiveness, according to the several remarks previously introduced. The second aspect regards the CCs and the economic and territorial effects produced by the enlargement, in order to complete also the CRP possible needs framework, both for the actual and the new Partners. The last aspect integrates the results of the previous ones towards a general view of the economic geography (deriving from the enlargement), according to which the different states/regions are set as regards to their regional development problems and the necessary structural adjustments to be adopted to achieve better competitiveness and welfare conditions.

This kind of research effort is essential for defining the reform needs of the CRP, in order to allow structural policies to perform well in front of the new challenges set by the enlargement.

BIBLIOGRAPHY

[1] ARMSTRONG H. W. - TAYLOR J., *Regional Economics and Policy*, Oxford, P. Allan Publishers Ltd., 1985.

[2] ARMSTRONG H. W., «European Union Regional Policy: Sleepwalking to a Crisis», *International Regional Science Review*, vol. 19, n. 3, 1996.

[3] BALDWIN R. E., «Measuring 1992's Medium-Term Dynamic Effects», *NBER Working Paper*, n. 3166, November, 1989.

[4] BALDWIN R. E. - FRANCOIS J. F. - PORTES R., «The Costs and Benefits of Eastern Enlargement: the Impact on the EU and Central Europe», *Economic Policy*, April, 1997.

[5] BARBIERI G. - PELLEGRINI G., «Coesione o sgretolamento? Un'analisi critica dei nuovi Fondi strutturali», *Rivista Economica del Mezzogiorno*, vol. XIII, n. 1-2, 1999.

[6] BEUGELSDIJK S. - VAN SCHAIK T., «Social Capital and Regional Economic Growth», Tilburg University, Faculty of Economics, *Discussion Paper*, December, 2001.

[7] BOLDRIN M. - CANOVA F., «Inequality and Convergence in Europe's Regions: Reconsidering European Regional Policies», *Economic Policy*, April, 2001.

[8] CECCHINI P., *La sfida del 1992*, Milano, Sperling & Kupfer, 1988.

[9] CEC - COMMISSION OF THE EUROPEAN COMMUNITY - *Libro Bianco sul completamento del mercato interno*, Bruxelles, 1985.

[10] — —, *Il costo della non-Europa*, Lussemburgo, 1988.

[11] — —, *Europa 2000: prospettive per lo sviluppo del territorio comunitario*, Bruxelles, 1991.

[12] — —, *Europa 2000+*, Bruxelles, 1994.

[13] — —, *First Cohesion Report*, Brussels, 1996.

[14] — —, «Agenda 2000. Pour une Union plus forte et plus large (Document synoptique)», *COM(97) 2000* - vol. I, Bruxelles, 1997.

[15] — —, *Conseil Européen de Berlin - Conclusion de la Présidence*, 24-25 March, 1999.

[16] — —, «The Economic Impact of Enlargement», *Enlargement Papers*, n. 4, June, 2001.

[17] — —, «Unity, Solidarity, Diversity for Europe, its People and its Territory», *Second Report on Economic and Social Cohesion*, Luxemburg, 2001.

[18] — —, «Common Financial Framework 2004-2006 for the Accession Negotiations», *SEC(2002) 102 final*, Brussels, 2002.

[19] — —, «Premier rapport d'étape sur la cohesion économique e sociale», *COM(2002) 46 Final*, Bruxelles, 2002.

[20] DARRIGUES F. - MONTAUD J.M., «Les pays du sud de l'Europe doivent-ils craindre l'élargissement de l'EUM aux PECO?», Université Montesquieu-Bordeaux IV, *Document de Travail*, n. 67, 2001.

[21] DELORS, J. - CEC, «Report on Economic and Monetary Union in the European Community», *Report to European Council*, Brussels, 1989.

[22] DAE - DIPARTIMENTO AFFARI ECONOMICI DELLA PRESIDENZA DEL CONSIGLIO, *Allargamento a Est dell'Unione Europea: sfide e opportunità per l'Italia*, February, 2001.

[23] DRESDNER BANK, «Herausforderung EU-Erweiterung: Wachstumschancen Nutzen - Reformen Vorantreiben», *Trends Spezial - Wirtscaftsanalysen*, May, 2001.

[24] EASTERLY W. - LEVINE R., «It is not Factor Accumulation: Stylised Facts and Growth Models», in *The World Bank Economic Review*, vol. 15, n. 2, 2001.

[25] EUROPEAN COUNCIL, «The Future of the European Union», Laeken, *SN 273/01*, December, 2001.

[26] FISCHER S. - SAHAY R. - VÉGH C. A., «How Far Is Eastern Europe from Brussels?», *IMF Working Paper*, April, 1998.

[27] HALLET M., «National and Regional Development in Central and Eastern Europe: Implications for EU Structural Assistance», *EU Economic Papers*, n. 120, March, 1997.

[28] HEINEMANN F., «The Political Economy of EU Enlargement and the Treaty of Nice», *Zentrum für Europäische Wirtschaftsforschung (ZEW)*, Mannheim, October, 2000.

[29] HOLLAND S., *Le regioni e lo sviluppo economico europeo*, Roma-Bari, Laterza, 1977.

[30] ISTAT, *Conti economici territoriali secondo il SEC 95 - anni 1995-98*, December, 2000.

[31] KRUGMAN P. - VENABLES A., «Integration and the Competitiveness of Peripheral Industry», *CEPR Discussion Papers*, n. 363, 1990.

[32] KRUGMAN P., *Geography and Trade*, Cambridge (Mass.), MIT Press, 1991.

[33] LUCAS R.E. jr., «Some Macroeconomics for the 21st Century», *The Journal of Economic Perpspectives*, vol. 14, n. 1, Winter, 2001.

[34] MCCRONE G., «Unione monetaria e sviluppo regionale», *Rivista economica del Mezzogiorno*, X, n. 3, 1996.

[35] MELE G., «Politica regionale comunitaria e riforma dei fondi strutturali», in *Mezzogiorno d'Europa*, n. 4, 1990.

[36] — —, «Allargamento a Est dell'Unione Europea: Il quadro di riferimento per le politiche comunitarie di sviluppo regionale e coesione», Roma, Centro Studi Confindustria, *Working Paper*, n. 29, 2001.

[37] NEVEN D. - RÖLLER L., «European Integration and Trade Flows», Fontainebleau, INSEAD, *Working Paper* n. 89/48, 1989.

[38] — — - — —, L., «The Structure and Determinants of East-West Trade: a Preliminary Analysis of the Manufacturing Sector», Fontainbleau INSEAD, *Working Paper* n. 90/56/EP, 1990.

[39] NEVEN D., «EEC Integration Towards 1992: Some Distributional Aspects», INSEAD, *Working Paper*, n. 90/23/EP/SM, Fontainebleau, 1990.

[40] — —, «Trade Liberalization with Eastern Nations: How sensitive?», in FAINI R. - PORTES R. (eds.), *European Union Trade with Eastern Europe: Adjustement and Opportunities*, CEPR, London, 1995.

[41] PADOA-SCHIOPPA T., *Efficienza, stabilità ed equità*, Bologna, il Mulino, 1987.

[42] PELKMANS J. - GROS D. - NÙÑEZ FERRER J., «Long-Run Economic Aspects of the European Union's Eastern Enlargement», The Hague, *WRR Working Documents*, n. W109, September, 2000.

[43] PREPARITY - INTERREG PROJECT CO-FINANCED BY EU, *Consequences of Eastward Enlargement for Border Regions on the External EU Borders*, 1997-99.

[44] SARCINELLI M., «Mezzogiorno e Mercato Unico Europeo: complementarietà o conflitto di obiettivi?», in *Moneta e Credito*, n. 166, 1989.

[45] SCHREYER M. - CEC, «Financing Enlargement of the European Union», *mimeo*, 2001.

[46] SENIOR NELLO S. - SMITH K. E., «The consequences of Eastern Enlargement of the European Union in Stages», *EUI Working Paper*, RSC n. 97/51, 1997.

[47] SMITH A. - VENABLES A., «Completing the Internal Market in the European Community: Some Industry Simulations», *European Economic Review*, vol. 32, n. 1, 1988.

[48] SVIMEZ, «Le infrastrutture e lo sviluppo del Mezzogiorno», Roma, *Informazioni Svimez*, Quaderno n. 12, February, 2002.

[49] VENABLES A., «Geography and International Inequalities: the Impact of New Technologies», Paper prepared for *World Bank Annual Bank Conference on Development Economics*, Washington, May, 2001.

[50] Williamson J. G., «Regional Inequality and the Process of National Development», *Economic Development and Cultural Change*, vol. XIII, n. 4, July, 1965.

[51] YUILL D. - MCMASTER I., *Benchmarking Regional Policy in Europe: A Review of National Regional Policies*, EPRC, mimeo, Glasgow, August 2001.

The Eastward Enlargement of the European Union and the Common Agricultural Policy: the Direct Payments Issue

Fabrizio De Filippis - Luca Salvatici*

Università «Roma Tre», Roma - Università «La Sapienza», Roma

Tenendo conto delle principali caratteristiche emerse nel processo di transizione nel settore agro-alimentare dei paesi dell'Europa Centro-Orientale, si procede ad una valutazione della recente proposta avanzata dalla Commissione UE per quanto riguarda l'estenzione a questi paesi delle misure previste dalla PAC. Il principale ostacolo sulla strada dei negoziati è rappresentato dalle conseguenze di un'eventuale piena estensione ai nuovi paesi membri dell'attuale programma di aiuti diretti agli agricoltori. Poiché tale estensione porterebbe ad una distribuzione dei trasferimenti tra paesi membri difficilmente sostenibile, vengono analizzate le implicazioni di possibili schemi alternativi per la suddivisione di costi fra bilanci nazionali e bilancio comunitario.

This paper traces the main features of the Common Agricultural Policy (CAP), and of the transition process in the agricultural sectors of Central and Eastern European countries. We argue that currently the main challenge is to extend the CAP to the new members without upsetting the net contributors to the EU budget, and we analyse the effects of different schemes that would allow

* Fabrizio De Filippis is Professor and Luca Salvatici is Assistant Professor. Financial support received by the Italian Ministry for Education, University and Research is gratefully acknowledged (Scientific Research Program of National Importance on "WTO negotiations on agricolture and the reform of the Common Agricultural Policy of the European Union"). Although the paper is the result of joint work, Sections 2, 5.1, and 5.2 should be attributed to Fabrizio De Filippis, and Sections 1, 3, 4, 5.3, and 6 to Luca Salvatici.

N.B., the numbers in square brackets refer to the Bibliography at the end of the paper.

some cost sharing between EU and national budgets. The main conclusion is that the CAP for an enlarged Union should be based on decentralization of expenditures and a system of subsidies and transfers among countries [JEL Code: E61, F15, P27, Q17, Q18].

1. - Introduction

Even more than in the case of earlier enlargements of the European Union (EU), agriculture is a key sector in the discussion of the likely economic impact of integrating the Central and Eastern European Countries (CEECs[1]) into the EU. The enlargement of the EU to the CEECs could add as many as 100 million new consumers and double the number of farmers under the subsidy schemes provided by the Common Agricultural Policy (CAP).

It was clear from the outset that, as CAP is the largest EU policy (at least in terms of budgetary expenditure) and as CEECs are considerably poorer and more 'agricultural' than EU-15, the eastward enlargement had the potential to be very difficult. Aligning domestic policies with those of the CAP has been a formidable challenge for most CEECs in light of the continued evolution of both support levels and types of policy interventions during the '90s.

This paper looks at the relationship between the enlargement of the EU and the reform of the CAP. Most of the literature dealing with these issues put the emphasis on the requirements of the enlargement in terms of CAP adjustments, arguing in most cases that the viability of the CAP will be threatened due to the budgetary implications of extending the present policy to the new members. Furthermore, the acceding countries are also members of the WTO, and thus the future configuration of the "enlarged CAP" must be consistent with the commitments of the Uruguay Round Agreement on Agriculture (URAA) and must be seen in connection with the ongoing multilateral trade negotiations within the World Trade Organization (WTO).

---

[1] The acronym CEECs refers to the ten Central and Eastern European candidates, namely: Czech Republic, Estonia, Hungary, Latvia, Lithuania, Poland, Slovakia, Slovenia, Romania and Bulgaria.

On the other hand, from the transition economies point of view, longer term structural change is particularly important when considering the role of their agricultural sector and by implication, the most appropriate set of policies for facilitating that role. The main issue here concerns the extent to which a policy designed for rich social democracies like the EU actual members is appropriate for nations in the midst of their 'take-off' stage of growth.

The aim of the article can be summarized as follows: *(i)* provide some background information on the CAP reform and some *stylized facts* about the agricultural sector and policy in the "new member countries"[2]; *(ii)* using the results of the most recent and updated literature, identify and discuss the central agriculture-related issues of EU enlargement; *(iii)* critically discuss and evaluate the EU Commission proposal for the integration of the new members into the CAP, and the implications for the multilateral trade commitments and ongoing World Trade Organization (WTO) negotiations; *(iv)* address the key issue of the CAP direct payments, studying the effects of a *co-financing* of expenditure.

Although the observations are based on the existing literature, we make no attempt to provide an exhaustive review of the huge number of contributions appeared over the last decade. Rather, we take a forward-looking perspective by briefly tracing the critical features of the transition process applied to the agricultural sector and relating them to the challenges ahead in terms of CAP reform.

Finally, an important caveat has to be made. Although the new members are often quoted as a group in the following, not all aspects discussed are of the same importance for each country. We are fully aware, as a matter of fact, that CEECs strongly differ in terms of economic structure, history, conditions at the start of transformation and policies subsequently implemented.

---

[2] The "new members" are the eight CEECs that are expected to join the EU on 1 January 2005, namely the Czech Republic, Estonia, Hungary, Latvia, Lithuania, Poland, Slovakia and Slovenia (we will refer to them as the new members in the following). Two more countries could join the Union in 2005 – Cyprus and Malta –, but the economic size of their primary sectors is so small that the agricultural chapter does not pose significant problems within the enlargement negotiations.

2. - The Reform of the Common Agricultural Policy: A Never Ending Story

As it is well known, the CAP has been the first EU common policy, and its objectives were explicitly stated in the *Treaty of Rome* (article 39). This pivotal role of the CAP can be explained by the presence in all the six founding member states of similar, very generous, agricultural policies. This was due to the importance of agriculture in the political market at national level, as well as to the commonly shared goal of accompanying and smoothing the process of structural adjustment in a period of rapid economic growth. Agricultural policies were largely based on price support and border protection: obviously, it would have been impossible to maintain the implementation of such policies at the national level within a single market. Hence, the implementation of the agricultural policy at the EU level was required in order to include the primary sector into the process of economic integration[3].

The chosen system, mainly shaped on the French model, included annually fixed minimum guaranteed prices, market intervention (purchasing and stocking surpluses), export subsidies and heavy border protection, based on variable import levies, calculated as difference between (fixed) domestic support price and world price. The original CAP, then, was fully consistent with the "coupled model" of agricultural policy prevailing in most developed countries, and based on guaranteed prices that made the farmers' benefit from the policy strictly proportional to the quantity produced. The price and market support soon became the core of the CAP, while the agricultural structural policy (investment aids granted for the modernization and cessation of farms) was pulled in an ancillary position, absorbing less than 5% of the total agricultural expenditure.

For a long time the CAP has remained the only effective common policy, capturing more than 80% of the EU budget, and this

---

[3] The literature on the CAP is huge. Other works of the authors (DE BENEDICTIS M. - DE FILIPPIS F. - SALVATICI L. [8]; DE FILIPPIS F. - SALVATICI L. [9]; DE FILIPPIS F. - SALVATICI L. [10] provide more detailed descriptions, as well as extensive lists of references.

contributed to reinforce its political importance as the cornerstone of European integration. The large amount of agricultural spending accurately reflects the role of agriculture as a key sector in the political agreement among member states, and this gave to the CAP strong momentum and resilience during the first two decades of application, including its extension to United Kingdom, Ireland and Denmark as a consequence of the first EU enlargement.

At the beginning of the eighties, though, some shortcomings of the coupled model of agricultural policy became apparent: uncontrollable budget expenditure, increasing public stocks of low quality, unsaleable products, market disruption for third exporting countries, environmental damages, uneven distribution of financial and economic costs and benefits among member states, as well as among products and producers. Therefore, milk production was brought under a quota system in 1984[4], and CAP outlays were further constrained through coresponsibility levies, as well as stabilising price adjustment schemes.

In a context in which both the political importance of agriculture and the public reputation of the CAP were rapidly declining, two main driving forces fueled the crisis. Domestically, the financial problems, both in terms of control of the agricultural expenditure, and in terms of distribution of costs and benefits among member Countries. Internationally, the growing interdependence between national agro-food systems and policies, which made agriculture a key sector in the multilateral negotiation for trade liberalization within the Uruguay round of the GATT, which had been launched in 1986.

In response to this, during the nineties, the CAP reform was strongly accelerated by the idea of "decoupling", which can be considered a turning point in the traditional slow, gradual and cautious process of change that had characterized the process during the previous decades. The decoupling of support from production implies that policy measures do not affect relative prices

---

[4] Before 1984 for sugar only a production quota system was in place with different price guarantees for separate quota segments.

of agricultural commodities or of the inputs used to produce them. Hence, a policy is decoupled if it has no or only very small effects on production and trade. As it is well-known, if the main objective of agricultural policies is to ensure a fair level of income to farmers relative to other domestic economic groups (and if there are not other distortions in the economy), then the most efficient instrument is a lump-sum transfer from the latter to the formers, i.e. a transfer as decoupled as possible from agricultural production and market conditions.

The first step of this process was the so-called *Mac Sharry Reform* (1992), which gradually reduced intervention prices for cereals and beef, implementing fixed per hectare or per head direct ("compensatory") aids, linked to historical base areas and based on historical yields, in order to compensate farmers for the price reduction. It is also to be noted that total outlays on these direct payments were upperbounded, since they were guaranteed only up to a maximum eligible reference area or reference herd.

The *Mac Sharry Reform* was a turning point for the CAP, since there was a shift from price support to a system of fixed direct aids, linked to (historical) factors of production rather than to quantity (actually) produced. It should be noted, though, that payments were decoupled from actual production decisions only to some extent, since they were differentiated according to the type of crop and farmers were still required to stay in production in order to benefit from the scheme[5].

The *Mac Sharry Reform* made possible for the EU to sign the *URAA* in 1994. Until the Uruguay Round, agriculture received special treatment under multilateral trade rules through loopholes, exceptions, and exemptions from most disciplines applying to manufactured goods. The *URAA* addressed the issues of improved access for imports, enhanced export competition and limits to domestic support. In terms of market access, a major step in the direction of liberalising agricultural trade has been taken by im-

---

[5] Many other factors could also reduce the degree of decoupling: labour decisions of the household, investment decisions, risk perception of producers, existence of a positive marginal cost of taxation.

posing the tariffs-only rule (through a process called "tariffication"). Nevertheless, due to the high level of the bounded tariffs, the agreed reductions proved to be poor in terms of a real improvement in market access (Anania [2]). Much more effective were the commitments to reduce the volume and the value of subsidized exports over the implementation period of the *Agreement* (1995-2000).

As far as domestic support is concerned, the *Agreement* required countries to reduce outlays on domestic policies that provide direct economic incentives to increase production ("amber box" measures). A "green box" was created as well, including nondistorting and decoupled measures of domestic support, which are totally exempted from any reduction commitments. In each country, the extent of the amber box is measured by the so-called *Aggregate Measure of Support (AMS)*, but it should be noted that the CAP direct payments introduced in 1992 were exempted from compulsory reduction, even if they were only partially decoupled[6].

In 1999, a second important step of the reform process was the *Berlin Accord on Agenda 2000*. As with the *Mac Sharry Reform*, *Agenda 2000* is intended to reduce support for commodities through market interventions and to increase support to farmers through direct payments, thereby relaxing the constraint on subsidized exports under the *URAA* commitments. *Agenda 2000* both deepens and broadens the principles of the 1992 reform, even if the reform of the dairy sector was postponed until 2005/2006 and the sugar sector was not considered.

Agenda 2000 also made clear that within the CAP a clear shift is taking place from the traditional agricultural policy (price and income support) towards rural policy. This is the so-called "second pillar" of the PAC, partially linked with the more general action of the structural funds of the European budget[7]. The CAP

---

[6] As a matter of fact, the EU direct payments, as well as the US deficiency payments, were considered in a special category, the "blue box" measures.

[7] It is worth recalling that after *Agenda 2000* the rural development action is mostly financed by the EAGGF Guarantee Section, i.e. by the fund that traditionally financed only the market intervention component of the CAP. The rural development policy has remained as a part of structural funds action (EAGGF Guidance section) only in Objective 1 regions.

shifting in the direction of rural development policy promotes the "multifunctionality" (from the environmental point of view) of the European agriculture, and makes the EU more in compliance with *URAA* guidelines, since the most of rural development policy falls in the "green box".

As a result of these reforms, it can be argued that the CAP has entered a slow but clear process of transition from the old totally "coupled" model of agricultural policy. However, the increase in compensation payments and the maintaining of production quotas in the dairy and sugar sectors intensify the difficulties to be faced in extending the full CAP provision to the new member countries.

Around 70% of current agricultural "market" expenditure is captured by partially decoupled hectare or livestock payments, whose nature has become ambiguous over time. These payments were (calculated and) implemented as an explicit compensation for the price reduction imposed by the *Mac Sharry Reform*. Then, they were increased as a partial (50%) compensation for the further reduction decided with *Agenda 2000*. Presently, the Commission seems to consider them as generic direct aids, which can be conditioned, modulated or reduced according to different criteria (e.g., environment compliance, quality standards, rural development). As we will see in Section 5, on the eve of the enlargement process, the most important problem of the agricultural chapter was exactly the definition, the nature and the destiny of the direct aids distributed by the CAP and, in relation to it, the decision about whether, to what extent, and in which time span, extending them to the new members.

3. - Transformation of CEEC Agriculture and Integration with the EU

The process of economic transformation in CEECs has been having a big impact on the agro-food sector. Although it is not possible to provide here a detailed review of the agricultural and food sectors of the CEECs, we will at least try to highlight the main differences in the performance of agriculture amongst the new members. However, given the policy focus of the paper, we put the emphasis on the agricultural policies pursued in these countries within the process of adjustment and integration with the CAP.

CEECs agriculture has undergone fundamental and rapid changes since 1989, as one might have expected given the fundamental legal reforms that have taken place. The issue of farm production structures is important for international competitiveness, since factor use and comparative advantage may be related to various farm production structures. Decollectivization and privatization reduced the share of area farmed by cooperatives and state farms, but also resulted in a highly fragmented ownership structure (INEA [23]). On the whole, semi-subsistence agriculture has resisted, and extended to small and average holdings, old or new, to various national degrees (Pouliquen [31]).

According to Lerman [25], agriculture is now largely individualized in Latvia, Poland and Slovenia, while large-scale collective or corporate farms continue to play an important role (40% of agricultural land) in Hungary, Czech Republic, Slovakia, Estonia, and Lithuania. In Slovenia and Poland the farm structure has always been characterized by predominance of small and medium-size farms.

There are many indicators that could be employed in the analysis of the sectoral performance. Looking at role of agriculture in the economy, Davidova and Buckwell [7] show that it was a relatively 'robust' sector in all the CEECs during the early years of transition, since agricultural output fell less than industrial output. Then, a more conventional development pattern emerged, due to a more rapid recovery in the industrial sector, as well as substantial growth in the service sector (OECD [30]).

After a short recovery around 1995, due to favourable climatic and economic conditions, production has generally fallen back or, at best, stagnated in real terms: the gross agricultural production per hectare of utilized area in the accession countries was in 1999 between 8.5% and 35% of the EU average, apart from the Slovenia exception[8]. Also using land and cattle productivity indicators, such as crop yields and milk per dairy cow, the gap appears to be substantial. Not only the land productivity of the new members is still below that of the EU, but the variability is much higher: this indicates the use of different farm technologies, with Hungary, Slovenia, and the Slovak and Czech Republics presenting consistently higher yields (Pouliquen [31]).

Since labour is relatively cheap, while material inputs (feed, fertilizer, etc.) are very expensive, and capital is both expensive and difficult to obtain, it is certainly not surprising that we register labour-intensive production and yields substantially below those of the EU. Development of primary agriculture, as a matter of fact, has been hindered in most CEECs by the lack of access to credit and high real interest rates. In this respect, it is also worth noting that foreign direct investment in the agro-food sector is low across the region, and in primary agriculture is even lower than in the upstream and downstream sectors (OECD [30]). Hopefully, full EU membership should have a positive impact, and substantial capital inflows should also be brought by policies specifically targeted to support agricultural and rural development.

Owing to a substantial reduction and then stagnation of agricultural consumption per capita, the CEECs have maintained slight trade surpluses in temperate agricultural products. However, the overall agro-food trade balance of the ten countries is negative and worsened during transition in all the countries. Due to the rapid growth in consumer demand for higher value added foodstuffs the proportion of processed products is much higher in imports than in exports, in particular in trade with the EU (Pouliquen [31]).

For quite a long time, the argument of the comparative advantages of less expensive and more abundant manpower and land has inspired the diagnosis of strong current and/or potential com-

---

[8] The OECD [30] reports that there has been an increase in the amount of uncultivated agricultural land across the region: this further reinforces the relative weakness of gross agricultural production per hectare in the CEECs.

petitiveness of agriculture in the CEECs in relation to the EU. This vision underestimates dramatically the capital intensity per worker of the main technical functions of agricultural production. The low effective competitiveness of CEEC staple products on the Single Market is evidenced by the fact that their exports to the Union often remained far from filling the tariff rate quotas, i.e., the import quotas at reduced duty granted by the EU.

More generally, although the EU has become the CEECs largest trading partner in agricultural and food products, it should be noticed that the EU trade barriers on agricultural imports coming from CEECs has remained high, since the *Association Agreements* merely provided bilateral trade liberalization for non-sensitive industrial products. Only in 2000, agreements were negotiated for the elimination of tariffs and export subsidies for a wide range of raw agricultural products ("double zero" option)[9].

There is a widespread agreement in the literature (Hartell and Swinnen [22]; OECD [30]) about the fact that agricultural price and trade policies in CEECs during the '90s can be divided into three broad stages. In the first phase, most countries removed or substantially reduced non-tariff barriers and production subsidies.

In a second phase, price and trade interventions were introduced or reintroduced to help maintain social and political stability: in Hungary, Czech and Slovak Republics, Poland and Slovenia, non-tariff interventions evolved into a market organization system including variable import levies in combination with minimum guaranteed producer prices. Such 'Old CAP-style' agricultural policy packages also include production quotas in the milk sector (Hungary and Slovak Republic) and in the sugar sector (Poland). However, even though policy choice frequently appeared in line with the pre-reformed CAP, it in fact often operated differently, and at significantly lower levels.

---

[9] The agreements usually includes three lists of goods: 1) all tariffs are to be abolished for goods on the first list ("non-sensitive products"); 2) for the goods on the second list, tariffs will be abolished up to a given quota (to be increased each year), provided that export subsidies are abolished as well ("double-zero products"); 3) the third list of goods will be subject to preferential tariff rates ("sensitive products").

Since 1996 the policy regimes of many CEECs have significantly changed, and following the falling of world market prices, agricultural protection and support to farmers has increased significantly. Market price support is becoming a somewhat less important component of support to producers, while budgetary support to direct aid measures has increased: this makes the new members' agricultural policies more aligned with the 'reformed CAP', if not in terms of the level of support, at least in terms of the choice of policy instruments. On the other hand, there are important divergences amongst the support levels given to specific commodities among the new members, and between them and the EU: the only product where the support level and ranking are similar is milk, while cereals are invariably much less supported.

According to Hartell and Swinnen [21] there are two different (extreme) explanations for interpreting the sequence and choice of agricultural policy instruments in the CEECs. The first, which they call the 'looking across the fence' explanation, presumes that CEECs' policy has converged towards the model of the potential integrator, in order to minimise adjustment costs at the time of EU accession. The second, which is labelled as the 'political economy' explanation, presumes that CEECs' policy was the outcome of a combination of political pressures and motivations, and economic/structural conditions, similar to the ones prevailing in the EU. Apparently, the two explanations have very different implications in terms of the new members' negotiating position on the agricultural chapter.

4. - Costs and Benefits of Enlargement: the Role of Agriculture

In the huge literature that attempt to quantify the impact of the enlargement, we chose a small number of applications — which are summarized in Table 1 — according to three main criteria: *(i)* they are *applied equilibrium models*, that is, we do not consider time series projection models, regressions based on political economy theory, or studies that use spreadsheet calculations; *(ii)* they are *CAP-focused*, since they make an effort to model the wide and complex set of instruments implied by the presence of the CAP. This is quite a peculiar feature, since recent surveys reveal that several modellers rely on highly stylised representations of the CAP instruments (Nielsen [27]; Nielsen *et* AL. [28]; Salvatici *et* AL. [32]); *(iii)* they are of a *recent vintage*, since life goes fast in CAP reform and enlargement, and to make the analysis relevant the scenarios should reflect the current situation of policies and markets. Recent estimates are often lower than earlier ones because they account for the 1992 CAP reform and additional reforms required by the *URAA*, and they rely on less optimistic productivity growth assumptions: a narrowing price gap implies that production will rise less, and consumption will not decline as much as projected before 1999.

Although the impact of the enlargement logically includes four main components – the costs and the benefits in the east, and the costs and the benefits in the west – efforts to date have been directed almost exclusively to the cost to the EU budget (Baldwin *et* AL. [4]). This is particularly true in the case of agriculture, since the large agricultural sectors and the comparatively low GDP of the CEECs were seen to threaten the EU budget with an unmanageable bill if the current CAP was to be adopted in those countries. In this respect, the breadth of the results reported in table 1 is extremely wide, with the range of the budget impact going from 0.6 to 16.2 billion euros.

One possible explanation is that the values presented in Table 1 refer to different time periods and different euros (sometimes in real, sometimes in nominal terms). This discussion leads naturally to the question of which base year the model is calibrated to. As a matter of fact, applied general equilibrium models link the simulation results to the structural characteristics of the economies in a particular year. Generally speaking, the process of integration and trade liberalisation is likely to change these structures over time, but the problem is exacerbated in the case of transition economies, which are supposed to rapidly change "by definition", and in the case of the agricultural sector, which is highly dependent on weather changes, and fluctuating world prices.

A second, more substantive, set of factors relates to the definition of policy experiments, as well as to the assumptions that

TABLE 1

ESTIMATES OF CAP BUDGETARY COST AFTER THE ENLARGEMENT

	Model structure	CEEC coverage	Base year/ Evaluation year	CAP modelling	Enlargement scenarios	Increased budget cost
FROHBERG K. et Al. [19]	partial equilibrium	Bulgaria, Czech, Republic, Estonia,	1995/2005	a) 1995-1996 CAP b) Agenda 2000 (proposals)	a)-b) CAP wihout compensatory payments + quotas = 1995 production duction level	a) 2.4 billion € b) 0.6 billion €
FULLER et AL. [20]	partial equilibrium	Czech Republic, Hungary, Poland	2000/2010	Agenda 2000	a) CAP vithout compensatory payments + requested quotas b) CAP with compensatory payments + historical (present pro-duction level) quotas	–
MÜNCH W. [26]	partial equilibrium	Czech Republic, Estonia, Hungary, Poland, Slovenia	1994-1996/2013	Agenda 2000 + Uruguay Round	a) CAP vithout compensatory payments + endogenous (WTO consistency) quotas b) CAP with compensatory payments + endogenous (WTO consistency) quotas	a) 3.5 billion € b) 10 billion €
BANSE M. [5]	general equilibrium (4 single-country models)	Czech Republic, Hungary, Poland, Slovenia	1992, 1994, 1995/2013	Agenda 2000	a) No CAP b) CAP without compensatory payments c) CAP with compensatory payments (90% decoupled)	a) 3.5 billion € b) 3.5 billion € c) 8.4 billion €

TABLE 1 *(cont.)*

ESTIMATES OF CAP BUDGETARY COST AFTER THE ENLARGEMENT

	Model structure	CEEC coverage	Base year/ Evaluation year	CAP modelling	Enlargement scenarios	Increased budget cost
WEYERBROCK S. [34]	general equilibrium	Albania, Bulgaria, Czech Republic, Slovak Republic, Hungary, Poland, Romania, former Yugoslavia	1987/1987	a) 1992 CAP reform + URAA b)a) + Agenda 2000	a)-b) Full implementation of the CAP (quotas = 1987 production level)	17% increase
FRANDSEN S.E. et Al. [17]	general equilibrium	Bulgaria, Czech Republic, Hungary, Poland, Romania, Slovak Republic, Slovenia	1995/2005	Agenda 2000 (proposals) + URAA	Full implementation of the CAP (quotas = 2005 production level)	–
BACH C.F. et Al. [3]	general equilibrium	Bulgaria, Czech, Republic, Hungary, Poland, Romania, Slovak Republic, Slovenia	1995/2005	a) 1992 CAP reform + URAA b) a) + Agenda 2000 (proposals)	a)-b) Full implementation of the CAP (quotas = 2005 production level)	a) 13.9 billion € (+ 35%) b) 13.8 billion € (+ 32%)
FRANDSEN S.E. - JENSEN H.G. [18]	general equilibrium	Bulgaria, Czech, Republic, Hungary, Poland, Romania, Slovakia, Slovenia	1995/2010	Agenda 2000 + URAA	a) CAP without compensatory payments (quotas = 2010 production level) b) CAP with the same level of existing payments (quotas = 2010 production level c) CAP with 2/3 of existing payments for all members (quotas = 2010 production level)	a) 5.5 billion € b) 16.2 billion € c) 3.9 billion €

form the integration scenarios. Table 1 shows that most applications perform baseline scenarios, which provide projections of the economies to a given year against which the enlargement effects can be compared (evaluation year). The assumptions made about the development of the economies in the baseline will of course affect the consequent impact of the enlargement scenario. Moreover, the various studies differ in terms of crucial features, such as: the number of entrants, the future of the CAP and extension of the CAP direct payments to new members, Eastern Europe's supply response to the CAP and productivity increases.

Turning to a third set of factors, these can be traced back to basic differences in model structure. Two broad dividing lines can be drawn here. The first separates partial from general equilibrium models. In the case of simulations concerning the creation of a customs union, or the enlargement of an existing one, considering the multi-sectoral nature of policy change and likely size of the related shock, the use of general equilibrium models seems the most appropriate.

The second separates single-region from multi-regional (or even global) models. Any attempt to evaluate a typical discriminatory trade policy such as the EU enlargement should be based on models that can simulate bilateral trade flows. All of the models reported in the Table 1 are able to model different tariff (and subsidies) according to the origin (and destination) of the traded goods thanks to the "Armington assumption" (that is, assuming imperfect substitutability in consumption of goods according to their country of origin). This is a dangerous and hardly justifiable hypothesis in terms of simulation results, if after the enlargement the goods produced by the original EU members will remain imperfect substitutes of those produced by the new members (Anania [2]).

It is clear that the largest budgetary consequences with regard to accession of new member states relates to granting direct payments to these new members. Models that provide a welfare analysis show that budget transfers (more than) compensate the allocative efficiency losses due to the extension of the CAP. Conclusions that emerge from the literature state that full payments would probably be too large to constitute a mutually beneficial solution for both the incumbents and the applicants. On the other hand, the other extreme solution – no payments – would be an unstable and discriminatory solution.

Assessing the effects on agriculture in the candidate countries stemming from the adoption of the CAP, there is a "pessimistic" scenario of an overall agro-food recession in the CEECs after accession, with increasing net imports from the EU-15. According to Pouliquen [31], sectors, such as sugar, beef and milk, are limited by weak internal purchasing power, and by the relative inefficiency of the relevant agro-food chains; while, for beef and milk, quality differences account for a large proportion of the price gap with the EU. On the other hand, the prices of cereals, oilseeds, pig, poultry and the eggs are on the whole very close to Community averages, especially at equal quality.

In any case, accession to the EU will have rather different implications for CEECs agriculture and CEECs food industry. For CEECs farmers it will alter the agricultural policies more or less dramatically, since in most acceding countries agricultural protection is much lower compared to the EU-level. Moreover, the potential impacts on land markets could be significant: upward pressure on land prices could result from any rise in producer prices or if foreigners are allowed to buy CEECs' land. However, the CAP reforms introduced in the last ten years have changed drastically the impact of the enlargement: contrary to what would have been the case in the absence of CAP reform, it now appears that future development of production in the CEECs will largely be dominated by the underlying trends in productivity (Tangermann, Swinnen [33]).

More generally, for much of the CEECs food industry the future is not very promising, since the current competitive advantage of low standards will disappear as a consequence of enforcing EU standards (Pouliquen [31]). It is therefore not surprising that some acceding countries are asking for long transition periods before the implementation of the full range of quality standards, during which those products not meeting EU standards would be sold only on the domestic market or exported to third countries.

The *acquis communautaire*, as it is well known, defines the rights and obligations that EU members have under Union law, and candidates are presented with the *acquis* as a rigid "take it or leave it" offer. However, the *acquis* originates from economies at a higher level of economic development, and it reflects the values and risk aversion of present members of the EU. There is no reason why the optimal quality standards should be the same for all countries: accordingly, enforcing higher standards than those the CEECs would have chosen may result in a welfare loss[10]. On the other hand, in the long run imposing EU food quality standards is the only way to sell on the EU markets.

5. - The Agricultural Chapter of the Enlargement Negotiations: Main Issues and Implications

5.1 *General Remarks*

As we anticipated in the previous sections, the most important problem of the agricultural chapter of the enlargement is the budget issue. The substantial increase of the agricultural sector within an enlarged Community makes the full extension of the present CAP not compatible with the agricultural guideline of the budget[11]. In principle, it could be argued that such a guideline is not really binding, since the budgetary cost of carrying out the present agricultural policies turns out to be a tiny share of GDP or total public expenditure, and it would be balanced with the political insurance of stable democratic neighbours to the east. Although the argument has the merit to remind us the grand picture — eastern enlargement is not really about budget transfers —, it overlooks the fact that budget concerns are very important

---

[10] According to COCHRANE N. [6] roughly half of Poland's meat output and 40% of Hungary's comes from processing plants that do not meet EU standards.

[11] According to the agreement reached in Edinburgh in 1992, the rate of growth for the agricultural expenditure within the EAGGF-Guarantee Section must not exceed the 74% of the rate of growth of the EU GDP. Given the increasing importance of the GDP resources in total budget contributions, this implies a progressive shrinking of the share of the agricultural component in the EU budget.

not only with respect to the level of the expenditure, but especially with reference to the redistribution of funds among the membership. In this respect, it should be clear that the full extension of the CAP would really disturb the actual delicately balanced political equilibrium.

The CAP financial compatibility issue is strictly related to the direct payments. Therefore, it is not surprising that the debate has been focusing on the modalities, the extent and the timing by which the direct payments scheme is going to be extended to the new member states. According to the Berlin agreement on *Agenda 2000*, Eastern farmers would have not been eligible for the current system of CAP direct payments, since they did not suffer for the price reduction that constituted their original justification[12]. On the other hand, the new member states argue that the compensatory role of the CAP payments could be justified only on a temporary (and decreasing) basis. Moreover, since the subsidies are only partially decoupled, granting them only to the farmers of certain countries would distort competition within the single market.

Apparently, there is an obvious link between the decision concerning the agricultural chapter of the enlargement and the next steps of the CAP reform process. In the short term, the mid-term review of the CAP indicated by *Agenda 2000* — i.e. the possible changes to be decided by the end of 2002. In the longer term, the decision about the "new CAP" post *Agenda 2000*, in the context of the budget planning for the period 2007-2013. Both the Commission and the group of "traditional defenders" of the CAP insist in keeping the two issues carefully separate. The Commission seems to be genuinely concerned with the pace of enlargement negotiations and does not want it to be linked with such a thorny issues like the CAP reform. The traditional defenders want to postpone as much as possible the discussion about the long-term CAP reform, in particular the revision of the direct aids system, probably hoping in the support of the new members in order to maintain it in an enlarged Union.

---

[12] As it was mentioned, in many cases agricultural prices in the new member states are expected to increase as a consequence of the enlargement.

5.2 The Commission's Proposal

In this context, at the and of January 2002 the Commission put on the table a proposal for the financing of the enlargement (EU Commission [15]), with the explicit goal to limit expenditure in the first years after accession, in order to respect the budgetary limits set by *Agenda 2000*. In the case of agriculture, such a short-term perspective does not provide any indications about the road to be followed after 2006.

According to the Commission's proposal, the new member states will have full and immediate access to CAP market measures, while for the direct aids a transition period is envisaged. The Commission proposes a ten-year phasing in period for the CAP direct aids to CEEC farmers, with payments beginning on 2004[13], at 25% of the full level of subsidy, and then increasing at 30% in 2005 and 35% in 2006. For the following years, the Commission states that direct aids would be organized in such a way as to ensure that the new member states reach in 2013 the support level then applicable. The new member states are allowed to top up the CAP direct aids with national funds. Moreover, in the framework of simplification, the Commission gives the option of granting direct payments in the form of a homogeneous area payment, totally decoupled from production and paid per hectare to all the farmers.

As far as the quota systems in milk and sugar sectors are concerned, the Commission proposes to extend them to the new member states, determining the amount of quotas on the basis of average production over the years 1995 to 1999. New members do not consider this an appropriate time frame, since they claim that the recent period was plagued by natural disasters and market disturbances: pre-transition data would better reflect the supply potential.

---

[13] For 2004 no direct payments have to be considered in the EU budget, since these payments are made to the farmers by national agencies and then, after one year, member states receive the reimbursement from Brussels. Accordingly, direct aids will be paid out in 2004 by new member states, but they will appear on the EU budget only in 2005.

Concerning rural development, a new special measure for the so-called semi-subsistence farms is proposed, that is for farms that produce for own consumption but market the larger part of their production. The measure will take the form of a flat rate aid of 750 Euro maximum, conditional on submitting a plan demonstrating the future economic viability of the enterprise. Moreover, for the programming period 2004-2006, the Commission proposes to increase the EU co-financing rate of rural development actions up to 80% also for the measures financed the EAGGF Guarantee Section[14], bringing it to the maximum level admitted for structural programs in Objective 1 regions.

Looking at the figures in Table 2, it could be argued that the Commission's proposal is fully consistent with the budget constraints, and with the principles stated in *Agenda 2000* for the continuation of the CAP reform process.

a) Gradualism: the direct aids are introduced gradually over a long transition period, in order to reduce the risks of slowing down the restructuring of the agricultural sector due to the tendency of direct aids to be capitalized in increased land prices. Moreover, it is not clear who could benefit more from the payments among landowners, users of land and commercial farms' employees. Thus, it is very important to monitor the whole process, in order to avoid the danger of creating large income disparities both within rural areas and between rural and urban areas.

b) Decoupling: the payments in the new member states are going to be "fully decoupled", since they may be applied to all types of agricultural land and there will be no obligation to produce.

c) Strengthening of the second pillar: the rural development action is reinforced, both in terms of new measures and of financial effort.

---

[14] For the new members these measures will be the following: early retirement of farmers, support for less favored areas or areas with environmental restrictions, agro-environmental programs, afforestation of agricultural land, measures for semi-subsistence farms, setting up of producers group, technical assistance. The additional rural development measures that are financed from the structural funds (EAGGF Guidance section) are investments in agricultural holdings, aids for young farmers, training, other forestry measures, improvement of processing and marketing, adaptation and development of rural areas.

TABLE 2

THE FINANCIAL COST OF THE ENLARGEMENT IN
AGRICULTURE IN 2004-2006
(million of Euros)

	2004		2005		2006		2002-2006	
	A.V.	%	A.V.	%	A.V.	%	A.V.	%
Market policy	516	25,2	749	20,8	734	18,7	1999	20,8
Direct aids	-	-	1173	32,6	1418	36,1	2591	27,1
Rural development	1532	74,8	1674	46,6	1781	45,3	4987	52,1
Total	2048	100,0	3596	100,0	3933	100,0	9577	100,0

Source: EU COMMISSION [15].

However, the proposal has at least two weak points, which make it nothing more than a short-term compromise. On the one hand, the consistency of the proposal with the long term needs of the new member states, in terms of development and restructuring of their agricultural sector; on the other hand, the link of the proposal with the more general CAP reform process, with particular reference to the role the direct payments will play after 2006.

As far as the first point is concerned, the discussion on the agricultural chapter of the enlargement has been directed almost exclusively to the costs to the EU budget. The adjustment costs in transition countries following their accession to the EU have received too little attention (Fidrmuc *et* AL. [16]). In the case of the agricultural sector, though, the traditional adjustment cost argument — maintaining that in the short run certain sectors of the economy face difficulties, since producers are not able to exploit their potential comparative advantage — could be reversed. In other words, the major problem for the agricultural sectors of the new members may not be the danger to be exposed to an unaffordable competitive pressure but, on the contrary, that restructuring of least efficient farms could be dampened by the too generous flow of direct payments and quota rents ensured by the CAP. Even if the impact of direct payments will depend on their use for investment rather than absorption in consumption, on this ground they appear poorly targeted instruments.

In this perspective, the cost of the enlargement for the agricultural sector would not be a short-term "adjustment cost", rather a long-term "structural cost" in terms of lower efficiency and lack of competitiveness. If the overall objective for the new members is to complete their transition, developing an efficient, productive, and competitive market oriented agro-food sector that will contribute to economic growth and welfare, it is far from sure that the present CAP provides the right mix of structural, trade and domestic policies. As a matter of fact, in some cases accession to the EU will lead to a deliberalization of markets, imposing highly distorting regulations. In this respect, the obvious reference is to the sugar and (above all) milk sectors, for which an extension of the quota system is proposed, even if in *Agenda 2000* it has been already decided of phasing it out in 2008.

As a consequence of the Commission's proposal, the new members share in EU agricultural expenditure will be lower in terms of direct compensation payments and higher in terms of rural development[15]. Given the large arrears with which the rural and agricultural sector in the CEECs must contend, this is arguably a more efficient use of resources than keeping income artificially high in the agricultural sector. On the other hand, the social and macroeconomic issues of rural development policies and migration towards urban employment are of very different scope and nature from those of the EU-15.

In the EU-15, rural development policy emerged after the very strong agricultural employment reduction resulting from modernisation and concentration of Community agriculture since the '60s: the support of multifunctional agriculture (i.e. preservation of the environmental and cultural heritage) is part of this process. These problems have a certain relevance in the most industrialised and urbanised regions of the Czech Republic, Slovakia and Slove-

---

[15] As it is shown in Table 2, in the period 2004-2006 the share of rural development actions on total agricultural expenditure in the new member states is more than 50%. Obviously, this figure is inflationed by the relatively low initial level of direct aids in the first years of the transition period. In any case, the share of rural development envisaged by the Commission for the new member states is much higher than in the current CAP.

nia. On the contrary, in countries with high levels of agricultural employment (Poland, Lithuania and Latvia), as well as in certain regions of other countries, the major issue of rural development is the alleviation of hidden agricultural unemployment. "Rural development" (whether through diversification, as in farm tourism, or services, as the environment) will be able to absorb only a very small fraction of it: its reduction will involve mainly migration towards urban jobs.

The emergence of viable professional holdings in the CEECs requires major qualitative (market integration) and quantitative (economic size) leaps forward. To reach only half of the average productivity of the EU-15 would involve, with constant production, the destruction of 4 million agricultural jobs (Zezza and Stamoulis [35]). Therefore, while in the incumbent members rural policy is important to prevent people from moving away and to keep rural areas from economically deteriorating, in the new members there is still the need to put the emphasis on the restructuring of the agricultural sector.

As far as the link with the CAP reform is concerned, between the two driving forces mentioned in Section 2, the international dimension related to the WTO commitments does not seem to play a crucial role. In terms of market access, where the tariff rates were lower in the candidate countries than in the EU, the EU should negotiate compensation with the WTO partners involved[16]. In practice, since partners submitted to preferential trade (which represents a substantial share of EU-15 and CEECs' imports) are excluded from negotiations, the total possible compensations within WTO framework will be weak[17].

No explicit regulation is provided by the WTO covering the calculation of maximum export support in the enlargement of a custom union. However, after the Doha Ministerial Declaration it

---

[16] The same sort of pattern emerged with the Iberian accession, and in that instance third countries, notably the US, demanded compensation for the hikes in farm protection: the US were granted a zero-tariff quota for their export of corn and sorghum on Spanish and Portuguese markets.

[17] Simulations of enlargement scenarios confirm, by far and large, that the impact on world agricultural markets is limited, and trade effects are mostly within the enlarged Union (FRANSEN S. *et* AL. [17]; FULLER F. *et* AL. [20]).

is likely that agricultural export subsidies will have to be phased out independently from the outcome of the enlargement negotiations (De Filippis - Salvatici [11]).

Finally, in terms of domestic support, the Commission claims that the headroom under EU AMS appears to be sufficient. This is not surprising, given that the payment scheme implemented in the new members could be totally decoupled, and this would exclude it from the AMS computation.

5.3 *The Budget Issue*

The real issue concerning the eastward enlargement, then, is going to be a domestic one, namely the level and the distribution of the agricultural expenditure. Despite the efforts by the Commission in order to keep the enlargement dossier separated from the CAP reform one, net contributors like Germany and the Netherlands does not seem willing to accept the enlargement without any guarantee about its effect on their deficits. As it was mentioned in Section 2, a mid-term review of the CAP is planned for 2002, but it is likely that a more radical reform could be necessary in order to correct the incoherence in the distribution of expenditures before the EU eastward expansion. As a matter of fact, if the CAP is not reformed, new and more obscure "rebate systems" will be necessary from the political point of view in order to correct the imbalances.

Looking at the proposals that were discussed during the negotiations on *Agenda 2000* (INEA [24]), it could be argued that there are 3 possible approaches to avoid the explosion of the cost (and of the related financial imbalances among countries) of the implementation of the direct aids scheme in an enlarged Community, namely *(i)* modulation; *(ii)* phasing-in/phasing-out, through a mechanism of degressivity; and *(iii)* national co-financing.

Modulation refers to limiting payments to the farmers based on the size of their business. In *Agenda 2000* this was an option to be implemented on a voluntary basis, and did not really benefit the EU budget since each member state was allowed to use the savings coming from modulation in order to increase the financial resources available for rural development programs. The use of modulation as a saving feature for the EU budget would impose both making it compulsory, and excluding the possibility of retaining the savings at the national level. This means that those countries with relatively larger farms would carry the cost of modulation, and this reduces substantially the chance of succeeding for this option.

Degressivity refers to gradually reducing direct aids over time in the old members, in order to find resources to finance their increase in the new ones. Obviously, this mechanism could be addressed to obtain in 2013 a system of direct aids of equal amount for all the farmers in the Community, but at a lower level than the present one.

Co-financing was an option proposed in a document tabled by the Commission in the latest stage of the *Agenda 2000* negotiation, in response to a twofold objective (EU Commission [14]). On one hand, the goal was to save money in order to finance the compensations for dismantling the quota system in the milk sector. On the other hand, co-financing was proposed in order to reduce the structural financial imbalances among member countries in the distribution and financing of CAP direct aids[18].

The Commission's proposal about co-financing was very simple. It implied the partial (75%) reimbursement of CAP expenditure — instead of the usual 100% — on direct aids to farmers. Obviously, this option would benefit those member states where the share in financing of the European budget is greater than the share in CAP direct aids, while it would affect adversely those member states where the opposite holds. Germany, for example, gets a smaller share of the total CAP payments (15%) than the share of its contribution to the EU budget (25%), with a deficit around 2.8 billion euros. France, on the contrary, gets 24% of the expenditure for direct payments, but contributes to the budget with a share of 17%, with a surplus around 1.9 billion euros (Table 3).

---

[18] It is worth noting that the study, issued by the Commission in the late 1998, had been prepared in response to an explicit request made by the Council in 1994, for exploring the possible solutions to the problem of the financial imbalances among member states.

TABLE 3

1999 - EFFECT OF *CO FINANCING* (25%) OF THE CAP DIRECT PAYMENTS (MILLION EURO) AND RATE OF MEMBER STATES ON EU GDP AND ON CAP DIRECT PAYMENTS (%)

	Current System				balance in CAP Aids (a)	Co-financing		
	direct payments	% CAP direct payments	national financing	% EU GDP		national financing share (25%) (b)	reduction of EU budget contribution (c)	difference d=(c-b)
Belgium	311.2	1.1	834.4	3.0	-523.2	77.8	208.6	130.9
Denmark	805.2	2.9	554.0	2.0	251.2	201.3	138.5	-62.8
Germany	4,231.2	15.2	7,048.0	25.3	-2,816.8	1,057.8	1,762.0	704.3
Greece	2,206.0	7.9	396.8	1.4	1,809.2	551.5	99.2	-452.3
Spain	3,974.0	14.3	1,854.8	6.7	2,119.2	993.5	463.7	-529.8
France	6,652.0	23.9	4,738.0	17.0	1,914.0	1,663.0	1,184.5	-478.5
Ireland	652.0	2.3	225.6	0.8	426.4	163.0	56.4	-106.6
Italy	3,509.2	12.6	3,890.8	14.0	-381.6	877.3	972.7	95.4
Luxemburg	15.2	0.1	59.2	0.2	-44.0	3.8	14.8	11.1
Netherlands	361.2	1.3	1,263.6	4.5	-902.4	90.3	315.9	225.6
Austria	482.0	1.7	702.4	2.5	-220.4	120.5	175.6	55.1
Portugal	426.0	1.5	351.2	1.3	74.8	106.5	87.8	-18.7
Finland	288.0	1.0	402.0	1.4	-114.0	72.0	100.5	28.5
Sweden	539.2	1.9	766.8	2.8	-227.6	134.8	191.7	56.9
United Kingdom	3,416.0	12.3	4,779.2	17.1	-1,363.2	854.0	1,194.8	340.8
Total	*27,867.2*	*100.0*	*27,867.2*	*100.0*	*0.0*	*6,966.8*	*6,966.8*	*0.0*

Source: DE FILIPPIS *et* AL. [12].

A mechanism such as co-financing would have implied a notable reduction of the financial distortion among countries, with a consequent effective reduction of the deficit for Germany and the Netherlands and, to a less extent, for United Kingdom, Sweden, Austria, Finland and Italy (Table 3). Although the co-financing proposal was rejected, especially due to the strong opposition from France, a degree of national co-financing (probably higher than the one envisaged by the Commission in 1998) seems unavoidable in order to guarantee the affordability of support to the agricultural sector in an enlarged EU[19]. This could happen either introducing the *co-financing principle* in the first pillar of CAP, or shifting resources in the direction of rural policy, where such a principle is traditionally applied.

6. - The Road Ahead: Subsidiarity and Co-Financing?

The analysis of financial transfers between the EU and the member states and of the effect of a *co-financing* mechanism is based on Graph 1. On the expenditure side, we focus on the direct aids to farmers, which account for the largest share of CAP expenditure. In order to cover this expenditure, we consider the national contribution based on the national share of the GDP of the Union (Table 3).

Agricultural expenditure *(A)* is measured on the horizontal axis, while non-agricultural expenditure *(NA)* is represented on the vertical axis. The 45° *(su)* line is a national "pre-EU" public budget line, i.e. before any transfers to or from the EU, since for a given budget any increase/decrease of the agricultural expenditure should be matched by an equal increase/decrease of the expenditure in favour of other sectors.

EU membership implies a parallel shift of the budget line toward the origin of the axes, since financing the EU reduces — *coeteris paribus* — the national financial resources. Accordingly, the

---

[19] According to the DUTCH GOVERNMENT [13] estimates, even a 25% *co-financing* would be hardly sufficient to compensate the necessary extra contributions as a result of granting the current direct income support to new members.

GRAPH 1

EU TRANSFERS AND THE NATIONAL GOVERNMENTS'
BUDGET CONSTRAINT

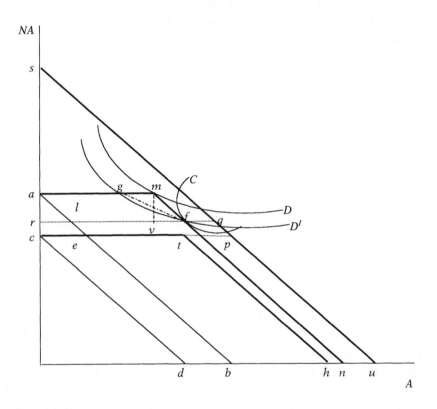

net (of the contributions to the EU) national budget constraint is represented by the *(cd)* line. The effect on the national budget constraint of the CAP spending is shown by the "post-CAP" budget line *(cth)*. The net budget line *(cd)* shifts to the right by the amount of the expenditure received by the national agricultural sector *(ct)*. National policy-makers can supplement CAP spending with national expenditure moving along *th* on the budget line (if such expenditure does not distort internal competition), but cannot reduce agricultural expenditure below the amount decided at EU level.

As a consequence of *co-financing*, the net budget constraint shifts from *cd* to *ab*, while the EU spending is reduced from *ct* to *am*. If the overall amount of financial resources available to the agricultural sector were required to remain (at least) the same, as in the *Agenda 2000* proposal, the point chosen could not be positioned to the left of *f (rf = ct)*.

This implies that the minimum level of transfers to the agricultural sector would continue to be decided within the CAP, at the EU level. The cost of these decisions, though, would be shared between the EU budget *(am = lf)* and the national exchequers *(rl)*. In other words, in the Commission's proposal, the *co-financing* did not deal with the "assignment problem", that is the allocation of responsibilities to various levels of government, only implying a joint financial support of a policy still designed and implemented at the EU level. Therefore, it should be clear that criticisms of the proposal on the ground that it would have fostered the dismantling of the CAP or a move toward its re-nationalisation were purely instrumental.

In terms of the budgetary position, the figure presents the case of a member state that is a net contributor to the CAP. In this case, the reduction in the contribution to EU *(ce)* due to *co-financing* exceeds the national financing share of CAP expenditure *(rl)*. This implies a reduction of the budgetary imbalance corresponding to the difference between *(tp)* and *(fq)*. On the contrary, countries with a share in financing lower than the share in CAP receipts would register a significant worsening of their budgetary position. Obviously, this goes a long way in explaining the strenuous opposition by France to the Commission's proposal. In the same vein, the higher the rate of *co-financing*, the lower the financial benefits that the new members could get from the extension of the direct payments' scheme.

According to the Commission, the "rationale for the partial reimbursement would be that direct aids to farmers constitute strict interpersonal redistribution, with no allocative aim" (EU Commission [14], Annex 5 p. 2). Although it is true that compensatory payments have no allocative aim, this does not certainly imply that they have no allocative impact (OECD [29]). In this respect, as long as the payments to farmers are not fully "decoupled", the Commission has a crucial role to play in ensuring the preservation of the internal common market. In order to ensure that competition is not distorted, strict EU controls on the amount of and the manner in which national subsidies can be given are necessary.

On the other hand, the literature on fiscal federalism suggests that the assignment of the responsibility for financing should go along with the possibility to decide the amount of the expenditure. In this respect, the co-financing proposal is not fully consistent.

Graph 1 shows that national governments are likely to benefit from the possibility to pursue their own objectives. With indifference curves of type D, for example, the chosen point would move from f to m, since the latter allows the achievement of a higher indifference curve ($D > D^1$). On the other hand, if national government's preferences are more biased toward the agricultural sector (as in the case of indifference curves of type C), it could still be the case that the chosen point is f. In such a case, though, the requirement to devote a certain amount of resources to the agricultural sector would not be binding. Hence, the proposal of making the CAP expenditure by member state compulsory should be considered either harmful (if binding) or redundant (if not binding).

Rather than introducing the *co-financing* mechanism, it would seem preferable to extend to the "first pillar" of the CAP the principles currently governing structural funds expenditure. In this area, the financial burden is shared, since member states are required to match EU spending. Moreover, in order to guarantee a certain degree of redistribution among member states on an equity ground, different rates of financial EU support could be envisaged.

Agricultural matching transfers from the EU change the slope of the national budget constraint, since at any level of non-agricultural expenditure the national government can obtain x-percent more of agricultural expenditure. In such a case the budget constraint is *(agfn)*, since in order to maintain the burden for the EU budget constant *(gm)* and *(vf)* must be equal. Apparently, this type of financial mechanism differ from the co-financing proposal, since it would allow some flexibility to member states in pursuing their own redistributive objectives.

In this respect, the adoption of a matching transfers system by the EAGGF Guarantee Section presents two major benefits. On the one hand, the national matching or cost-sharing component maintains to the EU a certain degree of control, since it requires a degree of accountability by national governments, ensuring that funds are directed toward expenditures on which the Union places a priority. On the other hand, such an approach can easily take into account some equity concerns, through the adoption of different reimbursement rates according to the national (regional) income levels.

According to Alesina *et* AL. [1] p. 4, «the element that is central to all federations is a tension between the heterogeneity between countries and the advantage of taking certain decisions in common». The heterogeneity within the EU will be greatly increased after the eastward enlargement, but moving away from traditional price support policies allows the CAP to move away also from an institutional set up in which every country has to follow the policy chosen at the federal level.

The main conclusion that we draw from the analysis developed in this Section is that a possible CAP for the enlarged EU could be based on a more "flexible" structure, in which the Union fixes a minimum expenditure for all countries and these can subsequently topped up. This would allow increasing the adaptability of agricultural policy to different national preferences and structures. In addition to the minimum expenditure, the future CAP would also provide for the possibility to induce national governments to make the "right" (from the Union point of view) choices through a system of financial support, in the form of matching transfers.

7. - Conclusions

This paper moves from the observation of the low effective competitiveness of the agro-food sector of the CEECs in relation to the EU and its continuing deterioration. Due to lack of access to functioning market services (competitive processors, marketers, and input suppliers), or general obstacles to efficient operation, (such as difficulties with legal enforcement of contracts, corruption in various levels of government, barriers to mobility in labour markets), most of CEEC agro-food production is still far from satisfying EU quality, sanitary and phytosanitary standards.

In terms of agricultural policies, the changes introduced in the EU and in the new members during the last ten years imply that (at least some of) the consequences of the EU accession are already there. It could be argued, though, that in both cases changes have taken place partly to minimize potential problems with the accession, but mainly for domestic political reasons.

As far as the agricultural chapter is concerned, we do not dare to make any forecasts about the changes that will be introduced into the Commission's proposal before the end of the negotiations. Although the proposal is fully consistent with the 2000-2006 financial guideline, we argue that the crux of the matter in the present negotiations is the agricultural expenditure for direct payments.

From the point of view of the incumbent members, net contributors to the EU budget show increasing fears that they will have to pay the brunt of the cost, if the CAP is extended in its present form to 10 or more new EU members. As far as the new members are concerned, it must be acknowledged that their negotiating position is quite comfortable, since they would not need to change pre-enlargement spending rules, but they would simply ask for an equal treatment. However, in order to evaluate the new members' negotiating position, it should be kept in mind that most of income support would end up in two countries, namely Poland and Hungary.

On the other hand, it is not possible to be overly optimistic about the outcome of a CAP reform negotiated after enlargement: reaching decisions is likely to become more difficult, given the greater diversity of needs and preferences. Political and bureaucratic gridlock in an enlarged EU is a real danger that should be taken seriously into account.

A possible solution could be provided by new institutional arrangements in terms of cost sharing between EU and national budgets. We have analysed the co-financing proposal that was discussed (and rejected) in the negotiations of the *Agenda 2000* CAP reform package. We find that the original co-financing proposal does not provide a satisfactory answer to the problem of allocating responsibilities between nationals and European authorities. In this respect, a better solution would be to make the first pillar expenditure consistent with the principle adopted for other components of the EU budget. In any case, both a reform of the financial rules for the traditional CAP subsidies, and a further shift in the direction of rural development, will increase the importance of intergovernmental grants in the new agricultural policy of the enlarged Union.

BIBLIOGRAPHY

[1] ALESINA A. - ANGELONI I. - ETRO F., «Institutional Rules for Federations», Cambridge (Ma), National Bureau of Economic Research, *Working Paper* n. 8646, 2001 (http://www.nber.org/papers/w8646).

[2] ANANIA G., *Modeling Agricultural Trade Liberalization*. A Review, paper presented at the Annual Meeting of the American Agricultural Economics Association, Chicago, August 2001.

[3] BACH C.F. -FRANDSEN S.E. - JENSEN H.G., «Agricultural and Economic-Wide Effects of European Enlargement: Modelling the Common Agricultural Policy», *Journal of Agricultural Economics*, vol. 51, n. 2, 2000, pp. 162-80.

[4] BALDWIN R.E. - FRANCOIS J.F. - PORTES R., «The Costs and Benefits of Eastern Enlargement: the Impact on the EU and Central Europe", *Economic Policy*, n. 24, 1997, pp. 127-76.

[5] BANSE M., «Does the CAP Matter? Macro-Economic Implications of EU-Accession in Central European Countries», paper presented at the 75th Conference on *Policy Modelling for European and Global Issues*, Brussels, July 2001.

[6] COCHRANE N., «EU Enlargement: Negotiations Give Rise to New Issues», *Agricultural Outlook*, January-February 2001, pp. 19-22 (http://www.ers.usda.gov/Publications/AgOutlook/Jan2001/AO278H.pdf).

[7] DAVIDOVA S. - BUCKWELL A., «Transformation of CEEC Agricutlure and Integration with the EU: Progress and Issues», TANGERMANN S. - BANSE M. (eds.), *Central and Eastern European Agriculture in Expanding European Union*, Wallingford Oxon, CABI Publishing, 2000.

[8] DE BENEDICTIS M. - DE FILIPPIS F - SALVATICI L., «Nature and Causes of CAP Changes in the 1980s and a Tentative Exploration of Potential Scenarios», in ANANIA G. - CARTER C. - MCCALLA A., *Agricultural Trade Conflicts and GATT*, Summertown (Oxford), Westview Press, 1994.

[9] DE FILIPPIS F. - SALVATICI L., «L'Italia e la politica agricola del mercato comune europeo», in *Storia dell'agricoltura italiana in età contemporanea*, vol. III, Venezia, Marsilio, 1991.

[10] — — - — —, «La politica agricola comunitaria: una riforma incompiuta», *Politica internazionale* n. 3, 1997.

[11] — — - — —, «Le prospettive del negoziato agricolo dopo la Conferenza di Doha», in DE FILIPPIS F. (ed), *Le vie della globalizzazione: la questione agricola nel WTO*, Milano F. Angeli, 2002, Cap. 6.

[12] DE FILIPPIS F. - HENKE R. - PUPO-D'ANDREA M.R. - SALVATICI L., «Cofinanziamento e rinazionalizzazione della Pac: questioni aperte», *La Questione Agraria* n. 76, 1999.

[13] DUTCH GOVERNMENT, *The Financing of the Common Agricultural Policy after Enlargement of the European Union*, The Hague, Interdepartmental Policy Study, 2001 *(http://www.euractiv.com/ndbtext/general/capo1.pdf)*.

[14] EU COMMISSION, *Financing the European Union: Commission Report on the Operation of the Own Resources System*, Brussels, Directorate General XIX, 1998.

[15] — —, «Common Financial Framework 2004-2006 for the Accession Negotiations», Brussels, Communication from the Commission, *SEC 102*, 2002.

[16] FIDRMUC J. - HUBER P. - MICHALEK J.J., «Poland's Accession to the European Union: Demand for Protection of Selected Sensitive Products», *MOCT-MOST: Economic Policy in Transitional Economies*, vol. 11, n. 1, 2001, pp. 45-67.

346   *Fabrizio De Filippis - Luca Salvatici*

[17] FRANDSEN S.E. - JENSEN H.G. - VANZETTI D.M., «Expanding Fortress Europe, Agricultural Trade and Welfare, Implications of European Enlargement for Non-member Regions», *The World Economy*, vol. 23, n. 3, 2000, pp. 309-29.

[18] FRANDSEN S.E. - JENSEN H.G., "Economic Impacts of the Enlargement of the European Union: Analysing the Importance of Direct Payments", in VAN TONGEREN F. - VAN MEJIL H. (eds.), *European Policy Issues in a Global Trade Analysis Framework*, The Hague, Agricultural Economics Research Institute, Report 6.01.06, 2001.

[19] FROHBERG K. - HARTMANN M. - WEINGARTEN P. - WAHL O. - FOCH A., «Development of CEEC Agriculture under Three Scenarios - Current CEEC Policies, CAP 1995/96, Agenda 2000», in BROCKMEIER M. - FRANCOIS J.F. - HERTEL T.W. - SCHMITZ M.P. (eds), *Economic Transition and the Greening of Policies: Modeling New Challenges for Agriculture and Agribusiness in Europe*, proceedings 50th *EAAE* Seminar, Kiel, Vauk Verlag, 1998.

[20] FULLER F. - BEGHIN J. - FABIOSA J. - MOHANTY S. - FANG C. - KAUS P., *Accession of the Czech Republic, Hungary, and Poland to the European Union: Impacts on Agricultural Markets*, Iowa State University, Center for Agricultural and Rural Development, *Working Paper* n. 00-WP 259, 2000.

[21] HARTELL J.S. - SWINNEN J.F.M., «Trends in Agricultural Price and Trade Policy Instruments Since 1990 in Central European Countries», *The World Economy*, vol. 21, 1998, pp. 261-79.

[22] HARTELL J.S. - SWINNEN J.F.M., «Europea,n Integration and the Political Economy of Central and Eastern European Agricultural Price and Trade Policy», in TANGERMANN S. - BANSE M. (eds.), *Central and Eastern European Agriculture in Expanding European Union*, Walllingford Oxon, CABI Publishing, 2000.

[23] INEA (Italian Institute of Agricultural Economics), «Peco e allargamento dell'UE», *Osservatorio sulle Politiche Agricole dell'UE*, Roma, INEA, 1998.

[24] — —, «La riforma della PAC in Agenda 2000», *Osservatorio sulle Politiche Agricole dell'UE*, Roma, INEA, 1999.

[25] LERMAN Z., «Agriculture in Transition Economies: from Common Heritage to Divergence», *Agricultural Economics*, Vol. 26 n. 2, 2001, pp. 95-114.

[26] MÜNCH W., «Effects of CEEC-EU Accession on Agricultural Markets in the CEEC and on Government Expenditure», in TANGERMANN S. - BANSE M. (eds.), *Central and Eastern European Agriculture in Expanding European Union*, Walllingford Oxon, CABI Publishing, 2000.

[27] NIELSEN C.P., «Enlargement of the European Union. A Survey of Quantitative Analyses», Copenhagen, Danish Institute of Agricultural and Fisheries Economics, *Rapport 106*, 1999.

[28] NIELSEN C.P. - STÆHR M.H.J. - FRANDSEN S.E. - JENSEN H.G. - RATINGER T. - THOMSON K.J., «Assessment of the Usefulness of GTAP for Analysing the EU Enlargement», in FRANDSEN S.E. - STÆHR M.H.J. (eds), *Assessment of the GTAP Modelling Framework for Policy Analyses from a European Perspective*, Copenhagen, Danish Institute of Agricultural and Fisheries Economics, *Rapport 116*, 2000.

[29] OECD, «Decoupling: a Conceptual Overview", *COM/AGR/APM/TD/WP(2000)14/FINAL*, Paris, 2000.

[30] — —, «Challenges for the Agro-food Sector in European Transition Countries", *OECD Policy Brief*, 2001 *(http://www.oecd.org/pdf/M00007000/M00007250.pdf)*.

[31] POLIQUEN A., «Compétitivités et Revenus agricoles Dans Les Secteurs Agro-Alimentaires des PECO», *Reports and Studies DG VI*, Bruxelles, European Commission, 2001.

[32] SALVATICI L. - ANANIA G. - ARFINI F. - CONFORTI P. - DE MURO P. - LONDERO P. - SCKOKAI P., «Modelling CAP Reform: Hype or Hope?», in HECKELEI T. - WITZKE H.P. - HENRICHSMEYER W. (eds), *Agricultural Sector Modelling and Policy Information System*, proceedings 65th EAAE Seminar, Kiel, Vauk Verlag, 2001.

[33] TANGERMANN S.. - SWINNEN W., «Conclusions and Implications for Food and Agricultural Policy in the Process of Accession to the EU», TANGERMANN S. - BANSE M. (eds.), *Central and Eastern European Agriculture in Expanding European Union*, Walllingford Oxon, CABI Publishing, 2000.

[34] WEYERBROCK S., «East-West European Integration: A General-Equilibrium Analysis of Alternative Agricultural Policies», *Review of International Economics*, Vol. 9, n. 3, 2001, pp. 462-81.

[35] ZEZZA A. - STAMOULIS K.G., «The Role of the Agricultural Sector in Transition Economies: Synthesis and Concluding Remarks», in POGANIETZ W.-R. - ZEZZA A. - FROHBERG K. - STAMOULIS K.G. (eds.), *Perspectives on Agriculture in Transition: Analytical Issues, Modelling Approaches, and Case Study Results*, Kiel, Wissenschaftsverlag Vauk, 2000.

The Political Economy
of Eastern Enlargement

Friedrich Heinemann*

Zentrum für Europäische Wirtschaftsforschung, Mannheim

L'allargamento ad Est coinvolge gli interessi personali dei politici e dei lobbisti dell'Unione Europea. Questo approccio teorico è indispensabile per una piena comprensione delle diverse decisioni che devono essere prese riguardo al Trattato di Nizza, *alla* Convenzione *sulle riforme costituzionali, nonché ai negoziati e al calendario dell'allargamento. In quest'ottica, si possono anche inquadrare gli effetti di lungo periodo dell'allargamento sulle politiche comunitarie. L'ingresso di 12 nuovi paesi condurrà a nuovi equilibri politico-economici, ad esempio nel caso della Politica Agricola Comune.*

Enlargement is affecting personal interests of politicians and lobbyists in many ways. This view is shown to be indispensable to a full understanding of many decisions that have been taken in regard to the Treaty of Nice, *the* Convention *set up in Laeken, the emerging results of the accession negotiations and the choice of first wave countries. This view is also helpful to assess the long-run impact of enlargement on EU policies. The accession of 12 new countries to the EU will bring about new political-economic equilibria, as argued here for the case of the Common Agricultural Policy.* [JEL Code: F02, H77]

1. - Introduction

The EU accession of twelve new member countries does not only constitute a significant change in the economic setting in Eu-

---

* Friedrich Heinemann is Senior Researcher in the Department of International Finance and Financial Management.

N.B., the numbers in square brackets refer to the Bibliography at the end of the paper.

rope, it will also have a major impact on political-economic processes. Politicians, bureaucrats and lobbyists of new members are appearing as new actors on the scene and are beginning to influence debates and decisions in EU politics. In this sense, enlargement can be understood as a shock to the stability of existing political-economic equilibria.

This papers tries to contribute to a better understanding of this dimension of enlargement. In particular, it is dealing with three issues: first, with the pre-enlargement behaviour of important EU-15 agents; second, with the different political-economic appeal of candidate countries and, third, with the likely long-run impact of enlargement on interest group power with a special focus on the Common Agricultural Policy (CAP).

With regard to the first issue, it is demonstrated that many pre-enlargement developments and decisions are heavily influenced by attempts of EU-15 government representatives and members of EU organs to protect their interests in an enlarged Community. The *Treaty of Nice*, some first results of the accession negotiations but also the characteristics of the *Convention* that prepares the next Intergovernmental Conference in 2004 can be interpreted in this way. All these opportunities are used by incumbent politicians of EU-15 countries to create facts that will protect their interests at least for a transitory period after enlargement.

With regard to the second issue, it is argued that the field of candidates shows considerable differences in terms of each country's appeal to the agents in the West. This analysis is helpful to understand the likely regional sequencing of enlargement.

With regard to the third issue, some likely characteristics of new long-run power equilibria will be discussed. Without doubt, the balance of power and of interests in EU-27 will lead to different results compared to that of EU-15. It is argued that accession might weaken the power of interest groups and thus increase the scope for major policy changes.

This paper is a complement to Heinemann [15]. The latter paper looks in detail at the political-economic driving forces behind the *Treaty of Nice*. Apart from that, studies on the political-economic dimension of the current enlargement process are scarce.

While public choice issues have attracted much interest in the transition literature (for example Hillman [16], Backhaus and Krause [1], Bastian [3]), the process of EU enlargement has rarely been analysed in this way. The early analysis of Bofinger [5] is largely restricted to the interests of trade related lobbies. Kohler [17] looks at the interests of EU-15 countries in regard to enlargement but largely abstracts from personal interests of decisive actors in EU institutions. Baldwin *et* Al. [2] is helpful insofar as it analyses the impact of past enlargements on the EU budget in a political-economic perspective.

The analysis proceeds in the following way. In a first step (Section 2), central political-economic challenges to enlargement are identified. After that, Sections 3 to 5 deal consecutively with the pre-enlargement behaviour of EU-15 agents, the political-economic appeal of candidate countries and the post-accession perspective of important EU policy fields. Section 6 concludes.

2. - The Impact of Self-Interest on the Enlargement Process

The political-economic approach offers a straightforward basis for the identification of major policy forces influencing the enlargement process: According to the standard public choice assumption the self-interest of decisive agents should have a major impact. On the side of EU-15 countries, members of national governments and of the European Parliament are decisive agents since any accession requires unanimous support in the Council and an absolute majority in the European Parliament (Art. 49 *Treaty on European Union*). The preferences of individuals in these institutions should have a particular impact on the enlargement process since they have the power to block enlargement in case it would threaten their interests to a considerable extent.

Economists tend to argue that enlargement produces a «win-win» outcome in terms of the general welfare of old and new member countries. Nevertheless, from the individual perspective of EU-15 politicians, the process is likely to have both positive and negative consequences (details together with a game theoretic formalisation in Heinemann [15]): On the asset side of the balance sheet there are advantages like the internalisation of externalities that, pre-accession, result from autonomous national policies of Eastern European countries e.g. in environmental policy. Furthermore, EU-15 governments can hope to limit the nuisance resulting from locational competition between Eastern and Western Europe. By obliging Eastern European economies to implement the full acquis communautaire (the existing EU law including all directives and regulations) it is possible to reduce disadvantages in competition resulting from high regulation in Western Europe. This motive corresponds to the well-known desire of «raising rivals' costs» (Goldberg [13]): Governments of highly regulated countries try to extend their regulation to competing countries.

However, there are also important lines on the liability side of enlargement's balance from the perspective of EU-15 politicians' self-interest. For national governments and members of EU organs alike, the EU budget today offers a valuable instrument to care for politically important interest groups such as farmers and voters in poor regions. 79.7% (2002) of the budget is being spent either on the Common Agricultural Policy or the Structural Funds. Thus, at least in budgetary terms the verdict is still justified that the European Union «has specialized in the supply of privileges to interest groups» (Vaubel [21], p. 175). From the EU-15 governments' perspective this function is likely to be damaged through enlargement since the relatively large agricultural sectors and the low per capita income of new member countries will result in redirecting substantial budgetary flows from the West to the East.

With the trade unions further important interest groups should be sceptical on enlargement due to the likely negative impact of relatively labour-abundant new member economies on real wages.

Voters' preferences cannot be expected to counterbalance these anti-enlargement interest of important lobbies. Relative to other policy issues, enlargements regularly gets the lowest marks in terms of political priority in recent polls (European Commission [7], p. 45). A majority of voters in old member countries is not particularly keen on a fast enlargement so that EU-15 governments cannot hope to be rewarded at the ballot box for accepting accessions.

In principle, these hazards to the personal interests of decisive policy makers could pose a threat to the success of the enlargement process. In order to reduce this risk for enlargement, rationally acting negotiators of candidate countries could promise to respect established interests of EU-15 countries e.g. on the budgetary field. However, there are two problems with any such promise. First, as examples like the Polish negotiation stance on agricultural subsidies clarify, policy makers in the candidate countries are often restricted by own domestic lobby pressure. This reduces their leeway for compromise and forces them to press hard for a significant share in EU redistributive spending policies because otherwise they risk to lose power in domestic political competition. Second, any pre-entry promise to respect EU-15 interests after accession lacks credibility. This lack of credibility results from the strong post-entry power of a new member that stands in sharp contrast to the weak pre-entry position: Pre-entry, a EU candidate has only the choice between accepting all accession conditions posed by Western partners or dropping the EU application altogether. With the entry, however, a country becomes a full partner represented in EU decision making bodies with rights equal to old members. Once accession is realised, there is an incentive to break all past promises since the decision on EU membership is an irreversible decision.

If promises lack credibility the usual remedy is the creation of institutional guarantees. Indeed, this creation is exactly what is characterising several decisions of the pre-entry period. Of course, protecting self-interest is no motivation appearing in official documents. Nevertheless, the analysis of the next section shows that EU-15 policy makers have so far already invested considerable efforts to protect their interests in an enlarged Community.

There are different approaches available to EU-15 agents for strategies of protecting self-interest in an enlarged EU. These approaches concern the EU constitution and the details of the accessions as analysed in Section 3 and the country sequencing of enlargement as analysed in Section 4. One insight applies to all of them: In order to overcome the political-economic obstacles to enlargement it might be sufficient to establish transitory guarantees as long as their validity extends beyond the relevant political time horizon of those politicians that decide on enlargement.

3. - The Protection of EU-15 Interests in Nice, in Laeken and in the Accession Negotiations

3.1 *Nice*

As long as the new members have not yet joined, the old member countries are free to change the constitution to their advantage without requiring consent from candidate countries. In Nice in December 2000, this opportunity was used in a consequent way: Important contents of the *Treaty of Nice* are not understandable without taking account of the motive of EU-15 governments to create guarantees for their interests after enlargement. The following examples (summarised from the detailed analysis in Heinemann [15]) support this view.

The analysis of council voting for the EU comprising 27 member countries (EU-27) as agreed in Nice shows a shift of power towards the 15 old member countries compared to an extrapolated pre-Nice constitution. This power shift is not simply explainable by the *Treaty*'s official objective of improving capability to act. The contrary is true since the new Council voting formula even leads to a deterioration of the capability to act measured on the basis of Coleman's decision probability.

Also in regard to the Parliament, Nice has been used to protect interests of EU-15 representatives relative to future members. These decisions are in obvious contradiction to the official objective of improving democratic legitimacy through a higher degree of population proportionality. In the Nice allocation of parliamentary seats the new member countries are discriminated against insofar population rankings are reversed in the ranking of a country's seats. Although in 2000, the Czech Republic had a larger population than Belgium and both Czech Republic and Hungary had larger populations than Portugal, the two Western European countries have been granted 10% more seats (22 each) than the two Eastern European countries (20 each). This is probably the least disguised example of EU-15 interest protection in the *Treaty of Nice*.

Furthermore, current members of the European Parliament find their reelection chances well protected at the 2004 regular election through the Nice results. These provisions have been decided on at the expenses of the past official objective of limiting the size of Parliament. Not only has the Amsterdam ceiling of 700 seats been lifted to 732 on a permanent basis. In addition, a comfortable transitory provision practically renders any enlargement driven reduction of seats per EU-15 country unnecessary at the 2004 election: During the enlargement process the number of seats is allowed to be extended even beyond the 732 limit. This is a good example that at least the transitory provisions are designed to protect incumbent individuals in the decisive EU organs.

3.2 *Laeken and the Convention*

Also the post-Nice constitutional development has elements that can be easily interpreted as driven by the desire to establish guarantees protecting EU-15 interests. The most important innovation of this development is the establishment of a Convention decided at the European Council in Laeken in December 2001. The *Convention*'s purpose is to prepare the next Intergovernmental Conference that is to decide the further reform of the EC and *EU Treaties* scheduled for 2004.

At the time of Laeken, progress in accession negotiations had it made increasingly likely that the first accessions would take place by 2004. Membership, however, implies necessarily veto power in constitutional reforms. Thus, EU-15 governments convening in Laeken had to reckon with the fact that in the next Intergovernmental Conference they would require consent from Cen-

tral European countries for any further constitutional change. This
veto power would obviously make further constitutional changes
impossible that would be unfavourable to new members.

With this background, the innovation of calling a preparato-
ry *Convention* was able to alleviate this problem from a Western
point of view. The *Convention* defines the options that will be available as basis for negotiations at the Intergovernmental Conference. The *Convention*'s output thus creates facts for the next reform of the EU's constitution since it does not seem realistic that
this body's recommendations could be completely ignored. The
treatment of the candidate countries in the *Convention* points to
the relevance of the suggested view: «The accession candidate
countries ... will be represented in the same way as the current
member states ... and will be able to take part in the proceedings
without, however, being able to prevent any consensus which may
emerge among the member states» (European Council [12], Annex 1). Thus, likely full members of the EU in 2004 are present
in the *Convention* but explicitly deprived of veto power. This is
hardly understandable without accepting the motivation to restrict
the influence of new members for the next step of constitutional
reforms.

3.3 *Emerging Details of the Accession Treaties*

The self-interest of the members of EU governments should
also have its impact on the details of the accession agreements.
Particularly revealing are deviations from the principle of the acquis communautaire. According to that principle politicians of EU-
15 have always insisted that temporary derogations from the full
rights and obligations of EU membership should be avoided as
far as possible. In contradiction to that general position, EU-15
politicians (from Germany and Austria in particular) have themselves pressed for a temporary derogation concerning the free
movement of labour. The emerging transitory provision in respect
to this basic freedom of the internal market grants EU-15 countries the right to protect their labour market against immigration

of new members' workers for a maximum period of seven years after accession (European Commission [11], Chapter 2: *Free Movements for Persons*). This provision is able to comfort concerns of important interest groups like trade unions and — assuming first accessions 2004 — extends to 2011 which is beyond the political time horizon of most current members of governments.

A further crucial policy field where the Western sides insists on a temporary differential treatment of the new members is the Common Agricultural Policy (CAP). A Commission "report" in January 2002 on the financing of enlargement (European Commission [10]) has defined the EU-15 position on direct payments in CAP. According to this position, current rules for direct payments shall not be fully applied to farmers in the new member countries before 2013. If this Commission proposal were realised farmers in new member countries would start with only 25% of the direct payments corresponding to the rules existing for Western Europe. Thus initially, Western farmers and taxpayers are largely protected from the consequences of an enlargement that would be consistent with the full acquis communautaire. Note that again the potential long-run conflicts between old and new members are not solved but simply shifted beyond the relevant political time horizon.

While the examples of labour movements and CAP are those most obviously being driven by EU-15 agents' self-interest there are further examples. In the negotiation chapter on environmental policy candidates are interested to obtain transitional periods before the full realisation of the acquis due to financial and economic restrictions. While the EU-15 side has accepted this necessity it has not missed the opportunity to raise rivals' costs at the earliest possible time at least «at the margin»: From the day of accession, all new investments have to respect the full environmental standards of EU-15 (European Commission [11], Chapter 22: *Environment*). Thus, enlargement is consequently used to export as quickly as possible the environmental standards reflecting the preferences of wealthy industrial countries to much poorer economies. This solution can hardly claim economic efficiency but is consistent with the desire of Western European governments to alleviate the restrictions from international competition.

4. - Country Sequencing

As the interests of Western European decisive agents have their impact on constitutional reform and accession negotiations these interests should also be helpful in understanding the choice of the first wave of entering countries. The choice of countries is a further degree of freedom available to old members' governments who seek to limit effects of enlargement detrimental to their self-interest.

Although uncertainties of the timing and sequencing still existed when writing this analysis, in its progress report of November 2001 (European Commission [8]) the European Commission has already articulated the Western preferences in this respect. This report's message is that the Commission regards accession of ten countries as possible by 2004 (European Commission [8], Chapter IV *Conclusions*). Apart from Turkey where accession negotiations have not even started Bulgaria and Romania are implicitly identified as not belonging to the first wave because, in the report's terminology, they are not yet regarded as «functioning market economies» (Chapter II *Progress*).

There is, of course, no way to measure in an objective way whether a country is a functioning market economy or not. The vagueness of this terminology thus offers rich opportunities to keep countries out of the EU whose membership would be particularly problematic in the light of EU agents' interests. The emerging choice of first wave countries seems to be in line with this political-economic interpretation of the enlargement process as can be seen from the following considerations and quantification.

As analysed above (Section 2) EU politicians from national governments and the European Parliament face a basic trade-off in choosing new members. On the one hand, they are interested to extend the size of the EU since this amplifies the political and economic usefulness of European integration (such as benefits from trade, power of EU in international negotiations, political cartel, internalisation of externalities). On the other hand, agents from EU-15 face a price for enlargement in terms of power losses in EU institutions, an increasing fiscal burden resulting mainly from the application of CAP and Structural Policies to new member countries and increasing migration pressure. This suggests that the candidate country is most attractive that for a given size implies the smallest power loss, the smallest fiscal burden and the smallest migration pressure.

Based on these considerations, some simple indicators can be constructed that describe the costs and benefits of a specific country's accession from the Western politicians' perspective. On the benefit side, it can be assumed that GDP (in purchasing power standards) is the variable EU actors are most interested to maximise. In the political dimension those countries are most attractive that for a given share of power in EU institutions offer the largest GDP. Thus, GDP/power ratios for candidate countries can be interpreted as indicators of attraction from the EU-15 perspective. For the calculation, it is made use of two power indicators: first a candidate's Shapley-Shubik power share in the Council according to the Nice constitution (taken from Heinemann [15]) and a candidate's number of seats in the European Parliament as agreed in Nice.

On the cost side those variables are helpful that are either determinants of EU transfers in the context of CAP and structural spending and/or indicate large emigration pressure for a candidate country since EU transfers and migration are highly sensitive issues for the self-interest of old members' governments. Per capita income, shares of agriculture in GDP and employment and the unemployment rate are relevant variables in this context.

Table 1 includes these benefit and cost indicators for 12 candidate countries. Indicators have been standardised by the mean and standard deviation of the original numbers so that zero stands for the average and the units are standard deviations of the underlying series. The sign has been adjusted so that a positive (negative) sign is assigned to a country with a political-economic attraction above (below) the average for all candidates.

TABLE 1

INDICATORS FOR THE RELATIVE ATTRACTIVENESS
OF CANDIDATES*

	«Benefits»			«Costs»		
	GDP/ Council power	GDP/EP seats	GDP p.c. (PPS)	Unem- ployment rate	Employ- ment share in agriculture	GDP share of agriculture
Poland	0.77	0.79	−0.17	−0.42	−0.44	0.48
Romania	0.43	0.10	−0.45	0.36	−2.44	−0.94
Czech Republic	0.71	0.83	0.32	0.21	0.57	0.40
Hungary	0.47	0.58	0.15	0.39	0.43	0.32
Bulgaria	−0.32	−0.29	−0.52	−0.42	0.13	−1.68
Slovakia	0.26	0.20	0.04	−0.66	0.41	0.52
Lithuania	−0.45	−0.44	−0.39	−0.36	−0.42	0.55
Latvia	−0.39	−0.46	−0.41	−0.25	−0.11	0.32
Slovenia	0.21	0.22	0.59	0.37	0.28	0.25
Estonia	−0.51	−0.44	−0.19	−0.16	0.44	0.01
Cyprus	−0.45	−0.36	0.85	0.54	0.30	0.33
Malta	−0.73	−0.73	0.16	0.40	0.85	−0.56

* Underlying data refer to the year 2000. For the values and sources of variables see appendix. Indicators are standardised (mean zero and standard deviation one). Positive values indicate above average attractiveness.

The following general picture emerges: Although countries with large populations tend to be attractive due to their low political power in EU institutions for a given GDP, some small and medium countries have an appeal for EU decision makers due to relatively low fiscal burdens.

Graphs 1 and 2 clarify the ranking for the benefit and cost side of the accession trade-off. The exclusion of Bulgaria and Romania from the first wave is obviously driven by cost considerations. Though both countries are in a medium position concerning the benefit aspects, cost indicators demonstrate the fact that an early membership of both countries would produce particularly high spending and migration pressure and thus damage EU-15 governments' interests.

GRAPH 1

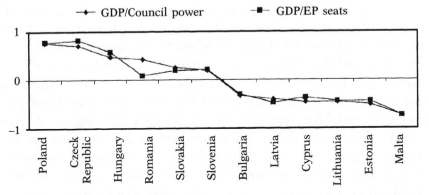

RANKING IN ATTRACTIVENESS ACCORDING
TO BENEFIT INDICATORS*

→ GDP/Council power   ■ GDP/EP seats

* First two columns of Table 1.

GRAPH 2

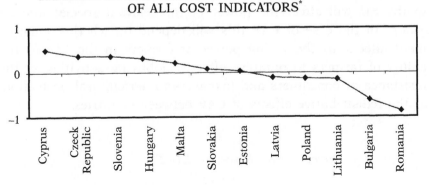

RANKING IN ATTRACTIVENESS ACCORDING TO MEAN
OF ALL COST INDICATORS*

* Mean of last four columns in Table 1.

5. - Enlargement's Long-Run Impact on Political-Economic Equilibria

5.1 *The Long-Run Dimension*

As has become clear by the preceding analysis, old members' governments have established a number of guarantees protecting established interests. As described, however, important guarantees (such as restrictions to CAP's direct payments, restriction to free movement of labour, exclusion of Bulgaria and Romania from the first wave) are only of a temporary nature. These measures effectively defend the *status quo* for one or two legislative periods but expire afterwards. Individuals currently represented in governments and EU bodies are naturally less interested in effects emerging well beyond their expected time in office. Thus, although vested interests are a hurdle for fast changes they might not prevent substantial long-run divergence from the starting point. This Section deals with this long-run impact of enlargement on EU policies where «long-run» stands for the time after the expiration of transitory provisions. This Section will focus on the example of CAP, nevertheless the results partly allow conclusions in regard to the future impact of interest groups on EU policies in general.

For the long-run impact of enlargement on a policy such as the CAP it is crucial whether the accession of 12 further countries to the EU will affect the power of the relevant special interest group. In the case of CAP this will depend on whether enlargement affects: *a)* the voting power of farmers in the EU; *b)* the ability of farmers to organise effective lobbying activities; *c)* the resistance of consumers and taxpayers to agricultural protection; *d)* the redistributive effects of CAP between countries.

5.2 *Farmers' Direct Voting Power in EU-27*

Enlargement will significantly increase farmers' voting power in terms of population shares. While on average 4.3% of the civilian working population work in agriculture, forestry, hunting and fishing in EU-15, the average is 21.5% for the ten countries from Central and Eastern Europe. The population weighted average agricultural employment share for EU-27 is 8.0 which is almost double the current value of EU-15 (all data refer to 2000, source: European Commission [9], see Appendix).

Even though a further shrinking of the agricultural sector in old and new member countries can be expected enlargement will thus tend to boost the direct voting power of farmers to a considerable extent.

This direct voting power will make some of the new members' governments to natural allies of farmers. For national politics in Romania (agriculture share in employment: 45.2%) but also in likely first wave countries such as Poland, Lithuania or Latvia (shares between 14 and 19%, see Appendix) farmers' voting power will often have a pivotal role for reaching domestic political majorities. Thus, these countries' representatives in the Council and the European Parliament must be expected to act as advocates for the farmers' interests.

5.3 *Organisation of Farmers' Interests*

Pioneered by Olson [19], the theory of interest groups has clarified that the sheer size of a group does not guarantee political influence. A further condition is that this interest can be organised. The smaller the size of a group and the more homogeneous its interests the better its chances to overcome the free rider obstacle to the successful establishment and smooth function of an interest group.

Taking account of these aspects, enlargement could pose difficulties to the effectiveness of farmers' lobbying. What is an advantage for a group's direct voting power is a disadvantage for its ability to organise and act in a united way: The large number of farmers in the candidate countries might be a burden for this group's organisational capability. With 12.3 million agricultural holdings, Poland on its own has a considerably larger number than all current EU countries together (7.0 million). With 30.3 million agricultural holdings, the seven Central and Eastern European countries for which data are available (Czech Republic, Estonia, Hungary, Poland, Romania, Slovakia and Slovenia) would increase the number of agricultural holdings in the EU by more than 400%, judging on the most recent available data from 1997 (European Commission [9]).

This also points to a considerable heterogeneity of interests between Western and Eastern farmers which could weaken the impact of farmers on EU politics. Important indicators show huge discrepancies between farmers in old and new member countries even if in the next years some convergence would take place: The average EU-15 agricultural holding has a size of 18.4 ha contrasting to 1.5 ha for the seven candidate countries listed in the last paragraph (1997 data from European Commission [9]). Furthermore, income differentials between Western and Eastern farmers are enormous: The average gross value added per worker employed in the Western agricultural sector is with 21,630 Euro more than ten times larger than for the candidate countries (2,030 Euro, calculations based on 2000 data from European Commission [9]).

Hence, it is extremely unlikely that Western and Eastern European farmers will be able to form a lobbying coalition. On the contrary, this substantial heterogeneity of interests is likely to weaken the power of the European farmer lobby as a whole. As pointed out by Kroszner [18] in the context of financial industry regulation, rival groups within a sector have an incentive to battle each other. They could dissipate their efforts in their internal struggle. Consumers and taxpayers could thus benefit from a kind of «divide et impera» outcome.

5.4 *Resistance of Consumers and Taxpayers*

Central and Eastern European consumers have to pay much higher shares of their total expenditure for food than consumers in the old member countries. While the EU-15 average for this ratio is 17% (1999, European Commission [9]), it ranges from 21% in Slovenia to 45% in Bulgaria (see Appendix). These ratios suggest that consumer resistance to protected agricultural markets should be more intense in the East. However, this consideration does not apply to the CAP's direct income support. The burden for direct payments falls onto the taxpayer and due to the EU financial system mainly onto the taxpayer of the wealthier countries. Therefore, new candidate's population might be opposed to price support but not to income support for domestic farmers.

A further aspect in regard to likely resistance against farmers privileges is the information issue. Resistance against interest group privileges is positively correlated with the degree of voters' information. A general problem detrimental to the political control of the European policy level is that European voters tend to be less well informed about the EU than about the national policy level (Vaubel [22]). It must even be expected that the population in new candidate countries is less informed than in the West. Recent polls support this expectation and show that voters in these countries are significantly less familiar with EU institutions than Western European voters. While, for example, in the EU-15 countries, 89 (77)% of citizens have heard of the European Parliament (the European Commission), these numbers are with 72 (60)% significantly lower for the candidates' populations (European Commission [6]). Most likely, this is not merely a transitory pre-enlargement problem since it is an established fact (Vaubel [22]) that the quality of information on the EU system increases with income and proximity to the centre so that according to all experience the new members will bring in voters with a relatively poor information on the EU's political system. In this sense, enlargement could tend to reduce the average information level of European voters and give more leeway to EU politics to care for special interest groups such as farmers.

5.5 *CAP and Distributive Effects between Countries*

The CAP results in substantial transfer of financial resources between countries. Generally speaking, those countries benefit that are relatively poor and/or have a relatively large agricultural sector. This is due to the characteristics of the EU's financial system (for details see Heinemann [14]). The revenues («own resources») are more or less proportional to a country's share in EU-GDP while the national share of CAP spending depends among other factors on the size of the national agricultural sector. These redistributive effects can be regarded to be among the most important political-economic functions of this policy field since it allows log-rolling deals like that between Germany and France (Vaubel [22]): While Germany was expected to benefit above average from the Internal Market, France was compensated through the generous growth of agricultural spending in the eighties and nineties.

With this background it is useful to calculate some rough indicators for the distributive effects of CAP in the enlarged EU. This is helpful in order to see which countries could in future become advocates in favour of or against a further expansion of CAP spending and in order to assess the likely preferences of a majority of countries.

Table 2 presents together with Council votes per country a CAP distribution indicator both for the situation before and after enlargement. This indicator is calculated as the ratio between a country's share in total EU agricultural sector (the benefit side from CAP spending) and a country's share in total EU GDP (the cost side because of the close link between a country's contribution to the EU budget and its GDP). The agricultural sector share is calculated as an average of the share in agricultural employment and the share in agricultural gross value added. A country with an indicator value below one tends to be a net payer in CAP since its share in payments to the EU budget exceeds its share in CAP spending. Obviously, the used indicator is only a very rough indicator for actual redistributive effects and the precise numbers must be treated with caution. Neither does this calculation account for the complexities of the own resources system nor does it incorporate the details of CAP's spending programmes. Nevertheless, the calculations should allow some insights into the main trends concerning distribution driven interests into the future of CAP.

With the exception of Ireland, Spain, Portugal and Greece all present EU countries will be net payers in the CAP after full enlargement according to this simple indicator. Hence, countries like France and Italy might start to rethink their position that until now have been tough opponents to any reductions of agricultural spending. On the long run, they could come into a position where a system of national agricultural subsidies becomes much cheaper than the present EU based system.

TABLE 2

CAP REDISTRIBUTION AND COUNCIL VOTES*

Pre enlargement			Post enlargement		
	CAP distri-bution indicator	Council votes (pre-Nice)		CAP distri-bution indicator	Council votes (pre-Nice)
Luxembourg	0.31	2	Luxembourg	0.23	4
UK	0.37	10	UK	0.26	29
Sweden	0.50	4	Sweden	0.32	10
Belgium	0.51	5	Belgium	0.38	12
Germany	0.57	10	Germany	0.39	29
Denmark	0.94	3	Finland	0.56	7
Finland	0.97	3	Austria	0.63	10
Netherlands	1.02	5	Malta	0.68	3
Austria	1.03	4	Denmark	0.70	7
France	1.09	10	Netherlands	0.76	13
Italy	1.30	10	France	0.80	29
Ireland	1.56	3	Italy	0.92	29
Spain	2.11	8	Ireland	1.06	7
Portugal	4.04	5	Spain	1.46	27
Greece	5.38	5	Cyprus	1.79	4
			Portugal	2.12	12
			Czech Rep.	2.15	12
			Slovenia	2.39	4
			Hungary	2.39	12
			Slovakia	2.66	7
			Greece	3.33	12
			Estonia	3.65	4
			Latvia	5.06	4
			Poland	5.23	27
			Lithuania	11.27	7
			Bulgaria	12.37	10
			Romania	37.48	14
Sum of Council votes (indicator < 1)		37			182
Total Council votes		87			345
Council vote shares of CAP's net payers		0.43			0.53

* Calculation of CAP distribution indicator: see explanation in text, calculated on basis of year 2000 data from European Commission [9] and Eurostat.

In terms of voting shares in the Council which for Agriculture is the most important organ enlargement will bring a loss of power to the country group that is benefiting from the redistributive effects of CAP. While in the EU-15 the CAP net payers command only over 43% of Council votes, this share will increase to 53% after the full enlargement. This indicates that the redistribution motive behind CAP is going to lose power with enlargement.

This development is even more likely if one takes account of the deadweight losses of the CAP based distribution system. According to Becker [4], the level of costs relative to the distributive benefits play an important role for the political-economic appeal of a particular distribution system. Already today, CAP is a negative sum game due to its high administrative and monitoring costs and its damage to market efficiency. Enlargement is likely to further increase these deadweight losses since the large numbers of farmers in new member countries will substantially increase administration and monitoring costs of CAP. With these increasing losses the system becomes less attractive as an instrument for both inter-personal and inter-country distributive objectives.

5.6 *The Overall Effect*

Summing up this section's analysis there are countervailing political-economic forces having an impact on the future of CAP after enlargement. The increasing direct voting power of farmers and the continuing low resistance of consumers and taxpayers will work in favour of keeping or even extending the high level of protection and subsidies for European farmers. Opposite pressure originates from the high West-East heterogeneity of farm interests which weakens European farm lobbies and the increasing Council power of countries that will be net payers in the system. The outcome which would be consistent with all these countervailing forces would be the renationalisation of agricultural subsidies. This would be compatible with the rules of a common market as long as the agricultural market rules including guarantee prices would further be defined on a European level. The financing of national farmers' income support out of the national budgets would set an end to a major part of the inter-country distribution effects of CAP that will become increasingly unpopular for a Council majority of countries. At the same time the interests of farmers in countries with powerful farm lobbies could be taken care of by the national policy level. In this sense, this analysis points to a likely long-run system change in the CAP where in future the national taxpayer would carry the burden for nationally agreed income support to farmers. This development would tend to reduce the overall level of subsidies since due to the better information of voters about national policies compared to EU policies interest groups would have to cope with harder resistance.

6. - Conclusion

As for many other fields of politics the political-economic view is also indispensable for a full understanding of the enlargement process. This process implies so profound economic and fiscal changes that politicians and lobbyists will use all available degrees of freedom to optimise the outcome from their individual perspective.

Indeed, this impact could be demonstrated for the pre-enlargement period in regard to the *Treaty of Nice*, the *Convention*, the emerging terms of accession and the choice of first wave countries. What might even be more interesting, however, is the question how the long-run changes to equilibria of interests will influence EU policies. The analysis of the CAP has offered only one example for this forward looking approach and there is the need for further research along these lines, for example, in regard to trade policy, labour market policy, structural policy or environmental policy. Some of the CAP example's insights, however, can be generalised. The political power of many pan-EU interest groups in general will come under stress in the coming years through an increasing heterogeneity of interests among its members. What was shown for the farm lobbies is also likely to hold for European trade unions, employers associations or European regions. This would be no bad development from the point of view of economic efficiency and from the perspective of European consumers and taxpayers. So the judgement seems justified that the political-economic consequences might not be the least important type of benefit resulting from enlargement.

BASIC DATA ON CANDIDATE COUNTRIES

Source	EUROPEAN COMMISSION [9]	EUROPEAN COMMISSION [9]	EUROPEAN COMMISSION [9]	EUROPEAN COMMISSION [9]	EUROPEAN COMMISSION [9]	EUROPEAN COMMISSION [9]	EUROPEAN COMMISSION [9]	HEINEMANN [15]	Treaty of Nice [20]
Year	2000	2000	2000	2000	2000	2000	1999		
Variable definition	population (1000)	GDP p.c. PPS	unemployment rate (% of civilian working population)	employment in the agriculture, forestry, hunting and fishing sector (number, 1000 persons)	employment in the agriculture, forestry, hunting and fishing sector (share in employment civilian working population, %)	Share of agriculture in the GDP (GVA/GDP, %)	Share of household consumption expenditure devoted to food (%)	Nice Shapley Shubik power share in Council	EP seats
Cyprus	755	18540	4.9	27	8.9	3.8	17.0	0.011	6
Malta	388	11920	6.5	2	1.6	9.1	21.5	0.008	5
Bulgaria	8191	5403	16.2	377	11.2	15.8	45.1	0.028	17
Czech Republic	10278	13480	8.8	244	5.3	3.4	23.3	0.034	20
Estonia	1439	8520	13.2	42	7	5.7	30.7	0.011	6
Hungary	10043	11832	6.6	246	7.2	3.9	25.0	0.034	20
Latvia	2424	6421	14.2	140	14.4	3.9	34.6	0.011	8
Lithuania	3699	6614	15.6	281	18.4	2.5	39.3	0.020	12
Poland	38654	8741	16.3	2711	18.7	2.9	31.2	0.080	50
Romania	22455	6030	7	4926	45.2	11.4	37.4	0.040	33
Slovakia	5399	10793	19.1	145	7.5	2.7	27.7	0.020	13
Slovenia	1988	16085	6.9	85	9.2	4.3	21.2	0.011	7

BIBLIOGRAPHY

[1] BACKHAUS J.G. - KRAUSE G. (eds.), *On Political Economy of Transformation: Country Studies*, Marburg, Metropolis, 1997.

[2] BALDWIN R.E. - FRANCOIS J.F. - PORTES R., «The Costs and Benefits of Eastern Enlargement: The Impact on the EU and Central Europe», *Economic Policy*, vol. 24, April 1997, pp. 125-176.

[3] BASTIAN J. (ed.), *The Political Economy of Transition in Central and Eastern Europe*, Aldershot, Ashgate Publishing, 1998.

[4] BECKER G.S., «A Theory of Competition among Pressure Groups for Political Influence», *Quarterly Journal of Economics*, vol. 98, 1983, pp. 371-400.

[5] BOFINGER P., «The Political Economy of the Eastern Enlargement of the EU», CEPR, *Discussion Paper*, n. 1234, 1995.

[6] EUROPEAN COMMISSION, *Applicant Countries Eurobarometer 2001*, Brussels, December 2001.

[7] — —, *Eurobarometer No. 55*, Brussels, October 2001.

[8] — —, *Making Success of Enlargement, Strategy Paper and Report on the Progress Towards Accession by Each of the Candidate Countries*, Brussels, 2001.

[9] — —, *Agricultural Statistics*, Website Agriculture Directorate-General, 2002.

[10] — —, «Commission Offers a Fair and Solid Approach for Financing EU Enlargement», Press Release IP/02/170, Brussels, 30 January 2002.

[11] — —, *Enlargement, State of Play Negotiations*, January 2002, Website Enlargement Directorate-General, March 2002.

[12] EUROPEAN COUNCIL, *Presidency Conclusions, European Council Meeting in Laeken*, 14 and 15 December 2001, Brussels, 2001.

[13] Goldberg V.P., «Peltzman on Regulation and Politics», *Public Choice*, vol. 39, 1982, pp. 291-7.

[14] HEINEMANN F., «Europäische Finanzverfassung: Zwischen Umverteilung und Effizienz», in: OHR R. - THEURL T. (eds.), *Kompendium Europäische Wirtschaftspolitik*, München, Vahlen, 2001, pp. 205-39.

[15] — —, «The Political Economy of EU Enlargement and the Treaty of Nice», forthcoming, *European Journal of Political Economy*, 2002.

[16] Hillman A.L., «The Transition from Socialism: An Overview from a Political Economy Perspective», *European Journal of Political Economy*, vol. 10, 1994, pp. 191-225.

[17] Kohler W.R., «Die Osterweiterung der EU aus der Sicht bestehender Mitgliedsländer: Was lehrt uns die Theorie der öknomischen Integration?», *Perspektiven der Wirtschaftspolitik*, vol. 1, n. 2, 2000, pp. 115-41.

[19] Kroszner R.S., «Is the Financial System Politically Independent? Perspectives on the Political Economy of Banking and Financial Regulation», Finanssektorns Framtid, Bilaga 23-28, vol. D, 2000, pp. 127-62.

[19] OLSON M., *The Logic of Collective Action*, Cambridge, Harvard University Press, 1965.

[20] TREATY OF NICE: CONFERENCE OF THE REPRESENTATIVES OF THE GOVERNMENTS OF THE MEMBER STATES, *Note, Subject: Treaty of Nice, SN 1247/1/01 REV 1*, Brussels, 14 February 2001.

[21] Vaubel R., «The Political Economy of Centralization and the European Community», *Public Choice*, vol. 81, 1994, pp. 151-90.

[22] —— —, «The Public Choice Analysis of European Integration: A Survey», *European Journal of Political Economy*, vol. 10, 1994, pp. 227-49.